Gendarmes and the State in
Nineteenth-Century Europe

Gendarmes and the State in Nineteenth-Century Europe

CLIVE EMSLEY

OXFORD
UNIVERSITY PRESS

OXFORD

UNIVERSITY PRESS

Great Clarendon Street, Oxford OX2 6DP

Oxford University Press is a department of the University of Oxford
It furthers the University's objective of excellence in research, scholarship,
and education by publishing worldwide in

Oxford New York

Athens Auckland Bangkok Bogotá Buenos Aires Calcutta
Cape Town Chennai Dar es Salaam Delhi Florence Hong Kong Istanbul
Karachi Kuala Lumpur Madrid Melbourne Mexico City Mumbai
Nairobi Paris São Paulo Singapore Taipei Tokyo Toronto Warsaw

and associated companies in Berlin Ibadan

Oxford is a registered trade mark of Oxford University Press
in the UK and in certain other countries

Published in the United States
by Oxford University Press Inc., New York

British Library Cataloguing in Publication Data

Data available

Library of Congress Cataloging in Publication Data
Emsley, Clive.
Gendarmes and the state in nineteenth-century Europe/
Clive Emsley.
Includes bibliographical references.
1. Police—France—History. 2. Police—Europe—History.
I. Title.
HV8203.E47 1999 363.2'0944'09034—dc21 99-23234
ISBN 0-19-820798-0

1 3 5 7 9 10 8 6 4 2

Typeset in Ehrhardt
by Hope Services (Abingdon) Ltd.
Printed in Great Britain
on acid-free paper by
Bookcraft Ltd,
Midsomer Norton Somerset

For Jack and Kyle

PREFACE

For roughly twenty years my research interest has been focused on the history of crime and policing. Much of my work has concentrated on the English experience, but in 1991 my good friend and colleague Bob Storch asked me to participate in a panel at the Annual Conference of the Social Science History Association. The panel was to review the recent historiography of police and policing and to highlight any areas which we considered ought now to be explored. The opportunity of a visit to New Orleans was too good to miss, and my presentation at the conference argued that it was time for some serious research to be undertaken on police institutions other than those of nineteenth-century towns and cities, and particularly on the gendarmeries. What follows is the result of trying to follow through the suggestion, and if it merely scratches the surface in many places it will, I hope, encourage others to look seriously at these institutions and their role.

Many friends and colleagues have been generous with help and advice as I progressed with the topic, notably Richard Bessel, Catherine Clémens-Denys, Charles Esdaile, Richard Evans, Cyrille Fijnault, Steven Hughes, Gwynne Lewis, Gunner Lind, Herbert Reinke, Xavier Rousseaux, Mario Sbriccoli, Vincent Sleebe, Terry Strieter, and Axel Tixhon. Sabine Phillips was of immeasurable assistance in tracking down various German and Austrian sources on my behalf and helping me with translations. My thanks to General Raffaele Benedetto Licci for authorization to use the Carabinieri archive in Rome, and to Rosemary Plum for helping me get into it in the first place, and then for helping me to translate and understand the material. Special thanks are due, first, to Mike Broers for his ready help and particularly for letting me use some archival material which he has found in Turin and which he has not yet used himself, and second, to René Lévy for his rigorous, critical reading of an earlier draft and for his (and Renée Zauberman's) generosity and hospitality during my visits to France. Any errors and inconsistences which remain are, of course, my own responsibility. Finally, I must thank Michel Fleury and Madame Aufray for providing me with the comfortable and peaceful accommodation of the Institut Francophone during my research visits to Paris.

The Research Committee of the Arts Faculty at the Open University has always generously supported my research. My particular thanks too to the Leverhulme Trust, which awarded me a fellowship enabling me significant respite from administration and various teaching duties at the Open University during the academic year 1996–97.

Last but not least, my thanks to my wife for living with this book for as long as I have, without being able to do anything about it. The dedication is to our grandsons.

CONTENTS

LIST OF TABLES

ABBREVIATIONS

AG	Archives de la Guerre, Vincennes
AMSC	Archivio del Museo Storico dell' Arma dei Carabinieri, Rome
AN	Archives Nationales, Paris
Arch. Parl.	*Archives Parlementaries (1ʳᵉ série)*
AST	Archivio di Stato di Torino
Cor. Nap.	*Correspondance de Napoléon 1ʳᵉ*, Paris, 1862

I

INTRODUCTION

This book attempts a broad-brush study of the development of a particular kind of police functionary and policing institution. During the last quarter of a century academic historians, and particularly social historians, have discovered crime and policing. From the late 1960s, as part of the movement for 'history from below', court records were seen as a new way of tapping into the lives and minds of the popular classes. Gradually, those responsible for policing, and hence for the initial decisions which led to the court records, also became the subjects of historical research. At first the attempt here was to investigate the imposition of what were perceived as new forms of social discipline developed during the nineteenth century, but increasingly police officers themselves—men generally drawn from the working classes and subject to a harsh and rigorous work discipline—became subjects of study in their own right. This book continues in the latter tradition, but surveys the development of the kind of police agent who has generally been ignored in the recent research—the paramilitary, or just plain military, gendarme.

From Robert D. Storch's seminal essays on policemen as 'domestic missionaries' in the eyes of one class, and a 'plague of blue locusts' in the eyes of another, to Jean-Marc Berlière's massive *doctorat*—three volumes, 1,300 pages, and possibly the smallest typeface ever used in a thesis—much of the recent research has focused on what were, essentially, civilian and largely urban policing institutions.[1] Such work has challenged the old certainties about police forces being developed as the successful solution to a real and rising tide of crime and popular disorder. The origins of policing institutions are now understood, at least in the academic world, as far more problematic, depending on aspirations for new thresholds of public decorum at least as much as on fears of

---

[1] Robert D. Storch, 'The Plague of Blue Locusts: Police Reform and Popular Resistance in Northern England, 1840–1857', *International Review of Social History*, 20 (1975), 61–90; id., 'The Policeman as Domestic Missionary: Urban Discipline and Popular Culture in Northern England, 1850–1880', *Journal of Social History*, 9 (1976), 481–509; Jean-Marc Berlière, 'L'Institution policière sous la Troisième République, 1875–1914', Thèse pour le doctorat, Université de Bourgogne, 1991.

crime and disorder. The pattern of police development is also recognized as being much more complex, and dependent on legislative debate in which both supporters of new policing structures as well as opponents had cogent cases to argue, on negotiation between central and local government, as well as on available finance. Yet the civilian, largely urban police institutions which have been the principal focus of so much of the recent research constituted only a part of the police power available in different countries across Europe during the nineteenth and twentieth centuries, and these police can be clearly subdivided into those organizations directly responsible to central government and those answerable to municipalities. The model most favoured for these civilian, urban institutions, in word if not necessarily in practice, was the Metropolitan Police of London established in 1829. Even Napoleon III, when he came to reorganize the police of Paris in the mid-1850s, sought to incorporate elements of the London model.[2] But Napoleon III also feted his Gendarmerie, the 20,000 men who had responsibility for policing outside the major towns of metropolitan France, for policing the French empire, and for providing the first line of defence against insurrection in his capital.

The French Gendarmerie, like the other gendarmeries discussed in this book, was principally stationed in the countryside, but this does not mean that the corps was merely a bystander in the history of nineteenth-century Europe. While the nineteenth century tends to be viewed as a period of major economic, industrial, and urban development in Europe, and rightly so, nevertheless, up to and indeed beyond World War I the populations of France, Italy, Spain, of much of Germany, and elsewhere continued to be rural dwellers. Moreover, while many nineteenth-century commentators described the burgeoning cities and towns as havens for the criminal and the dangerous classes, the countryside was not the idyll that this implied, and southern Europe still had traditional bandits as well as new, violent agricultural unions. At the turn of the century gendarmes were regarded by many governments as a valuable prophylactic against economic and social disorder.

According to the first Napoleon, a Gendarmerie was 'the most efficient way to maintain the peace in a country . . . it provides both a surveillance half civil, half military spread across the whole territory,

---

[2] Alfred Rey and Louis Féron, *Histoire du corps des gardiens de la paix* (Paris, 1894), 175–80; and for the different varieties of police see Clive Emsley, 'A Typology of Nineteenth-Century Police', *Crime, histoire et sociétés/ Crime, history and societies*, 3 (1999), 29–44.

together with the most precise information'.[3] Generally speaking, gendarmeries have been made up of soldiers and, in consequence, have been answerable to a ministry of war (or more recently a ministry of 'defence') for discipline, organization, and equipment. At the same time they have been at the call of civilian authorities, usually working under a ministry of the interior, to make arrests on warrants and to provide coercive force in the event of disorder, potential disorder, or criminal violence in the shape of, for example, banditry. Gendarmes also had, and have, the discretion of other police agents to act on their own in arresting those caught in the act of an offence, or identified as offenders by public clamour, which was often considered as tantamount to being caught *in flagrante*. They have carried, and continue to carry out many other functions performed by police officers in the Anglo-Saxon world, where such overtly military police are rarely found,[4] as well as by the civilian police in their own countries. This in itself poses an initial question: how was it possible for two different and distinct forms of police to develop side by side? The smug Anglo-Saxon response as to how gendarmerie-style police came to be developed was put by the doyen of traditional English police history, Charles Reith: Anglo-Saxon police were 'kin' police whose authority came from the people, and whose existence was a manifestation of successful democracy, while gendarmeries were essentially despotic, even totalitarian, since they represented force directed downwards from rulers on to the ruled.[5] A generation of academic historical research has challenged this comfortable assertion.[6] The stock response of gendarmes themselves is that two police forces are good for the maintenance of democracy, since the need to win over two distinct institutions creates problems for any group contemplating the organization of a coup.[7] But this is an assertion to justify the status quo. No one has sought to prove historically that this is why some states

---

[3] *Cor. Nap.*, vol. 12, no. 10,243, to Joseph Bonaparte, 16 May 1806.

[4] The principal exception is probably Canada, where the Royal Canadian Mounted Police is also known as La Gendarmerie Royale du Canada. While the Mounties have never been responsible to a war or defence ministry, the column of North-West Mounted Police that made 'the great march west' in 1874 was to all intents and purposes a military body equipped with a wide range of firepower, including cannon. The best general history of the early Mounties is R. C. Macleod, *The North-West Mounted Police and Law Enforcement, 1873–1905* (Toronto: University of Toronto Press, 1976).

[5] Charles Reith, *The Blind Eye of History* (London: Faber, 1952), 20 and 244.

[6] The most significant criticism remains Storch, 'The Plague of Blue Locusts' and 'The Policeman as Domestic Missionary'.

[7] I have heard this case argued with reference both to the French Gendarmerie Nationale and the Italian Carabinieri.

established two or more police institutions in the first place; moreover, it seems most unlikely that such historical proof could ever be satisfactorily provided. The first Napoleon, as will be shown below, had a policy of divide and rule with his various police organizations, though they were not initially developed to check each other, and democracy had no place on his agenda. Two or more police forces in a country can foster rivalries potentially inimical to good order and successful policing. Two police forces in Paris were relatively easily won over by Louis Napoleon in the preparations for his *coup d'état* in December 1851; two police forces did not prevent Mussolini's march on Rome, nor preserve the Second Republic in Spain. This, of course, is not to suggest that a centralized, single police institution is the ideal, but simply to urge, first, a critical approach to assertions regarding social and political phenomena, and second, a careful and critical approach to the historical development of institutions.

Curiously, while the history of the precursor of the French Gendarmerie Nationale, the *maréchaussée*, has been the subject of a significant amount of recent research and publication,[8] the history of the Gendarmerie itself has been left largely in the hands of members or former members of the institution. While this work has clearly described the major lines of development it has, like the traditional histories of English policing, tended to be celebratory rather than critical and analytical.[9] Such a tone is not surprising: élite military institutions need to be self-critical internally to improve and maintain their effectiveness, but their public face is one of pride in the corps, its traditions and successes. Moreover, institutional histories, especially those written by members or ex-members of the institution, invariably conceive of their subjects as perfectible and describe the overall direction of their development and growth as being driven by desirability, necessity, and progress. Perhaps what is most surprising is the failure of academic historians, as yet, to take much of a serious look at the gendarmerie institutions. Pierre Miquel's recent book *Les Gendarmes* is aimed at a

---

[8] Notably Iain A. Cameron, *Crime and Repression in the Auvergne and the Guyenne, 1720–1790* (Cambridge: Cambridge University Press, 1981), and Jacques Lorgnier, *Maréchaussée, histoire d'une révolution judiciaire et administrative*, 2 vols. (Paris: L'Harmattan, 1994).

[9] See *inter alia*, General L. Larrieu, *Histoire de la Gendarmerie, depuis les origines de la maréchaussée jusqu'à nos jours*, 2 vols. (Paris: Charles-Lavauzelle, 1927–33); Marcel Diamant-Berger, *Huit siècles de la gendarmerie* (Paris: J.F. Editions, 1967); Col. Louis Saurel, *Peines et gloires des Gendarmes* (Paris: Lavauzelle, 1973); Gen. Jean Besson and Pierre Rosière, *La Gendarmerie nationale* (Paris: Xavier Richer, 1982); and the articles in *Revue Historique de l'Armée*, 17: 3 (August 1961), *Numéro Spécial Gendarmerie Nationale*.

popular market and adopts a somewhat similar tone to the official and semi-official histories. François Dieu's important and perceptive *Gendarmerie et modernité* draws on history but is, essentially, a work of political science and an analysis of the contemporary role, values, and working milieu of the institution rather than a critical history.[10] The historiography of other European gendarmeries is similar. The Italian Carabinieri has published a celebratory part-work in its official journal,[11] and publishes books to help underwrite the costs of its museum in Rome.[12] It has also been the subject of popular histories by former members of the corps or by men closely linked with it.[13] The Austrian Gendarmerie published a history on its seventy-fifth anniversary, and another is plannned for its one-hundred-and-fiftieth.[14] But Helmut Gebhardt's volume on the Steiermark, while acknowledging a debt to the institutional histories and their authors, is a move to a rather more critical perspective.[15] The German Gendarmeries have attracted historians among the German police, but little in the way of serious historical monographs; Bernd Wirsing's thesis is path-breaking here.[16] Spain's Guardia Civil has had its share of celebratory histories; more recently Diego López Garrido has provided a more critical assessment tracing its role in the development of the centralized state,[17] but much remains to be done.

The aim of what follows is to draw some of this secondary material together and, leavened with a little primary research in Austrian, German, Italian, and especially French archives, to explore the development of gendarmerie-style policing across nineteenth-century Europe.

[10] Pierre Miquel, *Les Gendarmes* (Paris: Olivier Orban, 1990); François Dieu, *Gendarmerie et modernité. Étude de la spécifité gendarmique aujourd'hui* (Paris: Montchrestien, 1993).

[11] 'La storia dei Carabinieri', in *Il Carabiniere* (March 1992–March 1993).

[12] See, *inter alia*, Luigi Amadeo de Biase, *Carabinieri contro Briganti e Banditi, 1814–1934* (Rome: Museo Storico dell'Arma dei Carabinieri, 1995).

[13] See *inter alia*, Pompeo Di Terlizzi, *Quando frammenti di storia si ricompongono. Alle radici culturali e formative dell'Arma dei Carabinieri* (Bari: Levanti, 1991), and Francesco Grisi, *Storia dei Carabinieri. Imprese, battaglie, uomini e protagonisti: i due secoli della Benemerita al servizio della gente* (Spa: Piemme, 1996).

[14] Franz Neubauer, *Die Gendarmerie in Österreich, 1849–1924* (Vienna: Gendarmerie-Jubiläumsfonds, 1925).

[15] Helmut Gebhardt, *Die Gendarmerie in der Steiermark von 1850 bis heute* (Graz: Leykam Verlag, 1997).

[16] Bernd Wirsing, 'Die Geschichte der Gendarmeriekorps und deren Vorläuferorganisationen in Baden, Württemberg und Bayern, 1750–1850', Dissertation . . . des Doktors der Philosophie, Universität Konstanz, 1991.

[17] Diego López Garcia, *La Guardia Civil y los orígenes del Estado centralista* (Barcelona: Editorial Critica, 1982).

Gendarmes, as noted earlier, are usually soldiers, and as such they could be deployed as military units during international confrontations or conflicts. But while touched upon in passing, their role as soldiers and their battle honours are not the concerns here. Rather, I have set out to address questions concerning their internal policing role: what was it that made this kind of policing so attractive to governments, and was the attraction the same in each case? How did different political contexts shape and reshape the model? How were gendarmes recruited, deployed, and controlled? What roles were assigned to them, and how effective were they at fulfilling them? How, if at all, did their roles change and develop over time? What impact did they have on the communities in which they served, and on the development of the nineteenth-century states that deployed them?

In addressing these questions for France and the Napoleonic Empire I have used sources in the military archives at Vincennes and in the Archives Nationales. I have sampled material for the old *ancien régime* in the former, and particularly worked through the X^f series for the Napoleonic and post-Napoleonic periods. In the Archives Nationales I focused on the AF IV cartons which deal with the Gendarmerie in the Napoleonic period, and for the period after 1815 on the Gendarmerie reports for a cross-section of *départements* in the voluminous F^7 series. I selected some *départements* noted for their economic progress (Nord, Rhône), and others for their 'backwardness' (Finistère, Puy-de-Dôme); some from the north, some from the south. It is clear to me that more detailed research can be done on individual *départements* and regions, particularly drawing on local archives, but I felt that for my purposes a halt had to be called somewhere. I was even more restrictive with the primary source material sampled from elsewhere. There is no central archive containing material for the Prussian Gendarmerie, and since much of the recent police research has concentrated on the west of the kingdom, I opted to supplement this with material drawn from provinces to the east. For the Carabinieri I was fortunate enough to be authorized to use the corps's own archive on the top floor of its museum in Rome, and I have concentrated on material found here to supplement and amplify the work of others. The Habsburg Gendarmerie remains the least researched of any of the corps on which I have focused in any detail in what follows. For this organization I have simply sampled a small quantity of the material available in the Kriegsarchiv in Vienna.

For the traditional historians of the English style of policing, like Charles Reith, the overtly military nature of the gendarme counted against him and made him a very different being from the Anglo-Saxon police officer.[18] Yet, given the nature of policing, the military discipline, equipment, organization, and management of the gendarmeries was, arguably, an honest recognition of the police officer's role and specific attributes, especially in nineteenth-century continental Europe. Max Weber suggested that a useful minimum definition of the state was that collectivity of institutions which claimed and enjoyed a monopoly of legitimate violence within a continuous bounded territory.[19] Several of the states discussed below went through a period of formation, expansion, and/or unification during the nineteenth century in which their continuous boundaries were significantly shifted and redrawn. Soldiers were important in the initial period of expansion and unification, but small squads or even individual gendarmes could provide permanent manifestations of state power across the new as well as the old territories. Equally important, the gendarmes were professional soldiers/ policemen at a time when the armies of continental Europe were increasingly shifting from a professional mercenary to a conscript base. Within the state the police officer, or gendarme, is the only official empowered to use physical violence in day-to-day dealings with the citizens. Indeed, David H. Bayley, while recognizing that police officers are expected to fill a variety of roles, has argued that the use of physical force is the key distinguishing feature of the police.[20] This is not to say that contemporary police officers, or their nineteenth-century predecessors, spend, or spent, the whole time exerting or threatening the use of physical force. On the contrary, much of what police officers do and have done involves public assistance and welfare. But other agencies also have welfare tasks, and unlike the authority to use legitimate, physical force, such tasks cannot be held as constituting part of any definition of what is unique to the role of a specialized police force. With his military bearing, uniform, and weaponry the nineteenth-century gendarme manifested the threat of state violence and state power, but he also undertook other tasks. These may not have been the reason why gendarmeries were created, and they may have been taken over at different times by specialized agencies. Yet in some countries, and at some times, the welfare tasks and other

---

[18] The civilian nature of England's 'New Police' has been greatly overemphasized by Reith and others writing in the Whig tradition. See Clive Emsley, *The English Police: A Political and Social History*, 2nd. edn. (London: Longman, 1996), 26, 56–9, and 254–7.

[19] Max Weber, *The Theory of Social and Economic Organisation*, ed. and introduced by Talcott Parsons (New York: Free Press, 1964), 156.

[20] David H. Bayley, *Patterns of Policing: A Comparative International Analysis* (New Brunswick NJ: Rutgers University Press, 1985), 12–13.

responsibilities which did not involve the use of force were probably as significant in shaping the gendarme's own perception of his duties, and both government and civilian attitudes towards him and his utility.

The gendarme's presence in the states and empires of nineteenth-century Europe readily slots in with much of the recent conceptual and theoretical work concerned with the state. He can be seen as a significant manifestation of state power in both the despotic and infrastructural dimensions delineated by Michael Mann, since he enforced authority from above but also contributed to the co-ordination of social life.[21] The gendarme played an important part too in enforcing new forms of discipline within society, and was an instrument of the expanding bureaucratic surveillance capacity of the state.[22] But while such theoretical perspectives are important stimuli to historical research in shaping new approaches and new questions, it is not the task of the historian to set out to prove the theories of others. New forms of power and discipline, an expansion of state surveillance, organization, and bureaucracy contributed to the development of gendarmeries; they also benefited from, and were extended by them. But broad continental perspectives can mask national and regional differences and idiosyncracies. Similarly, frictions between different sections of the bureaucracy or the ruling élites, which can be crucial to the developments of individual institutions, are lost under the sweep of the very broad brush.

This book aims to trace the development of the different manifestations of an institution, to show how and why a basic model—the French Gendarmerie—was established and changed over time; it aims also to explore how and why the model was taken up, how it developed and with what particular emphases, elsewhere. The book is divided into three parts. The first two trace the history of the French Gendarmerie from becoming a national, state-directed force during the eighteenth century, through the revolutions and upheavals of the late eighteenth and early nineteenth centuries, to its role, and comparative neglect in the generation before World War I. Part III compares and contrasts developments elsewhere in Europe, with particular emphasis on the experience of Italy, Germany, and the Habsburg lands. Finally, a con-

---

[21] Michael Mann, *The Sources of Social Power*, 2 vols. (Cambridge: Cambridge University Press, 1986).

[22] For the disciplinary society see, *inter alia*, Michel Foucault, *Discipline and Punish: The Origins of the Prison* (Harmondsworth: Penguin, 1978); for 'bureaucratic surveillance' see Anthony Giddens, *The Nation-State and Violence: A Contemporary Critique of Historical Materialism*, vol. 2 (Oxford: Polity Press, 1985), and Christopher Dandeker, *Surveillance, Power and Modernity* (Oxford: Polity Press, 1990).

clusion first situates the gendarmeries in some of the broader changes in rural Europe during the nineteenth century, and then offers some comparative conclusions about the gendarmes themselves, their experience of their work, their attitudes and behaviour.

PART I
France: *The Coming of the Gendarmes*

2

'THE MOST USEFUL CORPS
FOR THE NATION . . .':
THE MARÉCHAUSSÉE

The Gendarmerie Nationale boasts of being the oldest institution of the
French state, claiming, at the close of the twentieth century, 'eight centuries of history'. Institutional tradition has it that the corps can trace
descent from the *sergents* entrusted with supporting legal officers by
Philippe Augustus when he embarked for the crusades in 1190. The
validity of this claim might be open to some debate, but it recurs throughout official and semi-official histories.[1] A lineage with the officers
appointed by the commanders of the royal army, the marshals
(*maréchaux*),[2] to supervise and to administer justice in the army, is more
secure. The expansion and increasing permanence of the king's army led,
in turn, to an expansion of these *prévôts des maréchaux* and to the creation
of companies of soldiers to assist them. In the sixteenth century the companies, known as *maréchaussées*, began to acquire jurisdiction over civilians. A defining moment in this acquisition came with the Edict of Paris
issued by François I on 25 January 1536. Brought about by anxiety over
armed brigandage and the apparent participation of royal troops in this,
the edict extended the *prévôts'* competence to include anyone involved in
highway robbery, be they civilian or military, vagabond or settled resident of a community. Within fifty years the *cas prévôtal* had been extended
to include poaching (1538), coining, and sacrilege with breaking and
entering (1564), smuggling and murder (1547), rape and arson (1585).

[1] Marcel Diamant-Berger, *Huit siècles de la gendarmerie* (Paris: J.F. Editions, 1967). See
also Capt. Louis Saurel, 'Regards sur l'histoire de la Gendarmerie', *Revue Historique de
l'Armée*, 17 (1961), 9–49; Col. Louis Saurel, *Peines et gloires des gendarmes* (Paris:
Lavauzelle, 1973); Gen. Jean Besson and Pierre Rosière, *La Gendarmerie nationale* (Paris:
Xavier Richer, 1982). For a critical discussion of the origins of the *Maréchaussée* see
Jacques Lorgnier, *Maréchaussée, histoire d'une révolution judiciaire et administrative*, 2 vols.
(Paris: L'Harmattan, 1994), vol. 1, *Les juges bottés*, chap. 1 *passim*.

[2] Originally there were three key royal officers, the *sénéchal*, the *connétable*, and the
marshals; the first disappeared in 1191, the second was left without a holder from 1626.

Louis XIV's Criminal Ordinance of 1670 further extended this jurisdiction by including burglary and popular disorder, though it sought to limit abuses by bringing the *cas prévôtal* under a degree of supervision by the local royal *présidial* courts. The Ordinance confirmed the *maréchaussées'* responsibility for arresting any offender, whether or not his or her offence came within the remit of a *cas prévôtal*. By the turn of the century the companies were also pursuing a variety of other policing tasks, such as the supervision of *cabarets* and of transport on both roads and waterways.

Louis XIV's reign witnessed significant developments in the policing of Paris with the creation of the *lieutenant-général de police de la ville* in 1667. This was a venal post, and had to function alongside a clutch of other feudal jurisdictions; but it was also a powerful position and the *lieutenant-général* had the direction of a large and increasing number of police agents and watchmen. The policing of provincial towns was in the hands of the local municipal oligarchies or, perhaps, the local *seigneur*. An ordinance of 1699 established *lieutenants-généraux de ville* for the principal towns. Again the posts were venal and seem to have been created more to meet the needs of Louis's fast-dwindling treasury during the War of the Spanish Succession rather than to rationalize urban policing or to respond to any perceived crime wave or increase in disorder. The principal purchasers of the office were often the existing oligarchies and *seigneurs*, who added the title to their others and took some responsibility for policing matters. As a reform this step may have been largely meaningless, though we still await detailed research on the policing of eighteenth-century French towns; in the countryside, however, there were no new moves either to raise money by creating new venal posts or to reform the system. When Louis XIV died in 1714 the *maréchaussée* companies were shot through with the idiosyncrasies of *ancien régime* institutions. There were, perhaps, 1,000 men in all to police the whole of rural France, with the companies ranging from a dozen men or less to around one hundred. Jurisdictions often overlapped; thus, in the Auvergne there were five separate and autonomous companies, and in the neighbouring *généralité* of Bordeaux there were eleven. Flanders was more fortunate; as a relatively new province of the kingdom it had only one company—a *prévôt général*, fourteen officers, and seventy *archers*; created in 1679, it had benefited from the monarchy's limited attempts to rationalize and to iron out complexities.[3]

[3] Iain A. Cameron, *Crime and Repression in the Auvergne and the Guyenne, 1720–1790* (Cambridge: Cambridge University Press, 1981), 3–4; Lorgnier, *Maréchaussée*, vol. 1, *Les juges bottés*, pp. 102, and 113–14.

Across France as a whole company commanders had a bewildering mixture of titles—*prévôt général, prévôt provincial, vice-bailli, vice-sénéchal, lieutenant de robe courte*. All ranks were venal, which made the men difficult to control and direct. The pay was poor and often infrequent, which fostered abuses and negligence. The companies were based in the larger towns; every three months they were supposed to make a sweep of the whole of their jurisdiction, though quite how effectively and thoroughly they did this remains an open question. In July 1716 an ordinance was issued regarding the *maréchaussée* companies, the first of any significance since that of 1670. It acknowledged that there were problems, but its principal solution was simply to order the companies and the *prévôtal* courts to do their duty.[4] Nor was it only the central government which recognized problems in the organization and behaviour of these companies; the Estates of Brittany, for example, petitioned the monarchy for reform in 1716, 1717, and again in 1719.[5]

In 1720 the minister of war, Claude Le Blanc, issued a series of edicts and orders which commenced a rationalization of the *maréchaussées* both in the way that they were recruited and administered and the way that they were deployed.[6] Le Blanc was an able and efficient administrator.[7] Born in 1669, the son of a former intendant of Normandy, he had become a councillor to the *parlement* of Metz in 1696—he married the daughter of the *parlement's* president the following year—and, using his powerful connections at court, he had secured the appointment of intendant of the Auvergne in 1704. In the Auvergne Le Blanc had come face to face with the problems of policing in the provinces. He found corruption at the Royal Mint in Riom and illegal trafficking in money. The recruitment of men for the French armies was hampered by the reluctance of the local inhabitants to serve; there was widespread desertion and a general resistance to ballots for the militia. There were also smugglers who defied the salt tax (*gabelle*) and who cocked a snook at the authorities; some members of both the *maréchaussée* and the salt police (*gabelous*) appeared to be in the smugglers' pay. Le Blanc

---

[4] Claude C. Sturgill, *L'Organisation et l'administration de la maréchaussée et de la justice prévôtale dans la France des Bourbons, 1720–1730* (Vincennes: Service Historique de l'Armée de la Terre, 1981), 19.

[5] Eliane Bertin-Mourot, 'La Maréchaussée en Bretagne au XVIIIe siècle (1720–1789)', Thèse pour le Doctorat, Université de Rennes, 1969, p. 30.

[6] The key texts were the ordinances of 9 and 16 March, and the *Déclaration* of 9 April 1720.

[7] The following is based on Claude C. Sturgill, *Claude Le Blanc: Civil Servant of the King* (Gainesville, Fla.: University Presses of Florida, 1975), esp. 4–10 and 154–66.

employed his own agents in his conflicts with the money-traffickers and the smugglers; he had some success against the former, but it was extremely difficult to get convictions against the smugglers. He drafted a plan for a complete reorganization of the *gabelous*, for an enlargement of, and improvements in, the *maréchaussée*, and for the deployment of troops, but the proposal foundered. The tax-farmers were reluctant to do more than order a strict enforcement of their regulations, and it is doubtful whether, in the midst of an unsuccessful war, Louis XIV's ministers could have found the inclination, the time, or the money for a major reorganization of the provincial police. After four years in the Auvergne Le Blanc was transferred to Flanders, a province then invested by enemy troops. After a shaky start he again showed himself a competent and energetic administrator, particularly as he sought to cope with the war and the famine conditions of 1709–10. When Louis XIV died in 1714 the Duke of Orleans, as Regent, experimented with government by council; Le Blanc was appointed to the War Council. The military reforms proposed by this Council were blocked by its stubborn, conservative president, Marshal Villars; the Council was dissolved in 1718, and responsibility for the military was handed over to Le Blanc as minister.

While a member of the War Council, Le Blanc had expressed concern that the late payment of *maréchaussée* pay fostered negligence; he had also suggested that it would be more sensible to have small brigades spread across the whole territory so as to be able to respond more quickly to problems of disorder.[8] At the beginning of February 1719, less than six months after taking office as minister, he appointed two paymasters for the *maréchaussée* and ordered a full audit of the force with a view to arranging a schedule of payments by which the crown could buy back purchased and hereditary offices. It was possibly because of his experience as an intendant that reform of the policing of the countryside was high on Le Blanc's agenda. There was nothing he could do about the *gabelous*, since these men remained the responsibility of the independent financiers who ran the tax farms.[9] The *maréchaussée* companies, in contrast, drew their authority from the commanders of the

[8] Gen. L. Larrieu, *Histoire de la gendarmerie depuis les origines de la maréchaussée jusqu'à nos jours*, 2 vols. (Paris: Charles-Lavauzelles, 1927–33), vol. 1, titre II, p. 63. Larrieu cites two circulars, dated 5 June 1716 and 21 Sep. 1716, from Le Blanc to intendants; but he describes Le Blanc wrongly as secretary of state during this period.

[9] There is no detailed study of the *gabelous*, but see Earl Robisheaux, 'The "Private Army" of the Tax Farms: The Men and their Origins', *Histoire Social/Social History*, 12 (1973), 256–69.

royal army. But there were other reasons for reforming the *maréchaussée* in 1720 which had little to do with Le Blanc's earlier problems as an intendant. With Louis XIV's death, and with the conclusion of his costly wars, the councillors and ministers of the Regency could turn their attention to the internal situation of France. They were alarmed by the scale of mendicity and vagabondage. Probably, as the French economy recovered from the wars and as the population renewed itself in the wake of the demographic disasters of 1693–4 and 1709–10, the situation was not as serious as they feared, and not as serious as it had been. Nevertheless, during the Regency a series of measures were introduced designed to suppress mendicity.[10] The unreformed *maréchaussée* companies already had a role in this suppression; it seems probable that the reform of 1720 drew at least part of its impetus from the Regency's general anxiety about beggars and vagrants. On 10 March, the day following the first of Le Blanc's reforming edicts, a Royal Ordinance expressed concern about the 'great number of vagabonds and disreputable individuals [*gens sans aveu*], most of whom beg with insolence, more often through idleness than genuine necessity'. It directed the *maréchaussée* and other policing agencies to pursue and arrest them.

The changes wrought by Le Blanc were remarkable in their extent for the France of the *ancien régime*. They laid the foundation for a professional state police organization which was a military body but which, nevertheless, had responsiblity for policing civil as well as military society. No other *ancien régime* state in eighteenth-century Europe had, or was to have, a comparable organization at its disposal. The system was to be further developed by declarations and ordinances, notably in 1768 and 1778, and then during the Revolution and under subsequent regimes; but Le Blanc established a basic uniformity of structure and appearance, of recruitment from former soldiers and deployment in small brigades across the country.[11]

Le Blanc abolished all of the old companies and the old titles, replacing them with a structured, hierarchical system. The new *maréchaussée* was attached to the elite troops of the royal household (*la Gendarmerie de la Maison du Roi*); it remained under the nominal direction of the marshals, but was, in reality, responsible to the minister of war. The men of the corps were also elite in another way. This was a period when

[10] Robert M. Schwartz, *Policing the Poor in Eighteenth-Century France* (Chapel Hill, NC: University of North Carolina Press), 1988, 26–34 and 40–1.

[11] Sturgill, *L'Organisation et l'administration, passim*; and Cameron, *Crime and Repression*, chaps. 1 and 2 for a survey of these reforms.

armies contained large numbers of foreign mercenaries, when desertion was a major problem, and when the tactics of the battlefield had led to strict, precise regimentation, obviating any need for initiative on the part of the soldier. The brigades of the *maréchaussée*, however, were deployed in small groups, which left a great deal to their personal discretion and initiative. In this respect they bore some resemblance to the light troops deployed for patrols and reconnaissance, for ambushes and fighting in broken ground, but who were not often found in the major European armies until the second half of the century.

The jurisdictional boundaries of the new *maréchaussée* companies coincided with those of the *généralités* which, in the eyes of the royal government, had become the most meaningful units of local administration. *Ancien régime* factionalism persisted to the extent that each of the new companies remained formally separate; and *ancien régime* dynastic politics created an anomaly in Lorraine, which came under French administration in the late 1730s, and saw an independent *maréchaussée* company established in 1739 with a unique and distinctive yellow uniform. Lorraine was not formally incorporated into the kingdom until 1766; its *maréchaussée* was assimilated the following year. The Ordinance of 1778 eventually pursued the logic of Le Blanc's reform by uniting all thirty-three companies into one single corps of six divisions. But the national nature of Le Blanc's *maréchaussée* meant that from 1720, where the boundaries of *généralités* did not conform to the pattern of geography, steps could easily be taken to ensure cross-boundary patrols. Thus, from the close of the 1730s instructions were issued authorizing men from the *maréchaussée* in the Dauphiné to act in the *Comté* de Grignan with the same powers as the *maréchaussée* in Provence; and following the annual inspection of 1771, it was suggested that remote areas of Poitou would be more sensibly patrolled by brigades based in Aunis and the Limousin.[12]

The *maréchaussée*'s jurisdiction was essentially rural. Neither Le Blanc not any of his successors contemplated extending it into the larger towns, which were administered by privileged oligarchies who took responsibility for their own police. There could be clashes between the *maréchaussée* and the rulers of these towns when the former appeared to the latter to be encroaching on their authority, or when municipal authorities sought to use the *maréchaussée* for their own purposes. The *Cour des Aides* in Montpellier, for example, wanted the local *prévôt* and

---

[12] Gérard Grand, 'La Maréchaussée de Provence (1554–1790)', Thèse pour le doctorat en Droit, Université d'Aix-Marseille, 1956, pp. 24–5: AG Y^b 789, Inspection 1771, Poitou.

his officers to attend the burial of its president dressed in black; the *prévôt* refused; and *maréchaussée* officers strongly disapproved when the brigades in Marseilles acted as theatre guards during the 1740s and the men stationed in Aix carried out the orders of the *procureur général* of the *parlement* and raided a gaming house.[13] But it was also possible for the *maréchaussée* and urban authorities to work together successfully and in harmony. Paris, the largest and principal city of the kingdom, close to the court at Versailles, provides a good example. Paris, of course, had special policing arrangements directed by its *lieutenant-général de police*. The *maréchaussée* company of Paris, known also as the company of Île de France, had its brigades stationed across the main roads into the city; none was more than fifteen miles from the city centre. Within Paris itself there were two other companies of roughly fifty men each. The *connétablie* was the elite of the corps and took precedence over all others; however, it regularly performed duties at the request of the *lieutenant-général*, notably supervising crowds outside the Comédie-Française, the Comédie-Italienne, and the Opéra. The second company within the city specialized in the repression of counterfeiting and worked closely with the *Cour des Monnaies*, but it too carried out arrests for the *lieutenant-général*. Indeed, the *lieutenant-général* acquired many of the attributes of a national police chief, and as such he employed any and all of the provincial companies as his eyes and arms when he considered it in the interests of Paris or the state. Thus, he circulated them with descriptions of important fugitives, directed them to watch out for poor parents sending unwanted infants to Paris so as to take advantage of the city's foundling hospital, and used them to assist in searches for subversive literature, as well as to make arrests.[14]

From 1720 each company possessed the same administrative structure and was subject to inspection by one of a group of five Inspectors General, increased to six in 1778. Each company was commanded by a *prévôt-général* who had between three and five lieutenants to command the subdivisions of his jurisdiction, and a group of legal officers and clerks to run the *prévôtal* court. The other ranks were divided into brigades and stationed in towns and villages across the *généralité*.

---

[13] Cameron, *Crime and Repression*, 92–4 and 99–101; Grand, 'La Maréchaussée de Provence', 95–6; Daniel Martin, 'La Maréchaussée d'Auvergne face aux authorités administratives et judiciaires au XVIIIᵉ siècle (1720–1780)', *Cahiers d'histoire*, 18 (1973), 337–49; for jurisdictional friction between the *maréchaussée* and the échevins of Lille, see Archives Municipales de Lille, Affaires générales, carton 102, dossiers 14 and 35.

[14] Alan Williams, *The Police of Paris, 1718–1789* (Baton Rouge, La.: Louisiana State University Press, 1979), 86–9, 196, and 214.

Initially these brigades consisted of an NCO (an *exempt*,[15] a brigadier (equivalent to a corporal or junior NCO), or a *sous-brigadier*, depending on his seniority) and four men, originally known as *archers*, but from 1720 increasingly referred to in official correspondence and ordinances as *cavaliers*. During the late 1760s attempts were made to spread the presence of the corps more widely; this was done partly through a small increase in numbers, but also by the reduction of some brigades to just three men, which meant that there could be more brigades on the ground. In 1778 the brigades were restructured to consist of an NCO (now a *maréchal des logis* or a *brigadier*) and three *cavaliers*. Le Blanc's reforms had led to the positioning of 565 brigades, providing something of a permanent police presence across provincial France. Rather than quarterly sweeps, the brigades were expected to make daily patrols, though in the early years at least there appears to have been some laxity in the way that patrols were organized.[16] The Ordinance of 17 April 1760 sought to systematize patrolling by stipulating that patrols should consist of two men and that they should be recorded in a *Journal de Service* which was to be submitted monthly for inspection, first by the local lieutenant and then by the *prévôt*. During their patrols the brigades were to link and liaise with their neighbours; these liaisons were formalized in 1769 into regular meetings, to be held at least once a week and known as *correspondances*. The reforms of 1778 increased the number of brigades to 800; yet as this number testifies in itself, the *maréchaussée* was never a particularly large body of men given the size and population of eighteenth-century France. Following Le Blanc's reforms there were 142 officers and 2,825 NCOs and *archers*; by 1789 these numbers had grown to 383 and 3,660 respectively. The *lieutenant-général de police* in Paris on the eve of the Revolution had 3,114 men at his disposal, of whom just under a half were made up of men available for deterrent patrols.[17] In 1789 the population of France was around 28 million, and the population of Paris was a little over 600,000.

As a national institution the *maréchaussée* was paid by the central government. Of course, the money had to be collected in the provinces and *ancien régime* privileges ensured that some subsidized others without any reference to their economic situation and ability to pay. There were

---

[15] The rank of *exempt* was almost midway between commissioned and non-commissioned rank. When, by the Ordinance of 28 April 1778, it was abolished, the best of the *exempts* were created *sous-lieutenants*, while the remainder became *maréchaux des logis*.

[16] Larrieu, *Histoire de la Gendarmerie*, vol. 1 titre II, p. 202.

[17] Williams, *The Police of Paris*, 68–9.

complaints about the injustice of this, countered by the determination of others to cling to their privileges. Equally, throughout the seven decades following Le Blanc's reforms, there were requests from across the length and breadth of France for new brigades, or for the restoration of brigades which had been moved elsewhere. Such requests were occasionally coupled with proposals for saving money, notably by establishing a foot, rather than a mounted, brigade—though the corps remained mounted throughout the century.[18] Sometimes the requests for a new brigade were met when the force was augmented, but the main concern of the central government, and of the officers who carried out the annual inspections, was always that brigades be sited on the main roads and in areas of particular sensitivity. Thus, in 1768 it was suggested, and rapidly agreed, that a brigade was needed in the expanding textile town of Elbeuf; it was feared that robbers and deserters were able to hide easily among the crowds of workers, but equally the town was in the middle of an important agricultural district which supplied Paris, Rouen, and Versailles.[19] Three years later, following the annual inspection of the Provence company, it was suggested that a new brigade be established just outside Avignon where the main road divided, with one branch heading to Orange and the other to Pont St Esprit; it was noted also that the local inhabitants were unruly and that the area was infested with smugglers. At the same time it was proposed to move the brigade of Pourcieux the short distance to St Maximin la Ste Baume, since the *cavaliers* had to travel there anyway for food and forage.[20]

The men of Le Blanc's reformed *maréchaussée* wore the same military uniform of blue tunic with red facings and silver buttons.[21] The *archers* and NCOs no longer purchased their positions; they were to be recruited from soldiers with four years service and a good disciplinary record; cavalrymen were preferred since the *maréchaussée* was a mounted force. The new recruitment regulations made it easier to dismiss NCOs and *archers* who were negligent, but it did not mean that it was easier to find good men with the necessary and desired attributes; indeed, the turnover of men in the decades immediately after Le Blanc's reforms

[18] Grand, 'La Maréchaussée en Provence', 52–4; Bertin-Mourot, 'La Maréchaussée en Bretagne', 186.
[19] AG X^f 5, Projets d'augmentation, 1768.
[20] AG Y^b 787, Inspection 1771, Provence.
[21] Except where specified, the next four paragraphs draw principally on Cameron, *Crime and Repression*, chap. 2; Clive Emsley, 'La Maréchaussée à la fin de l'ancien régime: note sur la composition du corps', *Revue d'histoire moderne et contemporaine*, 32 (1986), 622–44; and Schwartz, *Policing the Poor*, 203–5.

was considerable. The minimum period of army service was increased to eight years in 1769 and then to sixteen years in 1778. These changes were sharply criticized by the *prévôts-généraux* and the inspectors of the *maréchausée* for reducing the pool of potential recruits. They pointed out that, after sixteen years military service any man who was any good would be a senior NCO, greatly valued, and one that a regiment would not wish to lose; and any soldier who, after sixteen years service, was not such an NCO was probably not the kind wanted by the *maréchaussée*.

Le Blanc left the officer ranks open to purchase and these could still be handed down from father to son, but the government began to impose restrictions; in Brittany, for example, the family of Piquet de Melesse held the position of *prévôt-général* through three generations from 1720, though the inheritors were forbidden from carrying out any judicial functions until they reached the age of 25; the family of Gardin de la Glestière held the lieutenancy at Rennes through four genera-tions.[22] *Survivance* was finally abolished in 1768, and from 1778, when the office of a *prévôt* or lieutenant became vacant, it was no longer to be purchased but was filled by a royal appointee. Thus, a decade before the Revolution, and in spite of the parlous state of the royal finances, offi-cers as well as men of the *maréchaussée* were becoming paid appointees of the central state.

Family links in the corps remained, among the other ranks as well as the officers, but increasingly this was the result of sons choosing to fol-low fathers and brother following brother into the ranks; *enfants du corps*, as the sons of NCOs, *archers*, or *cavaliers* were termed, were exempt from the requirement of military service for most of the eighteenth cen-tury. There were also strong local links, since many seasoned soldiers appear to have requested an appointment in the *maréchaussée* as a means of returning to their *pays natal*. Detail drawn from inspections during the 1770s (see Table 2.1) shows that, overall, rather more than one man in ten was serving in his place of birth, and only about a quarter of the NCOs and *cavaliers* were serving outside their province of birth. The statistics show a decrease in the number of men serving in their place of birth during the decade, but probably the result of accident rather than design, since while the Ordinance of 1778 tightened up the entry qualifications, it does not appear that there was any deliberate govern-ment policy to reduce the number of local recruits. The pull of a man's place of birth was strong and, at the end of the eighteenth century at

---

[22] Bertin-Mourot, 'La Maréchaussée en Bretagne', 59–60 and 90–8.

least, *nostalgie*—home-sickness for the *pays natal*—was recognized in the French army as a serious psychological disorder which could render even a minor wound fatal for a peasant soldier.[23] There were also distinct advantages for the authorities in deploying local men; a variety of patois and local languages were spoken in eighteenth-century France, and it was useful to have policemen who could communicate with the peasantry. Thus, when the *prévôt* of Béarn wrote requesting the appointment of Hughes Fourouge to his company in December 1766, he stressed that 'he speaks the Basque idiom perfectly, very necessary in this region'; and twelve years later *cavalier* François Ferri, although a native of Lorraine, was considered unsuitable for the brigade at Reling because he knew no German. But the local links varied from province to province. In Brittany and the tiny province of Aunis the number of men serving in the *maréchaussée* who were born outside those provinces was noticeably above the average—just over a half in the former, more than two-thirds in the lattter. In Brittany this was possibly a reflection of the relatively small number of Bretons who served in the army; this was a province which provided recruits to the maritime service. Perhaps, too, it was the result of the fierce parochialism of the Bretons. Aunis too was a coastal province curling round the port of La Rochelle. However, the small number of local men may also have been the result of the region's obstinate Protestantism; after all, it fell to the *maréchaussée* to investigate reports of Protestant services.

As with any institution in which people work for their living, there were periodic problems over pay and conditions. While NCOs and *cavaliers* commonly earned more than the artisan and peasant stock in which they originated, their pay was often late in coming. The general inspection of 1771, for example, revealed that in the *lieutenance* of Carcassonne pay for the last part of 1770 had not been received until the following September, no pay had been received for 1771, and the men were being forced to borrow. The idiosyncracies of the *ancien régime* also led to problems: the prison at Mirepoix in Languedoc was seigneurial, and the local brigade complained that the gaoler regularly released their prisoners; in Ruffec in the Limousin the gaoler demanded fees from the *cavaliers*; brigades in the Beauvaisis found themselves compelled to pay *octrois* when royal troops were supposed to be exempt

---

[23] Marcel Reinhard, 'Nostalgie et service militaire pendant la Révolution', *Annales historiques de la Révolution française*, 30 (1958), 1–15.

TABLE 2.1. Origins of men by company, 1771 and 1779 inspections[1]

Company	Men serving		Vacancies		Serving in place of birth		Definitely serving outside place of birth		Origin unknown	
	1771	1779	1771	1779	1771	1779	1771	1779	1771	1779
First Division										
Paris	228	187	9	4	17 (7.4%)	9 (4.9%)	68 (28%)	81 (44.5%)	0	5
Voyages et Chasses	—	62[2]	—	18	—	0[3]	—	—	—	—
Soissonais	90	88	0	0	10 (11.1%)	10 (11.3%)	21 (23.3%)	24 (27.2%)	0	0
Picardie	106	87	0	1	20 (18.8%)	13 (14.9%)	19 (17.9%)	12 (13.7%)	0	0
Flanders	83	72	2	0	7 (8.4%)	5 (6.9%)	24 (28.9%)	29 (40.2%)	0	0
Hainault	62	52 + 1 sn	3	0	4 (6.4%)	6 (11.3%)	21 (33.8%)	22 (41.5%)	0	0
TOTAL	569	548			58 (10.2%)	46 (8.4%)	153 (26.8%)	168 (30.6%)	0	0
Second Division										
Alsace	75	71 + 4 sn	1	1	5 (6.6%)	3 (4%)	11 (14.6%)	15 (20%)	0	0
Champagne	201	165	1	3	26 (12.9%)	25 (15.1%)	22 (10.9%)	18 (10.9%)	0	0
Trois Evêchés	93	80 + 1 sn	1	0	2 (2.1%)	2 (2.4%)	32 (34.4%)	27 (33.3%)	0	0
Lorraine	176	135 + 4 sn	1	1	21 (11.9%)	9 (6.4%)	47 (26.7%)	39 (28%)	0	2
Franche Comté	93	90	0	2	8 (8.6%)	2 (2.2%)	15 (16.1%)	17 (18.8%)	0	0
TOTAL	532	541			62 (11.7%)	41 (7.6%)	127 (23.8%)	116 (21.4%)		2
Third Division										
Berry	119	94	1	2	24 (20.1%)	10 (10.6%)	12 (10%)	28 (29.7%)	0	0
Bourbonnais	110	96	0	0	28 (25.4%)	13 (13.5%)	12 (10.9%)	22 (22.9%)	0	0
Burgundy	—	103	—	1	—	22 (22.9%)	—	20 (20.8%)	—	7
Lyonnais	91	81	3	2	7 (7.6%)	7 (8.7%)	31 (34%)	15 (18.7%)	0	1
Orleans	178	147	2	13	28 (15.7%)	16 (11%)	71 (39.8%)	61 (42%)	0	2
TOTAL	498	521			87 (12.5%)	68 (13.5%)	126 (25.3%)	146 (28%)	0	2

Fourth Division										
Alençon	94	88	1	0	15 (15.9%)	17 (19.3%)	24 (25.5%)	13 (14.7%)	0	0
Brittany	199	154	2	6	18 (9%)	12 (7.7%)	112 (56.2%)	78 (50.6%)	0	0
Caen	79	79	0	1	12 (15.9%)	17 (21.5%)	4 (5%)	5 (6.3%)	0	0
Rouen	120	100	1	0	13 (10.8%)	17 (17%)	33 (27.5%)	18 (18%)	0	0
Touraine	241	199	1	0	37 (15.3%)	25 (12.8%)	28 (11.6%)	49 (25.2%)	0	5
TOTAL	754	620			95 (12.6%)	88 (14.2%)	201 (26.6%)	163 (26.2%)		
Fifth Division										
Aunis	72	53	2	7	2 (2.8%)	2 (3.8%)	51 (71.8%)	35 (67.3%)	1	1
Béarn	120	104	1	?4	12 (10%)	5 (4.8%)	8 (6.7%)	45 (43.2%)	1	0
Guyenne	120	102	0	10	17 (14.1%)	14 (13.7%)	13 (10.8%)	25 (24.5%)	0	0
Limousin	119	114	1	4	35 (29.4%)	22 (19.8%)	6 (5%)	17 (15.3%)	0	3
Poitou	106	111	0	9	16 (15%)	9 (8.2%)	29 (27.3%)	33 (30.2%)	0	2
TOTAL	537	484			82 (15.3%)	52 (10.7%)	107 (19.9%)	155 (32%)		
Sixth Division										
Auvergne	113	99	0	1	12 (10.6%)	12 (12.3%)	27 (23.8%)	24 (24.7%)	0	2
Dauphiné	114	96	0	4	14 (12.2%)	10 (10.4%)	31 (27.1%)	20 (20.8%)	0	0
Languedoc	227	193	1	7	39 (17.1%)	23 (12%)	51 (22.4%)	34 (17.8%)	0	2
Montauban	91	79	1	1	13 (14.4%)	14 (17.7%)	8 (8.8%)	17 (21.5%)	1	0
Provence	123	93	4	3	21 (17.2%)	14 (15%)	21 (17.2%)	15 (16.1%)	1	0
Roussillon	49	39	1	1	8 (16.3%)	5 (12.8%)	23 (46.9%)	12 (30.7%)	0	0
TOTAL	717	599			127 (17.6%)	78 (13%)	161 (22.4%)	122 (20.3%)		

Notes: sn = supernumerary.

[1] The divisional structure was not clarified until 1778. Three companies had been added since the 1720 reform: Lorraine 1739/67; Corsica 1769, though it is not included in these inspection reports; Voyages et Chasses du Roi, 1772, essentially for the protection of the king when on his travels and while hunting.

[2] No vacancies are given in the review, but the Ordinance of 1778 set the size of the company at 20 NCOs and 60 *cavaliers*.

[3] At least 14 of the company came from the area covered by the company of Paris, including four men from Versailles.

[4] The Lyonnais company had three brigades with only three men in 1779, the Béarn company had eleven brigades with only three men and three with only two. Possibly there were 'vacancies' in all of these instances, but the three-man brigades could have been left over from the pre-1778 brigade structure.

Source: AG Y^b 787, 788, 789, 790, 800, 801, 802, 803, 804, 805.

from the tax.[24] Though fees were paid for the arrest of criminals and beggars, and though expenses incurred on duty could be claimed in certain instances, securing payment of this money was rarely easy. Additional hardship resulted from the requirement that *cavaliers* provide their own horse, and this commonly meant going into debt. A horse lost on active service was likely to be replaced, but the *masse de remont*, a contributory fund organized to provide new horses for those which died or became useless to the service, was as much a burden as a boon before the mid-1770s. An order of 1769 which required men to live in barracks relieved them of the cost of housing; nevertheless, the insistence that they live in barracks without their families meant that any family man had to provide a separate lodging for his wife and children. The prospect of a financial bonus no doubt contributed to the enthusiasm with which *cavaliers* began apprehending beggars in 1767 after the government announced a reward for every such arrest; the courts and the new houses of correction were unable to cope, and the intendants promptly stopped paying the bounty.[25] Financial problems were almost certainly the spur to a few men 'moonlighting' in artisan trades or as innkeepers, and often insisting that the business was that of their wife. Financial problems may also have prompted some graft, corruption, and even criminal offences. Unsavoury and unsuitable men were regularly noted in the annual inspections. The most common problem, however, appears to have been drink. There were also men who were too old or too infirm to be of much value in the job; though the guarantee of a pension in 1778 went some way towards reducing this problem. For all these problems and difficulties, however, it seems fair to say that as the *ancien régime* in France drew to its dramatic end, the personnel of its *maréchaussée* was increasingly better disciplined, fitter, and carried out its duties in a systematic and reasonably rigorous way.

The duties of the corps were many and varied. It still had a significant military role in supervising troops on the march and in the pursuit of deserters. Also, in areas where there was a strong, permanent military presence, such as the north-east, much of the *maréchaussée's* time was taken up in dealing with soldiers who had committed civilian offences. The evidence from Flanders reveals soldiers as being particularly involved in violent crime, and their participation in various forms

---

[24] AG Y^b 787, Inspection 1771 (Languedoc); Y^b 789, Inspection 1771 (Limousin); Y^b 790, Inspection 1771 (Paris).

[25] Olwen H. Hufton, *The Poor of Eighteenth-Century France, 1750–1789* (Oxford: Clarendon Press, 1974), 223.

of theft also appears to have been far in excess of their proportionate numbers in the community.[26]

According to the brief *Instructions pour les cavaliers de maréchaussée* printed in 1775, the institution had been established 'to maintain public peace, facilitate commerce, and enforce the execution of the laws'.[27] The Ordinance of 1778 made a clear differentiation between ordinary and extraordinary service (*le service ordinaire* and *le service extraordinaire*). The former concerned the *maréchaussée*'s role in maintaining the peace and referred to the daily activities which this role required. Essentially the ordinary service involved the *cavaliers* in patrolling the main roads of their district, supervising fairs, markets, and village festivals. During such patrols they were expected to arrest suspects and vagabonds, to enquire into any incidents reported to them, to collect lists of all persons staying in the local inns or *cabarets*, to check on vehicles and make sure that they were not overweight and thus breaking up the roads. An account of a brigade's patrols had to be kept in the *journal de service*; this was supposed to be signed by a leading member of the community of each village or small town covered by their patrols, and, as noted above, was inspected monthly by officers.[28] While the pattern of patrols was similar across the whole of France, each region presented its own distinct problems. The Auvergne, for example, was a poor, isolated province with a stagnant economy; in the aftermath of a harvest failure in 1770 the commander of the Auvergne Company informed the minister of war that he had suspended the apprehension of beggars, fearing that a strict enforcement could lead to the arrest of more than 4,000 people of both sexes and of all ages before a day was over.[29] The Flanders Company, in contrast, patrolled a sensitive border region with large military garrisons. Following the annual inspection of 1779 the inspecting general noted that this company was constantly having to patrol alongside troops on the march, and was burdened by the pursuit and guarding of deserters. Moreover, differences within the region meant differences within within the company; the horses of

---

[26] Lorgnier, *Maréchaussée*, vol. 2, *Quand le gendarme juge*, 48, notes soldiers as making up 53.4% of those guilty of homicide, 51.6% of those responsible for attacks on the main roads, 20% of those responsible for incidents of grievous bodily harm; soldiers also comprised 13.96% of those guilty of petty theft, and 12% of those guilty of breaking and entering.

[27] Musée de la Gendarmerie (Melun), *Instructions pour les cavaliers de maréchaussée* (1775), 1.

[28] See the Ordinances of 19 Apr. 1769 (Section III) and 28 Apr. 1778 (Section IV, articles 3 and 22).

[29] AG X^f 12, Panay du Deffan to Choiseul, 19 Nov. 1770.

the men in the *lieutenance* of Arras were in good shape, unlike those in Lille and Bailleul where the local countryside furnished little and where, for two-thirds of the year, they patrolled up to their hocks in mud.[30] The *service extraordinaire* referred to those activities for which men were specifically requested by other authorities. These could involve, for example, escorting public coaches, those carrying tax receipts, or wagons containing gunpowder and ammunition. But the principal roles here were carrying out arrests on judicial warrants and providing coercive assistance (*main-forte*) for the civil authorities.

An edict of 1731 formally exempted nobles, clergy, *sécrétaires du roi*, and royal judges from the *maréchaussée*'s civilian jurisdiction, though in effect it had always been concerned largely with offenders drawn from the poor. Two kinds of *cas prévôtal* were defined: those relating to the accused—vagrants (who always constituted the largest single group of individuals arrested by the *maréchaussée*), gypsies, escaped felons, 'old offenders', and deserters; and those relating to the offence—highway robbery, burglary, coining, and disorder. Essentially, such offences and offenders were those regarded as presenting a threat to the security of the state. While *cavaliers* might be called upon to arrest offenders accused of petty theft or minor assault, and while they might seek to break up a small fight, their real concerns were those individuals on the margins of society, serious violence, whether in the form of rioting or connected with robbery, or the kinds of threats to the general good posed by, for example, the circulation of false money. It was these matters also with which the *prévôtal* courts were concerned.

The *prévôtal* courts provided speedy verdicts, and there was no appeal. The courts were military, but the Criminal Ordinance of 1670 had introduced a significant degree of legal supervision. A suspect apprehended for a *cas prévôtal* had to be interrogated within twenty-four hours of arrest by the local *maréchaussée* lieutenant who acted as the *prévôtal* judge. As a soldier, the lieutenant was most unlikely to have had any legal training and, during the interrogation, he had to be assisted by a legally trained *assesseur*. A dossier was then prepared and sent, within three days of the accused's arrest, to the nearest royal *présidial* court, which decided on whether or not the offence came within the competence of the *prévôt*. If the judges of the *présidial* court were satisfied, the dossier was returned and the lieutenant issued his final judgement in consultation with the *assesseur* and five local judges. The *prévôtal* court

---

[30] AG Xf 12, Inspections . . . 1779 . . . Deuxième division.

had the power to pass a variety of penalties—death, the galleys, banish-
ment; yet while the assumption might be that military justice was bound
to be harsh, the evidence does not bear this out. In the Périgueux
towards the end of the *ancien régime*, the *prévôtal* magistrates appear to
have been rather more moderate than other judges, particularly in the
treatment of beggars. In Flanders the *prévôt* worked in harmony with
other jurisdictions and contributed to the general trend in the ameliora-
tion of punishment. Furthermore, while overall the judicial role of the
maréchaussée was gradually giving way to a broader policing role, it
appears that country people were increasingly prepared to use the *prévôtal* courts, as they promised a justice that was at least as trustworthy as
that of other courts, but which was much less subject to long delays and
complacencies.[31] That said, however, it remains the case that rural communities generally sought to resove internal differences, including
assaults and crimes, among themselves; they only had recourse to an
external agency such as the *maréchaussée* as a last resort.

Understandably, the *maréchaussée* was not popular with those whom
it was charged to apprehend; and an officious *cavalier* demanding to see
an individual's passport or travelling papers was not going to make many
friends. The *procès-verbaux* of arrests reveal a colourful string of abusive
epithets directed at the *cavaliers*: *sacrés bougres, valets de bourreau, cheva-
liers de la Chaine, foutus gueux*.[32] Nor was it only from the individual
who had been apprehended that abuse and violence came. Some beggars
were able to call on the support of local communities since, in certain
instances, the medieval perception persisted of the beggar as a sacred
figure. Deserters, similarly, could call upon, and get, community support against *cavaliers* seeking to apprehend them. The unpopular ballot
for the *milice* might also provoke hostility towards the *cavaliers* charged
with supervising it; while during disorders over the high cost or shortage of food, it was the small brigades of *maréchaussée* which commonly
found themselves in the forefront of confrontations with angry crowds.
In the observations appended to his general inspection of the Brittany
company in 1771, Jean-Nicolas de Cambon reported that two *cavaliers*
had recently killed a man who had been verbally and physically abusing

---

[31] Cameron, *Crime and Repression*, chap. 4; Lorgnier, *Maréchaussée*, esp. vol. 1, *Les juges
bottés*, chap. 15, and vol. 2, *Quand le gendarme juge*, chap. 8.

[32] R. Samson, *Marginaux, délinquents et séditieux dans le beauvaisis, 1765–1790*, vol. 1,
Vagabonds et mediants à la veille de la révolution de 1789 (Beauvais: Centre départemental
de documentation pédagogique, 1980), 58. Most of such terms would lose in the translation; but 'knights of the chain' refers to the chain attached to offenders being led to the
galleys.

them. However, he did not consider their offence to be serious since 'the Breton peasant has a marked hatred of the *maréchaussée*, and the fact that [the peasants] got away with killing an *exempt* and a *cavalier* at Landerneau three years ago has only served to perpetuate their insolence'.[33] Yet even in Brittany it was not unknown for local people to assist *cavaliers* in making arrests. Moreover, some *cavaliers* were so well integrated into the communities where they were stationed that they were invited to weddings and asked to act as godparents.[34]

There were critics of the *maréchaussée* among the elite. Bertrand de Molleville, for example, the intendant of Brittany, protested that after the 1778 ordinance each *cavalier* had become 'the arbitrator and sovereign of his district'. Even the most respectable people were at his mercy, threatened by false denunciations or by financial corruption; moreover, the *cavaliers* did not pursue vagabonds as they ought, either because of negligence or because they could not be bothered. Yet de Molleville's complaints were probably coloured by his relations with the local *prévôt* and his dislike of the corps's independence. Few intendants liked the independence of the *maréchaussée*, which was guaranteed by its military nature and by its responsibility to the minister of war.[35] There were jurisdictional clashes, as noted above, but few among the privileged orders perceived of the *maréchaussée* as a serious and constant threat to their authority and privileges. Significantly, the brigades and the *prévôtal* courts were no challenge to seigneurial justice, which was often most concerned with enforcing feudal dues and rights. There were attempts by the central government to revive feudal justice during the eighteenth century, recognizing that it was in the interests of *seigneurs* and state to be allies in controlling the countryside; but few *seigneurs* were prepared to spend much effort, money, or time on providing local courts to try cases which did not involve their personal concerns.[36]

Overall, perhaps, the contemporary criticism of the *maréchaussée* has probably been rather too readily accepted by historians, and the praise

[33] AG Y^b 790, Inspection 1771 (Brittany).

[34] Eric Hestault, 'La Maréchaussée dans la lieutenance de Nantes à la fin de l'Ancien Régime (1770–1790)', Mémoire de maîtrise, Université de Nantes, 1992, p. 81.

[35] Hestault, 'La Maréchaussée dans la lieutenance de Nantes', 279–80, 305–6, 332–5, 342, and 364–7.

[36] John Mackrell, 'Criticism of Seigneurial Justice in Eighteenth-Century France', in J. F. Bosher (ed.), *French Government and Society, 1500–1850* (London: Athlone Press, 1973); Steven G. Reinhardt, *Justice in the Sarladais, 1770–1790* (Baton Rouge, La.: Louisiana State University Press, 1991), 60–4.

rather too readily dismissed.[37] Foreign observers like Sir William Mildmay were impressed with the institution which fought

a kind of perpetual war, not against a foreign enemy, but against such of the native subjects as disturb the peace and violate the laws of their country; and who, as such must be deemed the common enemies of all society. Happy therefore is it for the honest part of mankind, to find so formidable a force, ready to fight their quarrels, and protect their properties.

Of course, such a military institution would be quite out of place in his native England, but Mildmay considered that it might be possible to set up a similar sort of organization 'subservient wholly to the civil power' which would be of immense value on the roads around London.[38] Criticisms made by French people within France brought forth powerful responses:

There is no end to criticisms of the *maréchaussée*; from the traveller, because he does not often see them on the road; from country people, because they do not maintain a perpetual surveillance of the farms; from town dwellers, legal officials etc. etc. etc. Finally, everyone thinks he has the right to complain because the corps does not occupy itself with him solely. Yet these unjust men are sheltered from the enterprises of malefactors, live peacefully in the bosom of their families surrounded by their possessions, without doubt, because of the watchfulness and the ever-increasing, perpetual fatigues of this corps, which they criticise . . .[39]

---

[37] There is, for example, some debate about how the *cavaliers* interpreted and enforced the laws regarding beggars. Some historians have stressed evidence which suggests that they focused on serious offenders and let others slip by; others have concentrated on the evidence of enthusiastic arrests of easy targets, particularly when the government was offering a reward for every beggar apprehended. This, it has been suggested, implies a concentration on the harmless who offered no trouble to the *cavaliers*. Weighing up the controversy, Clay Ramsay concludes that, when it came to deciding on an arrest (the years of rewards apart), they took the signs of being a stranger—a pause at the crossroads, a curious accent or patois—as being most significant, and that they demanded passports and travelling papers as a substitute for a local character witness. Clay Ramsay, *The Ideology of the Great Fear: The Soissonais in 1789* (Baltimore: Johns Hopkins University Press, 1992), 54–6.

[38] Sir William Mildmay, *The Police of France: or, an Account of the Laws and Regulations established in that Kingdom for the Preservation of Peace, and the Preventing of Robberies* (London, 1763), 31–2 and 41. Tobias Smollet, having travelled from Paris to Lyons in the early autumn of 1763 without meeting a single *cavalier*, nevertheless believed that their existence kept the roads safe. 'It is a reproach upon England that some such patrol is not appointed for the protection of travellers', Tobias Smollet, *Travels Through France and Italy*, ed. Frank Felstein (Oxford: Oxford University Press, 1979), 68.

[39] Anon., *Réflexions sur le Corps de la Maréchaussée, addressées, en forme de lettre, à l'auteur du livre intitulé: Défense du système de guerre moderne* (Geneva, 1781), 64–5.

The same point was underlined in the annual report of the *maréchaussée* for the *généralité* of Soissons for 1788. After listing the number of deaths investigated and the number of arrests made by the company during the year, the report concluded that 'we cannot repeat too often that [the *maréchaussée's*] presence alone prevents far worse evils, and its utility in the provinces where it is active cannot be calculated'.

TABLE 2.2. *The statistics of the* maréchaussée *in the Soissonnais, 1788*

(a) *Reported crimes*	
Attempted murder	7
Highway robbery	11
	The above offences resulted in 3 fatalities
Thefts from churches	14
Other thefts	212
Threatened arson	5
TOTAL	249
(b) *Arrests*	
Thieves	24
Wanted on warrants	48
Beggars	63
Vagabonds	96
Prostitutes	26
Mad men	10
Mad women	5
Deserters	18
Soldiers for misconduct	6
TOTAL	324
(c) *Present at interments*	
Suicide because of mental derangement	6
Accidentally drowned	9
Road accidents	10
Quarry accidents	3
Frozen to death	5
TOTAL	33

Source: Constructed from information in AG MR 1957, Liasse, 'Ordonnances', *Extrait de la correspondance de la Maréchaussée de la Généralité de Soissons, résultat pour l'année 1788*.

The Soissonais company's stress on the effectiveness of its preventive role was, arguably, the best and, given the statistics, perhaps the only way in which the company could justify its existence (see Table 2.2). There were 141 men of all ranks in the company in 1788; 92 of these were *cavaliers*. Putting these figures alongside the theft and arrest statistics, the implication is that, even if the *cavaliers* alone are perceived as the most active members of the force, each man was responsible for following up only about two thefts and for arresting around three offenders in the course of twelve months. Of course, on the eve of the Revolution crime, vagrancy, and other social phenomena were not assessed nationally and in the statistical form which came to characterize the nineteenth-century state. Such national assessments, when they did come, probably contributed to the overall concerns about and conceptualization of such phenomena, and were used to formulate and drive policy. Eighteenth-century enlightenment thought was part of the process towards such formulations, but it was beginning to address problems of criminality and penal sanctions. Lawyers, philosophers, and policemen, including at least one officer of the *maréchaussée*,[40] presented a variety of proposals for the better supervision of the population, and more effective pursuit and punishment so as to check vagrancy and other forms of offending.

Cesare Beccaria's *Dei delitti e delle pene* (*On Crimes and Punishments*) was first published in 1764, and it appeared in French translation the following year. The pamphlet, with its call for just, equitable laws and for certain, rational punishments, crystallized much of the progressive thinking already developing in France. Even if Beccaria did not have much to say about policing structures, it was apparent that the *maréchaussée* was the kind of organization which could act as an important adjunct of a reformed system: an effective system of police contributed to the certainty of an offender's apprehension and thus to the certainty of punishment; it also ensured respect for the law, thus assisting in the prevention of crime. And even those less sympathetic to legal and penal reform saw value in the *maréchaussée* and the *prévôtal* courts as important auxiliaries to the justice system, not least because of their focus on vagrants and the poor, something which both played upon and reinforced prejudices about those responsible for crime.[41]

The *cahiers de doléances* drawn up at the outset of Revolution took up the desires expressed on and off throughout the century by both individuals and different local bodies for the *maréchaussée* to be enlarged. It

[40] M. Guillaute, *Mémoire sur la Réformation de la Police de France* (1749), introduction and notes by Jean Seznec (Paris: Herman, 1974).

[41] Nicole Dyonet, 'La Maréchaussée et la culture judiciaire française au temps de Beccaria', in Michel Porret (ed.), *Beccaria et la culture juridique des lumières* (Geneva: Droz, 1997). In 1780 Jean Charles Lenoir, *lieutenant-général de police*, was suggesting that the police should lose such judicial role as they had so as to concentrate on prevention (Williams, *The Police of Paris*, 37). Clay Ramsay (*The Ideology of the Great Fear*, 18) notes some government officials and large farmers seeing the *maréchaussée* as an instrument for disciplining labour, notably those workers who, in their perceptions, had opted for a life of begging and vagrancy.

was a common complaint of the *cahiers* that the force was simply too thin on the ground to be effective, and several small towns and villages protested that they hardly ever saw patrols.[42] The Third Estate of Étampes complained that governments in the past had been more interested in fighting wars outside France's frontiers than maintaining peace at home. 'Brigands lay waste towns and countryside, and all citizens want to be able to travel in safety, and to rest in their homes sheltered from the attacks of these enemies of their repose.' The *maréchaussée*, 'the most useful corps for the nation', should therefore be increased and better paid.[43] The fears and anxieties expressed in other *cahiers* were many and varied. The parish of Bures wanted the *cavaliers* to maintain a careful watch over cultivated land during their patrols, so as to arrest those who 'killed chickens, uprooted young fruit trees, cut green corn and stole other produce, broke down fences, and committed other damage'.[44] The clergy of Montargis were particularly concerned about the large number of poor in their district and considered that an enlarged *maréchaussée*, with some of the additional brigades being on foot, would serve to keep them in check. They could also be deployed

to uncover the obscure hideouts of brigands, to protect growing crops; perhaps they could be employed most usefully, and without danger, to protect hunting rights; and finally to break up brawls [*rixes*] which, if allowed to continue, can become murderous; to check, by their presence other disorders all too common among the ruder sort when they gather for pleasure . . .[45]

Other *cahiers* also called for foot brigades; they would be of much more use for the pursuit of offenders in mountainous regions, assured *cahiers* from the Auvergne; they would also be cheaper, explained the Third Estate of Dombes.[46] Although they were drawn up several months before *la grande peur*, it is striking quite how many *cahiers* sought an increase of *maréchaussée* because of 'brigands', because of the problems of dearth and the high cost of bread, and because of 'the evil-minded who go about in bands, arms in their hands, to extort charity'.[47] In the

---

[42] Victor Fourastié, *Cahiers des doléances de la sénéchaussée de Cahors* (Cahors, 1908) 73 (Cenac) and 326 (Sauzet); A. Le May, ed. *Cahiers des doléances des corporations de la ville d'Angers et des paroisses de la sénéchaussée particulière d'Angers*, 2 vols. (Angers, 1915), ii. 784 (La Pommeraye).

[43] *Arch. Parl. (1re série)*, iii. 288. [44] Ibid., iv. 385. [45] Ibid., iv. 20.

[46] Françisque Mège, *Les Cahiers des paroisses d'Auvergne en 1789* (Clermont-Ferrand, 1899: Geneva: Megariotis Reprints, 1979), 88–9; *Arch. Parl. (1re série)*, vi. 83. For other *cahiers* proposing foot brigades see ibid., iii. 647 (Le Mans), v. 360 (Peronne), 658 (St. Quentin), 757 (Sens), vi. 77 (Troyes), 123 (Vendôme), 273 (Cadenet), and 699 (Soissons).

[47] Ibid., iv. 783 (Palaiseau) and 641 (Lardy).

Vendée around Angers such brigands, it was alleged, had commonly been involved in smuggling salt across the Breton border and had learned their violent behaviour in clashes with the police of the tax farms; now they infested the wooded countryside.[48] Elsewhere, where main roads ran through large desolate woods, it was urged that travellers could be protected from brigands by new brigades of *maréchaussée*.[49]

The *cahiers* might have sought protection and the maintenance of order from an enlarged and better-paid *maréchaussée*, but they were not entirely uncritical of the institution. There were complaints about *cavaliers* vexing carters and waggonners with fines for infringements of regulations.[50] Some disliked *prévôtal* justice. The Third Estate of Gray urged that the *prévôt* be limited 'to the capture and imprisonment of offenders and suspected persons, and to delivering them to a judge within twenty-four hours'. That of Le Mans wanted an accused to be taken as soon as possible after arrest to the prison of an ordinary judge, since a lieutenant of the *maréchaussée* should not have jurisdiction over ordinary citizens.[51] But rather more common than any explicit criticism of the *prévôtal* courts was the desire to have the *maréchaussée* brought under the control of local judges and jurisdictions. For the *bailliage* of Beaumont-le-Roger the problem was the military structure of the institution which was 'absolutely contrary to the carrying out of its functions', since, as a result, 'there was no relationship, no subordination to formal justice, the sole reason for it to exist'.[52] Yet this, like the overwhelming majority of references to the *maréchaussée* in the *cahiers*, was a call for reform rather than abolition. In February 1789 a military commission proposed improvements to the administrative structure and organization of the *maréchaussée*.[53] The proposals seem to have been forgotten in the political effervesence of the following months. The *maréchaussée* itself became swept up in the liberal, reformist enthusiasm of the Revolution's early stages and was transformed into the

---

[48] Le May, *Cahiers . . . d'Angers*, ii. 255 (Mozé) and 649 (Saint Philbert-en-Mauges).

[49] *Arch. Parl.* (*1re série*), iv. 546 (Férolles), 644 (Lesigny), v. 146 (Triel), 766 (Sézanne), and vi. 212 (Vitry-le-François).

[50] Ibid., v. 202 (Villeneuve-sous-Dammartin) and vi. 658 (Orleans).

[51] Ibid., i. 780 and iii. 647. The *cahier* of St Cloud was so hostile to the vexations created, in part, by these powers of the *maréchaussée* that, exceptionally, they wanted the whole force abolished; ibid., v. 68.

[52] Ibid., iii. 314; and see also iii. 254 (Dourdan), iv. 212 (Vitry-le-François), 408 (Charonne), 699–700 (Soissons), 709 (Meudon), v. 95 (Saint-Maurice-Montcouronne), and 331 (Mortagne au Perche).

[53] AG MR 1957, Liasse 'Notes, ordonnances et mémoires sur la maréchaussée', Mémoire sur le projet d'une nouvelle distribution des Divisions de la Maréchaussée.

Gendarmerie Nationale. But the context in which the reforms took place, and the tasks which dominated the Gendarmerie's existence over the following quarter of a century, helped to ensure that it maintained its military nature.

3

'GOOD CITIZENS AND BRAVE SOLDIERS': GENDARMES AND THE REVOLUTION

The Declaration of the Rights of Man and Citizen, adopted by the National Assembly on 26 August 1789, proclaimed the sovereign people as the source of all political legitimacy and the law as the expression of the general will. All citizens had the right to participate in making the law, either in person or through their representatives, and all were equal under it. The maintenance of the rights of the citizen necessitated a public force (*une force publique*) which was to be funded, equally, by all citizens according to their means. The *maréchaussée* had the potential to be such a force, and the *cahiers de doléances* suggested that many people within France perceived it as such. However, the disorders of 1789 emphasized how thin the institution was on the ground, while the removal of the *présidial* checks on *prévôtal* justice by royal decree appeared quite contrary to the aspirations of those in the National Assembly who were seeking reform.

The Flour War of late April and May 1775 was a wave of popular disorder principally in the Paris region but stretching in a great rectangle from Amiens to Dijon and from Rouen to Blois. The disorder had been prompted by a poor harvest and the desire of the new *contrôleur général*, Turgot, for a free market in grain. At times small brigades of the *maréchaussée* could do nothing to prevent the crowds which they confronted from fixing prices in markets and preventing the movement of grain. But the disorder was relatively short-lived. Arrests and examples were made, particularly by the brigades functioning within a thirty- to forty-five-kilometre radius of Paris.[1] Yet there was no serious

---

[1] Cynthia A. Bouton, *The Flour War: Class, Gender and Community in Late Ancien Régime French Society* (University Park, Pa.: Pennsylvania State University Press, 1993), 100–1, notes that 92% of the 548 arrests during the Flour War were made by *cavaliers*

movement for political and social reform to add an extra, and more dangerous dimension to the riots. In 1789 the situation was quite different. The currents of the Great Fear swept much further; the rumours of brigands and famine plots went much deeper; while the excitement generated by the calling of the Estates General and peasant hopes for an end to feudal exactions, which in turn prompted attacks on chateaux, made the situation much more serious. In general the *maréchaussée* appears to have acted in a moderate, even-handed manner; it sought to repress crowds engaged in price-fixing or preventing the movement of grain, but it also sought to ensure that the markets were well stocked and initiated the prosecution of grain-hoarders. The corps continued the moderate attitude towards beggars which had been emerging gradually within the *prévôtal* courts, while the behaviour of some of its members suggested that they were as much inspired by the ideology of the nascent Revolution as anyone else.[2]

The scale of the disorder was such that on 21 May 1789 a decree from the royal council removed, temporarily, the requirement that the *présidial* court rule on the *prévôt*'s competence in cases where the accused were charged with participating in disturbances. There was a precedent for this; a similar decreee had been issued during the disorders resulting from a bad harvest in 1739–40, but in 1789 the political situation was quite different. The new decree created confusion, especially as it became enmeshed with measures proposed by the National Assembly for resolving problems of grain supply. Also, by restoring unchecked authority to 'booted justice', albeit as a temporary measure and in very specific circumstances, the decree appeared to run counter to the reforms being undertaken in the penal code. The situation was further confused in September when the Assembly instructed local judges of the ordinary *bailliage* or *sénéchaussée* courts to prosecute anyone engaged in preventing the free movement of grain. By this move the Assembly distanced itself from the exceptional tribunals of the *prévôts* but, at the same time, appeared to contradict the decree of 21 May, thus opening the way to local friction.[3] One local incident in particular drew hostile

based in the Beauvais (322), Brie and Champagne (78), Melun and Nemours (53), and Île-de-France (42).

[2] Iain A. Cameron, *Crime and Repression in the Auvergne and the Guyenne, 1720–1790* (Cambridge: Cambridge University Press, 1981), pp. 244–8; Clay Ramsay, *The Ideology of the Great Fear: The Soissonnais in 1789* (Baltimore: Johns Hopkins University Press, 1992), 117–19, for the restrained response and sensible analysis of the Great Fear in the Clermontais by the local *prévôt*.

[3] Ramsay, *The Ideology of the Great Fear*, 170 and 176–7.

attention to the judicial power of the *prévôts*. In early November the powerful oratory of Mirabeau was deployed against *prévôt* de Bournissac in Marseilles who, in violation of the new provisional law on criminal procedure, had denied new legal rights to a group of individuals charged with rioting. Moreover, de Bournissac had allegedly sided with the bourgeois militia against revolutionary patriots, and selected interested parties from that militia to act as judges alongside him. The *prévôt*'s justice, insisted Mirabeau, had degenerated into oppression and tyranny. Other deputies, notably Dubois de Crancé who denounced the *prévôt* of Champagne, echoed Mirabeau's outrage,[4] and across the country other examples of injustice and partiality by the *prévôts* were trumpeted and roused popular prejudice. There were those who defended the *prévôtal* courts as central to the efficiency of the *maréchaussée*. It was stressed that *prévôtal* justice was speedy and, unlike other courts, in normal times it was hardly arbitrary given the checks of the *présidial* court. The officers of the *maréchaussée* were 'intrepid warriors [and] accomplished magistrates, as familiar with the sword of war as with that of justice'.[5] But such arguments ran against the tide of opinion in the Assembly. In March 1790 all sentences passed in *prévôtal* courts were suspended and prisoners detained on such a sentence were released. The decrees of 6–11 September 1790 abolished *prévôtal* justice along with all other exceptional tribunals.[6]

Amidst the attempts to reform the laws and the penal system, the early revolutionary assemblies also recognized the need for instruments to enforce the laws. In 1790 and 1791 the old venal offices in urban areas were replaced with elected *commissaires*. In Paris the position of *lieu-tenant-général* was abolished and the police was decentralized to the city's forty-eight sections; each section was to elect its own *commissaire de police*. In addition to the *commissaires* in Paris, a small, centralized corps of twenty-four *officiers de paix* was established. Provincial towns and cities were also authorized to elect *commissaires* to serve as their principal police officers, supported by such additional force as the

---

[4] *Arch. Parl.* (*1re série*), ix. 696–7 (5 Nov. 1789); and see also ibid., x. 257–8 (25 Nov. 1789) and x. 427–8 (8 Dec. 1789), and S. Vialla, *Marseille révolutionnaire. L'armée nation* (*1789–1793*) (Paris: Chapelot, 1910), 27–8.

[5] *Précis important sur les maréchaussées* (Paris, 1791); quotation at p. 16.

[6] Edmond Seligman, *La Justice en France pendant la Révolution* (*1789–1793*), 2 vols. (Paris: Plon, 1913), i. 243–7; Cameron, *Crime and Repression*, 243–4. In Feb. 1813 Marshal Moncey suggested that a revival of the *prévôtal* courts 'presided over by a Colonel of Gendarmerie with whom all classes of society are in accord, would only strike terror into brigands', AN AF IV 1158, report to Emperor, 13 Feb. 1813. The proposal went no further.

locality thought necessary. *Commissaires* were expected to supervise the
maintenance and execution of municipal regulations, and were to take
depositions (*procès-verbaux*) in criminal cases. The rural communes were
authorized to employ *gardes-champêtres* whose task was to enforce the
new rural code of 1791 protecting property and crops. In many respects
the *gardes-champêtres* were simply a formalization of the customary village practice of recruiting crop watchers.[7] These legislative measures
show the state taking significant steps on the road towards establishing
uniform systems of policing across the whole of France; they also show
the importance which was conceded to local authority in the early stages
of the Revolution. But *commissaires de police*, *officiers de paix*, whatever
provincial municipalities were prepared to recruit and pay in the way of
watchmen, and the *gardes-champêtres* were never seen as the forceful
hand of the law capable of dealing with brigands or rioters; and, as the
minister of war commented in a letter to the Assembly in May 1791, it
did not seem a good idea simply to rely on the army for the maintenance of order in the provinces.[8]

While there were radicals who, like Robespierre,[9] expressed suspicion
of the *maréchaussée* because of its professional military nature, the con-
sensus was that the corps, now divested of its judicial power, might be
reformed to take on the role of providing a coercive force to back up the
law and its functionaries. But reform was unquestionably required, and
this was not simply because of concerns over 'booted justice.' The political effervesence of the early years of the Revolution encouraged the
washing of dirty linen in public, and members of the *maréchaussée* took
advantage of this to voice complaints through the medium of the press.
In the late summer of 1790 printed memorials were addressed to the
National Assembly, purportedly from the brigades in the Île de France,
complaining about one officer in particular for corrupt handling of the
uniform and remount kitties, about appointments and promotions
depending more on family and clientage than merit and qualification,
and suggesting ways of making significant savings in the costs of the
maréchaussée while, at the same time, paying the NCOs and *cavaliers* a

---

[7] Each of these posts was, at least in some measure, reorganized subsequently during
the Revolution and Empire, but the key laws establishing them were the law of 21 May–27
June 1790 (dividing Paris into 48 sections and establishing the *commissaires de police*), two
separate laws of 21–9 Sept. 1791 (establishing the *officiers de paix* in Paris, and authorizing the creation of *commissaires* in the provinces), and the law of 6 October 1791 (establishing the *gardes-champêtres*).

[8] *Arch. Parl.* (1re *série*), xxiv. 398–9 (26 May 1791).

[9] Ibid., xxi. 244–7 (5 Dec. 1790).

bigger and, by definition, more just wage.[10] Gauthier d'Auteville had been removed as *prévôt* of the company in Corsica in 1784 amidst allegations of pocketing monies due to his men. Five years later, restored to favour, he was appointed to command in the Dauphiné; but d'Auteville found the company in a particularly sorry state, and there were difficulties with his subordinate officers. In the summer of 1791 d'Auteville burst into print critical of the Dauphiné Company and of the behaviour of his superiors in the ministry of war.[11] But between these memorials the *maréchaussée* had been reorganized and renamed.

On 22 December 1790 the *vicomte* de Noailles outlined to the National Assembly the ideas of its military committee regarding 'the public force'. The pressures of the moment had suggested to the committee the need for an active force deployed across the whole country, and it was convinced that this was also 'the wish of the people'. It concluded that the best way forward was to develop the existing the *maréchaussée*. De Noailles stressed that the augmented corps was to be independent of any arbitrary influences in its composition and organization. Charged with watching over public safety, it was to be 'at the same time both civil and military'. Its men were to be drawn from the army but, in accordance with the new ideas of equality, promotion to the highest rank, that of colonel, was to be open to any man of talent. In accordance with the decentralization of the early years of the Revolution, it was also to have strong local ties. The men were to be enrolled by, take their oath in front of, and act on the requests of the directory of the *département* in which they served. Nevertheless, the force was specifically intended to be 'national', as was indictated by the proposed name, the 'maréchaussée et gendarmerie nationale des départements'.[12] The idea of developing and augmenting the existing *maréchaussée* did not prompt much criticism in the Assembly. There was some concern about what Jacques-Guillaume Thouret, deputy for Rouen, called the 'physiognomy *prévôtale*', and the shorter name 'Gendarmerie Nationale' seemed preferable, partly because it

[10] *A l'Assemblée Nationale, par addition au Mémoire présenté, le dix-neuf de ce mois, par les Brigades de la Maréchaussée de l'Isle de France, le 25 septembre 1790; A l'Assemblée Nationale, pour seconde addition au Mémoire présenté le 19 septembre et augmentée d'un plan economique de 2,005,233 liv. sur le traitement annuel de la Maréchaussée de l'Isle de France, même nombre de Chefs de Brigades et Cavaliers, avec augmentation de paie, le 14 octobre 1790.*

[11] *Mémoire présenté au temps par M. Gauthier d'Auteville, à Paris, ce 13 juillet 1791, suivi d'une lettre à M. Duportail, Ministre de la Guerre, Paris, 1791.*

[12] *Arch. Parl.* (1re série) xxi. 626–7 (22 Dec. 1790).

distinguished the new force from the old.[13] Discussions in December and again in January led to final agreement on set of regulations on 9 February 1791; they received royal assent one week later as the law of 16 February 1791.

The new law commenced by declaring that, from henceforth, the *maréchaussée* would be known as the Gendarmerie Nationale. The new name was an interesting mixture of the old and the new; the Gendarmerie had been an elite heavy cavalry regiment of the Royal Household which boasted of origins in the fifteenth century, and which had only recently been disbanded. The adjective 'nationale', however, removed the explicitly royal connotations and tied the organization to the new, reformed order in France. The corps was increased to 7,250 men divided into twenty-eight divisions; each division was commanded by a colonel, and was subdivided into three companies, each one of which was appointed to a separate *département*. The old deployment of five-man brigades commanded by a *maréchal des logis* or a brigadier was maintained. New recruits were to be 25 years old, literate, and were required to have served for three years in the army with a record of good conduct. While the Gendarmerie was to remain part of the army, most of the decisions about candidates for vacancies were to be decided by the directory of the *département* concerned. Recruits received their warrants and swore their oaths before the same directory, promising 'to be faithful to the nation, the law and the king', and to uphold the law 'as good citizens and brave soldiers in everything relating to public safety and tranquillity'. The insignia of the Gendarmerie emphasized its responsibility to the law and its elite military status: tunic buttons bore the words *force à la loi*, while the turnbacks of tunics carried no longer the royal *fleur de lys*, but the grenade of the army's elite grenadier companies.

The day-to-day tasks of the gendarmes remained largely those of their predecessors. They were charged with following up all information relating to both serious and petty offences, as well as with the pursuit of offenders. They could make an arrest if an offender was caught in the act, but they required a warrant to arrest an individual at home and, under penalty of prison, they were not to ill-treat any individual under arrest. They possessed greater freedom of action in the countryside, where they could take the initiative in dealing with trouble, than in the towns, where they were required to wait until called upon to act by the

---

[13] *Arch. Parl.* (*1re série*) xxi. 716 (30 Dec. 1790); and see also ibid. 628 (22 Dec. 1790).

local authorities. The system of patrols, of the supervision of markets
and fairs, remained as before, as did the requirement that their patrol
books be signed by a local mayor or, in his absence, by another local
official. But in discussing new legislation on the role of police officials
Thouret had emphasized the honest, impartial, and influential role
expected of the gendarme in the countryside. The officers, he explained,
were to maintain the public peace in conjunction with the new *juges de
paix*; and his explanation for the double authority is worth quoting in
full for the light that it sheds on how some of the advocates of the
Gendarmerie perceived both of its role and of problems in the countryside:

This competitive authority [*concurrence*] is necessary to remedy any partiality in
the *juge de paix*, who sometimes will be an enemy of the plaintiff, or a relation,
ally, or friend of the accused. Such links are frequent in the villages, and of
greater significance than in the towns. It is necessary therefore to establish a
counterweight to the *juges de paix* with men who do not have the family links
typical of the social groups most numerous among the inhabitants of the countryside. Such will be the officers of the Gendarmerie Nationale. This competitive authority is also necessary to remedy the weakness and timidity of certain
juges de paix in moments of difficulty, such as when confronting an accused who
has made himself a formidable figure in the canton, like those rogues who have
long braved the decrees of justice and insolently defied officers of the law; or
when it is a question of offences which, in a moment's distraction, are not considered as such by local opinion and of which a numerous proportion of the *juge
de paix*'s compatriots are guilty, such as armed smuggling, the prevention of the
free movement of grain or of the collection of taxes, or coercion in communal
or primary assemblies. Can we expect that in all such cases a *juge de paix*, left
to his own devices, will have the courage to start proceedings and deliver the
warrants for summons and arrest? It is therefore necessary to give authority to
men independent of the people, possessed of forceful and energetic characters,
and the bravery to confront dangers. Such are the officers of the Gendarmerie
Nationale. Finally, such authority is necessary to counterbalance the inexperi-
ence of the *juge de paix* in the pursuit of carefully planned crimes, the authors
of which have thought to cut all the threads which could lead back to them. The
officers of the Gendarmerie Nationale provide you with men well-practised in
collecting, evaluating, and following up evidence: they will be no less useful
in their experience of uncovering the guilty in hiding, than for their courage in
confronting the threats of brigands.[14]

Behind the rhetoric here of the courageous man of experience and probity, is the idea of the gendarme as the representative of the state's law

[14] Ibid. 716 (30 Dec. 1790).

which, by definition, is superior to local arrangements. As such a representative, the gendarme stands above, and is quite independent of, local rivalries and faction. This section of Thouret's speech was lifted virtually word for word and inserted in the *Manuel de la Gendarmerie Nationale* published in 1791 as a guide to the duties and role of the corps.[15]

The devolution of the appointment of gendarmes to the new *départements* was in keeping with much of the legislation passed during 1790. There was massive administrative improvisation in the *départements* as they sought to come to grips with their new, and short-lived authority; and while the achievements were significant, there was much that remained undone and much that developed according to local initiative and interpretation.[16] As early as July 1791 there were some who saw the Gendarmerie as the potential internal saviour of France and the Revolution. For anxious civil administrators in the Morbihan it was the Gendarmerie alone which could 'restore peace to the countryside, exposing and repressing ceaselessly the seditious behaviour of refractory priests and the manoeuvres which they constantly employ to inflame fanaticism and excite the people to revolt'.[17] Yet in spite of such concerns and more general worries about law and order, the appointment of gendarmes and the deployment of the brigades appears to have been one of the many matters that, in some areas at least, was delayed or implemented largely in accordance with local agendas. By the end of the year many *départements* had not appointed and deployed their quota of men and brigades, while some complained that the number of brigades allocated was insufficient for their needs. 'We cannot depend on the National Guard,' explained the president of the Council of the Mayenne, 'as it is too occupied in maintaining order in the towns and larger villages to be called upon to mount frequent expeditions and so it is absolutely essential to increase as much as possible the number of Gendarmerie brigades . . . for the security of the countryside.'[18] Since its emergence from among the local militias established to combat

---

[15] Auguste-Charles Guichard, *Manuel de la Gendarmerie nationale* (Paris, 1791), 137–9.

[16] Alison Patrick, 'French Revolutionary Local Government, 1789–92', in Colin Lucas (ed.), *The French Revolution and the Creation of Modern Political Culture*, vol. 2, *The Political Culture of the Revolution* (Oxford: Pergamon Press, 1988), 399–420.

[17] AN F⁹ 325, Dossier 6 (Morbihan), Commisaires civils du département to min. of int., 14 July 1791.

[18] AG Xᶠ 242, fos. 190–2, Président du conseil de la Mayenne, 30 Nov. 1791; and see in general, ibid., fos. 1–184, 'Depouillement des Tableaux des Brigades existantes en chaque Département, et celles demandées en augmentation'.

brigands during the disorders of 1789, the National Guard had created problems for, and a potential rival to, first the *maréchaussée* and subsequently the Gendarmerie. It was a local force, with a local power base, and as such could become involved in local conflicts and in maintaining, or challenging, local social and political structures.[19] Furthermore, in spite of the statements that the Gendarmerie should be the representative of the Law and stand above local prejudice and partiality, in practice in the decentralized France of 1790 and 1791 this could be difficult to ensure. In Cahors in October 1791 a church belonging to some regular canons who objected to the new Civil Constitution of the Clergy was attacked and sacked. Colonel Trouard de Riolle, the local commander of the Gendarmerie, protested that the municipality was implicated and had been slow to call on his men for assistance. The adminstration of the *département* of the Lot sided with the municipality, and the ministry of war reluctantly agreed to its suggestion that the colonel be removed.[20]

The failure of many *départements* to establish their quota of Gendarmerie brigades, together with the fact that some *cavaliers* of the old *maréchaussée* had been dismissed on the grounds that they could not read or write and in spite of promises that they would keep their posts, were highlighted in a report to the Legislative Assembly from its military committee on 24 December 1791. The need for a force to maintain the public peace was even more acute now, declared Claude-Marie Carnot-Feulint on behalf of the committee, when 'the enemies of liberty and equality were employing all their powers to destroy them'. The committee proposed increasing the number of brigades from 1,293 to 1,560; sixty of these were to be supplementary, available to be sent where the need was perceived to be greatest.[21] The report was the cue for heated debates about the policing of civil disorder and the use of a militarized police organization. Charles Danthon, a lawyer who had served as executive officer (*procureur syndic*) for the district of Vienne, considered the Gendarmerie to be very useful because it was both civil and military; the deployment of armed civilians against protesting civilians threatened civil war, while the deployment of troops of the line was the mark of despotism; the Gendarmerie, though, maintained a sensible balance. However, Danthon was concerned that the increase as proposed was too great, and potentially dangerous for periods of internal tranquillity; yet, in a period like the present, when part of Europe was

---

[19] Cameron, *Crime and Repression*, 247–52.   [20] AG X^f 242, fos. 205a–j.
[21] *Arch. Parl.* (*1re série*), xxxvi. 367–70; quotation at 369 (24 Dec. 1791).

promising succour to the internal opponents of the Revolution, it was insufficient. He proposed, therefore, that the Gendarmerie should consist of around 15,000 men divided into two groups; half of the force would then be spread over the country in brigades like the old *maréchaussée*, the other half would be stationed in garrisons like the regular army. Antoine-Louis Albitte, a radical lawyer from Dieppe, was completely opposed to the increase and urged, in contrast, a reduction. He did not openly suggest following the English example, but his speech had echoes of Sir William Mildmay's comments of nearly thirty years before:

> There are countries where there are neither *maréchaussée* nor gendarmerie, and I believe that we should not put into the hands of some authority or other an instrument so powerful as to stifle liberty. There, where individual liberty is most respected, there where policing is not entrusted to a military despotism, there also is the greatest respect for the laws.

Albitte's intervention was received with increasingly angry murmurs. Danthon's proposal was referred to the military committee for further consideration, but came to nothing.[22]

The Law of 14–29 April 1792 eventually increased the Gendarmerie to 8,700 men, deployed in 1,600 brigades, of which forty were designated as supplementary. The new legislation re-emphasized the corps's subordination to the civil power in matters of public order; however it re-established inspecting colonels and instructed the minister of war to revise the regulations concerning general service. As the new law was agreed so, on 20 April 1792, by its declaration of war on the Habsburg Emperor, France embarked on the succession of wars which were to convulse Europe for a quarter of a century. The wars were to have a profound impact on the duties of the Gendarmerie; they held up the revision of its regulations for nearly thirty years, but they also provided the opportunity for it to spread across continental Europe.

Preparations for war and the organization of a citizen army had already begun in 1791. In the summer and early autumn there had been calls for volunteers to come forward from the National Guard for such an army. As part and parcel of these preparations two divisions of Gendarmerie had been established in Paris in August: the first was a mounted division recruited from among former cavalrymen in disbanded National Guard units; the second was recruited from active National Guard infantry companies. A foretaste of a future, major

[22] *Arch. Parl.* (*1re série*), xxxvii, 98–9 (5 Jan. 1792).

Gendarmerie role was to be found in a query from the *département* of the Landes in November, when it was found that men who had volunteered for the army in haste from the National Guard were now repenting at leisure and deserting from the garrison in Dax. They had returned to their native parishes 'where, unquestionably they have supporters, where they find help in the bosom of their families, a place to hide and, perhaps, the means to throw off any pursuit'. The question was, did the Gendarmerie have the authority to set off in pursuit of such men? After all, these were free citizens who had volunteered their services for the motherland, and as such they did not appear to be the same as deserters from the old royal army.[23]

Initially the war went badly for the forces of the Revolution. In the north-east the new Gendarmerie brigades were caught up in the invasion and, at least among some officers, there seems to have been personal conflict over which side to back and what to do if their district was overrun.[24] Desperate demands for men to fill the gaps at the front prompted the decree of the *levée en masse* on 23 August 1792. In July and August three new Gendarmerie divisions, similar to those established the year before, were created for the army out of former soldiers. The revolutionary government also recognized that it had a significant cadre of veteran soldiers in the Gendarmerie brigades deployed across the countryside. A decree of 12–16 August announced that one man would be taken from every brigade so as to create two new cavalry divisions; then, following the fall of Longwy to the Prussians, the law of 26–7 August announced the organization of eight such cavalry divisions to be formed by taking four out of five men. The idea was that new brigades could be formed in the countryside around the single remaining gendarme with recruits chosen from the National Guard by the directories of the *départements*. The result in the *départements* was confusion and chaos: what were they supposed to do where the brigades were not yet up to five men? Or where men were old and infirm and awaiting their retirement and pensions? What was to be done where gendarmes had no equipment or horses? The scale of complaints and queries was such that, three weeks after the second levy on the Gendarmerie, the ministry of war felt it necessary to dispatch a printed

---

[23] AG X^r 242, fos. 204–5.

[24] AN F^9 325, Dossier 2 (Meuse), correspondence of Nov. 1792 concerning Lieutenant Oberhoff who allegedly deserted to the enemy and Lieutenant Martin who, when inspecting the brigade at Stenay, found the place occupied by Austrians and then allegedly directed the gendarmes to disarm the local population.

circular with answers to what it perceived as the principal questions.[25] But whatever circulars said or promised, many districts appear to have been stripped of their brigades.

Many gendarmes themselves had doubts about the turn that events had taken. There was the question of rank. A gendarme was regarded as having a rank one stage above that of his equivalent in the army: thus, a gendarme was the equivalent of a brigadier in the cavalry, a Gendarmerie brigadier was the equivalent of a *maréchal des logis*, and so on; would this distinction be maintained in the draft? They were concerned about going to war on their own horses; would these be replaced if lost as a result of war service? What was to happen to their families left in the district where they had been serving? There were general complaints about overdue expenses and pay, and individual complaints about injustices and corrupt officers and officials in the *départements* where they had been serving. Louis Charmoille from the Hautes-Pyrénées was angry that he had been charged more than his pay would allow for a stay in hospital, and he wanted reimbursing. François Bellein protested that he had been moved from his native Perigueux, first to one town, then to another where he had been the only gendarme and where there was no provision either for him or his horse. Mustering the men together into three large camps—at Chalons, for gendarmes from the northern *départements*, at Fontainebleau for men from the south and east, and at Versailles for men from the south and west—provided them with the opportunity for comparing wrongs and for seeking remedies in a body. The gendarmes at Versailles drafted a list of their complaints which concluded with the threat that they would not leave for the front without a positive response from the 'patriotic administration' in whom they felt they could trust. The document was endorsed by their commanding officer.[26] The appropriate promises were made.

The standards carried by the Gendarmerie divisions bore mottos illustrative of their civilian role—*Force à la loi*; *Discipline et obéissance à la loi*—even if these were scarcely relevant to either the campaigns on the frontiers or to the savage civil conflict in the Vendée where many of them were engaged. Such brigades as continued to exist during the Montagnard terror and for much of the Thermidorian period sought to get on with their day-to-day tasks, but were overshadowed on the one hand by the *armées révolutionnaires*, made up of highly politicized urban

[25] AG X^f 4, Circulaire, 16 Sep. 1792.

[26] AG X^f 4, 'Mémoire sur les réclamations que font les Gendarmes qui composent la 2e Division organisée à Versailles pour le service des armées', and *passim*.

radicals organized to ensure the supply of grain to the towns, who meted out ferocious revolutionary justice to their opponents and recalcitrant peasants, and on the other by regular troops deployed to crush federalism and the western rebels. In the Loire region most notably, the *représentants en mission*, and particularly Claude Javogues, deployed the local *armée révolutionnaire* to search for suspects, carry out arrests, protect food supplies, keep order at markets, pursue vagabonds, and enforce recruiting regulations; all of which were essentially tasks belonging to the Gendarmerie. When Javogues was recalled to Paris in February 1794 the local *armée révolutionnaire* was disbanded and efforts were made to increase the Gendarmerie in the region with additional brigades in St Étienne and Feurs.[27] Moreover, in the absence of civil war and/or terror, brigades of gendarmes, no matter how numerous, were vulnerable to economic resistance on the part of the peasantry. In 1792 peasants were reluctant to take payment from gendarmes in the inflationary paper *assignats*; during the food shortages of 1795 they increased their prices, and even after the *assignats* had been replaced in 1796 the problems continued. The situation appears to have been particularly acute in the Vendée where, in the aftermath of civil war, the economic needs of the gendarmes provided the peasantry with a means of striking back against *les bleus*. 'Here [the gendarmes] cannot find a penny credit either for their own existence or for that of their horses', wrote the company commander of the Maine-et-Loire in *prairial* Year V (May 1797). 'The citizens of this region discourage them by their scant regard, and the authorities do not show the energy necessary to maintain them in their provisional accomodation.'[28]

There was a plan to reorganize the entire Gendarmerie during the Terror; it was couched in the fiery rhetoric of the day which attributed weakness to feeble peacetime laws and suggested a new name more in keeping with a republican regime—*la Cavalerie de Sureté*.[29] But the name remained unchanged, as did the sorry state of the corps. Under both the Thermidorian regime and the Directory the Gendarmerie was under strength, the mounted men lacked horses, pay was always in

[27] Colin Lucas, *The Structure of the Terror: The Example of Claude Javogues and the Loire* (Oxford: Clarendon Press, 1973), esp. 181, and J.B. Galley, *Saint-Étienne et son district pendant la Révolution*, 2 vols. (St Étienne: Imprimerie de la Loire Républicaine, 1904–6), ii. 551.

[28] Catherine Garnier, 'La Gendarmerie dans le Maine-et-Loire de 1791 à 1815', Mémoire de Maîtrise, Université d'Angers, 1996, pp. 84–5 and 108–9.

[29] AG MR 2003, 'Projet d'une nouvelle organisation de la Gendarmerie nationale' (1793).

arrears, and at every level the men found their authority challenged by other functionaries; and such a situation could not but have an unfavourable impact on the behaviour of many of the men. In *frimaire* Year IV (December 1795) the *départemental* administration of the Hérault exhorted the local Gendarmerie commander to bring an end to the inertia in his company, to ensure frequent patrols on the post roads, particularly at daybreak and at dusk, and to have arrested all deserters and travellers without passports. The exhortation was forwarded to the minister of the interior, lamenting the daily occurence of theft and acts of brigandage on the roads which were attributed to the negligence of the Gendarmerie.[30] It may well have been this letter which prompted the minister of *police générale* to send a circular, dated 19 *nivôse* Year IV (10 January 1796), to the administrators of provincial cantons requesting information on the scale of crime and mendicity and the state of the National Guard and the Gendarmerie. The replies varied from region to region, and indeed from canton to canton. Most wooded areas reported widespread forestry offences; many districts, not just those in the west, were anxious about brigands. A few districts were satisfied with their National Guards, though many others described them as inactive. On the subject of the Gendarmerie, some cantons commented simply that they had no brigade or, if they had one, that it performed its tasks with 'exactitude'. Others gave rather more detail, and the range of comment was wide. There were complaints about the men themselves. From the Ardennes came the criticism that not only was the corps inactive, it was also unpatriotic; it 'often let the guilty escape [and] in general needed a major reform'. The canton of Arbois (Jura) proposed that brigades be moved around regularly so as to prevent corruption, something which implies that such problems had been experienced. Épineu le Chevreuil in the Sarthe reported that its brigade had moved itself to Le Mans. 'I do not know their motives,' explained the correspondant, 'their departure has not caused much of a sensation, three out of five of them refused to take arms against the Chouans.' From Le Mans itself it was reported that, while the commanders were highly regarded, the behaviour of gendarmes on patrol was poor. Belley (Ain) was critical of many of the men in the local company who were not right for the service, and they were always complaining about their poor pay; but the reply also noted that the men were too few for the tasks required of them. Meyssac (Corrèze) protested that their local

---

[30] AN F⁹, Dossier 1 (Hérault).

brigade commander was illiterate, 'which is contrary to the law and prejudicial to the service'; but went on to explain that the whole company lacked arms, equipment, and uniforms. The paucity of numbers, the lack of equipment and pay, and the sorry state of their horses—when they had them—was echoed in other replies, and many of these showed a distinct sympathy for the gendarmes. Le Cateau (Nord), for example, commented: 'The Gendarmerie performs its service with exactitude, but it is too few in number. We have only four gendarmes and a brigadier; they are overburdened with work; they get no rest; we need at least ten.'[31] Other correspondence to the minister of the interior reflects a potential faith in a reorganized and revived Gendarmerie as, throughout the period of the Thermidorians and the Directory, commune after commune petitioned to keep a brigade, to have a brigade established for its district, or to have an additional brigade.[32]

The war ministry itself was not unaware of the state of the *départmental* brigades; a draft reform proposal, apparently prepared in 1796, noted that there were men who were 'too young, many who could neither read nor write, many insufficiently irreprochable to be confided with functions of such importance'.[33] In 1797 the company of the Maine-et-Loire was found to have several men who could do no more than sign their names; 'however, their morality, public spiritedness [*civisme*] and long service' appeared sufficient reason for keeping them on; and when 26-year-old René Delhumeau requested an appointment, the company was prepared to accept him since, while he could neither read nor write, he seemed otherwise an ideal recruit and had promised to rectify his illiteracy as soon as possible.[34] The inspection of the Meurthe Company in *fructidor* Year V (September 1797) revealed problems similar to those of the *maréchaussée* before the reforms of the 1770s, together with a clutch of new ones. Some men were proposed for removal as unsuitable for the rank of gendarme: Jean-Baptiste Dumas, from the Puy-de-Dôme, and Nicolas Frénot, a native of the Meurthe, for example, were both considered as lacking in intelligence and zeal, and Frénot was alleged to have done nothing for the past two years. Pierre-Antoine Culaut, from the Vosges, was accused of a string of petty offences; Jean Curé, from the Moselle, was always arguing with his

[31] AN F⁷ 3065 *passim*.

[32] See, *inter alia*, AN F⁹ 324, Dossiers 13 (Loire Inférieure), 14 (Loiret), 21 (Marne); F⁹ 325, Dossiers 10 (Nord), 11 (Oise); and F⁹ 326, Dossier 8 (Seine-et-Marne).

[33] AG MR 2003, 'Mémoire sur la Gendarmerie nationale' (pencil annotation: 'Présumé de l'année 1796').

[34] Garnier, 'La Gendarmerie dans le Maine-et-Loire', 73.

superior; Pierre Oberhaussen, from the Meurthe, was permanently sick and incapacitated by 'a considerable hernia'. Of the eighty NCOs and men who were to remain in the company, over half (forty-eight) were born in the Meurthe itself, and just under a quarter (eighteen) came from the three neighbouring *départements* of the Meuse, the Moselle, and the Vosges. Half-a-dozen men were singled out for immediate dismissal on the grounds that they were too young for the Gendarmerie and were fit, and of an age, for service in the line army; most (fifty-six) of the men who were to remain were aged between their mid-thirties and mid-forties. At the time of the inspection, seventy-five of the eighty were technically mounted, and forty-three of them owned their own horses. But whether owned by the gendarmes themselves or the property of the Republic, the horses were in a sorry state: thirty-nine of them were considered unsuitable, six of these were described as 'old and worn out', and another three were blind. Sixty-eight of the men were noted as requiring 'the complete uniform, tunic and boots', which suggests that gendarmes at this point in their history were patrolling in a mixture of old army uniforms, probably well-worn, and, perhaps, some civilian clothing. But these men were still old soldiers, and even if they looked a motley, threadbare crew, the inspectors noted that 'the rest of the equipment and the arms were good'.[35] This was just as well given the internal problems of France, notably an upsurge of brigandage which emerged out of the war, worsened under the Directory, and helped to ensure a future for the corps.

There had been a little administrative tinkering with the Gendarmerie during the Montagnard ascendancy and then under the Thermidorians, but significant reorganization did not come until well into the Directory. As a result of the law of 24 *nivôse* Year V (13 January 1797), gendarmes had to swear an oath declaring 'hatred of royalty and anarchy' together with 'attachment and loyalty to the Republic and the Constitution of the Year III'. The laws of 25 *Pluviôse* and 7 *germinal* Year V (13 February and 27 March 1797) set out to remove Jacobin—or in the parlance of the time and the new Gendarmerie oath, 'anarchist'—elements in the corps and to establish clear ties with central government. Jacobin sympathizers among the gendarmes based in Paris had provided anxious

---

[35] AG X^f 234. (This carton is catalogued as 'Gendarmerie: Voltigeurs Algériens, correspondence'. Most of the material in the carton concerns the Algerian *voltigeurs* during the Second Empire, with the principal exception of three large sheets relating to the inspection of the Meurthe Company in *fructidor* Year V.)

moments for the government during the troubles of 1795.[36] Nor was the problem confined to the capital: in Thermidorian Dijon gendarme Bellemel was denounced for boasting of being a *terroriste*, lamenting that the Terror had finished too soon since now 'Patriots were vexed by aristocrats', and threatening to disembowel *muscadins*.[37] The first of the two new laws reduced the corps by 100 brigades; it also made the appointment of officers the prerogative of the Directory itself, while the final selection of NCOs and men was to be made locally by a *jury d'examen départemental* composed of representatives from the local authorities and officers of the Gendarmerie. It was this law which the *jury d'examen* in the Meurthe appears to taken advantage of the following *fructidor*, when identifying men for removal from the company; two of the three officers proposed for removal by the *jury* may have been singled out for their political links—a former *cavalier* of the *maréchaussée*, Lieutenant François André, had been appointed lieutenant by one *représentant du peuple* in Year II, dismissed by another in Year III, and then reappointed by the *départemental* administration in Year IV; Lieutenant Nicolas Laroche had also served in the *maréchaussée* and owed his lieutenancy to a *représentant*, but his age probably also counted against him, at 70 he was the oldest man in the company. The rank and file, however, were not simply passive actors in the working of this law, and the behaviour of two men suggests the continuation of close links between some men and local communities: Jean-Paul Perette made it clear that, if the brigade in which he was serving was one of those to be abolished, then he would prefer to be retired than have to serve elsewhere; brigadier Claude Guillaume, on the other hand, appears to have used the law to organize a move back to the Vosges, where he had been born.[38] The *germinal* law specified that the Gendarmerie was responsible to the ministry of war for discipline and equipment, while its role in the maintenance of public order brought it within the remit of the ministry of *police générale*. It looked forward to a future reorganization which was,

[36] Jean-Paul Berthaud, *La Révolution armée. Les soldats-citoyens et la Révolution française* (Paris: Robert Laffont, 1979), 301 and 303.

[37] Richard Cobb, *The Police and the People: French Popular Protest, 1789–1820* (Oxford: Oxford University Press, 1970), 366–7.

[38] AG X^f 234, 'Département de la Meurthe: État des Officiers susceptibles du traitement de Réforme, et de sous officiers et gendarmes susceptible du même traitement.' Georges Lefebvre, *The Thermidorians* (London: Routledge & Kegan Paul, 1964), 15, notes how in the Meurthe, following the law on Revolutionary Government of 7 *fructidor* Year II, Michaud restored to office the sans-culottes imprisoned as Hébertists before the fall of Robespierre. Such upheavals account, at least in part, for the promotions and dismissals of officers in Years II to IV.

in the event, introduced almost exactly one year later by the Law of 28 *germinal* Year VI (17 April 1798).

The 1798 law opened with a statement of the Gendarmerie's role: 'to ensure within the Republic, the maintenance of order and the execution of the laws. A constant, ever-watchful surveillance constitutes the essence of its service.' The law was drafted against a background of internal disorder which the Directory was combating with an increasing use of tough, military repression, reminiscent of the kind of behaviour sanctioned by the *ancien régime* in time of crisis, and behaviour which had been specifically repudiated by the National Assembly in the early stages of the Revolution.[39] There was also a recognition that, given the military drafts and reorganizations of the institution during the previous decade, there was a need to provide a new and precise delineation of the Gendarmerie's aims and structure. The law was the work of Jean-Gilles-Denis Laporte, a deputy from the Haute-Garonne in the Council of Five Hundred, and of an experienced solder and administrator, General Jean-Gérard Lacuée, in the Council of Ancients. They drew on the advice of General Louis Wirion, who had begun his military service as a royal dragoon, risen, via the Paris National Guard, to be a general in the Gendarmerie, and who had organized the new Gendarmerie companies for the annexed Belgian *départements* in Year IV.[40] The law enlarged the force to 2,000 brigades with an effective strength of 10,575 officers and men. The system of appointment to the different ranks, which had been established in 1797, was maintained; candidates were expected to be between 25 and 40 years of age, 1.73 metres in height, to have fought in three of the campaigns since the beginning of the Revolution, to have served for four years in the cavalry, to know how to read and write, and to have certificates of good morals, good conduct, bravery, and loyalty to the republic. The pay was increased; the company kitty was reorganized, based on an annual deduction from the pay, to provided expenses for remounts and replacement uniforms and equipment; a pension was to be available to men on retirement at the age of 60 years. The gendarme's role in the maintenance of internal order was re-emphasized by the new motif for the plaque on the belts crossing his chest: *Respect aux personnes et aux propriétés.* However, his role in enforcing the state's claims to young male citizens for its army—

---

[39] Howard G. Brown, 'From Organic Society to Security State: The War on Brigandage in France, 1797–1802', *Journal of Modern History*, 69 (1997), 661–95.

[40] For Wirion's organization of the Gendarmerie in the Belgian provinces see AN F⁹ 320.

claims which were to be renewed with provision for conscription on a more systematic basis by the Jourdan Law of 19 *fructidor*, Year VI (5 September 1798)—were soon to reveal some of qualifications to this respect.

4

'THE MOST EFFICIENT WAY TO MAINTAIN . . . TRANQUILLITY': GENDARMES IN NAPOLEONIC FRANCE

Napoleon's correspondence is sprinkled with laudatory references to the Gendarmerie and its various tasks. When one of the four regional directors in the ministry of *police générale*, André-François Miot, was critical of the corps, Joseph Fouché, the minister, was informed sharply that this was the body of men to whom Napoleon owed the restoration of order in France. Shortly after his appointment as King of Naples, Joseph Bonaparte was instructed, in the words quoted earlier, that the Gendarmerie was 'the most efficient way to maintain the tranquility of a country . . . it provides a surveillance half civil, half military spread across the whole territory together with the most precise information'. As the *Grande Armée* crossed the Nieman at Kovno on its way to disaster in Russia, Marshal Berthier, the able and dependable chief of staff, was reminded that the gendarme was 'not just a man on a horse', rather, his role was 'was the most important police service in the rear of the army' and his time should not be wasted on escorts and baggage security.[1] Throughout the period of the Napoleonic regime the Gendarmerie fulfilled a multitude of roles within the *départements* of France and the Empire, and with the armies. The model was imposed on subject peoples, but it was also adopted by allies and enemies who perceived it as being efficient, effective, and adaptable to their own circumstances.

The general acquiescence over the *coup d'état* of *brumaire* owed much to the belief among the propertied classes in France that General

---

[1] *Cor. Nap.*, vol. 10, no. 8,375, to Fouché, 10 *ventôse* Year XIII (1 Mar. 1805); vol. 12, no. 10,243, to Joseph Bonaparte, 16 May 1806; vol. 23, no. 18,871, to Berthier, 26 June 1812.

Bonaparte was a strong and able military man who could restore internal tranquillity to a country wracked by a mixture of civil strife and brigandage. The Directory had introduced ferocious policies involving tough military repression to deal with these problems. The law of 10 *vendémiaire* Year IV (2 October 1795), for example, required a community to compensate the victims of violence and/or property damage when the attacks occurred on its territory. When some *départemental* authorities had shown themselves reluctant to use the law, the Directory in Paris had prompted army officers to petition the courts to apply it and to direct their soldiers to enforce it. The law of 29 *nivôse* Year VI (18 January 1798) empowered military courts to prosecute civilians for crimes such as brigandage, burglary, and highway robbery when two or more offenders were involved. The young First Consul took an active interest in the suppression of brigandage, and his new regime appreciated that providing security was a key element in ensuring its authority. The military repression deployed under the Directory and the early part of the Consulate gradually gave way to a system of surveillance. Howard Brown has described this as a 'security state . . . the new tutelary administrative and judicial apparatus which supplanted the democratic institutions of the Revolution's and which was to rely more on surveillance and regulatory control to maintain public order rather than on the deployment of coercive force to restore it.[2] Central to this surveillance and regulatory control, and ready with a degree of coercive force should the need be perceived, was an improved Gendarmerie.

Four months after the coup, in March 1800, Bonaparte was writing to Lacuée, now a councillor of state, outlining what he perceived as the problems which persisted in spite of the Gendarmerie law of 1798, or which had not been resolved by it. Amongst other things, he echoed comments made in the *Cahiers de doléances*; he believed that gendarmes on foot were probably of much more use than mounted men in mountainous districts and those regions significantly broken up by rivers and other natural barriers; there was also the implication that he thought they would be cheaper. In April he issued an order with his own plans for reorganization. This provided for an increase in the number of gendarmes on foot in those areas where he thought they were needed but, more interestingly, it also outlined a proposal to have detachments of gendarmes drafted from the regional companies and posted to the four major cities of Paris, Bordeaux, Lyons, and Marseilles for tours of duty

---

[2] Howard G. Brown, 'From Organic Society to Security State: The War on Brigandage in France, 1797–1802', *Journal of Social History*, 69 (1997), 661–95, at p. 694.

of just one year. Each of these cities had witnessed serious disorder during the revolutionary decade, and the three latter had all, at some stage and to varying degrees, been in revolt against the authorities in Paris. State military policemen, with limited opportunities for developing links with the populace, must have appeared to the young consul as the ideal way of checking any recurrence of disorder in these cities.[3] In the event this proposal came to nothing, but even as he drafted his initial thoughts to Lacuée, Bonaparte was also dispatching General Wirion to the west to reorganize the Gendarmerie companies there, to purge the mounted brigades, and to establish 200 new foot brigades in the region.

Wirion was proud of his record of having establish the Gendarmerie companies in the thirteen new *départements* of the north, the former Austrian Netherlands. He set about his new commission with vigour and determination. He addressed his new command with all the bombast and enthusiasm of the revolutionaries. They were, he told them, to be an 'anti-Vendéen' force. They had obligations towards both individuals and the state, and they had to know these, and the relevant laws, thoroughly. It was not enough for a gendarme to be strong and courageous: 'bravery and boldness must be joined with moral standards, and a thorough understanding of them.' The officers were urged to seek their model in the heroes of ancient Rome.[4] Wirion himself swept through the region dismissing the old and infirm, the useless and the drunkards, changing the posting of others as a means of punishment, and assessing the most sensible places for stationing brigades of both foot and mounted men. His ideal gendarme was a tall, courageous veteran, honest, moral, sober, able to read and write, and a man who stood apart from the local population in which he was stationed. Wirion also had very clear ideas about the kind of knowledge that the men should acquire of the districts in which they were based:

This positive knowledge can only be acquired by frequent, multiple patrols until the point is reached when there is not a *single village, a single hamlet, a single house, a single wood, ravine, a single road, or even a single bush* which is not recognized and known to the new gendarmes. I attach such a great importance to this local knowledge that I expect that, by both day and night, a gendarme could

---

[3] *Cor. Nap.*, vol. 6, no. 4,657, to Lacuée, 21 *ventôse* Year VIII (12 Mar. 1800), and no. 4,720, Order, 29 *germinal* Year VIII (19 Apr. 1800). For examples of the First Consul's directives concerning the supression of brigandage in particular regions, and the deployment of gendarmes to this end, see ibid., vol. 6, nos. 4,665 and 4,679.

[4] AN AF[IV] 1154, Wirion to First Consul, enclosing printed proclamation to the new gendarmes, 23 *germinal* Year VIII.

leave his barracks and go to any point to which he was directed in his brigade's district with his eyes closed.[5]

Many of these attributes had been expected of the *cavaliers* of the old *maréchaussée* but, taking the cue from the rhetoric of the Revolution, Wirion and men like him articulated the gendarme's role with a new slant towards probity and the idea of personal sacrifice on behalf of fellow citizens and, above all, the state. This new articulation was to become central among advocates of, and apologists for, the gendarmeries which were to spread across Europe in the next half-century; they were also to become central to the self-perception of these institutions.

At the beginning of May 1800, while Wirion beavered away in the west, General Étienne Radet was instructed to prepare a general reorganization of the whole Gendarmerie, particularly to improve the ways in which the corps functioned. Radet was competent, honest, and loyal; he was also blunt, straightforward, and he had a conscience, traits which, in some respects, may have checked his career. A native of Stenay in Lorraine, he had enlisted in the army during his eighteenth year, in 1780; rising to sergeant two years later, he had transferred to the *maréchaussée* in 1786, and was promoted brigadier the following year. The Revolution offered the chance of advancement, initially through the National Guard and then once more with the colours. In February 1798 Radet, in poor health and recovering from wounds, was promoted to colonel and ordered to take command of the 24th Gendarmerie Division whose four companies were based in the *départements* of the Bouches-du-Rhône, Gard, Hérault, and Vaucluse. The region was notorious for its brigandage. Radet had no particular desire to take up the posting, and he found his division in poor shape. Horses and men were worn out; he feared that this could mean that soon the whole division would be on foot. Some men were in league with brigands, others were drinkers and/or lax in their duty. The pay was often months in arrears, the barracks were in poor shape, and local authorities often tried to use the brigades as their own 'pretorian guard'. Radet applied himself to the difficulties with vigour and determination; he made enemies, but he also improved morale, got rid of the worst officers and men, and began to turn his command into a force to be reckoned with. Bonaparte was obviously impressed when, on his return from Egypt, he met Radet in Avignon and, in a ninety-minute meeting, heard his account of the problems which still faced his division. Bonaparte was also given a

---

[5] Ibid., Wirion's final report to General Bernadotte, 30 *thermidor* Year VIII.

first-hand introduction to the brigandage problem when his own baggage was pillaged.[6]

Radet's deliberations in Paris resulted in the organizational order (*arrêté*) of 12 *thermidor* Year IX (31 July 1801) which enlarged the corps to 16,500 men and, in keeping with Bonaparte's own thinking, increased the number of gendarmes on foot. There were to be 2,500 brigades of six men each; 1,750 of these brigades were to be mounted and 750 on foot. The structure of one company for each *département* was maintained, with four companies grouped into a regional legion; an elite legion was also organized with two mounted squadrons whose task was the protection of the First Consul, and later the Emperor, wherever he went, and two foot companies who were responsible for guarding palaces. A further attempt was made to weed out undesirable men: officers were to receive their commissions directly from the First Consul, and later the Emperor; other appointments were to be vetted by a *départemental* council consisting of the prefect and two gendarme officers. Finally, a headquarters staff was to be established under a divisional general, who was to be Premier Inspecteur Général de la Gendarmerie, supported by two brigade generals. Radet suggested General Leclerc for the job,[7] who was married to the First Consul's sister Pauline. By Radet's own subsequent account, however, the First Consul offered it to Radet himself, and he refused it, twice, on the grounds that he believed that some of the political tasks which Bonaparte had in mind for the Gendarmerie would undermine the esteem which he sought for it and weaken the corps's moral authority.[8] Radet promptly fell from favour; he was sent to reorganize the Gendarmerie in Corsica, and for the next decade he was employed outside the old frontiers of France establishing Gendarmerie legions in Italy, northern Germany, and the Netherlands. The position of Premier Inspecteur Général was accepted by General Moncey, who, with one or two absences commanding military corps on campaign, notably in Spain, served in the post throughout the periods of the Empire and the First Restoration, rising to Marshal of France in 1804 and being created Duke of Conégliano in 1808.

Moncey was another soldier from the *ancien régime* who had profited from the Revolution, but in origin he was very different from Radet. His

---

[6] Étienne Amadée Combier (ed.), *Mémoires du général Radet, d'après ses papiers personnels et les archives de l'état* (Saint-Cloud: Belin Frères, 1892), 96–116.

[7] AN AF[IV] 1154, Radet to First Consul,? *ventôse* Year IX.

[8] Combier (ed.), *Mémoires du général Radet*, 148.

real name was Adrien-Jeannot Bon, but he had taken the surname Moncey from the place of his birth. The son of an advocate in the *parlement* at Besançon he was also destined for a career in the law, but he left his studies and in 1769, aged only 15, he enlisted. He was only a junior officer when the Revolutionary Wars began, but promotion came swiftly to men of his ability, and by the close of 1793 he was a general. He distinguished himself in the fighting with Spain in the Pyrenees; and he urged on his men the need to win the hearts and minds of the Basque people rather than terrorizing them.[9] After the coup of *brumaire* he had been appointed commander of the 19th Military Division, with his headquarters in Lyons. His time here was short, only two months, before he was back campaigning in northern Italy. Yet during this period he showed himself an able administrator in a difficult region, and notably organized gendarmerie patrols on the main roads which were infested with brigands. It was also during this period in Lyons that Moncey clashed for the first time with Fouché and the ministry of *police générale*.[10]

Moncey was a prickly individual with a determination to maintain the gendarmerie's independence. This suited well with what Fouché called Napoleon's 'Machiavellian maxim of "divide and rule" ' among his police organizations, though Moncey could, and on at least one occasion did, go too far in asserting the Gendarmerie's independence—something which earned him a severe imperial rebuke.[11] Napoleon's divide-and-rule policy meant that, throughout most of the period of his empire, there were four police organizations functioning side-by-side: in addition to the Gendarmerie and the men working within, and under the direction of, the ministry of police, there were also the men responsible for the policing of Paris who were answerable to the Prefect of Police, together with a separate military organization under General Duroc in his capacity of Grand Master of the Palace. Even when the subtle Fouché was replaced by a military man, General Savary, in 1810, there was still tension between Moncey and the ministry of police, notably when Savary suggested that Gendarmerie officers might send their reports on particularly serious offences directly to him rather than via

[9] Benjamin Kennedy, 'Crisis in the Borderlands: General Moncey in the Western Pyrenees, 1794–1795', *Proceedings of the Annual Meeting of the Western Society for French History*, 19 (1992), 139–47.

[10] C. A. G. Duchesne de Gillevoisin, Duc de Conegliano, *Le Maréchal Moncey: Duc de Conegliano, 1754–1842* (Paris: Calmann Lévy, 1902), 102–17.

[11] Joseph Fouché, *Les Mémoires de Fouché*, ed. Louis Madelin (Paris: Flammarion, 1946), 145; *Cor. Nap.* vol. 10, no. 8,570, to Moncey, 10 *germinal* Year XIII (31 Mar. 1805).

the Inspector-General. Moncey's response was that his men were already burdened with paperwork and that this would mean them having to write the same report twice.[12]

Four police organizations or not, the forces available for the maintenance of public order in case of an emergency in the capital remained slender; and when the problem was finally resolved in the last days of the empire, there were, once again, opportunities for jurisdictional resentment and argument. On 9 *frimaire* Year IX (1 December 1800) Wirion presented plans for a force of 566 foot and 570 mounted gendarmes to patrol Paris, but he warned that its duties would be very different from those of the provincial companies and suggested that this should be taken into account in appointing the officers.[13] Wirion's proposal was shelved and a Municipal Guard was established for Paris by Consular Order on 22 *vendémiaire* Year XI (14 October 1802). This was an elite military unit, but separate from the Gendarmerie; its battalions were constantly removed by Napoleon for his campaigns, and it was compromised during General Malet's republican conspiracy of October 1812. Malet's bold coup came close to success. The troops in Paris had been easily convinced by his performance, and Prefect of Police Pasquier, who had no significant coercive force at his disposal, had been chased from the prefecture at bayonet-point. In consequence, in April 1813, Napoleon agreed to the creation of four Gendarmerie companies for his capital. These companies were to be under Pasquier's direction; they were to be recruited from the Gendarmerie companies across the empire, and Savary helped him in the selection of the men—all of which infuriated Moncey. 'No one was more pernickety and touchy than [Moncey]', recalled Pasquier:

> He came up to me, his eyes flashing: 'Well, *monsieur le préfet*,' he said to me, 'at your pleasure you are going to take all the men you want from my Gendarmerie; and when I, a marshal of France, the Inspector-General, meet one of these fine men, wearing your uniform, in the streets of Paris, I won't be able to say: "Rascal, why is your hat on cock-eyed?" ' '*Monsieur le maréchal*,' I replied, 'you won't even do him the honour of looking at him, you'll take him for a civilian.'[14]

---

[12] AN AF[IV] 1158, Savary to Moncey, 25 Mar. 1812, and Moncey to Savary, 28 Mar. 1812.

[13] Ibid. 1154, Wirion to Fouché, 9 *frimaire* Year IX.

[14] *Souvenirs du Chancelier Pasquier 1767–1815*, introduction and notes by Robert Lacour-Gayet (Paris: Hachette, 1964), 144–5; Jean Tulard, *Paris et son Administration (1800–1830)* (Paris: Ville de Paris Commission des Travaux Historiques, 1976), 153–6.

The kind of man who served in the Gendarmerie under Moncey, and who, from 1804, was to swear 'obedience to the constitution of the Empire and loyalty to the Emperor',[15] was much the same as had served in the old *maréchaussée*. In part, of course, this was because the regulations required that gendarmes be former soldiers with a good conduct record; but once again it appears that many men were using the corps as a way of returning to their home region. When regimental colonels forwarded lists of volunteers for the Gendarmerie, they commonly stated that the men wanted to serve in their *département* of origin. In the summer of 1805, for example, Colonel Darricau of the 32nd Infantry recommended Sergeant-Major François Monfraix who, though only 29, had fourteen years service behind him. Monfraix's conduct was irreproachable: 'he knows arithmetic and has good standards of behaviour. He is only leaving the regiment in the hope of being employed in his [native] *département*.'[16] There was also the advantage that local men would know the local patois or language. Thus, in March 1812 Lieutenant Nicolas Bach was preferred over another officer for appointment in the Haut-Rhin 'because he knows German.'[17]

Table 4.1, based on the reports of company inspections in 1814 and 1819, shows the number of men serving in their *département* of origin. As in the case of the statistics from the 1770s discussed earlier, it shows that not every region was the same. The figures for 1814 are skewed by the problems resulting from the end of the war: released prisoners of war and companies from territories restored to their former princes were deployed in various *départemental* companies, sometimes in considerable numbers. The company from the former Rhenish *département* of the Roër, for example, was broken up with thirty-four men going to the Vendée, twenty-four to the Yonne, three each to the Moselle and Paris; only one of these men, one of those sent to the Moselle, was going to his *pays natal*.[18] The relatively small percentages of local men serving in the western *départements* of the Finistère, Morbihan, Loire-Inférieure,

[15] Sénatus consulte, 28 *floréal* Year XII (18 May 1804).

[16] AG X^r 246, Gendarmerie, recruitment, an II–1806, Darricau to minister, 27 *thermidor* Year XIII, and *passim*. Eric A. Arnold, jr. *Fouché, Napoleon, and the General Police* (Washington, DC: University Press of America, 1979), esp. chap. VII, is highly critical of Moncey and his men, but his account is based on very limited sources and on one occasion (pp. 109–10) he appears to have assumed, first, that the Garde départementale de la Seine was a company of Gendarmerie, and second, that its dubious membership of thieves and worse was typical of the Gendarmerie. See Ernest d'Hauterive (ed.), *La Police secrète du Premier Empire*, 5 vols. (Paris: Perrin (later Clavreuil), 1922–64), iii. no. 969.

[17] AG X^r 104, Gendarmerie, compagnies départementales . . . Year XIII–1814.

[18] Ibid. 133, Gendamerie, Pô à Deux-Sèvres, 1813–1814.

TABLE 4.1. Départemental *origins of gendarmes*

Département	Total men	Native to Dept.	Neighbouring Dept.	Origin unknown
(a) *1814*				
Ain	96	30 (31.25%)	17 (17.7%)	18
Allier	55	24 (43.6%)	4 (7.3%)	–
Basses-Alpes	99	39 (39.3%)	9 (9.0%)	–
Drôme	99	30 (30.3%)	10 (10.1%)	–
Gers	83	39 (46.9%)	9 (10.8%)	–
Finistère	140	8 (5.7%)	6 (4.3%)	–
Loire-Inférieure	207	40 (19.3%)	18 (8.7%)	–
Maine-et-Loire	241	59 (24.5%)	19 (7.8%)	–
Morbihan	207	26 (12.5%)	10 (4.8%)	–
Puy-de-Dôme	149	48 (32.2%)	5 (3.3%)	–
Hautes-Pyrénées	66	32 (48.8%)	6 (9.0%)	–
Pyrenées-Orientales	104	23 (22.1%)	5 (4.8%)	–
Bas Rhin	119	68 (57.1%)	26 (21.8%)	–
Haut Rhin	141	70 (49.6%)	22 (15.6%)	1
Saône-et-Loire	96	40 (41.6%)	17 (17.7%)	8
(b) *1819*				
Eure	120	82 (68.3%)	21 (17.5%)	–
Oise	161	103 (69.9%)	14 (8.8%)	1
Seine-Inférieure	132	78 (59.0%)	20 (15.1%)	2

Source: (a) AG X^f 128, X^f 130, X^f 131, X^f 132, X^f 133; (b) AG X^f 257, Gendarmerie, revues d'inspection.

and Maine-et-Loire appear to have been the exceptions rather than the rule. These exceptions can probably be explained in some measure by tradition, but also by the recent history of the region. The Loire-Inférieure and Maine-et-Loire were centres of the Vendéen uprising, and dissaffection simmered well beyond the defeats of the 1790s. As part of the policy of pacification, the Vendée was subjected to a lighter burden of conscription than other regions during the Napoleonic period, which meant that there was a much smaller pool of potential local recruits for the Gendarmerie. The Breton *départements* like the Finistère and Morbihan were subject to similar pacification policies as a result of the *Chouannerie*. But local men had been relatively few in the *maréchaussée* companies in Brittany, where men probably had looked to sea service rather than soldiering if they decided to take the king's bounty; there was, in consequence, only a relatively small reservoir of potential Breton *cavaliers*. Similarly, the recruitment and labour for the revolutionary and Napoleonic military in Brittany was geared rather more to naval then army needs—the largest town in the Finistère was the great port and arsenal of Brest.

As Moncey and Radet had profited from the new opportunities offered by the idea of the career open to talent, so too did men in lower ranks of the corps. A cluster of promotion orders for September 1812 provide a series of examples. *Maréchal des logis* Debar, serving in the Vendée, was gazetted as *sous-lieutenant* quartermaster of the company in the Charente-Inférieure. Born in Joiny au Moulins (Marne) in 1774, Debar had enlisted in a demi-brigade of light infantry shortly after his nineteenth birthday in 1793. He fought in eight campaigns and was twice wounded, reaching the rank of sergeant major; in *brumaire* Year XII he transferred to the Gendarmerie, rising to *brigadier* in 1806 and *maréchal des logis* in 1811. *Maréchal des logis* Ripau, a native of the Orne, serving in the Mayenne, and gazetted to be lieutenant in Fontenay (Vendée), had a longer career stretching back into the *ancien régime*. Born in 1765, he had enlisted as a grenadier in 1782; he fought in five campaigns, also reached the rank of sergeant major, and transferrred to the Gendarmerie in the Year VI. *Maréchal des logis* Lavigny had a less illustrious military career—only three campaigns—but his experience as a gendarme was longer. Born at Beaumont (Manche) in 1753, he had served as a dragoon from 1770 to 1778. In 1779 he transferred to the *maréchaussée* and was serving in his native *département* when, in 1812, he was promoted to be lieutenant at Dinan (Sambre-et-Meuse).[19] It was not that these men saw the Gendarmerie as a career and vehicle for social mobility when they first enlisted; rather, once in the military system, men rose through their courage and ability, and of course as in any institution, sometimes because of the favouritism of their superiors. Moreover, the rapid expansion of the empire provided greater opportunities for promotion to commissioned ranks, particularly in the new *départements* or subject territories.[20]

No institution can be sure of getting exactly the kind of personnel that it wants, and the Gendarmerie was no exception. Wirion had shown himself to be an immensely capable organizer and planner, but he failed to live up to the high standards that he demanded of his men. After his energetic and successful career establishing different Gendarmerie legions, Wirion was appointed commandant of the prisoner-of-war headquarters in Verdun. Here he acquired an unsavoury reputation among the British prisoners for extorting money. Early in 1810 he was summoned before a court of enquiry. Perhaps recognizing how far short

---

[19] AN AF^{IV} 1158 for these promotions, dated 23 and 30 Sept. 1812, and several similar.

[20] See below pp. 166.

he had fallen of the high standards that he had demanded from his gendarmes, Wirion pre-empted the court's verdict by committing suicide.[21] The idea of the regular inspections of the *départemental* companies was, in part, to weed out those men who were not considered suitable as well as those too old or infirm; and courts martial could do the same. Early in 1801 a *Conseil du Discipline Extraordinaire* in the Haute-Saône heard the case against Gendarme Lieffroy for being incapable, badly turned out, and generally useless. In his defence, Lieffroy protested that he simply did not have the physique for the rigours of Gendarmerie life, though he said nothing in response to the charges of incapacity and insouciance. The officers on the council accepted that his physique was poor, and recognizing that 'the position of Gendarme demands constant activity and vigilance of which Lieffroy was incapable . . . he was dismissed'.[22] Some gendarmes appear to have been rough and brutal, and none too keen to take at face value the word or the papers of a suspect, particularly in the early years of the empire.[23] Rank was no guarantee of avoiding dismissal, whether the offence was having manifested the wrong political principles, particularly at the beginning of the Consulate, or dishonouring the uniform through general unseemly behaviour.[24] Gendarmes were disciplined for arbitrary arrest, drunkenness, and insubordination, with short prison sentences, sometimes coupled with the requirement that they be moved to another brigade. Surprisingly, petty thefts from both civilians and comrades, while they might lead to a prison sentence, did not necessarily lead to expulsion from the corps. Gendarmes Chapelain and Louis, serving in the Côtes-du-Nord, were charged with the theft of 42 francs and thirteen sausages at the beginning of 1801. They were acquitted on the first charge, but found guilty

---

[21] Michael Lewis, *Napoleon and his British Captives* (London: Allen & Unwin, 1962), 125–34, for a very critical portrait of Wirion, based largely on the memoirs of British prisoners.

[22] AG X^f 254, Gendarmerie: Jugements, Conseil de Discipline extraordinaire, Haute-Saône, 15 *pluviôse* Year IX.

[23] d'Hauterive (ed.), *La Police Secrète*, i. nos. 939, 976, and 1,167. In the first of these incidents a gendarme mortally wounded a sailor in Marseilles, suspecting him of being a deserter. The problem was exacerbated by the reward of 12 francs offered to gendarmes for the arrest of any seaman without the appropriate papers, and the charge was made that gendarmes simply destroyed legitimate papers when presented so as to claim the bounty.

[24] AN AF 1154, Gouvion to First Consul, 8 *frimaire* Year II and Moncey to First Consul, 28 *pluviôse* Year II; AG X^f 104, Gendarmerie: Compagnies départementales, Compagnie . . . du Bas-Rhin, État Nominatif des Officiers, 18 May 1812, for case of Lieutenant Lintot 'uneducated, lacking ability, his age [56] does not suggest that he can improve. Addicted to wine, drinking with his subordinates . . . deaf in one ear and shortsighted. He dishonours the uniform . . .'

on the second and sentenced to three months imprisonment, after which they were to return to their brigades. Two months later Gendarme Latour, serving in the Var, was sentenced to six months for stealing from a comrade, after which he too was to return to his brigade.[25]

The rivalry at the centre of the administration between Moncey and officials of the ministry of *police générale* had echoes further down the line as, occasionally, gendarmes and other functionaries clashed over interpretation of the law and jurisdiction. A brigadier in the Alpes-Maritimes found himself before the local criminal tribunal accused of showing a lack of respect for the mayor of Nice; he had queried the mayor's right to issue a permit for gaming.[26] The brigadier of La Ferté (Seine-et-Oise) ran into trouble when he was sucked into a squabble between the curé of Bouray and his flock. The curé was a difficult individual who, leaving the parish, appears to have wanted to take property from the local church with him. The mayor and the local community objected and demanded that the property be handed over to the church-warden. The priest claimed that his life was in danger and demanded protection from the Gendarmerie when he quit Bouray. The brigadier responded by sending an escort of two men, and was promptly condemned by the mayor and adjoint for siding with the curé. In the brigadier's defence, the Gendarmerie lieutenant in Versailles insisted that the brigade had responded to a call for assistance and that it could not know whether this was true or false. Moreover, he pointed out, the mayor's deputy (*adjoint*) had been quite happy to sign the patrol sheet presented to him by the two-man escort.[27] Moncey protested to Napoleon that many local officials needed to be told where their duty lay, and drew attention to the lack of support that his men often received from both mayors and tribunals.[28] Early in 1805 Pelet de la Lozère, director of the second regional division of the ministry of police, sent a circular to the *départmental* prefects and to the principal police *commissaires* of the main towns, stating that, irrespective of its activity and zeal, the Gendarmerie was showing too much independence of local authority: 'The Gendarmerie, situated exclusively under the authority of the ministry of *police générale* for the use, the movement, and the deployment of force, is the instrument [*arme*] of the police, it is the executive

---

[25] AG X^f 254, Gendarmerie: Jugements, Jugement rendu par le Conseil de Guerre, St Brieuc, 19 *nivôse*, Year IX, Jugement rendu par the Conseil de Guerre, Marseille, 18 *ventôse* Year IX.

[26] Ibid., extract from criminal tribunal of the Alpes-Maritimes, 6 *fructidor* Year IX.

[27] d'Hauterive (ed.), *La Police Secrète*, i. no. 846.

[28] AN AF^{IV} 1156, report to Emperor, Apr. 1806.

arm [*bras*] of it, it is essentially dependent on it, and ought not to be the police itself.'

Pelet went on to note the relevant articles of the law of *germinal* Year VI, and a government order of the Year XII, and to request that local company commanders be apprised of these.[29] The responses suggest, however, that relations between the prefects and the company commanders in their respective *départements* were generally good. The most critical, the prefect of the Hautes-Pyrénées, thought the circular timely. He had recently experienced the problem of a high-handed brigadier making an official complaint against the mayor of Maubourguet; though the prefect had to admit that, when he informed the company commander, 'he was the first to acknowledge the brigadier's offence . . . and to order him to make his apologies to the mayor'. From the remote Ariège, where the representatives of central government commonly faced difficulties with the peasantry, the prefect noted that, while there might be some problems with one or two of his subordinates, it would be difficult to find a better and more agreeable officer than the company commander. The prefect of the Drôme similarly wrote in the most effusive terms of his company commander and their successful relationship. In Marseilles, however, Pelet's letter itself prompted friction which had not existed before; the Gendarmerie commander felt it necessary to respond to the comments of the local *commissaire* of police stressing the military and independent nature of the corps. In later years there were complaints from prefects about over-zealous or clumsy gendarmes creating problems with pointless arrests or charges.[30] But the overall impression is that the senior men on the ground, both prefects and company commanders, did their best to ensure that the system worked as well as possible; they kept in touch with each other, and sought to ensure that any problems did not grow out of proportion. While the evidence is fragmentary, it would seem that, as the administration of the empire became better established, there was a decline in the friction and rivalry between the Gendarmerie and senior civilian administrators. Not every clash or complaint in the provinces had the administrators in Paris immediately taking sides, and many senior civilian administrators were keenly aware of the Gendarmerie's problems with local government

---

[29] AN F[7] 3001 (Dossier 27, fos. 27–8) Pelet to Prefects, *ventôse* Year XIII. AN F[7] 3053 (Dossier 4) contains the replies from the prefects, which suggest that the circular was actually sent in *pluviôse*.

[30] d'Hauterive (ed.), *La Police Secrète*, iii. nos. 227 and 912.

officials, particularly mayors.[31] However, Moncey could not resist a riposte to Pelet's circular. In February 1807 he wrote to Fouché, satisfied that the relations between his men and the prefects were working well, but feeling duty-bound to draw attention to the pretensions of some subprefects who had been demanding unnecessary escorts. 'If the Gendarmerie wishes to satisfy all the requests for the useless escorts that various public functionaries think they have the right to demand, then it will have to renounce its duties, it will have to change the nature of the institution so as to become exclusively an object of luxury and pomp.'[32]

The gendarmes were instructed by Moncey that the anticipation and prevention of offences was a better policy than pursuit and punishment.[33] The old division between *le service ordinaire*, with its regular round of patrolling the main roads and supervising fairs and markets, and *le service extraordinaire* was continued, but major new tasks were added. Alongside instructions regarding patrolling the highways, protecting tax convoys and ammunition trains, and suppressing smuggling, there were new forms of surveillance and supervision, as well as requests for information about what was going on in the provinces, particularly the state of the public mind. A decree of 11 June 1806 required the Gendarmerie to register and supervise the *gardes-champêtres* in their district. A circular of November 1810, concerned about false rumours spread by people journeying from Paris, instructed gendarmes to post themselves at the stopping places of public coaches, to listen to the conversation of the passengers, and to get the name and address of anyone uttering such rumours.[34] But most time-consuming of the new tasks during the Consulate and Empire were those emanating from the regime's military adventures and policies—the supervision of prisoners

---

[31] In Feb. 1808, for example, a sub-prefect in the Lot-et-Garonne protested that a lieutenant in the Gendarmerie had failed to arrest a local tax official following an insult. Fouché scrawled on the report to the Emperor: 'This sub-prefect is a blockhead [*une mauvaise tête*], incapable of administering affairs.' d'Hauterive (ed.), *La Police Secrète*, iv. no. 85. In contrast, following the death of a rioter in Molines (Lozère) towards the end of 1804, the sub-prefect of Florac noted that 'rebellions' against the Gendarmerie were frequent in his district because the courts did not punish the guilty. Moreover, since in this case the local magistrate had issued an arrest warrant against the gendarme who had killed the man, it was suggested that all proceedings should be dropped. Ibid., i. nos. 503 and 741.

[32] AN F⁷ 3053 (Dossier 4), Moncey to Fouché, 5 Feb. 1807.

[33] *Ordres généraux*, 15 *nivose* and 25 *pluviôse* Year X.

[34] Musée de la Gendarmerie (Melun), Correspondance du Maréchal Moncey, 1805–14, no. 150, and see also nos. 142, 173, and 179; with reference to tax convoys see nos. 115 and 161; for ammunition waggons see nos. 193 and 201; for the patrolling of roads, no. 164; for the upkeep of roads, no. 143; for the supression of smuggling, no. 157.

of war, particularly while on the move, and, above all, the conscription process.

Gendarmerie officers assisted the subprefects in conducting the ballots, while small squads of gendarmes escorted the conscripts to their muster points and pursued refractory conscripts and deserters. In the aftermath of Ulm and Austerlitz, apparently concluding that the demand for conscripts would now decline and that his men could settle down to their ordinary service, Moncey announced:

Surveillance by the Gendarmerie will now be less difficult, but not less necessary. Conscription requires permanent care to ensure recruitment for the army and no circumstance can let this slacken. The safety of persons and property, that of the major roads and of all the communes of the Empire, will never cease to be the usual object of [the Gendarmerie's] duty. Protecting good citizens, containing the malevolent, apprehending the guilty when it has not been possible to prevent the crime, these are the tasks of every hour and every moment. And when, after glorious battles, the army rests on its laurels, the Gendarmerie will still be waging continous war, never less active, against all the enemies of good order.[35]

But Napoleon and his army rarely rested on their laurels. From 1806 the routine, bureaucratized system of conscription called upon at least 80,000 men annually, and in the crisis years towards the close of the Empire, the demand was much higher. The gendarme's various roles in the process were central. Moncey's General Orders make constant reference to the need to be vigilant in enforcing conscription legislation and vigorous in the pursuit of deserters and refractory conscripts.[36] The surviving letters sent by Moncey to Colonel Martin-Charly, commandant of the 8th Legion (Corrèze, Dordogne, Haute-Vienne, and Lot-et-Garonne), while containing instructions regarding the supression of smuggling, the supervision and the upkeep of roads, the protection of tax and of munition convoys, similarly emphasize military needs.[37] The demands of the Napoleonic military machine provided opportunities for

---

[35] *Ordres généraux*, 6 Jan. 1806.

[36] e.g. ibid, 5 *fructidor* Year X; 5 *ventôse* and 5 *thermidor* Year XI; 25 *brumaire* Year XII; 4 *pluviose* Year XIII; 8 Jan. and 25 Apr. 1807.

[37] There are 103 letters in the collection of Moncey's correspondence in the Gendarmerie Museum; 100 of these are to Martin-Charly. Of these 103 letters, 10 refer specifically to the problem of desertion or to specific deserters (nos. 138, 140, 171, 160, 178, 189, 203, 204, 207, 214); 3 concern the detatchment of gendarmes to the mobile columns which swept through particular *départements* in 1810 and 1811 in pursuit of deserters (nos. 47, 168, 169); another 4 are concerned with more general matters relating to conscription (nos. 124, 154, 199, 213).

some gendarmes to collude with local communities and to make money either by accepting bribes or by extorting money to turn a blind eye towards young men liable for conscription and dodging the draft.[38] But rather than collusion and corruption, more often, and especially in the more remote regions of France, these demands brought confrontation between gendarmes and local notables and violent clashes between gendarmes and local communities.

In *messidor* Year IX (June/July 1801) it was estimated that, across the whole of the extended territory of France, attacks on gendarmes engaged on conscription duties or the pursuit of deserters were running at an average of two a day.[39] A central role in the conscription process was played by the local mayor. The mayor was charged with keeping his commune's register of births, marriages, and deaths, the *état civil*, as well as issuing certificates of residence and passports. Such papers were essential for ensuring that all the right young men were present for the conscription ballot, and for ensuring that gendarmes could check the validity of the claims of any young men whom they suspected of desertion or of being refractory conscripts. The Napoleonic mayors were no longer elected but were appointed by the prefects; the job was shunned by the wealthy and respectable, and the typical mayor in a region of widespread peasant holdings was himself a peasant of modest income and modest education, whose sympathies were much more likely to be with his community and its needs rather than with the central government and its demands.[40] While Napoleon wanted soldiers, peasant communities wanted young men for local labour, or to bring back money from the traditional seasonal migrations. Unlike gendarmes, the *gardes-champêtres* did not live together in the comparative safety of barracks, and attempts on their part to enforce the conscription legislation could bring down terrible retribution from their neighbours, and on their families as well as themselves.[41] The appearance of gendarmes in a district hunting for deserters and refractory conscripts could provoke serious disorder, and disorder in which the mayors often demonstrated a greater sympathy for their neighbours than for the state. In July 1805, for example, *maréchal des logis* Nicolas Malhieu, brigadier Michel Saucher, and five gendarmes rode into Ségura (Ariège) in pursuit of a group of

---

[38] d'Hauterive (ed.), *La Police Secrète*, i. no. 1541, iii. no. 281, iv. no. 905, v. no. 440.

[39] AN AF[IV] 1154, Minister of War to First Consul, 7 and 13 *messidor* Year IX.

[40] Isser Woloch, *The New Regime: Transformations of the French Civic Culture, 1789–1820s* (New York: Norton, 1994), 127–33.

[41] d'Hauterive (ed.), *La Police Secrète*, ii. nos. 1,378, 1,473, iii. nos. 58, 427, and 726.

refractory conscripts. They apprehended some of their quarry, but found themselves obstructed by the mayors of Ségura and of the neighbouring commune of Mailliou, publicly abused by the local curé, and finally assaulted by the populace. Malhieu and his men got away with five conscripts, their personal weapons, and their lives; other squads were less fortunate. The *département* of Deux-Sèvres was not particularly noted for serious opposition to conscription, with the exception of the area close to the Vendée around Bressuire which, in August 1792, had been a centre of the first serious bloodshed in the counter-revolutionary activity in the west.[42] On 27 January 1806 three gendarmes were directed to escort two refractory conscripts to Bressuire. They were ambushed *en route*. Gendarmes Bourgeat and Chatelain were shot; their comrade escaped, as did the conscripts. The lieutenant in Bressuire learned subsequently that Bourgeat was not dead when his assailants reached him; they finished him off by smashing his carbine over his body.[43]

The hostility shown towards gendarmes in the pursuit of refractory conscripts and deserters led to some brigades sending advance parties of men into villages wearing civilian clothes to check on their quarry and on the potential for trouble. There were instances when the men in civilian clothes themselves made an arrest, but such action gave rise to legal concerns. The court of cassation ruled against charges of 'rebellion against the Gendarmerie' when men were not identifiable by their uniform, and the minister of justice warned that, engaged in such delicate tasks, gendarmes should always carry some mark of their identity.[44] Nor was the ruse always successful; disguised or not, men from local brigades could be recognized, while strangers with a military bearing were likely to be viewed with suspicion, especially if they started asking questions.[45]

---

[42] Charles Tilly, *The Vendée* (London: Edward Arnold, 1964), 306–8.

[43] AN BB[18]7, Malhieu's report, 2 *thermidor* Year XIII; AN AF[IV]1156, report to Emperor, 3 Feb. 1806, and for the general calm in the Deux-Sèvres, except for Bressuire, see report to Emperor, 7 Jan. 1806. For the Gendarmerie's conscription difficulties in general see Alan Forrest, *Conscripts and Deserters: The Army and French Society During the Revolution and Empire* (Oxford: Oxford University Press, 1989), 232–6; and Arnold, *Fouché, Napoleon , and the General Police*, 118–20.

[44] d'Hauterive (ed.), *La Police Secrète*, iii. no. 1,121; Forrest, *Conscripts and Deserters*, 229.

[45] AN AF[IV] 1155, report to Emperor, 14 *messidor* Year XII, describes an occasion in the Maine-et-Loire which went wrong when the two gendarmes in civilian clothes were recognized. Gendarmes also wore civilian clothes on occasions to get information about 'brigands'. The results could be embarrassing, as when, in the Finistère in August 1808, two gendarmes claiming to be *chouans* were reported by local peasants and arrested by customs officers; d'Hauterive (ed.), *La Police Secrète*, iv. no. 674. But they could also be

It was not only the pursuit and arrest of refractory conscripts and deserters, however, which provoked violence towards gendarmes. In December 1807 Gendarmes Perrin and Felix of the brigade in Saigne (Cantal) were given a warrant from one of the courts in Mauriac for the arrest of Pierre Delors, who was charged with forestry offences. They met no trouble in Delors's village, but they were viciously attacked by five individuals on the road back. Delors escaped; Felix died on the following day from the beating that he had received.[46] Individuals could also respond violently to a gendarme's demand, as Gendarme Ninguel in the Gard discovered in October 1806, when his order to a poacher to hand over his gun cost him his life.[47] Such violence is difficult to quantify. It appears to have been more serious in the more remote regions of France like the Ariège, where the violent *rixe* between young men of different communes was accepted as the way to defend the community and its borders. Faced with such violence, the Napoleonic gendarmes had to be tough and, at times, courageous; they may also have been prompted, on occasions, to behave in a rough fashion and to get their retaliation in first.

More life-threatening, though less common than the violence which sometimes accompanied conscription, were the battles with brigands. The word 'brigand' was a catch-all embracing the remnants of the royalist rebels, particularly in the west, groups of armed deserters or *réfractaires*, and individuals who saw opportunities for profit in highway robbery and other forms of offence; often there appears little distinction between such groups. A gang active in the *arrondissement* of Segré (Maine-et-Loire) towards the end of 1806 was allegedly composed of deserters, but commanded by an ex-*chouan*. In May 1807 there was an attack on the carriage carrying the tax receipts of Bergerac by four members of the same family, but not, it seems, either deserters or

successful. Towards the end of 1802 *maréchal des logis* Cotte, serving in the Orne, infiltrated a gang of robbers by acting as a receiver for their stolen goods. Cotte was given money from the company chest to pay the robbers for their booty, which he then returned to the victims in Alençon. As a result of Cotte's information the robbers were ambushed while on a raid: one was killed, one badly wounded, two were apprehended, and one escaped. Cotte was praised and rewarded, as were two other gendarmes and a civilian policeman who worked with him. Unfortunately Cotte's reward of 200 francs did not cover the money which he had been given from the company chest. Correspondence between the local prefect and Fouché, with the former seeking full reimbursement for the costs, continued until the end of 1804; AN F7 3260; d'Hauterive (ed.), *La Police Secrète*, i. no. 132.

[46] AN AF^IV 1156, report to Emperor, 9 Jan. 1808.

[47] d'Hauterive (ed.), *La Police Secrète*, iii. nos. 78 and 88; and for similar instances see nos. 103 and 417.

former rebels—indeed, several other members of the family held public office in the Dordogne. The two gendarmes guarding the carriage fought a gun-battle with the robbers, and while the attackers succeeded in getting away with roughly half the money, at least three of them were in custody within six weeks.[48] In a similar incident in the Calvados, the gendarme escorting the money was wounded in the shoulder, and the brigadier who, with another gendarme, galloped to the scene on hearing of the attack, was shot in the leg and had his horse killed under him. Here the company's failure rapidly to identify and apprehend the culprits led Moncey to replace its commander with the energetic Captain François Manginot, who had earlier distinguished himself in hunting down brigands in the Eure. Manginot's investigations began with the driver of the tax carriage, and the discovery of 400 francs hidden in the matress on the man's bed; from there he proceeded to unearth a conspiracy of former *chouans*.[49] But Moncey was never content with arrests in such circumstances; he wanted to use examples to encourage his men in what he felt was the proper behaviour for a gendarme. While the captain commanding the Dordogne company praised his men for their efforts in the Bergerac affair, the local prefect complained that they had not followed the procedures laid down for such escort duty. Moncey was sceptical: 'Their conduct will be carefully examined, and even if they are found to be without reproach, I will punish them as an example and to teach the corps that a gendarme ought to die rather than yield to brigands, whatever their number.'[50] The two gendarmes wounded in defence of the tax receipts in the Calvados, however, he considered worthy of some recompense. It was common for Moncey to seek a reward— a promotion, a sabre, a carbine, sometimes monetary payment—for men who had shown gallantry in such encounters, or who had apprehended a notorious offender. Just over 40 per cent of the paragraphs of the General Orders for the Gendarmerie published during his period as Inspector-General deal with such praise and recompense.[51] This policy was strongly approved by Napoleon.[52]

---

[48] AN AF[IV] 1156, report to Emperor, 13 May 1807; d'Hauterive (ed.), *La Police Secrète*, iii. no. 660.

[49] AN AF[IV] 1156, report to Emperor, 13 May 1807; d'Hauterive (ed.), *La Police Secrète*, iii. nos. 722, 728, 775, 818, 834, 849, 858, 871, 907.

[50] AN AF[IV] 1156, report to Emperor, 13 May 1807.

[51] Chef d'escadron Dominique Renault, 'Les convictions du Maréchal Moncey', *Revue historique des armées*, 4 (1991), 15–21. Regnault has broken down the 806 separate paragraphs of Moncey's 137 General Orders as follows:

see next page/

In spite of the legislation increasing their numbers under first the Revolution and then under Napoleon, the Gendarmerie brigades remained thin on the ground and short of numbers; promised increases appear often to have amounted to little more than statements of intent on paper. Early in 1805 the prefect of the Gironde explained that he had no criticism of the company in his *département*:

It gives me a periodic account of its operations regarding the arrest of conscripts, vagabonds, and those of no fixed abode. The orders which I give are carried out with zeal. If some operations are not conducted with the activity that could be wished, the officers' excuse is the multiplicity of their tasks and the vacancies in the company. Seven gendarmes and two brigadiers are lacking, the two NCOs died and have not been replaced. To complete the brigades on the main roads, where the service is unrelenting, it would be necessary to deplete those in the countryside where one can see the weakness of the brigades from the multiplicity of field and forest offences and the marked reluctance of the young men to serve the state.[53]

Two years later the prefect of the Maine-et-Loire reported an even greater shortfall. Here, in old Vendéen rebel territory, brigands were still active; they had only recently ambushed two gendarmes on the road, killing one outright—yet the company was sixty-two men under strength, roughly half its complement.[54] Sometimes the problem was that men had been seconded out of their *département* for other duties, such as the mobile columns organized temporarily for the pursuit of

Heading	Number	%
Reward	328	40.72
Punishment	74	9.18
Regulations of Service	169	20.96
Administration (Barracks, equipment, etc.)	113	14.01
Organization (New Companies, etc.)	75	9.30
Others	47	5.83

For a more detailed analysis see Captain Dominique Renault, 'L'Inspection Générale de la Gendarmerie au Début de l'Empire', Mémoire de Diplôme Technique, Enseignement militaire supérieur scientifique et technique, 1986–7.

[52] *Cor. Nap.* vol. 19, no. 15,915, to Moncey (8 Oct. 1809).

[53] AN F⁷ 3053, Prefect of the Gironde to Pelet de la Lozère, 15 *ventôse* Year XIII. There was a similar complaint from the Prefect of the Côtes-du-Nord in Jan. 1810. There were only 76 gendarmes available in his *département*; they had to be stationed on the main roads, but this left a great many important points without surveillance, in a region where the English were keen to land brigands to stir up trouble: d'Hauterive (ed.), *La Police Secrète*, v. no. 510.

[54] d'Hauterive (ed.), *La Police Secrète*, iii. no. 1,060; and the situation was no better in Mar. 1810 when the same company had only 60 men available for its brigades: ibid., v. no. 590.

deserters in 1809 or, more permanently, to provide cadres for companies newly formed elsewhere in the empire.[55] There were times too when, as had happened in the dark days of 1792, Napoleon's demands for men depleted the brigades still further.[56] In February 1808 the Gendarmerie as a whole was reported to be lacking 3,942 men.[57] Napoleon himself had little time for such complaints; he was not sure that gendarmes were always employed to their best advantage, and his response to the concerns of early 1808 was that, with the pacification of the west and without any need to continue the surveillance of nobles and refractory priests, the Gendarmerie might sooner be reduced rather than augmented.[58] Even so, when early in 1813 he demanded 750 gendarmes to reinforce his heavy cavalry regiments, Moncey protested that this was hardly possible since there were already 4,373 men on detachment.[59]

In spite of the gaps in its ranks, brigandage did decline, the conscripts did come in, the numbers of *réfractaires* diminished,[60] and the Gendarmerie could, and did, boast of playing a significant role in this. Early in 1809, standing in for Moncey who was absent campaigning in Spain, General Louis-Léopold Buquet wrote an assessment of the corps's achievements in the previous year. In spite of the fact that men

[55] d'Hauterive (ed.), *La Police Secrète*, v. no. 349; and for the detachment of gendarmes as cadres for new companies in the Empire see below pp. 161, 164, 166–7.

[56] On 24 Nov. 1812, as the scale of the Moscow disaster began to be recognized, the minister of war started chasing round for a force of 561 gendarmes to be detached from their ordinary duties and sent to army headquarters in Magdebourg: AN AF[IV] 1158.

On 15 Mar. 1813 a muster of the gendarmes who had embarked on the Moscow expedition itself revealed only 283 men present; 318 had been lost: AG X[f] 256. AG X[f] 248, Gendarmerie: Divers, consists mainly of the death certificates of gendarmes who were killed, or who died, while serving on campaign with Napoleon's armies—men like Pierre-Jules Maubert and Philibert-Nicolas Morin. The former, born in Calais in 1772 enlisted in October 1792 and served in the cavalry before transferring to the Gendarmerie as a brigadier in the Deux-Nêthes in Year V. In 1809 he was promoted *maréchal des logis* in Quesnoy (Nord), but two years later he was moved to the army of Portugal. He died in Salamanca in 1813. Morin was born in Rouen in 1772. He was serving as a *maréchal des logis* in Lippe when he was detached for service with the *Grande Armée* in 1812. He died in Berlin in March 1813 as a result of the fatigue and privations of the Russian campaign.

[57] d'Hauterive (ed.), *La Police Secrète*, iv. no. 92.

[58] *Cor. Nap.* vol. 16, no. 13,660, Note . . . (17 Mar. 1808); see also ibid., vol. 17, no. 13,759, to Clarke (18 Apr. 1808), infuriated that mounted gendarmes were being used to supervise a conscript depot. In Napoleon's eyes, this was tying up valuable cavalry horses; foot gendarmes should be used for such service, and he demanded that, in future, he receive regular reports of how brigades were being deployed.

[59] AN AF[IV] 1158, report from Moncey, 13 Feb. 1813.

[60] Woloch, *The New Regime*, 418, notes that the number of draft-dodgers declined at precisely the moment when, because of the larger and more frequent levies from 1810 onwards, they might be expected to have increased. He puts this down primarily to 'the cumulative impact of bureaucratic and coercive pressure'.

had been detached from the brigades for other duties, he insisted that the brigades were successfully reducing both the vestiges of *chouannerie* in the west and the incidence of brigandage elsewhere.

Never, perhaps, has the movement of prisoners been so great, and the number of escapes so few. . . . The policing of the main roads and markets is carried out with exactitude; the great movement of troops which has taken place has been faithfully shadowed and observed; everywhere good order has been maintained. It would be difficult to evaluate the number of offences which [the Gendarmerie's] vigilance and activity have prevented. This aspect of the service, for which there are no measurable results, is not however, the least dignified to be provided for Your Majesty.

In the repression of offences which the Gendarmerie could not prevent, the guilty rarely escape their investigations. The number of arrests made in 1807 was 57,981, this rose in 1808 to 59,719. However, it would be wrong to conclude from this increase that crime itself had increased in the course of the year since many of these arrests related to very minor trouble. The number of beggars and vagabonds arrested was 3,008, it was only 2,323 in 1807; strangers arrested for being without passports were around 5,000, and only 3,000 in 1807; 13,099 deserters were handed over to the army and the navy, 16,812 late or refractory conscripts were delivered to the colours.[61]

Of course Buquet was likely to have over-egged the pudding as far as his men were concerned, yet his comments on the inability of measuring prevention and the mass of petty offences are worth some reflection. It was violent confrontations, especially those with brigands or with refractory conscripts and their families, which tended to fill the Inspector-General's reports to Napoleon or to the minister of war, and which, at the same time, highlighted the sparse deployment of the often-depleted brigades. But fights, gun-battles, and riots were not the experience of gendarmes every day. A peaceful patrol or escort duty could suddenly end in a flurry of excitement, but the day-to-day experience was more commonly the humdrum patrol of a district watching for suspects, asking locals for news, getting mayors or other local worthies to sign the patrol book. Moreover, it probably is the case that, with the brief exception of the disorder created by the disintegration of the empire under the allied military onslaught in 1813 and 1814, such experience was becoming ever more the norm.

[61] AN AF[IV] 1157, Buquet to Emperor, Feb. 1809.

PART II
France: *Consolidation*

5

'ONE OF THE MOST SURE GUARANTEES OF ORDER': THE GENDARMERIE AND THE RESTORATION

During, and partly as a direct result of the quarter of a century of revolutionary upheavals, wars, and the massive administrative change in France between 1789 and 1815, the Gendarmerie had been increased more than fourfold. On Napoleon's fall it provided the French state with a much greater penetration into the provinces and, by its greater presence in the towns and villages and its patrols along the roads, it gave the French people a greater awareness of the state, particularly the state's demands and its claims to impose and to maintain its definition of order. The restored Bourbons changed little of the legal and administrative structures which had developed in their absence; the Gendarmerie survived along with everything else. Of course, the restored regime could point to the long tradition of its *ancien régime* progenitor, the *maréchaussée*. In the summer of 1815 there were discussions on whether or not to revive the old name, but the decision was taken to keep the new.

As for the occasional wrongdoings that can be attributed to the Gendarmerie, these were principally attributable also to the old *maréchaussée* which was the basis of the forces of public order in the very worst of times. The Gendarmerie that currently exists, as a result of the pains taken over its composition and the care given to its morale, can be regarded as one of the most sure guarantees of order and internal tranquillity.[1]

The Gendarmerie's role had developed considerably from that of its predecessor. Le Blanc's reform one hundred years before appears to have been sparked by anxieties about the numbers of vagrants. The

---

[1] AG MR 1957, Liasse 'Gendarmerie, 1814 à 1830', Rapport sur la dénomination de Maréchaussée à substituer à celle de Gendarmerie (no date).

provincial brigades of the *maréchaussée* and then of the Gendarmerie had always seen it as their duty to apprehend such offenders, but dealing with more general problems of brigandage, crime, and disorder had commonly constituted the public role of *cavaliers* and gendarmes alike. The demands of the revolutionary and, particularly, the Napoleonic wars had demonstrated the value of the Gendarmerie for mustering conscripts and for the apprehension of deserters; peace in 1815 did not mean an end to conscription, just a change to the system. The gendarme's role in enforcing the state's demands for soldiers was not particularly popular with the majority of the population; his role in maintaining the state jurist's view of order might also run counter to the views of local communities. As a regulation enforcer and crime fighter he could be regarded with ambivalence; victims of petty offences as well as of more serious crimes came from every section of society. Where he was more certain to be warmly regarded by the population was as a provider of aid and assistance in time of natural or man-made disaster; recognition of this role was not clearly articulated during the Restoration, and it was a role which the gendarme acquired almost by default—there was no other organized state institution available throughout the provinces to provide assistance in an emergency. The welfare role, arguably an extension of public order maintenance and of the protection of the population, was, however, a means of developing bonds between the gendarmes and the communities in which they were stationed; it was also a way for the state to demonstrate that it had the interests and safety of its citizens at heart.

Moncey distinguished himself in the defence of Paris against the allied armies early in 1814, but on Napoleon's abdication he rallied to Louis XVIII and continued in his post of Inspector-General. As Napoleon's empire was contracted into the kingdom of France, so, in July 1814, Moncey's command was reduced to twenty-four legions consisting of 15,350 men; he directed his inspecting generals to use the reduction as an opportunity for purging the force of any men too old, infirm, or not suited for their tasks.[2] During the Hundred Days Moncey refused to break his oath of allegiance to the king and retired to Franche-Comté. But on Napoleon's second abdication he fell from favour with the Bourbons when he refused to preside over the court martial of his former comrade-in-arms Marshal Ney. This refusal earned Moncey some ten months imprisonment in the fortress of Ham,

---

[2] AG MR 1957, Liasse 'Gendarmerie, 1814 à 1815', Instructions pour MM les Inspecteurs généraux de la Gendarmerie . . .

and though he was restored to his rank and honours towards the end of 1816, he never again served in the Gendarmerie. Radet, in contrast, opted for half-pay during the first Restoration, then, apparently without any great enthusiasm, he rejoined Napoleon during the Hundred Days. He commanded the Gendarmerie in the Midi, and in this capacity escorted the Duke of Angoulême into exile following the latter's abortive attempt to lead a Bourbon rising in the south. Wounded at Waterloo, Radet took over briefly as Inspector-General of the Gendarmerie, before being removed, tried, and sentenced to nine years imprisonment for supporting 'the usurper'. In the event he was released after just over two years in the citadel at Besançon, but he never saw active service again.

The courts martial which tried Moncey, Ney, and Radet were just the tip of the official purge of the army and the Gendarmerie. The Inspection-General of the Gendarmerie was itself abolished as expensive, smacking too much of the Napoleonic system, and 'not in harmony with the constitutional regime'.[3] The corps was brought directly within the remit of the ministry of war by the creation, within the ministry, of a department of Gendarmerie and Military Police. The Ordinance of 10 September–27 October 1815 reorganized the corps once again; the twenty-four legions were now to have a strength of 18,000 men divided into 1,550 mounted and 620 foot brigades. A supplementary ordinance of 18 November re-established *départemental* juries of senior civilian administrators and Gendarmerie officers, which vetted applicants for the corps, and subsequently these juries were urged to purge the companies of men who had served Napoleon.

The number of men dismissed or requesting to leave after the investigations of these juries suggests that the severity of the purge varied from *département* to *département*; nor does it appear that the juries interpreted the various criteria for dismissal in the same way (see Table 5.1). In the Oise, for example, thirteen of the men designated for retirement with a one-off gratuity payment were noted for 'conduct and for professing principles which no longer permits them to remain in the Gendarmerie'. The particularly detailed information provided by the juries in the Finistère and the Manche suggests that almost half of those under the simple heading 'dismissed' were got rid of for reasons similar to those which had led to dismissal in the past, rather than for showing any suspect political principles (see Table 5.2); the one man dismissed in the Lot-et-Garonne, Pierre-Joseph Massen, had blotted his

---

[3] Ibid., Liasse 'Gendarmerie 1814 à 1815', Rapport au Roi de 20 juillet 1815.

TABLE 5.1. *Purge of Gendarmerie companies, 1815–1816*

Company	Complement	Pensioned	Retired with a one-off gratuity payment	Dismissed or leaving on own request	Named new recruit	Men to be kept	Vacancies
Basses-Alpes	120	15	–	12	38	63	19
Calvados	156	32	11	12	62	84	7
Dordogne	138	23	13	28	67	62	9
Eure	108	20	–	8	32	70	6
Eure-et-Loir	120	11	–	24	17	85	18
Finistère	186	2	5	15	54	96	36
Loiret	150	19	–	22	11	93	46
Lot-et-Garonne	96	15	6	1	44	46	6
Maine-et-Loire	228	42	8	48	116	109	3
Manche	150	56	16	15	74	74	2
Nord	156	37	1	33	29	98	29
Oise	162	33	19	6	26	117	19
Puy-de-Dôme	156	38	15	13	54	94	8
Basses-Pyrénées	162	23	1	8	40	106	16
Rhône	162	28	4	14	36	65	59
Seine	252	24	13	23	30	209	13
Seine-et-Marne	150	23	20	–	17	94	39
Seine-et-Oise	234	27	–	32	7	191	36

Source: Sampled from AG X^c 10 and X^c 11, Gendarmerie, Décisions ministerielles rendues sur les rapports du jury d'organisation.

TABLE 5.2. *Reasons for dismissal of gendarmes in 1815–1816*

Rank	Name	Age	Reason
Gendarme	C.-J.-C. Lepaige	36	Own request
"	J.-G. Legall	29	Drunkard
"	C. Domergue	25	Bad principles
"	J. Legall	31	Ex-royal volunteer, admitted into the Gendarmerie 2 Oct. 1815, no education, drunkard
"	J.-Bte. Vasseler	30	Own request, being wrong for the service
"	C.-M. Moreau	29	Own request
"	F. Dubois	27	No education
"	P. Niauder	40	Bad conduct
"	A. Royer	–	"
"	J.-M. Duparc	35	Drunkard
"	B. Charpentier	23	"
"	J.-A. Denoid	28	Very poor soldier (*très mauvais sujet*)
"	D. Milloz	35	Very poor soldier, no education, and bad principles
Brigadier	N. Trusson	34	Very poor soldier, always drunk
Gendarme	M. Rennebach	39	Bad principles
(b) *The Manche*			
Gendarme	P.-G. Grissepierre	27	Misconduct
"	G. Cornu	35	" and drunkenness
"	J. Niderlander	34	Foreigner
"	H. Felten	38	" and very bad principles
"	J. Hardouin	24	Drunkard and insubordinate
Maréchal des logis	J. Prat	33	Piedmontese, principles contrary to the royal government
Gendarme	C.-J.-J. Beillard	32	Bad principles
"	J.-C. Picquerey	31	Partisan of the usurper
"	J.-F. Legeard	28	idem
"	P. Vildier	29	idem
"	P. Corbeau	28	Cannot read or write
"	J.-D. Perrin	29	Troublemaker and insubordinate
"	L.-F. Gauvin	26	Very bad principles
"	J.-L. Guillot	28	Incorrigible drunkard
"	G. Guignard	27	Sentenced to six months imprisonment for seditious words

Source: AG X^f 10, Gendarmerie, Décisions ministerielles . . .

copybook during 'the usurpation' but, in addition, the jury found him to be 'immoral . . . as well as suffering from epilepsy'. There is evidence of the purge being used to enable some men to return to their *départe-ment* of origin. Thus, gendarme Pierre Bridonneau succeeded in getting transferred from Auch (Gers) to Champdeniers in the Deux-Sèvres, where he had been born and where he still had family. Among the list of those to be dismissed from the Basses-Alpes was Gendarme Jean-Joseph Bridet. The jury noted that he had requested to leave the company so as to return to his *pays natal*. 'As there is no unfavourable comment against Bridet, who is only 30 years old and who has the means to provide his own horse, we propose to nominate him for the vacancy of mounted gendarme in the brigade of Pont-à-Mousson, Meurthe.' The same jury also suggested the reinstatement of two men purged in 1815 who had repented past conduct and who had demonstrated their loyalty to the king. Recognizing that it could cause anxiety if they were reappointed in the Basses-Alpes, particularly amongst those who had previously given evidence against them, the jury proposed that, as they were both married men, they might be appointed to a neighbouring *département* such as the Var or Vaucluse.

Amongst the most severe purges revealed in Table 5.1 was that in the Vendéen *département* of the Maine-et-Loire. It may be that the tradition of royalism and 'royalist brigandage' here had fostered an alternative, staunchly Bonapartist sentiment among the Gendarmerie company. But it may also be that the *départemental* jury felt it necessary to reflect local prejudices, or was itself particularly suspicious of Napoleonic gendarmes and determined to make major changes. Seventeen of the new recruits to the company had served in the royal army in the Vendée in 1815 and one, 42–year-old Victor Charles Delamare, designated *maréchal des logis* in Angers, was a former cavalry captain who had served in the émigré armies during the Revolution. Explanations for the large number of new men in the Dordogne, the Lot-et-Garonne, and the Manche are not so easy to come by; most probably the reasons here for change lay simply in the attitudes of the particular juries. A final point worth stressing is the large number of vacancies that remained. Some juries requested that the regulations on age and military service be waived; nine out of the new recruits to the Manche, and four each of those to Eure-et-Loir and Maine-et-Loire were under 25 years old. Moreover, twenty-one of the men listed under those who were to be kept on in the Oise, and eleven of those to be kept on in Seine-et-Marne were also included among those on the list for pensions.[4]

Of course the purge could not have removed all men who had served during the Empire; that would have required re-creating the entire corps. Probably only those who had made their Bonapartist tendencies particularly apparent during the Hundred Days were dismissed or

---

[4] AG X^r 10 and X^r 11, Gendarmerie, Décisions ministerielles rendues sur les rapports des jurys d'organisation.

TABLE 5.3. *Length of Gendarmerie service of men in the 3rd Legion, 1819*

Département	5 years and less	5–10 years	10–15 years	Over 15 years	Total
Eure	45 (23)	42	10	23	120
Oise	83 (72)	44	7	27	161
Seine-Inférieure	60 (29)	39	12	21	132
TOTAL	188 (124)	125	29	71	413

Note: The brackets in the first column show the number of men who are clearly specified as having served in the army at some point before 1814.

pressed to resign In spite of the purge, the Gendarmerie of the early years of the Restoration remained a force of Napoleonic veterans. The evidence surviving from the inspection of the 2nd Legion in 1819 (see Table 5.3) reveals that more than half of the men had joined the Gendarmerie before the first Restoration, and of the men who had joined since Napoleon's first abdication around two-thirds had served in his armies. A few men who could date their Gendarmerie service back to the early days of the Revolution were still in post. Three men serving in the brigade stationed in Barentin (Seine-Inférieure), for example, Jean-Marie-Antoine Doumene, Robert Degouy, and Gabriel Lesacheu, had all served in the army of the *ancien régime*; the first had joined the *maréchaussée* in 1789, the other two had joined the Gendarmerie in 1792 and 1798 respectively. There were others who had found their way into the Gendarmerie largely as a result of the French Empire and who had survived the post-Napoleonic purge; one member of the Eure company had been born in Bruges, Belgium, and another in the Roër.

The inspections reveal the old problems of a few men who were rather too fond of drink or in bad health. The brigade in Fécamp (Seine-Inférieure) seems to have been in a particularly bad way; of its six men, Charles Beuzeboc was in poor health, Pierre Brunen was criticized for both drunkeness and always being sick, Louis Chapeau was noted for his very bad conduct. Following the standards demanded by Moncey and Wirion, the inspectors were keen to maintain a high standard of morality and respectability among the men; gendarmes were criticized for contracting debts, for a lack of discretion, and for negligence, and superior officers were directed to maintain a careful surveillance of these individuals. Several such had slipped through the *départemental* juries. Jean-Baptiste Sotta and François Pattin had served briefly in the imperial armies before joining the Gendarmerie company of their native *département*, the Oise, in 1817. They were both dismissed in 1819. Sotta's name was followed in the inspection report with 'very bad conduct, libertine'. He was untidily turned out and wrote badly. Pattin was also poorly turned out and illiterate; '[he] will never make a good gendarme.' Some offenders were moved from one brigade to another so as to give them a fresh start and another chance to prove themselves. Gendarme Louis Hautavoine, for example, serving at Senlis in his native Oise, was noted as a man who needed watching; he had a good stature, but was poorly turned out, rather too fond of drink, and had acquired a bad reputation in Senlis. He was moved to Bresle in place of Benoît Honoré Billet, 'a mediocre gendarme, of good morals, but poorly turned out', who had a reputation for quarrelling with his brigadier and his comrades. Billet was sent to St Just, the commune of his birth; and the fact that the Gendarmerie appears to have had little concern about a man having strong local ties is underlined by the simultaneous decision to move Gendarme Pierre Delaruelle. Delaruelle was 48 years old, with twenty-five years of service in the Gendarmerie, a wife, and five children. His conduct was excellent; he was zealous and active, and could read and write well. Following the 1819 inspection he was moved to Formerie, near to where his wife owned property and where 'he could live more at his ease'.[5]

A further point revealed by the 1819 inspection is the fact that some two-thirds of the men were married, and the majority of these had children (see Table 5.4). In some instances the number of children must have made the barracks appear as much child centres as police posts. Brigadier Pierre Bourdin, a 43-year-old native of the Calvados with twenty-seven years of army and Gendarmerie service serving in the Seine-Inférieure, was noted by the inspector as having received a reprimand from his legion colonel for blundering in the writing of his

TABLE 5.4. *Men married and with children in the 3rd Legion, 1819*

Company	Total men	Married		Widower		With children	
		No.	%	No.	%	No.	%
Eure	120	79	65.8	6	5.0	60	50.0
Oise	161	117	72.8	2	1.2	87	54.0
Seine-Inférieure	132	90	68.2	4	3.0	60	45.4

Source: AG X^f 257, Gendarmerie, revues d'inspection.

[5] AG X^f 257, Gendarmerie, 2nd Legion Inspections, Aug.–Sept. 1819.

reports and for pestering and annoying his subordinates. It is possible that the pressure of responsibility for his six children contributed to Bourdin's poor leadership. In addition to Bourdin's children, there were another four belonging to men in his brigade which could well have contributed to life in the barracks being noisy, crowded, and fraught. In the same company Gendarme Louis Forchez, a 30-year-old native of the *département*, married with three children, was noted as being burdened by his family and finding it difficult to make ends meet. The members of Forchez's brigade also had ten children between them. Children in the barracks, however, were not necessarily a burden and a trial; they could work, provide information, or carry messages and, on their own initiative, warnings.[6]

In October 1820, when the trials and purges were over, when the allied armies of occupation had gone, and when, in spite of government anxieties about the behaviour of liberals, or *doctrinaires* as they were sometimes called, and the very occasional extreme incident like the assassination of the Duke of Berry, France had settled down to life under the Bourbons, a new ordinance was issued detailing the duties of the Gendarmerie and a further reorganization. The Ordinance of 29 October 1820 was the first complete revision of Gendarmerie regulations since legislation of 1792 had directed the ministry of war to instigate such. The Ordinance began by stating the Gendarmerie's *raison d'être*. It was 'a force established to watch over public safety and to assure in every part of the kingdom, in the military camps and with the armies, the maintenance of order and the execution of the laws'. The corps was now to be composed of three distinct bodies. Two elite companies, each of 117 men, were charged with guarding royal residences and protecting the monarch. The Gendarmerie Royale of Paris, already reorganized in 1816 into a force of 1,000 men, was now increased to 1,500. The provinces were to be patrolled by the twenty-four Territorial Legions; there were usually four *départemental* companies to each legion and the total provincial force comprised 14,086 men divided into 1,600 mounted and 650 foot brigades.[7] Applicants for the corps were to be literate,

---

[6] In the spring of 1843, for example, the brigade at Rochefort (Puy-de-Dôme) arrested one Annet Ganne for assault. While the majority of the brigade were away supervising a local fair, Ganne's friends sought to rescue him, initially by persuasion and then by setting upon the gendarme left guarding the barracks. One of the children of the brigade ran to find the gendarmes, who returned, prevented the rescue, and arrested the ringleader: AN F⁷ 4122, Report Apr., 1843.

[7] Corsica was the main exception within the territorial system. There were two Gendarmerie companies on the island and these alone made up the 17th legion. Concern

between the ages of 25 and 40 years, with at least four years of military service and a good conduct record. Appointment was now through a military chain of command; the commander of a *départemental* company passed a man's name on to the commander of a legion who, in turn, communicated with the minister of war. In Paris, however, where the company became an elite unit, men were recruited from the provincial companies as well as directly from the army, and the Prefect of Police also had a say in selection. Officers held their commissions directly from the king. The lowest officer rank was lieutenant, and all Gendarmerie officers were required to start their career in the corps from this rank. Two-thirds of the lieutenants were to come from the army from among men who had already held the rank for two years; the other third were to be drawn from men who had been NCOs in the Gendarmerie for at least four years and whose first step was to be promotion to sub-lieutenant. Lieutenant La Roche recalled that the officer corps of the Gendarmerie was popular with young men of little fortune since the pay was above that of an ordinary army officer; his career also reveals that, under the restored Bourbons, influence and patronage enabled some men to jump the queue.[8] All men were to swear before a Tribunal of the First Instance: 'to serve the king faithfully and well, to obey their superiors in everything concerning his majesty's service and in the performance of their duties, and never to use the force entrusted to them except for the maintenance of order and the execution of the laws.'

The 1820 Ordinance confirmed the military nature of the Gendarmerie. The ministry of war was responsible for its organization and administration, for its barracks, its discipline, and its equipment. Relations with other ministries were clarified. The ministry of *Police générale* had been abolished in 1818, and along with it went some of the opportunities for friction and rivalry. The corps was, however, to report to the ministry of the interior on matters relating to public order, and to forward to the minister accounts of its regular patrols. Any matters of *police judiciaire* were to be conducted under the authority of the ministry of justice; any cases regarding the supervision of naval personnel were to be carried out under the authority of the ministry for the navy.

about Corsican banditry and feuding convinced the authorities in Paris that an additional force was required and in November 1822 a battalion of 421 men, the Voltigeurs Corses, was established to assist the Gendarmerie. The battalion remained in existence until the Second Republic and a third company was established for the Gendarmerie in 1851.

[8] Vicomte Aurélien de Courson (ed.), *Souvenirs d'un officier de gendarmerie sous la Restauration*, 3rd. edn. (Paris: Plon, 1914), 93–5 and 152.

Civil authorities could request, but never order, assistance from the Gendarmerie; and any operational measures taken in the aftermath of such a request were to be the decision of the local gendarme commander alone. As soldiers, the gendarmes were directed always to wear their uniforms when on duty. However, as during the Napoleonic period, there were instances of gendarmes infiltrating gangs of brigands in plain clothes,[9] and of using men in civilian clothes to reconnoitre a situation before uniformed men went in to arrest a refractory conscript or deserter.[10] Such actions worried the Restoration authorities, whose legal officials were concerned that resistance to gendarmes in plain clothes could not easily, and legally, be defined as 'rebellion' against lawful force.[11]

But if the abolition of the ministry of police and the clarification of relations between the Gendarmerie and different ministries had reduced the opportunities for friction at the centre, there could still be problems in the provinces. The 1806 decree which had given the Gendarmerie the supervision of the *gardes-champêtres* was largely a dead letter. In 1812 the ministry of the interior had proposed brigading the guards and bringing them directly under the control of the Gendarmerie; this, it was believed, would transform local policing into an efficient system, staffed with reputable and responsible individuals. Some prefects saw problems; the Prefect of the Nord, for example, was concerned about the quasi-militarization of an organization whose tasks were principally local, and a few of his colleagues expressed reservations about what this would mean for financing the guards and the effect of removing them from the mayor's authority. But others warmly endorsed the proposal, seeing the guards as too often the creatures of the mayors and the powerful members of the communes, and too likely to be influenced by the dominant attitudes of their locality. The proposal disappeared in the confusion of the collapse of the Empire. Moncey appears to have been making moves to reintroduce it during the first Restoration, but again it disappeared in the excitement of the Hundred Days and its

---

[9] See above, p. 71.

[10] AN AF^{IV} 1154, Report of 20 *prairial* Year XII (Meuse-Inférieure); AF^{IV} 1155, Report of 8 *messidor* Year XII (Maine-et-Loire).

[11] Instruction d'application, 10 Apr. 1821, quoted in Colonel R. Coulin, *Historique et traditions de la Gendarmerie Nationale* (Melun: École des Officiers de la Gendarmerie Nationale, 1954), 67. See also BB^{18} 1017 (dossier 282), Interdiction aux gendarmes de se présenter déguisés pour opérer des arrestations. See also Ernest d'Hauterive (ed.), *La Police Secrète du Premier Empire*, 5 vols. (Paris: Perrin (later Clavreuil), 1922–64), iii. no. 1,121 esp.

aftermath.[12] The upshot was that throughout the Restoration rural policing below the Gendarmerie remained the unreformed system of *gardes-champêtres*, who were responsible to the local mayor. In some places, at least at the beginning of the restoration, the *gardes'* dependence on the local mayors was reinforced by the fact that, for convenience sake, they had taken their duty oath before the mayor rather than, as required by the law, the cantonal *juge de paix*.[13] The Gendarmerie commonly disparaged the *gardes* as useless and, at times, downright obstructive. 'There are few *gardes-champêtres* in the *département*,' complained the company commander of the Finistère in August 1821, 'it is hard to get information from them and we have to consider this area of policing as non-existent.'[14] But the real problems arose when the Gendarmerie came to enforce legislation which had little or no legitimacy in rural areas.

In 1818 and, word for word again in 1819 and 1820, the company commander in the Cantal reported that the local mayors were not interested in preventing *dévastations* of property, especially in forests and particularly in those owned by the government; by *dévastations* he seems to have been referring to local people taking wood for building and fuel. Equally serious was the lax interpretation which local tribunals gave towards the various regulations about carrying arms, and which enabled poaching in the Cantal to be practised with impunity.[15] In February 1821 the minister of the interior received a furious report from the company commander of the Gers of events the previous month. Poaching was a major problem here also, and when the Gendarmerie made arrests the accused were treated with indulgence by the courts. In a recent case an individual who had threatened gendarmes with a gun had been fined a mere 16 francs and acquitted of being a poacher; his excuse was that

---

[12] AN F²I 1203, Police Rurale (Objets généraux), Year III–1830; (Dossier 'Gardes-Champêtres'), Prefect of Nord to minister of interior, 14 Sept. 1812; Moncey to minister of interior, 28 Oct. 1814.

[13] AN F² 136¹, Circular from Minister of the Interior to Prefects, 25 July 1818. Of course, any *garde-champêtre* who did not get on with the local mayor was bound to have problems. Bernard Fraisse, who served the municipality of Penautier (Aude), was one such. He had his annual salary cut from 400 to 300 francs. The problem here appears to have been a political one involving friction between large and small proprietors. The former were satisfied with Fraisse; the latter, linked with the decisive mayor, who was opposed to the Restoration government, were not. The local prefect resolved the situation by conciliation; the commune Penaultier exchanged Fraisse for the *garde-champêtre* of the neighbouring municipality of Arayon: ibid., Prefect of Aude to Minister of the Interior, 2 Jan. 1821.

[14] AN F⁷ 3997, Report, Aug., 1821.

[15] Ibid. 3947, Annual reports 1818, 1819, and 1820.

he was carrying a gun to protect his master's property. At the same time the case had been dropped against a local mayor accused of insulting the Gendarmerie in the execution of its duty.[16] There could also be serious difficulties with local officials, as during the Empire, over the pursuit of refractory conscripts and deserters. In November 1824 the company commander in the Gers reported that the tribunal in Condom had released a mayor who had been sheltering a recalcitrant conscript in his own house. Eighteen months later he protested that, of the 500 mayors in his *département*, only five would help his men arrest a laggard conscript, while on several other occasions he complained of the ease with which young men could get false papers from local authorities.[17] It was the same story from the Puy-de-Dôme: 'The local authorities generally enjoy the confidence of those they administer. However, the Gendarmerie has to report that when it comes to the information that it requires, some mayors do not reveal the zeal which it has the right to expect of these officers in the performance of their duties.' The commander of the Rhône company reported that his brigade commanders complained 'of not being seconded in their pursuit of deserters by the mayors and the *gardes-champêtres*.'[18]

These details of the conscription problems were included in the monthly and annual reports which were sent by the commanders of the *départemental* companies, via the legion commanders for additional comment, to the ministry of the interior. Overall these reports give a broad picture of what the gendarmes were doing in the provinces. They exist, more or less complete, from roughly 1817 to 1847. They were made on printed forms, requiring statistical information of the numbers of arrests made and the number of individuals in custody moved from brigade to brigade through the *département*, and details of events likely to excite the public mind. Statistics were the great social science of the early nineteenth century; to minds educated in Enlightenment rationality they appeared pure and uncontroversial facts. The Napoleonic regime had made great efforts to collect and categorize economic and social statistics so as to provide what appeared to be an accurate, modern basis for

[16] Ibid. 4009, Report of Jan. 1821; see also F[7] 4143 (Rhône), Report of Nov. 1821.

[17] Ibid. 4009, Reports of Nov. 1824 and Apr. 1826; on the subject of false papers see the reports of July 1823 and June 1828; the report of Apr. 1824 notes proceedings commenced against the mayor of Villefranche for supplying a false certificate to a *retardataire* who had been apprehended by the Gendarmerie.

[18] Ibid. 4119, Annual report for 1818, see also reports for Feb. 1821, Sept. 1823, June 1824; F[7] 4144, Annual report for 1819, see also reports for Jan., Feb., and Mar. 1826 and Nov. 1829.

discussion.[19] Not the least of such statistics were those relating to judicial and penal matters. The Restoration governments continued the policy, and the Gendarmerie companies provided one valuable source of such information. In the early years of the Restoration some company commanders also presented written monthly reports on the state of the local economy, including grain prices in the principal markets. Whatever the aggravation that company and legion commanders may have felt over the problems deriving from conscription and poaching, the reports during the period of the restored Bourbons do not portray a society on the brink of social upheaval, with the Gendarmerie and the populace permanently at each other's throats. Rather, they suggest that, as the excitement of the Napoleonic adventure faded, so the Gendarmerie's existence began to be governed more and more by an almost mechanical routine of patrolling; and it is routine and a picture of general passivity across the country which dominates the reports. One bureaucratic way of seeking to demonstrate the corps' effectiveness was to be able to contrast the general passivity of a *département* with the scale of activity by the local company; the implication was that, by demonstrable zeal and activity, the local company was preventing crime and disorder. Thus, in addition to the statistics of arrests, some commanders began detailing the day-to-day activities of their men and the scale of their duties. The annual résumé from the Finistère in 1817, for example, contained the following statement:

Regular and daily service of the brigades, expeditions, patrols, conference points: All the Brigades have maintained an active surveillance, both day and night, to inspect the papers of travellers; frequent patrols have been made on the roads and in the countryside to ensure the free passage of travellers and public vehicles, and to pursue malefactors. They have escorted the waggons loaded with funds for the Royal Treasury, and ammunition convoys, etc.

They have made the rounds of the communes of their respective *arrondissements* and patrolled at the time of troop movements; they have escorted the Prefect of this *département* on his visits. Periodic conference points have been made with exactitude, together with service in their place of residence such as the inspection of inns and public vehicles.

They have attended all the markets and fairs to maintain order and ensure that the laws are respected.

The appropriate service has been undertaken in the ordinary tribunals, the assize courts, and the military courts.

[19] Jean-Claude Perrot and Stuart J. Woolf, *State and Statistics in France, 1789–1815* (Chur, Switzerland, and London: Harwood Academic Publishers, 1984).

The brigades have participated in full dress uniform at all festivals and public ceremonies.[20]

The commander of the Rhône company sent a similar account two years later; he also emphasized the fact that prisoners were brought to and from Lyons along eight separate roads, and that the brigades on the two routes northwards to Paris, one into Burgundy the other into the Bourbonnais, had a particularly difficult district to supervise requiring military assistance for the protection of the mail coaches.[21] By the mid-1820s such information was being detailed statistically by some commanders. Thus, in 1823 *chef d'escadron* Renault in the Nord reported the *service ordinaire* and *extraordinaire* of his men as illustrated in Table 5.5. He also began listing the number of incidents noted by, or reported to, his men during the year (Table 5.6).

While it is possible to perceive general trends in the activity of the territorial legions from these reports—the overall passivity of the country, the humdrum nature of the gendarmes' patrols, arrests and movement of prisoners—they also draw attention to the different problems faced by companies in different *départements*. The companies stationed in remote regions, and especially mountainous districts where life was hard, where the local peasantry scratched their subsistence from a poor soil and often embarked on annual seasonal migrations for work, were commonly those which found the most acute problems with mayors and local communities over conscripts and deserters. In his report for 1820 Captain Carrelet noted from the Puy-de-Dôme that, 'for part of the year the inhabitants, men, boys, and children, migrate to work in other

TABLE 5.5. *Service of the Nord Company, 1823*

Ordinary	Extraordinary
3,624 conference points	213 coercive assistance
11,645 patrols	608 escorts of taxes and ammunition
2,031 instances of service at fairs, markets, and fêtes	89 escorts of troops or detachments on the march
566 service at tribunals	58 honour escorts
63 service at revision tribunals	1 execution of a constraint over tax-collection
Daily visits to inns and public vehicles	768 executions of extraordinary ordinances
Daily a duty gendarme on duty in each residence	

Source: AN F⁷ 4103, Annual Report for 1823.

---

[20] AN F⁷ 3997, Annual report for 1817. [21] Ibid. 4143, Annual report for 1819.

TABLE 5.6. *Crimes and offences recorded by the Nord Company, 1823–1826*

Crime/offence	1823	1824	1825	1826
Murder, attempted murder, infanticide, attempted poisoning	13	10	10	8
Fires (accidental)	48	51	83	66
Fires (arson)	23	14	2	13
Fires (threats)	9	20	14	10
Thefts and attempted thefts	160	162	178	183
Misdemeanours	152	226	336	526
Investigations of individuals suspected or wanted by warrant	3,061	890	869	865
Attendance at burials	136	134	138	130
Prison escapes	8	3	1	5
Escapes from custody of Gendarmerie	–	2	1	1
Seizure of weapons of war	–	–	–	1
Seizure of contraband	26	29	17	18
New information on offences and events already reported	19	7	6	1

Source: AN F⁷ 4103, Annual Reports 1823–6.

départements, which often makes the Gendarmerie's searches for deserters difficult and almost useless'.[22] In the neighbouring Cantal the young travelled beyond the French frontiers in search of work, sometimes for nine months at a time, sometimes for years at a stretch. At least partly as a result of this only a quarter of the young men of the class of 1820 were present at the *tirage* for conscripts in May 1821.[23] Such rural *départements* were also the ones where village fêtes appeared to need the closest supervision. The commander in the Gers commented that, for his men, August was one of the most tense months on account of the high number of village fêtes. The young men often got drunk at these fêtes and the drinking sessions could end with ferocious brawls between the youth of different communes. Gendarmes were then called in by the local mayors to restore order, at which point the combatants might decide to join forces against the uniformed interlopers, who were perceived as complete outsiders by the fighting factions interfering in traditional contests which were none of their concern.[24]

Yet it would be wrong to suppose that all poor rural *départements* gave similar problems. The reports from the Basses-Alpes, for example, suggest few *rixes* and little problem over recruitment. The *arrondissement* of Barcelonnette was noted for smuggling, but even this, according to the

---

[22] AN F⁷ 3997, Annual report for 4119, Annual report for 1820.
[23] Ibid. 3947, May report, 1821.   [24] Ibid. 4009, Aug. report, 1826.

report of January 1821, was not as serious as it had been. 'The lesser offences [*délits*] are rare in this valley, except for that of smuggling. Crime [*crime*] is viewed with horror and is not committed here.' There were occasional seditious notices, notably in Sisteron, and there could be the occasional fracas over the arrest of a deserter, or when gendarmes involved themselves in matters, such as personal fights, which individuals thought were their own, private affair.[25] By and large, the reports from the Basses-Alpes suggest that the brigades had little to do beyond their daily patrols. Similarly, the reports from the Eure-et-Loir suggest a broadly peaceful *département*. The occasional fire periodically agitated the population; arsonists were invariably blamed by suspicious local communities, yet, as often as not, the fires seem to have been the result of accident or stupidity. In April 1822, for example, a fire in Dreux was caused by three young men who, in spite of the local mayor's prohibition, lit roman candles during a wedding celebration. Two major house and barn fires in November 1827 were suspected as being, respectively, the work of children and the result of the owner's imprudence; the following month a letter threatening arson in another commune led to the arrest of a 14-year-old boy. The general peace of the *département* received a rude shock in 1826 with two separate mail-coach attacks; on the second occasion gendarmes were quickly on the scene and one offender was shot and killed while a second was arrested. The lack of incident in the Eure-et-Loir, and elsewhere, may have encouraged some gendarmes to generate their own excitement; but it would, of course, be very difficult to prove that some men were enforcing regulatory ordinances over *cabarets*, roads or whatever, simply to reduce their boredom factor.[26] It would be equally difficult to show that some of the more

[25] Ibid. 3917, Jan. report 1821; for seditious placards in Sisteron see reports of Mar. 1822, Jan. 1823, Mar, June, and Aug. 1826; for trouble following the arrest of a deserter see Aug. 1821; and for trouble following the break-up of a fight see Sept. 1821.

[26] While, of course, the utmost care should be taken in drawing parallels between different centuries and different police cultures, it is at least worth noting Simon Holdaway's comments on English police officers in the inner city area of 'Hilton' during the 1980s. 'As far as Hilton's constables are concerned, real police work involves action—the sensation of speeding to an emergency call, time spent on crime, a fight or scuffle with a prisoner, ideally before making an arrest. When these events take place time passes quickly; work is being done; policemanship is being practised. "Action" defines time. However, we know that policing is a rather slow, spasmodic type of work which is largely concerned with mundane incidents . . . The problem for the lower ranks is that this "reality" of police work conflicts with their own view and, indeed, with their experience . . . Speed and hedonism appeal to the officers, and emphasis is placed on the interdependency between them . . . The technology of routine policing is reworked to create an experience which the officers define as typical and important.' Simon Holdaway, *Inside the British Police: A Force at Work* (Oxford: Basil Blackwell), 1983, 52 and 55.

disreputable behaviour of the men was fostered, at least in part, by the general lack of incident; but there is possibility of such a link. On the last day of 1821 Gendarme Dupuis, quartered in Chartres, got fighting drunk and attacked two civilians with his sabre. In May 1823 two gendarmes sexually assaulted a young woman whom they had been ordered to escort from Maintenon to Chartres.[27]

Départements with large military garrisons and/or growing industrial districts presented a different work experience for their Gendarmerie brigades. The Nord and the Rhône, for example, both had large garrison towns and these experienced occasional savage clashes between members of different regiments, or between the troops and the local population.[28] The situation was especially fraught in the immediate aftermath of the Napoleonic wars when, like other *départements* of the north and east, the Nord was occupied by allied troops. In August 1817 the company commander in the Nord reported the British army executing five of its infantrymen for quitting their post and robbing an innkeeper in Valenciennes of brandy, cheese, and other goods; elsewhere the allied troops were involved in fights with locals, and most kinds of criminal offence including smuggling.[29] The Nord of the 1820s was not yet the industrial centre that it was to be later in the century, yet already there were problems emerging in its larger towns and cities. In 1819, and again in 1823, the workers of Roubaix fought outsiders. On the second occasion, when the foreigners were identified as Flemish, there were fatalities; in both cases the Gendarmerie was forced to step in to aid the local police.[30] It was in the *département* of the Rhône, and particularly the turbulent city of Lyons with its well-organized silk-weavers, the *canuts*, where the most dynamic economic development of early nineteenth-century France was to be found. The local company and legion commanders were not unaware of this, but during the 1820s they did

---

[27] AN F[7] 3993.

[28] Ibid. 4103, Annual report 1820 (fights between troops in garrisons of Lille and Cambrai, leading to a stepping-up of patrols by the Gendarmerie), reports of Mar. and July 1822 for fights between troops in Valenciennes, and between troops and townsmen in Landrieu. F7 4143, Aug., Sept., and Dec. reports 1822, Jan. 1822, Jan. and Feb. 1823; F7 4144, Annual report 1828 noting trouble between inhabitants of Lyons and troops, but adding that it was caused by drink and 'did not have any serious character'.

[29] AN F[7] 4103, Aug. report 1817; for British troops involved in violent incidents see, *inter alia*, BB[18] 1036 (côte 1877), BB[18] 1037 (côte 1905), BB[18] 1039 (côte 2111)—this latter was an attempted rape at Vergnigneul, Pas-de-Calais; for allied troops involved in smuggling see, *inter alia*, BB[18] 962 (côte 2196)—Russians in the Nord—BB[18] 963 (côte 2379)—Bavarians in the Moselle.

[30] AN F[7] 4103, Annual report 1819, Mar. report 1823.

not perceive the industrial ferment as constituting any serious threat to the regime.

Everywhere the Gendarmerie sought to keep its finger on the pulse of public opinion. It informed the minister of the interior of rumours, however bizarre; during the French incursion into Spain in 1823, for example, stories began circulating in the Puy-de-Dôme that Napoleon was not dead but in Spain, that his old enemy, the guerrilla leader Mina, had joined up with him, that French troops were deserting to them, and that Mina at least was invading France.[31] Gendarmerie officers also responded to direct enquiries from the minister about matters likely to cause anxiety, as when, in the summer of 1822, the *Gazette de France* reported horrific murders in the Nord and attacks by brigands in broad daylight.[32] The commanders generally perceived the towns as more likely than the countryside to contain individuals and ideologies that were a political threat to the regime. 'The inhabitants of the country-side are generally motivated by a good spirit and appear devoted to the king and his government,' declared the colonel of the 5th Legion (Île-et-Vilaine, Côtes-du-Nord, Finistère, and the *Arrondissement Maritime de* Brest) in 1820, 'but on every possible occasion those in the towns reveal opinions and principles opposed to those of the government.'[33] From the Gers, where there was little in the way of either seditious comment or political agitation, the company commander nevertheless reported local anxieties about the corrupting ideologies circulating in faraway Paris. 'Several heads of families . . . complain that having sent their children to Paris to complete their studies they see them return with political and religious principles less than favourable to the social order.' He went on to identify one of the 'most dangerous' colleges involved.[34] Commanders regularly commented on public attitudes and behaviour at the time of elections, and especially on the machinations of the opponents of the regime. Yet it was rare that they appeared to view liberals, or any other opposition group, as a serious threat; the reports suggest that the officers of the Gendarmerie considered any political threat as containable.[35] Political feeling was running high in the seven

[31] Ibid. 4119, reports of Mar. and Apr. 1823.

[32] Ibid. 4103, letter from company commander, Nord, to commander of 24th Legion, 12 Aug. 1823, admitting that two women had been murdered, but insisting that the stories as reported in the *Gazette* were largely fiction.

[33] Ibid. 3997, Annual report 1820; see also Ibid. F7 4104, letter from company commander, Nord, to commander of 24th Legion, 5 Oct. 1829.

[34] Ibid. 4009, Oct. report 1822.

[35] See e.g. ibid. May and Dec. reports 1821 (Gers, liberal excitement particularly over Spain), Apr. and May reports 1822 (election); F7 4143, May and June reports (Rhône,

months of 1830 before the July Revolution, as liberals sought to make electors aware of what they considered to be a threat to the Constitutional Charter in particular and to liberty in general. Gendarmerie officers in the provinces, together with prefects and other police agents, were always on the lookout for conspiracies and plots, but even though there was an escalation in the price of basic foodstuffs and an increase of beggars and vagrants on the roads, the gendarmes could only report very rare political invocations in the form of Bonapartist or revolutionary slogans, and not a single 'Vive la République!'[36]

The elite Gendarmerie Royale in Paris worked at the political heart of the country, yet its daily reports reveal its principal tasks to have been dealing with petty offending and prosaic order maintenance. Based in large barracks in the capital, the Paris gendarmes also manned small police posts across the city and carried out regular patrols. They provided assistance to the agents of the Prefect of Police—the forty-eight *commissaires de police*, one of whom was resident in each *quartier*, the *officiers de paix* with their roving commission, and the subordinate *inspecteurs*.[37] They also arrested any offenders caught *in flagrante* by their patrols, usually individuals such as drunks or prostitutes whose activites could be labelled as disturbing the peace. It has been common to accept contemporary criticism of the Paris gendarmes as arrogant, aggressive, and brutal, and there is so much testimony to this effect that it is impossible to ignore. Yet there appears at times to have been some ambivalence towards the gendarmes. Their arrest of prostitutes could provoke crowd hostility, as could their interventions in other instances involving, for example, drunks or a popular assembly in the street. Early in January 1820, for example, a brigadier told two drunken apprentice tailors to desist from pestering two women in the Champs Elysées; he was assaulted and had to call on assistance from some soldiers who were nearby. At the same time people, often in distress, turned to a Gendarmerie patrol or ran to a Gendarmerie post to report a crime or a problem. *Cabaretiers* and *limonadiers*, whose customers had refused to pay, were common complainants; but there were also other, more serious incidents as when, for example, in November 1826 a patrol was

liberal agitation), Aug. report 1822 (royalist homes daubed with bloody daggers); F7 4144 Nov. report (Rhône, election).

[36] David H. Pinkney, *The French Revolution of 1830* (Princeton, NJ: Princeton University Press, 1972), 44–52; Pamela Pilbeam, *The 1830 Revolution in France* (London: Macmillan, 1991), 41–2.

[37] For the structure and organization of the police in Paris see Clive Emsley, 'Policing the Streets of Early Nineteenth-Century Paris', *French History*, 1 (1987), 257–82.

stopped and given information about a violent robbery in the Place Victoire, or when, in February 1829, a trembling night-watchman ran, pistol in hand, to the post on Boulevard Amelot to report having fired on thieves who had raided the building-site which he was guarding.[38] It would appear to have been the Gendarmerie Royale's public and prominent role in defending Charles X's regime in July 1830 which sealed its fate.

Charles X's coup was abysmally planned. The four ordinances issued on 26 July which virtually abolished press freedom, dissolved the Chamber, modified the electoral laws, considerably reducing the electorate, and set a new date for elections, were issued without any consultation with, or advice from military or Gendarmerie officers. Vicomte Jacques de Foucauld, the commander of the Gendarmerie Royale, had just returned from a week's leave and only learned of the ordinances when his adjutant passed him a copy of *Le Moniteur*, at roughly the same time as the news was beginning to circulate in Paris. The Gendarmerie made up about a tenth of the men available to Marshal Marmont in Paris for suppressing trouble; the loyalty of the 5,000 line infantry who made up roughly half of this force was questionable. The gendarmes certainly had a better knowledge of the city than many, perhaps most, of the other troops. They were the first units involved in confrontations with the crowds, since their role as back-up to the police meant that they seconded those *commissaires* charged with confiscating printing presses. Crowd hostility towards the gendarmes was manifested in shouts of 'Vive la ligne! À bas les gendarmes et la garde!' and 'Mort aux gendarmes!' before any serious fighting started.[39] Just over two weeks after the July Days, on 16 August, the Gendarmerie Royale was abolished. Its rank-and-file were dispersed among the territorial legions.[40] A new force, the Garde Municipale, was created for Paris. It was given a new uniform and made directly responsible to the Prefect of Police. But this did not convince the Parisians. They continued to refer to the new guards as 'gendarmes'. Attacks on them in their first days of duty were so persistent and serious that an *avocat-général* felt compelled to write a special report to the minister of the interior before the end of August; and their unpopularity was such that they do not

[38] AN F7 4168, Report, 4–5 Jan. 1820; F7 4172, Report, 18–19 Nov. 1826; F7 4174, Report, 27–8 Feb. 1829.

[39] The fullest account of the events is to be found in Pinkney, *The French Revolution of 1830*. For these incidents see esp. 81, 94, 102, 105, and 111.

[40] AG X^r 135, Gendarmerie, *passim*, and see below p. 104.

appear to have been used for anything other than routine guard duty, even when disorder threatened the city in October and December 1830.[41]

In the provinces only a few Gendarmerie brigades were engaged in confrontations during the July Revolution; these clashes were in the big towns, generally the *chefs-lieux* of *départements*. They occurred where the authorities were ardent supporters of Charles X, as in Rouen, where an attempt was made to enforce the ordinance against the liberal press, and as in Nantes, the only provincial city where opposition to the ordinances cost lives. Clashes also happened in the rare instances where local gendarmes acted against demonstrators on their own initiative; in Toulouse a Gendarmerie officer sought to seize a tricolour, and provoked an attack on himself and his men while troops stood by and watched.[42] Much more typical was the situation in Lyons where, apart from excitement on the streets and some disorder in the prison, the change of regime was trouble-free. The news had reached Lyons by telegraph, and just over a week after the Revolution the commander of the 19th Legion reported to the minister of the interior that:

All the officers, NCOs, and gendarmes are at their posts with the exception of Captain de la Martinière, commander of the Saône-et-Loire company, who, on the 4th instant, was dismissed from his duties by the provisional central administration of this *département*.

The tricolour flag flies over all four *départements* of the 19th Legion, his excellency the Duke of Orleans has been recognized in his position of Lieutenant-General of the Kingdom. These events have been orderly and sensibly undertaken, no bad incidents have occurred, and at this moment the greatest tranquillity reigns everywhere.[43]

At the other side of the country, with a very different economic base, the Gendarmerie reports were the same. 'The Gendarmerie's service has not been interrupted, it has watched constantly, day and night, over the maintenance of order and tranquillity', declared the company commander of the Finistère; and the commander of the 5th Legion explained that 'the restoration of the national colours has served as the motif for many fêtes in which attachment to the constitutional government and to the

---

[41] Patricia Ann O'Brien, 'Urban Growth and Public Order: The Development of a Modern Police in Paris, 1829–1854', Ph.D, Columbia University, 1973, pp. 75–88; Pinkney, *The French Revolution of 1830*, 237.

[42] Pinkney, *The French Revolution of 1830*, 200, 209–12, and 217–18.

[43] AN F7 4144, July report, 1830, and commander of the 19th Legion to minister of the interior, 9 Aug. 1830.

King of the French has been demonstrated'.[44] A sprinkling of Gendarmerie officers, like de la Martinière, were dismissed. A few others, like La Roche, transferred from the Gendarmerie Royale to a lieutenancy at St Pol, opted for half pay and retirement; La Roche felt that he could not break his oath to Charles X, and possibly one or two in the non-commissioned ranks felt similarly.[45]

[44] AN F7 3998, Aug. report, 1830.
[45] De Courson (ed.), *Souvenirs*, 102 and 219–22; La Roche reported that Gendarme Touret, who served with him in the Vendée, was so devoted to the king that he also resigned; yet Touret had begun his service in the armies of the Republic and had fought in battles against royalists.

6

'A SACRIFICE TO RANCOUR . . . POPULAR PREJUDICES AND . . . JEALOUSY': GENDARMES AND THE JULY MONARCHY

Louis-Philippe came to the French throne as a result of an uprising in Paris; there was thus, at the beginning of his reign, a need felt by the men around him to consolidate power. The Gendarmerie Royale of Paris was disbanded because of its unpopularity and, particularly, its aggressive behaviour during the July Days; the men were sent to the provinces but, given that many of them were sent to the new mobile battalions established in the west as a preventive measure in case of Legitimist counter-moves, it seems that there was not much concern about the men's loyalty.[1] The Garde Municipale, established under the authority of the Prefect of Police, was initially the same size as its predecessor and, as noted above, continued to be referred to by suspicious Parisians as 'the Gendarmerie'. In 1838 it was restored to military control, and its numbers were steadily increased until, on the eve of the Revolution of 1848, it had a strength of just under 4,000 men. The corps' duties involved the supervision of all public events and festivities in the capital, as well as the supervision of the city's ports, Les Halles, and the other markets. It acquired the same unenviable reputation for brutality as its immediate predecessor and, at least in its early years, also carried out some of its surveillance duties in civilian clothes.[2]

---

[1] The Ordinance of 4 Sept. 1830 established the first two of these battalions at Angers and Rennes. A third was established at Nantes by Ordinance on 11 Dec. 1830. They were abolished in Oct. 1841 with the men being distributed among the ordinary brigades in the west.

[2] Jean Tulard, *La Préfecture de Police sous la Monarchie de Juillet* (Paris: Imprimerie Municipal, Hotel de Ville, 1964), 66; Patricia Ann O'Brien, 'Urban Growth and Public Order: The Development of a Modern Police in Paris, 1829–1854', Ph.D, Columbia University, 1973, p. 81.

The provinces may have been relatively quiet during the July Revolution, with the Gendarmerie companies, largely oblivious of events in Paris, continuing with their routine duties, but it was not exempted from the general purge of administrative offices instigated by the prime minister Casimir Périer. A comparison of the names of Gendarmerie officers in the *Almanach Royal* of 1830 with the *Almanach Royal et National* of 1831 shows the extent to which the Revolution provided the opportunity for a significant reorganization. Of the twenty-four legion commanders in 1830, only three remained at their posts in 1831; of the ninety-two company commanders only ten; and of the 466 other officers, 153. Of course some men were promoted and others were moved sideways; the 24th Legion stationed in the north-east saw a particularly large amount of internal movement (see Table 6.1). So too did the 17th Legion based on Corsica. Here, in 1831, there were no officers new to the island, apart from the captain for the second company based in Ajaccio. Colonel Degasq had been transferred to command the 18th Legion (Isère, Drôme, Hautes-Alpes, and Basses-Alpes), and was yet to be replaced; eight other officers remained in their former residences, while another six were moved. The 12th Legion (Lot, Lot-et-Garonne, Aveyron, and Cantal) experienced the biggest changeover; only one company commander, Captain Jammé in the Aveyron, remained in place, together with a lieutenant in the Lot and another in the Cantal; two lieutenants from the latter two companies exchanged residences, but all of the other eighteen officers in 1831 were new.

The Revolution of 1830 has been seen as a key moment in a period of economic and social crisis which brought a series of latent social conflicts to the surface, and certainly a wave of disorder rippled across France over the following two years.[3] In rural areas the turbulence was often directed against the taxation system or against moves to abolish old rights of communal use, especially in forests. One liberal deputy in the new assembly called for the abolition of the Gendarmerie and its replacement with a civilian police body; he drew his examples from new English and American alternatives,[4] but his suggestion was ignored. Given the manner in which it had come to power and the need to consolidate its position, and given the disorder in the provinces and the

---

[3] Paul Gonnet, 'Esquisse de la crise économique et sociale en France de 1827 à 1832', *Revue d'histoire économique et sociale*, 33 (1955), 249–92; James Rule and Charles Tilly, 'Political Process in Revolutionary France, 1830–1832', in John M. Merriman (ed.), *1830 in France* (New York: New Viewpoints, 1975).

[4] Col. Louis Saurel, *Peines et gloires des gendarmes* (Paris: Lavauzelle, 1973), 52.

TABLE 6.1. *Officers of the 24th Legion, 1831*

Département	Name	Residence	Previous residence
	Colonel Ravier (Legion Commander)	Arras	Continuing
Pas-de-Calais	*Chef d'escadron* Clément	Arras	Continuing
	Captain-Lieutenant Gallois	Arras	Château-Thierry (Aisne)
	Captain-Treasurer Beaugrand	Arras	Continuing
	Lieutenant Flamen	Béthune	Continuing
	Lieutenant Belot	Boulogne	New
	Sub-Lieutenant Floure	Montreuil	New
	Lieutenant Saulnier	St Omer	Continuing
	Sub-Lieutenant Bresne	St Pol	Continuing
Nord	*Chef d'escadron* François	Lille	Company commander, Haut-Rhin, with rank of captain
	Lieutenant Delorne d'Alincourt	Lille	St Quentin (Aisne)
	Lieutenant-Treasurer Lemire	Lille	New
	Lieutenant Hamont	Avesnes	Continuing
	Lieutenant Dupuis	Cambrai	Boulogne (Pas-de-Calais)
	Lieutenant Cotton	Douai	New
	Lieutenant Delfosse	Dunkirk	Continuing
	Lieutenant Janssens	Hazebrouck	Continuing
	Lieutenant Blocaille	Valenciennes	New
Aisne	Captain Tilman	Laon	Arras (Pas-de-Calais) with with rank of Captain-Lieutenant
	Lieutenant Caillard	Laon	New
	Lieutenant-Treasurer Michel	Laon	Continuing
	Lieutenant Denu	Château-Thierry	New
	Lieutenant Capitain	St Quentin	Vervins (Aisne)
	Lieutenant Bonnay de Nonancourt	Soissons	Lille (Nord)
	Sub-Lieutenant Delacourt	Vervins	New

uncertainties generated by economic change, few deputies and no one in government seem to have been prepared to contemplate a relatively untried civilian system of police as the regime's first line of defence. It was better by far to rely upon the tried and trusted half-military, half-civilian gendarme.

Throughout the July Monarchy the Gendarmerie was on the lookout for political disaffection. There were occasional reports of trees of liberty being planted and of seditious words being written or uttered. Suspicious rumours were followed up, as, for example, when towards the end of December 1836 a *cabaratier* in Thouzy (Eure-et-Loir) informed the local brigade commander of a stranger from Paris promising 'an event concerning the *King*' before the beginning of the next month.[5] The abortive rising organized by the Duchess of Berry provoked excitement and anxiety in the west in 1832. It led to an enhanced Gendarmerie presence that was eventually regularized by the law of 23 February 1834. But Gendarmerie officers were not taken in by every rumour of political agitation or incident; the company commander in the Morbihan concluded that the alleged 'political' murder of a tobacconist was, in reality, simply an elderly, unsteady man falling off his horse.[6] Overall there was little serious political agitation to occupy Gendarmerie brigades across provincial France in the months and years following the July Revolution. The company commander of the Rhône was concerned that republicans were seeking to influence the workers of Lyons during the early 1830s, but the massive worker insurrections in the city in 1831 and 1834 were prompted, first and foremost, by problems in the silk industry rather than political opponents of the regime.[7] The second of these insurrections led to the company commander of the Nord, the *département* whose economy would soon overtake that of the Lyonnais to become the powerhouse of French industrialization, to investigate the attitudes of the employers and their workers in his jurisdiction. He concluded that 'the firm attitude and energy of the government had given

---

[5] AN F⁷ 6780, Dossier 5 (Eure-et-Loir), Company commander to minister of the interior, 1 Jan. 1837, and for seditious placards in Chartres see letters of 30 Apr. 1831 and 3 Aug. 1833; for other reports of seditous words or placards see, *inter alia*, AN F⁷ 6782, Dossier 9 (Gers), Company commander to minister of the interior, 24 May 1832 and 4 Feb. 1834; ibid., Dossier 6 (Nord), Company commander to minister, 20 Mar. 1831, 6 Oct. 1832, 9 May 1833, 9 Aug. 1834. In his annual report for 1831 the company commander in the Basses-Alpes reported four trees of liberty planted and five seditious placards, AN F⁷ 3918.

[6] Pamela M. Pilbeam, *The 1830 Revolution in France* (London: Macmillan, 1991), 116.

[7] AN F⁷ 4144, Rhône, Jan. and Apr. 1832, Oct. Nov. and Dec. 1833, Feb. and Mar. 1834.

the textile masters confidence. They had not needed to dismiss work-men as had been feared, and commerce continued to flourish.' Subsequent Gendarmerie reports dealing with industrial strife in the Nord over the next decade tended to stress that there was nothing 'polit-ical' about the workers' activities.[8] It was the same with reports from elsewhere. Indeed, it was possible for a Gendarmerie officer to be as crit-ical of employers for exploiting their workers as he was of the workers for taking industrial action.[9]

But if disorders involving industrial and urban workers were rarely overtly political, it would be equally wrong to assume that they were always economic. Drink, a sense of justice and/or morality, young men's high spirits and/or sheer bloody-mindedness could all play their part in fomenting popular action. In the textile town of Roubaix in August 1842 gendarmes were deployed with troops after the high-handed arrest of two 14-year-old girls by the local *commissaire de police* had provoked a riot. Again in Roubaix, in June 1845, and on La Croix Rousse, the hill-top silk-workers' enclave to the north of Lyons, in September 1847, the local gendarmes found themselves dealing with street disorders involv-ing young male workers and their sexual behaviour. In the first instance men had been denied entrance to a brothel because they were drunk; in the second a lodging-house for young silk-workers was stoned following reports of mysterious acts *contraires aux moeurs*.[10] The problems of drunks and of rowdy behaviour in *cabarets* and at dances were com-monplace for gendarmes. Yet the deployment of gendarmes to protect capital during strikes and to quieten worker behaviour in the name of public order and tranquillity did not mean that they were permanently ostracized by workers. When, in August 1833, a gendarme was insulted—'Voilà encore un grippe-jesus!'—and then assaulted by a group of young workers in Clermont, it was local people who came to his aid; and when the carpenters of Vaise, on the north-western edge of Lyons, held their annual fête in March 1835—'usually so tumultuous'—they invited both the local *commissaire de police* and the local Gendarmerie brigade.[11]

---

[8] Ibid. 6782, Dossier 6 (Nord), company commander to minister of the interior, 19 Apr. 1834; and see the report of 10 July 1837 concerning a strike by the miners of Anzin: 'Nothing political appears to be driving the rebels who are seeking a wage increase.'

[9] Pilbeam, *The 1830 Revolution*, 178.

[10] AN F7 4106, Nord, June 1845; 4146, Rhône, Sept. 1847.

[11] Ibid. 6782, Dossier 10 (Puy-de-Dôme), company commander to minister of the inte-rior, 28 Aug. 1833. The insult hurled at Gendarme Cossen is not translatable; *grippe-jesus*, a slang term for policemen used at least as early as the eighteenth century, could be ren-dered literally as 'Jesus 'flu'. F7 4145, Rhône, Mar. 1835.

Of course, disorders over work practices and wages were not simply the prerogative of urban and/or industrial workers. In July 1844 an attempt to introduce a new system of payment for harvesters in the Ardennes precipitated a large demonstration at Rethel. Initially the thirty gendarmes deployed to deal with the crowds could not cope, as angry men and women seized their bridles and forced them to retire.[12] While popular protest and disorder reached peaks at the beginning and again at the end of the July Monarchy, throughout the period across rural France the Gendarmerie brigades had to confront such manifestations, especially where communities perceived traditional land-use rights under threat. The Forest Code of 1827 and its accompanying ordinance were intended to bring about the better management of royal and communal forests principally by abolishing local use-rights. Local communities were given two years to prove their use-rights in law; a few were successful, but many more were not. The problems came to a head in the winter of 1829 to 1830 and continued beyond the July Revolution, since the change of regime did not mean a change of policy on the forests. For peasants dependent on a pastoral economy the rights to graze their livestock in the forests and to forage in them for fuel were essential. The best-known and most serious disorders erupted in the Ariège with the 'war' of the *desmoiselles*, but the problems were not confined to the more remote regions of the Pyrenees. In spite of the efforts of his men, the colonel of the 13th Legion (Haute-Garonne, Tarn-et-Garonne, Gers, and Hautes Pyrénées) reckoned that over 300 trees had been cut down by the poor in the royal forest of Saramon (Gers) early in 1830. Five years later trouble occurred on the other side of the *département* during the sale of a forest at Riscle; five Gendarmerie brigades had to be deployed. In November 1830 two landowners were brutally killed when they brought in the local Gendarmerie brigade to arrest villagers for cutting wood at Villesèque close to Narbonne. In April 1844 the captain of the Eure-et-Loir company reported that his men were redoubling their efforts to combat an outbreak of arson in the forests of Senonches and Chateauneuf. Local opinion, he explained, held it that the fires were the direct result of 'the rigour of the forest administration which no longer permits the poor to enter state forests to collect dead wood'.[13]

---

[12] Ibid. 12241, minister of justice to minister of the interior, 8 Aug. 1844.

[13] Ibid. 4009, Gers, Feb. 1830; 4910, Gers, Annual Report, 1836; Peter MacPhee, 'Une meurtre dans le Sud de la France en 1830: violence, mémoire et tradition démocratique', *Bulletin du centre d'histoire contemporaine du Languedoc Méditerranéen Roussillon*, 56 (1995),

Peasants also cherished what they saw as their right to hunt, and the attempts of Gendarmerie brigades to enforce laws against poaching could lead to serious confrontations and even fatalities. In January 1845 an unknown 'poacher' made two attempts on the lives of Brigadier Lavouez and Gendarme St Martin of the Masseube brigade in the Gers. In November the following year Brigadier Boutan of the Saramon brigade, only recently commended for his role in the detection and arrest of a thief, was shot and killed when he came across a labourer in the act of poaching.[14]

The explicit demands of the state for taxes—particularly the *contributions indirectes*—for the upkeep of roads, and for conscripts also brought gendarmes into conflict with rural communities. The local roads of rural France, which linked neighbouring communes and, through their junctures with *départemental* and national highways, linked these communes with the rest of France, had passed to the control of local administrations during the Revolution. Some were relatively well maintained, but many were not. Peasants sometimes ploughed up parts of them, stacked stones on them, drained their fields on to them, or, by ignoring them, allowed them to become rutted and overgrown. Furthermore, as under previous regimes, overweight carts broke up the stone beds of the roads and worsened the ruts. Legislation under both the Restoration and the July Monarchy, notably the laws of 28 July 1824 and 21 May 1836, sought to improve the situation, but even in *départements* where the state of the roads was notorious the peasantry could resent the resulting interference. The Finistère had a particularly primitive road network, but when a brigadier issued a summons against a small proprietor for encroaching on a road in May 1836, he and his men were assaulted. The jump in *Contraventions à la police du roulage* in the Gers from four in 1837 to sixty-seven the following year suggests the company's brigades were suddenly taking a firm line to enforce obedience to the laws and regulations regarding the roads.[15]

3–30; AN F⁷ 3996, Eure-et-Loir, Apr. 1844, and see also May for more fires. For the war of the *desmoiselles* see Peter Sahlins, *Forest Rights: The War of the Desmoiselles in Nineteenth-Century France* (Cambridge, Mass.: Harvard University Press, 1994).

[14] AN F⁷ 4011, Gers, Jan. 1845, Aug. and Nov. 1846, see also Annual Report 1844; for poaching disorders and other instances of gendarmes being shot at, see 4122, Puy-de-Dôme, Sept. 1842; 4146, Rhône, Dec. 1846.

[15] Ibid. 3999, Finistère, May 1836; 4010, Gers, Annual Reports 1837 and 1838. For the roads see Eugen Weber, *Peasants into Frenchmen: The Modernization of Rural France, 1870–1914* (Stanford, Cal.: Stanford University Press, 1976), chap. 12; and Isser Woloch, *The New Regime: Transformations of the French Civic Order, 1789–1820s* (New York: Norton, 1995), 164–71.

Young men, especially in the more remote regions, continued to resist conscription. Those in the Cantal, and especially in the Haute-Auvergne district, previously noted for their absences looking for work, were described by the company commander at the end of 1830 as having 'an invincible distaste for military service'. Four years later, while the *tirage* passed off without obstacles, he commented that 'none of the young men of the Cantal have any wish to serve; they employ all means possible to avoid recruitment, many wound and mutilate themselves'.[16] Probably, as far as the members of the individual Gendarmerie brigades were concerned, it was preferable to have the young men maiming themselves rather than injuring gendarmes. And while precise measurement of the change is impossible, the scale and the frequency of confrontations over conscription never approached that of the Napoleonic years; rather, it appears gradually to have declined. Early in 1833 Gendarme Pierre Marouzet was killed by a deserter whom he had pursued to his native town of Lignan (Gironde). There was no local support for the deserter, and the villagers directed Gendarme Jean-Baptiste Lequin to where his comrade's body was lying in a field. Significantly, however, Lequin initially suspected this to be a ruse to enable the deserter to escape.[17] On occasion gendarmes still resorted to civilian clothes to facilitate their movements when in pursuit of deserters or men avoiding conscription;[18] and they still found some mayors and *gardes-champêtres* who sought to impede them. Twice in 1832 the company commander in the Puy-de-Dôme complained about mayors preferring to maintain their popularity with their communities rather than assist the Gendarmerie in the pursuit of young men seeking to avoid army service. In February 1837 the company commander in the Côtes-du-Nord, who regularly complained of conscription difficulties, added that his men 'could not get information from the local authorities'. The following year the company in the Nord demanded the removal of a *garde-champêtre* in the *arrondissement* of Valenciennes for his refusal to assist a gendarme seeking to arrest an *insoumis*.[19]

There were other areas, besides conscription, where the local Gendarmerie commander could clash with the local civil administration. During a festival in Auch in September 1846, for example, there was a

---

[16] AN F7 3948, reports of November and December 1830 and Annual Report 1834.
[17] AN F7 6780, Dossier 10 (Gironde), reports of 9 and 10 Jan. 1833.
[18] Ibid. 6782, Dossier 16 (Rhône), report of Brigadier Claude Barra, n.d. (Aug. 1831).
[19] Ibid. 4121, reports of Jan. and Mar. 1832; F7 3974, report of Feb. 1837; 4105, report of June 1838.

difference of opinion between the local police and the Gendarmerie over illegal gaming; the former were prepared to tolerate it, while the latter wanted to stop it and began citing sections of the Penal Code.[20] For the disciplined Gendarmerie the *gardes-champêtres* continued to appear as a weak link in the maintenance of the public peace. In the summer of 1836, following a rowdy scenes in Valcivière (Puy-de-Dôme), the Gendarmerie called for the local *garde* to be dismissed on the grounds that he had stood idly by while his sons had been instrumental in the disorder. The sub-prefect of Ambert felt that this was an over-reaction. He understood the resentment of the gendarmes towards the commune, which was particularly troublesome and where the local administration was characterized by 'a deplorable inertia'.

The sons of *garde-champêtre* Gourbeyre were among the pack of drunken men and squalling children who followed the three rowdies whom the gendarmerie were taking to the town hall; but Gourbeyre senior did what he could to restrain his sons.

On the mountain of Valcivière the peasants are coarse and crude, and wine makes them mad. What happened on 14 August will have no unfortunate consequence, and no one in the region will see it as seriously undermining authority.[21]

But even in the Puy-de-Dôme, as well as in less remote *départements*, rural mayors seem increasingly to have acknowledged new thresholds of order and respectability that were being sought and sanctioned by the authorities in Paris and by the propertied classes of the larger towns. These mayors seem increasingly to have been prepared to call on gendarmes to enforce regulations and to underpin their authority, particularly when they feared that a certain *cabaret* or the behaviour at dances during communal fêtes were exceeding the new, tighter boundaries of order and respectability.[22]

Fights at fairs and village fêtes were part of a traditional way of life in which the young men sought to prove the superiority of their commune over their neighbours. Even the day of the conscription ballot could witness such conflicts, as the young men of different communes brought their traditional local rivalries to the scene of the nation state's

---

[20] AN F7 4011, report of Sept. 1846.

[21] Ibid. 12241, sub-prefect of Ambert to Prefect of Puy-de-Dôme, 2 Nov. 1836, forwarded to minister of the interior, 19 Nov. 1836.

[22] In Jan. 1841, for example, the mayor of Limous called in gendarmes to enforce police regulations which had been ignored hitherto in his community. The gendarmes were stoned: AN F7 4122, Rapports de Gendarmerie, Puy-de-Dôme, Jan. 1841.

small military ceremony. Such *rixes* were labelled by the state jurist and state functionary as 'disorder' and something for the Gendarmerie to suppress, though this was often easier ordered than done, since once the gendarmes began to interfere the combatants were likely to unite against them as outsiders. Conscription day in the canton of Monsol (Rhône) in March 1842 offers a good example. The young men of Ouroux and St Igny began fighting each other, but then turned violently on the gendarmes who tried to separate them. A brigadier was knocked unconscious and several gendarmes were injured. It appears to have been persuasion by the sub-prefect and the communal mayors which eventually brought the fighting to an end.[23] As an affront to order and respectability, the traditional *charivari* was similar to the *rixe*. Officers of the Gendarmerie agreed with civilian administrators that such behaviour was primitive and vulgar and, as the company commander in the Finistère put it in September 1835, 'foreign to the system espoused by the gendarmerie'. Like civilian administrators, they were at pains to stress that disorders directed at old men who took young wives were local customs, not serious threats to authority and not 'political'.[24] However, as with a *rixe*, the deployment of gendarmes to suppress a *charivari* could prompt crowds to turn on the state's men of order. In June 1834 gendarmes seeking to disperse a *charivari* directed against a widow and a widower who had married at St Pol de Léon (Finistère) were greeted with shouts of 'À bas les gendarmes!' Nine years later, in a similar incident at Mariac (Gers), the popular response was physical as well as verbal.[25]

Crowds seeking to defend their rights, asserting claims to fair wages or fair prices, or objecting to the demands of the state were bound to show hostility to the force deployed against them. Similarly, individuals travelling without papers, or already in custody, could seek to rouse a crowd against the gendarmes by claiming arbitrary behaviour and making appeals to populist sentiment. A lawyer stopped by gendarmes in the Finistère and found to have no travel documents raised the cry 'à l'arbitraire!' Two gendarmes escorting seven prisoners into Lyons ran into difficulties when two of the prisoners began shouting 'Vive la charte, à bas les gueux de gendarmes!', and urging crowds to stone the

---

[23] Ibid. 4146, Rhône, Mar. 1842, and see also Feb. 1844.

[24] Ibid. 3999, Finistère, Sep. 1835; see also 4010, Gers, Mar. 1835. Sahlins, *Forest Rights*, 101–2, provides some similar comments by civilian administrators, and notes also a growing concern among these administrators that there was a linkage between *charivari* and certain forms of political subversion.

[25] AN F7 3999, Finistère, June 1834; 4011, Gers, Annual Report 1843.

escort. Three gendarmes of the brigade of Allanche (Cantal) arrested a man in a local *auberge*; he shouted 'au secours!' and the community assembled to rescue him. The mayor's deputy brought the matter to a peaceful conclusion, but only by persuading the gendarmes to let their prisoner go.[26] But while the reports from the Finistère during the 1830s suggest considerable tension in some areas between the gendarmes and the populace, this is not the case in reports from the Nord and the Rhône, where the gendarmes were commonly the first units to be deployed against workers during industrial confrontations. Of course, it may be that the company commanders simply did not consider abuse hurled at their men in these *départements* as worthy of inclusion in their monthly reports; nevertheless, it would be presumptuous to conclude that hostility was the usual attitude of local communities towards the Gendarmerie. On occasions peasants went to the gendarmes either to tip them off about a particular danger or for help. In the Finistère in April 1832 it was the villagers of Kerneval who informed a Gendarmerie brigade about vagrants in their neighbourhood.[27] Of course, this may have been perceived by the villagers as in their own interest; there were concerns about arson attacks in the region, while the cholera outbreak had fostered fears of poisoners at work. But it also indicated a recognition and tacit acceptance of the Gendarmerie's role. In June 1843 a woman in the Puy-de-Dôme turned to the local gendarmes for help when her husband was being attacked at a village fête. The husband, however, appears to have considered this as a slight on his manhood, and joined forces with his attacker to fight the gendarmes.[28] Sometimes gendarmes stepped in to protect individuals—and not always deserving or sympathetic individuals—from the wrath of a local community. In August 1837 a woman, married to a man in Mauriac (Gers), infuriated the inhabitants of a neighbouring commune by moving in with one of their own menfolk. Brigadier Guerin of Mauriac took the woman under his protection, remonstrated with a crowd for an hour, but eventually escorted her back to Mauriac. In the following year the brigade of l'Îsle Jourdain (Gers) had to protect a curé who was being run out of town following accusations that he had made a young woman pregnant.[29] In the short term such actions may not have made the gendarmes popular, but they helped to underline their claims to impartiality.

---

[26] AN F⁷ 3999, Finistère, Jan. 1835; 4144, Rhône, Aug. 1831; 3949, report of June 1842.

[27] Ibid. 3998, Finistère, Apr. 1832.   [28] Ibid. 4122, Puy-de-Dôme, Apr. 1843.

[29] Ibid. 4010, Report of Aug. 1837 and Annual Report, 1838.

The Gendarmerie's role of providing assistance in times of natural disaster similarly may not necessarily have transformed the institution's popularity, yet it probably contributed to building respect, even if at times grudging. In October 1846, for example, heavy rain brought serious and widespread flooding to the Loire. Of course the Gendarmerie's brigades were as threatened as the local communities, but they were able to organize relief on the spot. Scores of men were praised for their behaviour and for carrying out rescues at great personal risk. *Maréchal-des-logis* Bertrand, a veteran of the Spanish intervention of 1823–4 who was serving as brigade commander in Orleans in his native Loiret,

exposed his life to save a great number of persons and on one particular occasion, while in a small boat, he demolished a wall and then went on to remove the roof from a house so as to rescue a family that had sought refuge in their grain loft. The mayors of St Jean le Blanc, St Denis en Val, and the *Commissaire de Police* of Orleans have all attested to this NCO's gallant conduct.

Nor was it just the NCOs and gendarmes who got themselves wet and their uniforms dirty by organizing and carrying out rescues. Bertrand's company commander, *chef d'escadron* Soufflet, was commended for ignoring threats to his own property from the floods and going with a boatman to the rescue of eighty-two people.[30] Less extensive floods prompted similar behaviour in other *départements* and at other times. Elsewhere gendarmes fought fires, pursued rabid animals, and provided assistance in the case of epidemics like cholera. Though in the latter situations, again, their assistance was not always appreciated; in the cholera epidemic of 1832, for example, Breton peasants were reluctant to accept the problem as one of sickness and believed the illness to be the result of poison.[31]

Crime was a traditional area in which the gendarmes could and did provide assistance. They apprehended offenders caught in the act, and pursued others. When in March 1837 the five robbers of a *laboureur* of Plouisy were promptly arrested by his men, the company commander of the Côtes-du-Nord was pleased to report 'numerous decent expressions of public satisfaction'. Laxity on the part of a brigade commander in reporting an offence, which might lead to a slow pursuit, would bring a reprimand. Some armed gangs continued to create anxiety, yet very little of the old brigandage was to be found during the July Monarchy,

[30] AG E⁵ 160, Inondations, 1846.
[31] AN F⁷ 3998, April report 1832, and see also 3919 May 1841 (floods), 3974 , Dec. 1841 (fire), and 3949, Jan 1842 (rabid dog) and June 1842 (floods).

and the Gendarmerie reports suggest that most crime was of a petty nature. 'If the number of crimes . . . is unfortunately up,' commented the company commander in the Gers in his annual report for 1842, 'it is true to say that none has been committed in circumstances likely to influence the overall tranquillity and public order.'[32] While comments from elsewhere were not as specific, the way in which crime was chronicled in the monthly and annual reports suggests that this was the general assumption.

In the same way that crime does not appear to have been a serious threat in the countryside, so Gendarmerie reports suggest an overall lack of any other incident likely to excite the public mind or threaten the security of the state. This does not mean, however, that patrols were always uneventful and did not, sometimes, have violent or even tragic conclusions. A patrol could hit an unexpected event resulting in a tragedy for someone, not least to the gendarmes themselves. On 25 April 1845, as he set out on a morning patrol of Dreux, Gendarme Hamel fell off his horse. His foot caught in the stirrup and he was dragged 400 metres. He died in hospital later the same day, leaving a widow and two young children.[33] And if patrols could have accidents, they could also find suspects simply through the routine of checking people's papers.[34] It was, perhaps, because the day-to-day patrols appear to have yielded little of note that the officers during the Restoration had been so keen to demonstrate their men's zeal and activity by detailing the nature of their different tasks. By the appearance of the July Monarchy the bureaucratic machine in Paris was automatically expecting that such detail be filled in on printed forms. The statistics were evidence that patrols were being conducted and that gendarmes were making arrests. Failure to keep records in good order could land a man in serious trouble. In July 1841 Lieutenant Duchesne Bressy, recently promoted to the Garde Municipale in Paris, was ordered back to Vire at his own expense to sort out the mess in which he was alleged to have left the records of the Calvados company. 'The initial examination of these archives, which have been thrown higgledy-piggledy in the room of a gendarme, suggests that they are missing the correspondence of the last four commanders of the company, the analytical registers of the *procès-verbaux*, those of the

---

[32] AN F⁷ 4010, Annual Report, 1842.   [33] Ibid. 3996, April report, 1845.
[34] Ibid. 12241, for example, has correspondence dated Aug. 1843 relating to the arrest, by a routine patrol, of two men in an auberge in the Ariège. The suspects, born in Avignon and Lyons and believed to be members of a large gang, were carrying weapons and instruments for conducting a robbery. The information was forwarded, via the minister of the interior, to the prefect of police in Paris

daily reports of 16 November 1839 to 28 February 1841 . . .'[35] The annual inspections sought to pick up problems like this, as well as others. Lieutenant La Roche, who recalled these inspections under the previous regime, wrote of the anxiety that they generated among the officers and of the relief which he himself felt when he received no critical comment.[36] No doubt the NCOs and men felt similarly.

Following his inspections in the north-east in 1845 General Duvergier wrote to the ministry of war suggesting a raft of reforms to improve the Gendarmerie; not the least of these was his plan for inspections without advanced warning which, he believed, would avoid the general smartening-up that preceded an inspector's visits and would thus provide a better picture of the different companies. Overall Duvergier believed that the corps had developed into an indispensible force in French life, 'but the men need encouragement, it is necessary to look after them and to seek to procure for them, in compensation for their labours and fatigues, that standard of well-being appropriate to their position and to the importance of their service'. He also urged policies to foster the recruitment of local men in those *départements* where they were few in number. The problem was that such *départements* too often had brigades composed of men who were new to the corps, learning their duties, lacking knowledge of the region, and who appeared keen to move closer to their own *pays natal* when the opportunity arose.[37]

Other officers were expressing different concerns. A year after Duvergier's proposals, *chef d'escadron* Lallement complained:

Its strong constitution its sole support, it [the Gendarmerie] continues to function, but look today, regardless of party concerns, at what the July Revolution has done to this great and fine institution which covers France as a protective network, and which the whole of Europe envies; it has been sacrificed to rancour, to popular prejudices, and to the jealousy of the army . . . [as a result] at the top there is discouragement and often inertia, at the bottom misery and its cortège, in the middle stagnation and the lack of a future.[38]

Similar dissastisfaction among the rank and file, as well as that among the officers, found a voice in the *Journal de la Gendarmerie* which began

---

[35] AN X^f 250, Dossier Duchesne Bressy.

[36] Aurélien de Courson (ed.), *Souvenirs d'un officier de Gendarmerie sous la Restauration*, 3rd. edn. (Paris: Plon, 1914), 148–9.

[37] AG X^f 257, Duvergier to minister of war, 18 Dec. 1845.

[38] AG MR 1957, Liasse 'Gendarmerie depuis 1830', Lallement to Préval, 7 Dec. 1846; see also 'Considerations de la Gendarmerie', 10 Jan. 1846.

publication in 1839 under the editorship of Pierre-Claude-Melchior Cochet de Savigny. Cochet came from an established Burgundian family, though his letters patent of nobility dated only from 1821. He had not followed a traditional military career. Born in Autun in 1781, he had passed most of the Napoleonic period as a tax official. However, in 1813 the *Contributions indirectes* formed a cavalry unit which he joined as a sub-lieutenant. The following year he transferred to Louis XVIII's Gardes du Corps and in 1816 moved to the Gendarmerie as a lieutenant in the company of the Seine-et-Marne. Cochet was suspected as politically unreliable at the beginning of the July Monarchy, but he was not formally pensioned until June 1839, when he held the rank of *chef d'escadron*. His career as a gendarme appears to have given him the confidence of men of all ranks, and he relied upon them for information to fill the pages of his journal. Yet there were some for whom he appeared too closely linked with governments and in 1842 the more outspoken *Bulletin de la Gendarmerie* began publication.[39] These journals provided an outlet and a focus for the gendarmes' dissatisfaction with their conditions and treatment, but however much they may have considered themselves neglected and ignored by the July Monarchy, when it came to the crunch towards the end of the regime the Gendarmerie proved both dependable and loyal.

Bad harvests and an economic downturn could prompt food rioting, industrial disorders, and scares about vagrants and vagabonds, as well as political agitation. Such was the case in 1839 and 1840;[40] and the problems became even more acute in 1846 and 1847. The Gendarmerie brigades were ordered out on more frequent patrols to quieten the public mind, deal with disorder, and clamp down on vagrancy. The arrest figures of beggars in the Eure-et-Loir increased from a total of just over 200 a year for most of the 1840s to 475 in 1847; in the Pas-de-Calais the increase was even greater, from around 100 to over 500, and here the

[39] Captain Louis Saurel, 'La Gendarmerie dans la société de la Deuxième République et du Second Empire', Thèse pour le doctorat, Université de Paris, 3 vols., 1964, vol. i, pp. 207–38. For a critical assessment of the state of the Gendarmeries during the 1840s, which draws significantly on the content of the *Journale la Gendarmerie*, see Jean-Noël Luc, 'La Revalorisation de la Gendarmerie sous la Monarchie de Juillet (1841–1847)', *Revue historique des Armées*, 213 (1999), 15–25.

[40] AG E⁵ 152, Troubles occasionés par la cherté des grains 1839–40. The report of brigadier Lautour to his company commander in the Mayenne (6 Nov. 1839) shows how such disorders could acquire a revolutionary tinge when the hungry sought to frighten their social superiors into providing food at a 'fair price'. A notice posted in a grain market in Latour's district contained a string of republican expressions and was dated '14 *brumaire* year 48 of the republic'.

category of 'strangers without passports' also increased from 100 a year to just over 400. The annual report for 1847 from the Nord described large numbers of Belgian *mendiants* being arrested and taken to the frontier.[41] Crowds sought to prevent the movement of foodstuffs out of their district, or to fix prices. Sometimes the gendarmes tried to interfere with the free market themselves, possibly in the interests of maintaining order, possibly through sympathy with the poor—they were themselves tired from the intensive patrolling during the emergency, and their families were also hit by the shortages and high prices. But more often, it seems, the gendarmes could be relied upon for firm action in the name of the government administrator's and state jurist's perception of order[42]—and this was also noticeably the experience in Paris in February 1848.

On the evening of 21 February 1848, expecting disorder in Paris as result of the opposition's planned banquet in favour of reform, General Sébastiani, the garrison commander, held a meeting of his senior officers. He urged moderation and instructed his men to act through civil mechanisms, in particular the *commissaires de police*, before seeking to disperse crowds. Given the divided command between army and police in the city, officers of the Garde Municipale were not present at the meeting. The result was that the Parisian gendarmes were much more energetic than other military units against the crowds. In some instances they successfully controlled disorder, but there were also situations where their appearance and actions seem rather to have aggravated matters. Probably the stories of wanton brutality and slaughter by the gendarmes against the crowds, and vice versa, were embroidered on both sides. On 24 February the new provisional government disbanded the Garde Municipale and all policing in Paris passed into the hands of a short-lived civilian police recruited from veterans of the barricades.[43] As in 1830 the *départemental* legions learned of the revolutionary events in Paris and their outcome only after they had occured. Much more than in 1830, the upheaval in Paris was followed by prolonged political agitation in the provinces, which contributed significantly to the expansion and fêting of the Gendarmerie by the regime which emerged out of the Second Republic.

[41] AN F7 3996, Annual Reports, 1842–7; 4117 and 4118, Annual Reports, 1840–7; 4106, Annual Report, 1847.

[42] Roger Price, 'Techniques of Repression: The Control of Popular Protest in Mid-Nineteenth-Century France', *Historical Journal*, 25 (1982), 859–87; at 865–7.

[43] Patricia Ann O'Brien, 'The Revolutionary Police of 1848', and Jonathan M. House, 'Civil–Military Relations in Paris, 1848', both in Roger Price (ed.), *Revolution and Reaction: 1848 and the French Second Republic* (London: Croom Helm, 1975), 135–6 and 152–3.

7

'A GENUINE AND DEPENDABLE ARMY OF THE INTERIOR': GENDARMES IMPERIAL AND REPUBLICAN

Drawing on an apocryphal comment of Hegel, Marx famously compared Louis Napoleon's seizure of power with that of his uncle fifty years before; history repeats itself, he wrote, 'the first time as tragedy, the second as farce'.[1] There were considerable similarities between the experiences of French gendarmes during and immediately following the revolutions of 1830 and 1848; 'farce' is not the word that readily springs to mind in describing the developments on either occasion, but 'tragedy' may well suit the events which surrounded the crushing of the popular effervescence released in 1848.

As in 1830 the gendarmes of Paris, the Garde Municipale, were disbanded; their reputation for arrogance and brutality during the July Monarchy and their fierce defence of the regime in February 1848 had left them with few friends; and when some of them enlisted in the new National Workshops established in the immediate aftermath of the revolution, they had to be sent to a special project outside Paris because of friction with other workers.[2] The maintenance of order in Paris fell briefly into the hands of Marc Caussidière, a republican revolutionary who established himself as Prefect of Police. Caussidière established a police force recruited from barricade fighters, popularly known as *La Garde rouge* or *Les Montagnards*. A decree of 24 April re-established a

---

[1] Karl Marx, *The Eighteenth Brumaire of Louis Bonaparte*, in Karl Marx, *Surveys from Exile, Political Writings*, vol. 2, edited and introduced by David Fernbach (London: New Left Review, 1973), 146.

[2] Mark Traugott, *Armies of the Poor: Determinants of Working-Class Participation in the Parisian Insurrection of June 1848* (Princeton NJ: Princeton University Press, 1985), 202–3, n. 2.

military-style police by creating La Garde Républicaine. But a lack of uniforms and the interchanging of personnel meant that these forces, together with others such as that recruited by and dependent upon the mayor, were not always distinguishable one from another. Caussidière's *Montagnards* were disbanded in May. The suppression of the workers' insurrection of June was left largely to the army, though some 200 officers and men of the new Republican Guard were killed or wounded during the fighting. By the close of 1848 the old system of policing was re-emerging in the capital—a civilian force, the Gardiens de la Paix, directed by the Prefect, and a Gendarmerie unit, the Republican Guard, initially paid by the municipality, but back under the remit of the ministry of war for equipment and discipline by the late spring of 1849. The Republican Guard was smaller than its predecessor of the July Monarchy—2,600 men as opposed to 3,900—but the concern for order in Paris prompted the creation of a mobile Gendarmerie battalion of 700 men at Versailles in July 1848. A second battalion was established and stationed in Paris in May 1850, increasing the total number of men to 1,200.[3]

In the countryside the Gendarmerie companies knew little or nothing of the events of February 1848 in Paris until they were over, and in consequence there was little that they could have done to preserve (or, had they so wished, contribute to the demise of) the July Monarchy. The old problems continued of deserters, petty fights and disorders, fires, floods, food riots, forest offences, friction between native and foreign workers, industrial troubles, and traditional *charivaris*. Yet once the ripples of revolution spread into the provinces, other problems flared and/or the old ones took on new political dimensions. The 45 centimes tax, introduced by the provisional government to save the new republic from bankruptcy, provoked disorder among the peasantry whom it hit the hardest; often the gendarmes were incapable of dealing with these disorders alone and regular troops had to be summoned to assist. The gendarmes were instructed to watch for democratic-socialist emissaries who were feared to be stirring up disorder and subverting both the peasantry and workers. They listened for seditious words such as, for example, the addition of the word 'sociale' to the slogan 'Vive la

[3] Patricia Ann O'Brien, 'The Revolutionary Police of 1848', in Roger Price (ed.), *Revolution and Reaction: 1848 and the French Second Republic* (London: Croom Helm, 1975), 133–49; Colonel R. Colin, *Historique et traditions de la Gendarmerie Nationale* (Melun: École des Officiers de la Gendarmerie Nationale, 1954), 61–2. For the casualties in the Republican Guard during the June Days see Colonel Louis Saurel, *Peines et gloires des gendarmes* (Paris: Editions Lavauzelle, 1973), 81.

République démocratique!', and apprehended offenders when they could. They ordered the removal of, or themselves removed, red flags. Sometimes they were assisted by the local population, as when a group of workers in Denain (Nord) arrested and handed over an agricultural labourer who had been urging them to go to Paris to aid the worker combatants of the June Days. Sometimes, and probably rather more often, attempts to arrest agitators, or to stiffen and support local authorities, led to attacks on both mayors and gendarmes, as happened at Badonvillers near Luneville (Meurthe-et-Moselle) on Christmas Day 1848 when an attempt was made to disperse a crowd shouting 'A bas les riches, à bas les bourgeois, vive la guillotine!'[4] In the politically charged atmosphere of the Second Republic even the closing of a *cabaret* could acquire a political texture. In February 1850 the mayor of a small commune summoned a squad of three gendarmes from Auxonne (Côte d'Or) to help him close a *cabaret*. The closure was effected, but a crowd assembled, began to shout 'Vivent les rouges à bas les blancs', and then ran away. As the gendarmes returned to their barracks the crowd reassembled and began to follow them, shouting and throwing stones. The gendarmes turned and charged. Injuries were inflicted on both sides; one man was arrested.[5]

In *Le Journal de la Gendarmerie* Cochet de Savigny urged that gendarmes should be politically neutral, but neutrality in the turbulent aftermath of revolution is difficult, especially for an organization charged with the maintenance of order. The more critical and outspoken *Bulletin de la Gendarmerie* continued to brand Cochet as an instrument of government and, in particular, of General Charles Rebillot, who had served briefly as Prefect of Police and who, in November 1849, had been appointed to supervise the Gendarmerie from within the ministry of war. The *Bulletin*'s venomous campaign against Rebillot contributed to its suppression in 1850, and *Le Journal*, while not the passive instrument that its rival claimed, did indeed pedal a line which sat well with the policies of the new President, Louis Napoleon Bonaparte. Coupled with Cochet de Savigny's insistence on political neutrality was his desire

---

[4] For these and similar incidents see AG F¹ 16, Rapports quotidiens, 1–9 divisions militaires. The daily reports in series F¹ run throughout the Second Republic; unfortunately many reports are little more than blank sheets. For the role of the gendarmes in the harrassment of democratic socialists see also John Merriman, *The Agony of the Republic: The Repression of the Left in Revolutionary France, 1848–1851* (New Haven, Conn.: Yale Univerity Press, 1978), 48, 94, and 103–4.

[5] AG F¹ 31, Correspondance Générale, Colonel of 20th Legion to Minister of Interior, 19 Feb. 1850.

for the Gendarmerie to be restored to what he considered to be its proper place as the elite of the army; he also hoped for its augmentation to 50,000 men, so as better to ensure the surveillance and repression of those who threatened order. Understandably, *Le Journal* voiced support for Louis Napoleon when government policies appeared to be moving in the general direction of Cochet de Savigny's dreams. The Gendarmerie was fêted by the Prince-President, and in July 1850 provision was made for 461 new brigades; this enabled the establishment of one brigade in each *canton*, and brought the overall complement of the corps to 19,323 men.[6]

When Louis Napoleon carried out his *coup d'état* in December 1851 the gendarmes in Paris acted solidly in his support. Most notable were men from the mobile battalions, who provided the coercive support for the Duke de Morny when he took over the ministry of the interior; and they also ejected from the Assembly those deputies who assembled to protest against the coup.[7] But, of course, such activities cannot be put down solely to the politics of the individual men, the influence of *Le Journal*, or the fêting; all of these probably contributed, but soldiers do, usually, obey orders. In those provinces where reaction to the coup was particularly hostile, however, initially at least many brigades appear to have considered discretion to be the better part of valour.

The peasant columns which came together in the south to resist the *coup d'état* appear to have taken the government by surprise. There had been concerns about democratic-socialist propaganda in the provinces, which the local brigades had been expected to investigate and suppress, but rural uprising on the scale that occurred was unexpected and consequently the authorities were unprepared. During the initial stages clashes between gendarmes and insurgents were rare. Gendarmes were fired on in only three places, and here they were protecting town-halls. While the men in some barracks were disarmed, in many instances the

[6] Howard C. Payne, *The Police State of Louis Napoleon Bonaparte* (Seattle: University of Washington Press, 1966), 232–3; Saurel, *Peines et Gloires*, 53–5. Pierre Miquel, *Les Gendarmes* (Paris: Olivier Orban, 1990), 175–6, describes how, in the pages of *Le Journal de la Gendarmerie* in the aftermath of the February Revolution, Cochet de Savigny urged gendarmes not to bear grudges for the treatment of the Municipal Guard. The dead were simply soldiers who had done their duty: 'the fault was not with the arm that struck the blow, but with the head that gave the orders.'

[7] Georges Carrot, *Le Maintien de l'ordre en France depuis le fin de l'ancien régime jusqu'au 1968*, 2 vols. (Toulouse: Presses de l'insitut d'études politiques de Toulouse, 1984), ii. 529–8. Carrot notes the story of General Espinasse instructing that the deputies should be removed courteously: 'Gendarmes emportez ces messieurs.' But this was translated by the commander of the 1st battalion of the Mobiles into the rather more earthy: 'Foutez les tous dehors.'

peasant columns simply marched by Gendarmerie barracks and did not interfere unless the gendarmes sought to obstruct them. The gendarmes' lack of enthusiasm in opposing these columns may in part have stemmed from the sheer size of the insurgent bands, but occasionally it may also have been linked with the fact that many gendarmes were also local men who did not wish to confront their neighbours unless directly ordered. The bloodiest confrontations occurred where gendarmes inflicted the first casualties or where foolhardy attacks on insurgents left them exposed to the fire-power and counter-attack of overwhelming odds. The fiercest fight was at the barracks in Bédarieux (Hérault). Here three gendarmes and a gendarme's wife were killed, and the dead body of the commanding brigadier was mutilated. The battle was provoked by the brigadier's foolhardy sally against the insurgents, which resulted in the death of a passing youth, and had reawakened the populace's angry recollection of the brigade's pursuit of a young baker for illegal hunting some two months earlier—the baker had died shortly afterwards.[8] The implication is that, in spite of the harrassment of the democratic-socialists, the rural population did not automatically perceive the Gendarmerie brigades to be either enemies or physical manifestations of the new regime which they were rejecting.[9] The peasant columns of December 1851 lacked co-ordination and clear objectives. Once the authorites had regained their composure they were quick to win back the initiative. Their repression was swift and brutal: *départements* were put under a state of siege, martial law was imposed, and mixed columns of gendarmes and troops of the line swept the countryside imposing the Prince-President's order.

The reluctance of a few brigades to get involved at the outset of the protests against the *coup d'état* was scarcely mentioned and rapidly forgotten. As under the first Napoleon the Gendarmerie was acclaimed as an institution which had helped to restore order. In the years imme-diately following the coup and the restoration of the Empire the gen-

---

[8] Ted W. Margadant, *French Peasants in Revolt: The Insurrection of 1851* (Princeton NJ: Princeton University Press, 1979), 266, 268, and 275–85.

[9] The insurrection of the Marianne secret society and the quarry-workers around Angers in Aug. 1855 reveals similar perceptions on the part of the insurgents. They were aroused by shouts that: 'We are going to Angers to demand a reduction in the price of bread, the former mayor and *the gendarmes are with us*, Napoleon has gone, the railway lines are cut, all France will rise at midnight.' (My italics.) The Gendarmerie barracks at Trélazé was only attacked after the gendarmes had arrested one of the insurgents armed with a pistol: Jacques-Guy Petit, 'Marianne en Anjou: l'insurrection des ardoisiers de Trélazé (26–27 août 1855)', *Annales de Bretagne et des Pays de l'Ouest*, 104 (1997), 187–200.

darmes were deluged with praise, while ministers and confidants of the new Emperor saw their role as central to the maintenance of the new regime. General Saint-Arnaud, for example, rejected the idea from the President of the Court of Appeal in Poitiers that it would be a good move to replace all the *gardes-champêtres* with gendarmes. This, he believed, would spread the corps too thinly across France and reduce its importance in the overall military structure. Nevertheless, he looked forward to its augmentation and the day when it would become 'a genuine and dependable army of the interior'.[10]

The imperial decree of 1 March 1854 announced a reorganization that was to last for half a century. It built upon previous Gendarmerie regulations, particularly the Ordinance of 1820. Article 1 declared that the corps was 'to watch over public safety so as to maintain public order and the execution of the laws'. The 'essence' of its service was a 'continual and repressive surveillance'; and in particular it was responsible for 'the safety of the countryside and of communication routes'. There were to be twenty-five legions covering provincial France and Algeria, a Colonial Gendarmerie,[11] two elite battalions—these were the mobile units first established in 1848, and which were incorporated into the Imperial Guard that was re-created in May 1854—and the Paris Guard—the term Republican Guard was, of course, no longer appropriate for the gendarmes in the capital. The military nature of the corps remained unchanged; the Gendarmerie was responsible to the ministry of war for all matters of organization, discipline, and equipment, but it was to work in liaison with, and at the request of, the representatives responsible to other ministries, namely, those of the interior and of justice. As before, the gendarme's duties were divided between ordinary and extraordinary service. Duties, it was stated in Article 119, were always to be carried out openly in uniform; and at no time, either directly or indirectly, were gendarmes to embark on secret missions since this would jeopardize their military nature. But, of course, what the regulations stated is one thing; how they were interpreted, and how they worked in practice was quite another.

The administrative and organizational headquarters of the Gendarmerie remained firmly established within the ministry of war

---

[10] AG F¹ 65, Correspondance général, 'Minute de la lettre écrite par le Ministre . . .', 25 Sept. 1852. See also Payne, *Police State*, 233–5.

[11] The Colonial Gendarmerie consisted of five companies (Martinique, Guadeloupe, Guiana, Île-Bourbon, and Indo-China) and four detachments (Saint-Pierre et Miquelon, Senegal, Tahiti, and New Caledonia).

thoughout the Second Empire, and the corps never reacquired the independence that it had enjoyed under Marshal Moncey. Yet, during these years there were clashes between ministers reminiscent of the clashes between Moncey and Fouché under the first Napoleon. Ministers of war and their senior Gendarmerie commanders were determined to maintain the distinctiveness and independence of the corps over the claims of other ministers. This friction appears to have been at its most acute at the end of the Second Republic and beginning of the Second Empire, as ministers jockeyed for position and sought to extend and/or ring-fence the competence of their fiefdoms within the emerging regime of the new Bonaparte. In a series of confrontations Saint-Arnaud successfully resisted both suggestions that the Gendarmerie be annexed to the ministry of police and attempts by the minister of police and some of his functionaries to employ gendarmes for political policing.[12] Yet this did not prevent Saint-Arnaud himself from using gendarmes in this way, and continuing to do so even after the 1854 Decree. In November 1849 one of his predecessors, General d'Hautpoul, had sent a 'very confidential' circular to the legion commanders requesting that officers and brigade commanders send regular reports that would enable him to take measures necessary 'to combat socialism [and] halt the progress it [was] making in the countryside'. These reports were to be sealed in two envelopes, the interior one being marked 'For the minister alone'. This policy was developed further by General Aristide de La Ruë who, in 1851, became an Inspector-General of the Gendarmerie and presided over its consultative committee within the ministry of war. In January 1854 La Ruë addressed a circular to legion commanders regarding 'political correspondence'. He urged that the Gendarmerie should be constantly on the watch for matters likely to have an impact on popular opinion or likely to trouble society, and he suggested that there were three categories on which such political reports should focus:

1. Those which have an impact on the whole country, such as the effects produced by general measures of government, anxiety caused by important occurrences such as, today, the high cost of grain and the possibility of war, or by political actions directed against the government . . .
2. Those which have most impact on a part of the country, a *département*, or an *arrondissement*, such as local measures required by the government or by administrative authorities, elections, assemblages of workers . . .

---

[12] Saurel, *Peines et gloires*, 56–7; Payne, *Police State*, 90–91. The Ministry of Police was briefly revived by decree in Jan. 1852 under the direction of Charlemagne de Maupas; it was suppressed in June the following year.

3. Those which have a particular impact on a social class, amongst the superior classes the conduct of the leaders of the old parties who remain outwardly in opposition, amongst the inferior classes the conduct of the leaders of the socialists . . . the relations between the Gendarmerie and other authorities, notably the brigades and the *commissaires de police*; the causes of discontent amongst agricultural and industrial populations, the lack of work, the insufficiency of wages, the complaints of workers, strikes, unemployment, etc.[13]

In 1857 Captain Frédéric De Bouyn of the Gendarmerie company in the Cantal requested an audience with the Emperor expressing concern that he was being required to act in a manner contrary to Article 119 of the 1854 decree.

You have wished, Sire, that the Gendarmerie should watch over the public peace, that it should ensure respect for the law, that it be the protector of all, that it be paternal, but feared only by offenders. Nothing in its behaviour should excite suspicion, nothing should imply that its duties are mysterious and shadowy . . . It cannot be within the Gendarmerie's competence to seek to penetrate people's political tendencies. It must not abuse the dignity that it is supposed to have.[14]

Nothing came of De Bouyn's complaint, other than that his career stalled at the rank of captain. La Ruë, in contrast, prospered. He was promoted to be permanent Inspector-General of the Gendarmerie in 1859, and then a senator; he also became an unofficial chief of political police, bypassing the minister of war and relaying the information received from the gendarmes directly to Napoleon III. La Ruë retired officially on 31 December 1865 at the age of 70, but he continued to supervise the political reports and pass on their contents. Four years later, after a *maréchal des logis* in the Haute-Loire had been accused of taking an active role in an electoral campaign, the minister of war called for an assessment of the legal situation which would demonstrate that the Gendarmerie was not a political institution. An undated report, which appears to have been the response, explained in words which probably satisfied the minister that: 'A political role, in the general sense of the expression, requires the performance of some action that involves

---

[13] AG MR 2003, 'Droit et usage du ministre de correspondre directement avec les chefs de légion, 27 Jan. 1870', includes both Gen. d'Hautpoul's circular of 12 Nov. 1849, and La Ruë's of 6 Jan. 1854.

[14] Quoted in Captain Louis Saurel, 'La Gendarmerie dans la société de la Deuxième République et du Second Empire', Thèse pour le doctorat, Université de Paris, 3 vols., 1964, vol. i, p. 90.

the exercise of policing or secret surveillance which is nothing to do with public acts, but with the opinions and the private lives of citizens.'[15]

The close relationship between Napoleon III and the Gendarmerie cooled somewhat after the reorganization of 1854 as the Emperor turned his attentions elsewhere, not least towards the development of civilian police. Cochet de Savigny and Saint-Arnaud saw Napoleon III's behaviour as moving in the direction of their dreams for a big Gendarmerie policing the interior of France; they missed the point that he was seeking to reorganize and improve all forms of policing within the state. At the same time that he was fêting the Gendarmerie he was also providing for a more hierarchical, more professional supervisory cadre for the municipal police, with new regulations for the *commissaires de police* and an extension of their authority. The organization of *gardes-champêtres* in rural communes, and of *sergents de ville*, or whatever other local name was used, in the towns remained the responsibility of the mayors, but an attempt was made to bring greater uniformity to the largest urban areas. The turbulent city of Lyons, together with its expanding suburbs, was singled out as a special case and brought under a single police authority, which was taken out of local hands and made the responsibility of the Prefect of the Rhône. Paris had long since been a special case, and in September 1854, six months after the Gendarmerie decree, the civilian police of Paris was significantly reorganized and greatly enlarged, drawing heavily on the model of London's Metropolitan Police.[16] It seems likely that Napoleon III found himself pulled in two directions: on the one hand he sought to emulate his uncle, and to this end he sought to play up the military pomp of his regime; but on the other, he was impressed by many things English, including London's overtly civilian policemen, and he may, reluctantly, have perceived such a policing style as the way of the future. For his generals and his gendarmes, of course, there was no such uncertainty, but they had little say in the overall development of internal policing policies.

The creation of the new *commissaires de police* provided new opportunites for friction between gendarmes and their civilian counterparts at the local level; this was due in part to the fact that the division of responsibilites was not always clear. But, as ever, clashes could also be

---

[15] AG MR 2003, 'Droit et usage du ministre . . .' for the undated document (Nov.–Dec. 1869?) relating the minister's call for 'un rapport tendant à prouver que la Gendarmerie n'est pas un corps politique'; see also Payne, *Police State*, 238–9.

[16] Payne, *Police State, passim*; see also Alfred Rey and Louis Féron, *Histoire du Corps des Gardiens de la Paix* (Paris, 1896), chap. 4; and Henry Buisson, *La Police: son histoire* (Vichy: Imprimerie Wallon, 1949), 226–7, 233, 275–80, and 291–2.

the result of an obstinate individual seeking to assert his authority or insisting on the correctness of his particular interpretation of the law or specific regulations. The mayor of Le Change (Dordogne) was outraged when a local gendarme began questioning local people about the mayor's role in the *Te Deum* held to celebrate the victory of Magenta. In the Tarn two gendarmes arrested the mayor of Courris when he did not immediately sign and return their *Journal de Service* but insisted on first reading it.[17] In February 1870 *maréchal des logis* Midel, the commander of the Gendarmerie brigade stationed on La Croix Rousse, the hilltop district which was home to of some of the most turbulent textile workers in Lyons, decided that he was not going to permit conscripts to sing revolutionary songs such as *La Marseillaise* or *Le Chant du Départ*. The local police advised him that they had been instructed to ignore such behaviour, but this did not deter Midel, who first seized the cane which a conscript had been swinging like a drum major and then later arrested three members of a larger party of singing conscripts. On each occasion it was the local civilian police which had to move in to disperse angry crowds; Midel himself was injured by a stone which struck him on the head.[18] Rather more common seem to have been tensions resulting from local functionaries constantly calling on the gendarmes for assistance, and gendarmes insisting on a recognition of their autonomy and the fact that they acted only upon requests from civilian authorities, not demands or orders. Such assertions of autonomy exasperated prefects, who pointed out that this did little to help the policing aspirations of the Empire; yet, probably, arguments and serious tensions between gendarmes and their civilian opposite numbers were the exception rather than the rule. *Le Journal de la Gendarmerie* commonly carried the approbations of mayors, their *deputies*, or *commissaires de police* following some courageous or intelligent action by an individual gendarme or brigade. The prefects were also generally complimentary about the Gendarmerie's abilities and professionalism. While policing may have been improving marginally in towns with the creation of new *commissaires*, in the eyes of the prefects the gendarmes remained their most dependable instrument for the maintenance of order in the countryside. 'The statutory service of the Gendarmerie is well done', wrote the Prefect of the Allier in July 1859. 'The service of the *gardes-champêtres* . . . leaves much to be desired because of the small number of men and the incapacity of most of them . . .' Six years later the Prefect of the

[17] Saurel, 'La Gendarmerie,' ii. 77–82 and 165.
[18] Archives Municipales de Lyon, 1² 44, Troubles politiques, 1869–71.

Oise commented on the attentiveness of the Gendarmerie to the super-
vison of drinking establishments, 'but it gets little support from the local
authorities who are made more indulgent by the approach of local elections'.[19]
    Gendarmes complained about the burden of their tasks, and particu-
larly about paperwork. According to the Prefect of the Aisne in 1859,
they felt that they spent less time on carrying out their duties than they
did in giving an account of them.[20] In addition to the political reports
for La Rüe and the special reports on particular incidents for all interested ministries, each month and each year every company had to complete a return for the ministry of the interior. The size of these report
sheets had grown significantly since the Restoration, and during the
Second Empire company commanders had to report not only the number of arrests and patrols that had been made, but also the number of
depositions sworn. Thus, in his annual report for 1855, for example, the
chef d'escadron in the Finistère noted that his men had performed 81,560
activities under the nineteen headings of *services ordinaires* and 3,431
under the eighteen headings of *services extraordinaires*. The former
included 11,915 separate patrols of individual communes, 14,134 visits
to inns, the supervision of 2,030 fairs and markets, and 421 village fêtes;
the latter included escorts for ammunition (165), for taxes (188), and for
troops on the march (44). The same report, under four headings and
thirty-nine subheadings, listed 6,658 depositions (*procès-verbaux*), the
largest single group of which (1,683) concerned traffic and roadway
offences, with petty theft a poor second (754). Some 300 miles to the
east, from the industrializing *département* of the Nord, the *chef d'escadron*
completed an identical form listing 12,397 depositions, of which 2,400
concerned traffic and roadway offences and 1,348 petty theft.[21] It was
manifestly impossible for the bureaucrats in Paris to do anything con-
structive with this mass of numbers, but what the information did provide, indirectly, was a means of supervising the Gendarmerie and
ensuring, as far as possible, that the brigades were doing what they were
supposed to do. Each table of service statisitics was signed off: 'Certified
as accurate after checking the journals and service reports, by me, *chef
d'escadron*, commandant of the company.' The space on these forms for
details of incidents likely to influence 'internal tranquillity and public

---

[19] AG G⁸ 180, Rapports de Prefet, Dossier Allier; G⁸ 182, Rapports de Prefet, Dossier
Oise; Payne, *Police State*, 240–4.
[20] Payne, *Police State*, p. 241.
[21] AG F⁷ 4002, Finistère, Annual Report, 1855; F⁷ 4106, Nord, Annual Report, 1855.

order' is rather more obvious in its intention, but it was common for this section to be scrawled with the simple comment—'None' (*Néant*). A section on the *gardes-champêtres* gave Gendarmerie officers the opportunity to comment on the efficiency and abilities of these local police. The old complaints were still made; the company commander in the Nord in particular thought them 'blind instruments of the mayors, however many show themselves devoted to the Gendarmerie'.[22] And if, elsewhere, the guards were occasionally drunk, reluctant to give information to the gendarmes, and sometimes dismissed for corruption, the reports in this section of the form were commonly brief and probably comforting to the Paris bureaucrat—'The conduct of the *gardes-champêtres* leaves nothing to be desired', or simply 'No complaint'.[23]

The annual averages by decade constructed for Table 7.1 show the largest number of arrests by the provincial gendarmes, from the Restoration until well into the Second Empire, were those made on warrants (*mandats de justice*) rather than as a result of catching offenders in the act or of popular clamour. These warrants steadily increased across the period, reaching a particularly high number in the industrial Nord. The arrests of criminal offenders showed a much more gradual increase; indeed, the incidence of crime does not appear to have given the Gendarmerie much cause for concern. In his inspection of the company of the Deux-Sèvres in 1863 La Rüe noted that petty theft and poaching were the principle offences in the *département*. 'Crimes are rare (something which is demonstrated by the fact that there has been no assize court here in the first third of the year), they are principally rapes and infanticides . . .' Table 7.1 shows that arrests which resulted from pro-active policing—the apprehension of beggars and strangers without passports—were always consistently higher than those of criminal suspects, though of course, in the eyes of officialdom in general and the gendarme in particular, the beggar and the stranger, especially one without papers, were suspect by definition. It also underlines the contrasts between regions. The Rhône formed part that region which had been the powerhouse of early nineteenth-century industrial development in France; by the 1840s this region was being superseded by the north-east,

---

[22] Ibid. 4106, Nord, June 1855; see also Feb. 1856.

[23] Ibid. 4002, Finistère, Annual Report 1856 notes that some guards are drunks and give no information to the Gendarmerie, but in general they 'conduct themselves well and perform their duty with zeal and intelligence'. F7 3949, Cantal, Annual Reports for 1856 and 1858 note corruption among individual guards, and that for 1859 comments that their conduct was 'quite steady, but as they are insufficiently remunerated the standard of their service leaves something to be desired'.

TABLE 7.1. *Annual averages of arrests by Gendarmerie Companies, 1817–1859*

Offence	1817–20	1821–30	1831–40	1841–7	1855–9
Basses-Alpes					
Homicide	2	4	4	2	1
Thieves	12	28	12	21	49
Disturbers of the peace	1	6	6	15	20
Arrests on warrant	41	45	93	77	150
Beggars	7	9	14	15	65
Strangers without passport	26	33	56	62	78
Escapees	–	1	–	1	6
Others	–	2	3	1	10
Deserters	–	14	22	20	9
Other military	–	–	–	–	3
Cantal					
Homicide	–	2	5	3	1
Thieves	2	8	29	37	50
Disturbers of the peace	–	4	22	43	20
Arrested on warrant	113	77	99	108	150
Beggars	12	14	21	28	65
Strangers without passports	18	25	71	61	78
Escapees	3	1	2	1	6
Others	17	4	1	1	10
Deserters	–	7	56	21	9
Other military	–	–	4	2	3
Gers					
Homicides	1	1	4	2	2
Thieves	34	18	50	65	68
Disturbers of the peace	3	3	9	16	3
Arrested on warrant	86	92	88	165	223
Beggars	11	4	50	128	77
Strangers without passports	35	41	126	470	182
Escapees	9	1	4	3	3
Others	9	3	11	42	8
Deserters	–	54	27	13	6
Other military	–	–	–	–	–
Nord					
Homicide	14	7	4	2	2
Thieves	94	58	46	68	107
Disturbers of the peace	–	18	14	9	6
Arrested on warrant	191	326	486	702	866
Beggars	68	219	142	181	161
Strangers without passports	46	340	169	111	163
Escapees	1	2	3	1	4
Others	101	–	–	–	39
Deserters	–	159	176	88	24
Other military	–	–	–	–	52
Rhône					
Homicide	4	6	6	3	3
Thieves	76	74	97	152	122
Disturbers of the peace	50	44	78	159	36

Offence	1817–20	1821–30	1831–40	1841–7	1855–9
Arrested on warrant	64	78	138	182	237
Beggars	373	395	298	392	317
Strangers without passports	8	32	132	265	152
Escapees	2	2	1	–	2
Others	–	29	64	49	36
Deserters	89	78	122	62	26
Other military	–	–	–	–	34

Source: Various annual tables in AN F7 3917–19, 3947–9, 4009–11, 4103–6, and 4143–6.

especially the *département* of the Nord. These areas had bigger concentrations of police than elsewhere, with urban forces lining up alongside the Gendarmerie companies; nevertheless, the gendarmes in these regions appear to have been kept much busier in responding to problems and in completing the inevitable reports on working-class attitudes, conditions, and wages, strikes, and the potential for political capital to be made from economic difficulties and unrest. In his report on the Rhône company in 1863 General Berger de Castellan stressed the difficult service undertaken by the brigades in Lyons, notably in maintaining a surveillance of the textile workers; moreover, the brigades had no rapport with the population, and gendarmes from outside the city were often called in to assist. In the Nord that same year the construction of railways was noted as contributing to the increased workloads of some brigades and a corresponding decrease in that of others. 'This situation is prejudicial to the service, it is desirable that the positioning of the brigades be revised so as to overcome the problem.' In the Moselle the situation was noted as being greatly complicated by the proximity of Bavaria, Belgium, the Netherlands, and Prussia, which required 'a very special surveillance and a redoubling of activity because of the number of idle men, vagabonds, and malefactors, *people of no country* who hang around these districts so as more easily to slip from one land to another and thus to escape the punishment which they have brought upon themselves by their misdeeds'. The problem was seen to be aggravated still further, first, by the large number of metal-works and other factories in both France and the neighbouring territories, which encouraged a constant coming and going among numerous workers, and secondly, by the employers being none too scrupulous about a worker's identity or morality.[24]

[24] AG X^f 210, Inspections of the Moselle, the Nord, and the Rhône, 1863.

While still charged with checking the papers of persons travelling on the roads, which generally meant the poorer individuals who looked shabby and/or suspicious, gendarmes could act for the benefit of the working classes. In October 1856, for example, two brothers, grain merchants from the Corrèze, were arrested in the Cantal for buying up grain in the hopes of forcing up prices.[25] Gendarmes were known sometimes to hand over their rewards to charity, to contribute to national subscriptions for the unemployed, to assist poor people rather than simply apprehend them as beggars, and even to pay, or organize a subscription to pay, the fines of unfortunate petty offenders. In December 1858, following a series of press reports of gendarmes assisting petty offenders, they were specifically ordered to stop doing this.[26] They could be the resort of other people in trouble, such as the victims of crime, and popular folk tales commonly ended with the evil brigand being beheaded or burned alive by gendarmes.[27] But the point was never lost on workers, both industrial and agricultural, that it was the Gendarmerie which was, generally, the first instrument of the state to be deployed in the event of a strike, for surveillance and, if considered necessary, for making arrests. The law of 25 May 1864 permitted combinations and, in consequence, strike activity. This meant that gendarmes were no longer concerned with dispersing assemblies and getting people back to work. However, the new law upheld the right to work and thus ensured the continuing potential for friction with strikers when gendarmes were ordered to protect blackleg labour. Gendarmes also incurred popular odium as enforcers of the 1844 law which forbade hunting to anyone who had not purchased a 25 francs permit; 'I know you well,' complained the mayor of Mezidon (Gers) to a squad of gendarmes, 'you would rather spend four nights waiting to catch a poacher in the act than catch a thief.'[28] They provided the coercive support for bailiffs conducting evictions, and for mayors and *commissaires* seeking to close *cabarets*. Equally, it was the Gendarmerie which conducted what, in the eyes of most prefects, was the most efficient supervision of those bars which lay beyond the surveillance of municipal policemen; and on Sundays and holidays urban workers commonly travelled beyond the limits of towns to enjoy themselves in these *guinguettes*. Yet for all the possibilities of confrontation, the numbers arrested for disturbing

[25] AN F7 3949, Cantal, Annual Report, 1856.

[26] Saurel, 'La Gendarmerie,' iii. 359–64; id. *Peines et gloires*, pp. 75–6.

[27] Eugen Weber, *Peasants into Frenchmen: The Modernization of Rural France 1870–1914* (Stanford, Cal.: Stanford University Press, 1976), 512–13, n. 12.

[28] Saurel, 'La Gendarmerie,' iii. 398.

TABLE 7.2. *Resistance to, or insults towards, gendarmes, 1855–1859*

Département	1855	1856	1857	1858	1859
(a) Arrests					
Basses-Alpes	14	3	4	12	9
Finistère	33	36	45	52 (including 10 soldiers)	64 (including 14 soldiers)
Gers	0	3	5	5	4
Nord	16	8	11	0	0
Puy-de-Dôme	8	22	26	41	16
Rhône	25	7	47	19	53
(b) Depositions					
Eure-et-Loir	10	10	9	35	11
Finistère	15	14	13	9	11
Gers	0	1	3	1	2
Nord	12	2	3	12	3
Rhône	0	0	9	14	0

Source: Tables in AN F⁷ 3919, 3996, 4002, 4011, 4106, 4122, and 4146.

the peace in the annual reports remain relatively low; and so too was the incidence of 'resistance or insults towards the Gendarmerie' (see Table 7.2).

The popular attitude to the gendarme appears often to have been dependent upon the context in which he was met. Probably he was respected, even feared, rather than liked by workers and peasants. Those gendarmes who lived by the strictest interpretation of the laws were doubtless detested by many in their communities. But those who helped people could find themselves helped, even in the most dangerous circumstances. Gendarme Cirq escaped death during the fight at Bédarieux when a radical café proprietor intervened in his favour; a few months earlier Cirq had broken regulations and allowed the proprietor to attend the funeral of a fellow radical.[29] Possibly because of the mixture of respect and fear, the gendarme could be a humourous character in some of his manifestations within popular culture. In the celebrated Lyons puppet plays, Guignol, the sensible, anti-authoritarian silk-weaver, always bests the pompous, authoritarian gendarme in argument. But the humourous character was established most effectively with Gustave Nadaud's popular song *Pandore, ou les deux gendarmes*. Gendarme Pandore, raised to fear God and, most of all, his brigadier, never opens his mouth except to agree with his NCO: 'Brigadier, vous-avez raison!' Pandore became the name synonymous with the blindly obedient

[29] Margadant, *French Peasants in Revolt*, 281–2.

gendarme. Obedience to the law, open-handedness, and probity were the qualities ascribed to gendarmes in two popular novels published towards the end of the Second Empire, the *Vicomte* de Ponson du Terrail's *Mémoires d'un gendarme* (1867) and Hector Pessard's *Les Gendarmes*; *Fantasie administrative* (1869).

The Gendarmerie remained popular among those of the propertied classes who had formed the backbone of the Party of Order that was established during the Second Republic; if nothing else, the military uniform, with its distinctive bicorne hat, provided reassurance and gave the wearer a smart military appearance which was a world away from the *garde-champêtre*, who may or may not have worn a uniform or part of one, and the *sergent de ville*, whose outfit depended upon the funds provided by an often parsimonious municipality. Cochet de Savigny died in 1855, and *Le Journal de la Gendarmerie* lost both its passion and its campaigning edge. Its pages became a simple chronicle of promotions, retirements, and details of heroic actions by members of the corps with accompanying approbations; it also contained rather dry, factual discussions of legal points and regulations. But the Gendarmerie still had its eulogists. A hagiography of Moncey had appeared in 1848, with a glowing description of the ordinary gendarmes who showed themselves to be 'slaves of duty, facing up to the greatest perils with calm', and who, it was claimed, were admired by all the powers of Europe.[30] Pierre Larousse's *Grand Dictionnaire Universel du XIXe Siècle*, which began publication in the mid-1860s, noted the jokes made about the gendarme in every music-hall, but then went on to quote Baron Ambert, an Inspector-General of Gendarmerie:

The gendarme is the expression most eloquent, most complete, most true, of the dedication and sacrifice that characterize religion. The gendarme is the direct descendant of the orders of chivalry born in the twelfth century. The knights spoke of 'Dying for the faith and protecting the weak'. The gendarme speaks of 'Dying for the law and defending justice' . . . Their barracks are little monasteries where the faith of duty is kept pure . . . In the midst of our modern civilization, the man most worthy of respect is the gendarme because he is the law's sentinel. In the midst of our gallant army, the most courageous man is the gendarme because his enemy is invisible and he is as intrepid in the shadows as he is in the sunlight. In the midst of our vigilant magistracy, the most observant man is the gendarme for he sees all when all hide from him. In the midst of our robust countryfolk, the strongest man is the gendarme since,

[30] Louis-Joseph-Gabriel Chénier, *Éloge historique du Maréchal Moncey* (Paris, 1848), 40–1.

in times of danger, everyone calls on him for help . . . Simple man, forgive those who lack the secret of your grandeur . . . I can never pass your doors without reading, engraved upon them, those mysterious, invisible words, which you have carved by your entire lives:

Without fear and without reproach.[31]

Many of Ambert's colleagues reported on the gendarme in rather less elevated terms. The inspectors of the 1860s drew a picture not greatly different from those of their predecessors. Some companies, and many men were competent, hard-working, and devoted to the government, but there were still ignorant gendarmes and the occasional drunk.[32] The company in the Ardennes was one singled out for praise, coping well with the difficult surveillance of a region part rural, part industrial, and heavily forested. The Ariège company got a less fulsome report. Several gendarmes were reported for heavy drinking, others for getting into debt, and some for sending anonymous denunciations of their superiors—though the latter behaviour seemed to be in decline. While their presence was essential for breaking up the *rixes* which commonly erupted at fairs and village festivals and which so easily degenerated into serious conflicts, the brigadiers in the Ariège were thought to lack the courage necessary for confronting large crowds. In the districts of the Alpes-Maritimes and the area around Nice, which had been recently acquired from Italy, the men, many of whom had transferred from the Piedmontese Carabinieri, were generally too short, spoke poor French, and did not carry out their duties as well as they might; but at least they knew the language of the local peasantry and appeared proud of their new French uniforms. It was still considered useful for the men in several of the eastern *départements* to know German. Those in the Finistère, where recruits to the company continued to be generally strangers to the region, were thought to be disadvantaged by not knowing the local Breton language.[33]

The reality of the Gendarmerie barracks was also rather different from Ambert's romantic picture of chivalrous, monastic knights transplanted into the nineteenth century. Visits to the barracks by a

---

[31] Article on 'Gendarmerie' in *Grand Dictionnaire Universel du XIXe siècle* (Paris: Pierre Larousse); for other examples of Ambert's purple prose (and that of others) see Saurel, *Peines et gloires*, pp.74–5.

[32] The number of men noted for excessive drinking appears to have been smaller than under the old *maréchaussée*; when the offence was repeated and in public, the punishment meted was severe. Terry W. Strieter, 'Drinking on the Job: *Ivresse* Among the French Gendarmerie in the Nineteenth Century', *Proceedings of the Annual Meeting of the Western Society for French History*, 13 (1986), 173–81.

[33] AG X^f 210, *passim*.

gendarme's family may have been restricted, and strict regulations were imposed on wives and children who lived in the barracks, but then few monks were expected to live with wives and children. The problem of men being burdened by wives and children had been noted under the *ancien régime* and again during the Restoration. In May 1860 Commandant Lebouvier submitted a report on the corps to the Emperor. He explained that, while marriage was encouraged 'in the interests of morality', the result was that the men had large numbers of children. Army regulations provided for the maintenance of five children per company, but the fecundity of gendarmes and their wives meant that some companies had 100, some 200 children, and this resulted in financial hardship for the men—unlike other working-class men, a gendarme's wife was forbidden from taking a job to help with the family budget. It seems that the settled existence of the gendarme encouraged him to marry at a rate similar to the rest of the population— nearly four out of five men were married; in contrast, amongst long-serving professional soldiers, well under a half were married.

Lebouvier emphasized the value of men knowing both the district in which they served and their neighbours; frequent changes of residence he considered prejudicial to the service. The evidence suggests that, as under earlier regimes, Napoleon III's gendarmes often served in their *département* of origin, though service in a man's village of birth (or that of his wife) was not permitted; others commonly served in a *département* neighbouring that of their birth. And if the Finistère had few Bretons, by the 1860s this was not the case with other Breton *départements*, such as the Côtes-du-Nord and the Morbihan. In addition to the significant presence of local men, some *départements* stand out for providing a dis-proportionate number of gendarmes, most notably those to the east of a line running from Abbeville to Macon. Transfers from one brigade to another were usually for promotion or personal reasons, and occasion-ally as a punishment. Lebouvier, like other contemporaries, stressed the increasing burdens on the corps: 'and in very many districts the brigades have become insufficient; moreover, the authorities and the population demand the creation of new posts in different places.' To meet these demands Lebouvier suggested a slight reduction in the army, which would provide the necessary finance, and the creation of more brigades of foot gendarmes, which were far cheaper to maintain and to pay than the mounted brigades.[34] In the event it was another nine years before

[34] AG MR 2003, 'Notes soumises à l'Empereur par le commandant Lebouvier, avec l'autorisation de Sa Majesté', 25 May 1860; for the origins of the gendarmes see the

anything was done. The regulation of 25 September 1869 introduced changes similar to those proposed by Lebouvier; an infantry regiment of the Imperial Guard was disbanded, mounted brigades in the Gendarmerie were reduced from six to five men, and twenty-five mounted brigades were transformed into fifty foot brigades. This raised the provision of men to 19,400, and the financial saving also allowed a pay increase.

Within a year of this change France was embroiled in the disastrous war with Bismarck's Prussia. The gendarmes' plethora of ordinary duties gave way to the demands of the emergency; some men were called back to the colours, others were deployed to police the army, especially after German troops had penetrated deep into French territory and encircled Paris. The end of the war brought the Paris Commune, with gendarmes fighting ferociously for the Versailles army, fired, at least in part, by the fact that some forty of their fellows were among the hostages shot by the Communards. As with the previous upheavals in nineteenth-century Paris, the Commune's impact rippled throughout the French provinces. Local Gendarmerie brigades were ordered to remove red flags and to look out for fugitives from Paris; sometimes their actions were supported by local communities hostile to the Communards, but sometimes the highly charged political atmosphere brought new clashes between gendarmes and local mayors and their communities.[35]

The early years of the Third Republic saw some tinkering with the organization of the *départemental* legions, but the broad policies which had emerged under Napoleon III were continued. There were some who urged a significant augmentation of the Gendarmerie, arguing that it, and its predecessor, had brought peace to the countryside and that the corps was now needed to bring peace to the burgeoning towns, increasingly the focus of problems and disorder.[36] Yet few in the assemblies of the Third Republic were interested in seeing policing significantly developed along military lines, for while the army remained steadfastly politically neutral, it was initially feared that the officer corps was Bonapartist and subsequently, during the Dreyfus affair, that it was

reports in AG X^f 210 and Saurel, 'La Gendarmerie,' ii. 58–77; for the detail on gendarme marriages and posting transfers see Terry W. Strieter, 'The Faceless Police of the Second Empire: A Social Profile of the Gendarmes of Mid-Nineteenth-Century France', *French History*, 8 (1994), 167–95; at 175–6.

[35] Saurel, *Peines et gloires*, 106–8; Miquel, *Les Gendarmes*, 256–60 and 269–70.
[36] Saurel, 'Les Gendarmes', i. 457.

right-wing, aristocratic, and Jesuit-educated. The loss of Alsace and Lorraine meant the disappearance of the companies that had patrolled this region, but the overall complement of the corps did not decline; the *départemental* legions continued to fluctuate at around 20,000 men into the new century. The alarm created by the Commune generated a massive, but relatively short-lived, increase in the gendarmes posted to Paris, once again rechristened as the Republican Guard; there were 6,100 of them in 1871, reduced to 4,000 in 1873 and to 3,000 in 1887. The uniformed *gardiens de la paix*, in contrast, numbered just under 8,000.

Some of the 6,100 men serving as gendarmes in Paris in 1871 appear to have transferred into a mobile legion based in Versailles. This legion was confirmed by decree on 28 March 1872. It was composed of a squadron of cavalry and a battalion of eight infantry companies, in all some 1,220 men. The legion was designed to provide rapid and significant support to the *départemental* companies should they be confronted with an emergency. Yet, whatever the fears, there was little serious threat in the aftermath of the Commune. The legion did little more than act as a guard for the Senate. Its numbers were gradually whittled away, and it was formally abolished in March 1885.[37]

The 20,000 provincial gendarmes continued to perform the daily tasks that they had accrued over the previous century. Occasionally the action of apprehending a deserter or seeking to ensure that conscripts turned up for their duty could still develop into a nasty confrontation; occasionally, too, poachers turned their guns on gendarmes. The Gendarmerie remained essentially a rural force, and France was becoming increasingly urban: just over 11 million people were classified as urban in 1872, about 31 per cent of the total population, and thirty years later the number had increased to nearly 16 million and the proportion to 41 per cent. Overall, the statistics of cases brought before the courts reveal that the actual number brought by gendarmes began to decline from the mid-1890s (see Table 7.3). Yet from the end of the Second Empire through to the outbreak of World War I they were generally more productive in this respect than the *commissaires* and their subordinates (see Table 7.4). Of course such figures have to be handled with extreme caution; the urban police had far less occasion to deal with vagrants or infringments of road regulations.

---

[37] Jean-Charles Jauffret, 'Armée et pouvoir politique. La question des troupes spéciales chargées du maintien de l'ordre en France de 1871 à 1914', *Revue historique*, 547 (1983), 97–144; at 110–11.

Table 7.3. *Average number of incidents brought before the courts by gendarmes and police respectively, 1865–1913*

Years	Gendarmes	Police
1865–9	128,500	109,300
1870–4	144,000	90,800
1875–9	185,000	104,600
1880–4	207,500	135,000
1885–9	237,500	147,800
1890–4	269,000	161,900
1895–9	265,000	157,300
1900–4	260,000	167,300
1905–9	255,600	175,600
1910–13	253,000	188,500

Source: Constructed from statistics in Bruno Aubusson de Cavarlay, Marie-Sylvie Huré, and Marie-Lys Pottier, *Les Statistiques criminelles de 1831 à 1981. La base Davido, séries générales* (Paris, CESDIP, 1989), Tableau 2, pp. 160–3.

TABLE 7.4. *Average number of offences brought before the courts by each man serving as a gendarme, policeman, or mayor and* garde-champêtre, *1865–1913*

Year	Gendarme	Policeman	Mayor and garde-champêtre
1865	6	9.4	0.6
1869	7.2	9.5	0.5
1875	8.9	8.5	0.6
1880	9.8	9.0	0.4
1885	10.9	9.8	0.4
1890	11.8	9.9	0.4
1895	13.4	9.6	0.3
1900	12.5	9.7	0.3
1905	12.4	10.0	0.3
1910	11.3	8.8	0.3
1913	11.9	9.5	0.3

Source: Constructed from statistics in Aubusson de Cavarlay, Huré, and Pottier, *Les Statistiques criminelles*, Tableaux 1 and 2, pp. 159–63.

As France was becoming more urbanized, so too was it becoming more industrial and experiencing significant industrial unrest. In the turbulent first year of the Third Republic Émile Zola wrote the first novel in his Rougon-Macquart series. *La Fortune des Rougon-Macquart* was set in the south during the violent peasant response to Louis-Napoleon's *coup d'état*; it contains unflattering images of the Gendarmerie. At the climax, the unfortunate Silvère is arrested by a gendarme while clutching his lover's body still draped in her red flag; and later, when the soldiery have no stomach for more killing, it is the terrible half-blinded Gendarme Rengarde who executes him and his companion. While gendarmes did not go round executing dissidents during the Third Republic, they were repeatedly criticized by the Left for political repression under the previous, Bonapartist regime; they also continued to have a repressive image amongst the growing number of industrial workers, since gendarmes were still commonly called out to supervise public order in cases of workers' demonstrations or strikes. Agents of the local police were often regarded as too few or insufficiently disciplined and organized for such a task, and there was a reluctance to use the conscript army. In February 1884, for example, Waldeck-Rousseau, then minister of the interior, issued a circular advising the deployment of gendarmes in preference to others in public-order emergencies; he considered gendarmes to be experienced professionals who believed in the strict application of the law. The journal *L'Avenir militaire* believed that the disastrous shooting of demonstrators at Fourmies on May Day 1891 could have been averted if the situation had been handled by thirty or forty gendarmes rather than by the army. The problem was that the Gendarmerie was thin on the ground, even in the most populous industrial districts. Men had to be detached from distant posts for service in emergencies, and as the incidence of strikes grew and their duration became longer, so rural districts could be left for lengthy periods with skeleton brigades. When it appeared that the gendarmes were insufficient, there was no other recourse but the deployment of troops. Almost a year after the shooting at Fourmies a proposal was drafted for a squadron of 100 mounted gendarmes who could act as a mobile support unit, but the plan was never implemented.[38]

But it was not only the political Left and worker activists who could sneer at the Gendarmerie for the tasks which it undertook for the state. When the Third Republic turned on the Catholic Church it was gendarmes who brought the order for the closure of a church school and the eviction of priests or nuns, and gendarmes who, sometimes in considerable numbers and backed by troops, were called upon to enforce such closures.[39] And if Zola, socialists, worker activists, and

---

[38] Miquel, *Les Gendarmes*, 297–303 and 313–16; Jauffret, 'Armée et pouvoir politique', 112–13.

[39] Caroline Ford, *Creating the Nation in Provincial France: Religion and Political Identity in Brittany* (Princeton N.J.: Princeton University Press, 1993), 140–6.

Ultramontanes portrayed gendarmes as tough and heartless, there were also journalists, caricaturists, and popular song-writers who saw them as figures of fun—men in large, old-fashioned hats, with big boots and big moustaches. Nadaud's Pandore continued to be an archetype during the Third Republic. This criticism and joking at the Gendarmerie's expense appears to have contributed to recruiting problems for the corps at the turn of the century, when there were more vacancies than applicants. Poor pay, which remined unchanged from 1874 until the outbreak of World War I, contributed to the problem, with gendarmes receiving less than the *gardiens de la paix* in Paris. Yet, as was the case with young men of little fortune during the Restoration, the Gendarmerie still appeared to offer opportunities for advancement. Ignace-Émile Forestier, for example, the son of a cooper and small farmer near Vichy (Allier), had served nine years in the cavalry in the spring of 1899. Still only 26 years old, he was encouraged to enter the school for cavalry officers at Saumur, but declined on the grounds that cavalry officers were generally wealthy and titled and that the sons of peasants or workers had difficulty in maintaining the dignity necessary for such a rank simply on the pay of such a rank. Forestier opted instead for marriage and the Gendarmerie.[40]

Forestier began his career in the Gendarmerie in the spring of 1901 stationed in the Indre, close to his native Allier. He served in the *départemental* brigades for twenty years, rising to the rank of captain; he then transferred to the Republican Guard in Paris where he completed his career with six years as a company commander. In addition to the Great War, which contemporaries and subsequent historians have portrayed as the cataclysmic end of the progressive nineteenth century, the years of Forestier's service witnessed an array of changes to the Gendarmerie. Some were largely superficial, like the disappearance of the bicorne hat and Condé boots in 1904. Others were more significant and paralleled developments in the civilian police, seeking to establish a new professionalism and a positive embrace of the technological and bureaucratic modernity which seemed epitomized by the progress of the nineteenth century and the dawn of the twentieth. A training school for NCOs, established early in 1901, was a new underpinning of the corps' professionalism; the authorization of the use of bicycles which preceded

---

[40] Ignace-Émile Forestier, *Gendarmes à la belle époque* (Paris: Editions France-Empire, 1983), 54; for the poor state of the corps at the turn of the century see, *inter alia*, Jean-Marc Berlière, L'institution policière en France sous la Troisième République 1875–1914', 3 vols., Thèse pour le doctorat, Université de Bourgogne, 1991, vol. ii, pp. 792–3.

this by a few months might be seen as a move towards modernization, though the Gendarmerie had to await the end of World War I before it got its first automobiles.

At the turn of the century, aspirations to a new professionalism and modernization notwithstanding, the mundane day-to-day duties of the gendarmes remained largely unchanged. Forestier made daily patrols, like his predecessors a century before. Economic and social change, however, were giving other, exceptional duties a greater prominence. For roughly three months towards the end of his first year of service Forestier found himself on detachment as part of a body of twenty mounted and twelve foot gendarmes quartered in St Vallier (Indre) because of a miners' strike.[41] In the decade before the war proposals were again brought forward for mobile brigades of Gendarmerie, distinct from the ordinary *départemental* brigades, that could be deployed to deal with public-order emergencies. Again the idea foundered. The Left was suspicious of a paramilitary body which it feared would be deployed primarily against the workers. The Right was suspicious of a corps which it feared could be deployed by a government of Freemasons to enforce extreme anticlerical policies. Officers of the Gendarmerie protested that the money for the mobile brigades would be better spent improving and augmenting the *départemental* companies which, they insisted, were continuing to provide a valuable service of honest men, always on duty, quite independent of other local police, and readily identifiable by their uniforms.[42] The Republican government eventually decided to invest such additional money as it could find for policing in mobile detective police patrols, equipped with modern motor cars and committed to dealing with 'criminals' as opposed to public-order emergencies. Gendarme historians have been tempted to portray their institution as a Cinderella service in the decade before World War I,[43] yet it is also clear that functionaries within the French penal system generally held the corps in high regard. Moreover, perhaps warmed by the comfort of retirement and of seeing a son follow in his footsteps, Forestier looked back on his early service with pride and spoke of his oath with reverence:

5 June 1901 . . . I was admitted to take the oath before the Tribunal of the First Instance at Châteauroux. It is a milestone in the career of a gendarme, for it is

[41] Forestier, *Gendarmes à la belle époque*, 66–7.

[42] Jauffret, 'Armée et pouvoir', 116–26.

[43] See e.g. Gen. Jean Besson and Pierre Rosière, *Gendarmerie Nationale* (Paris: Editions Xavier Richer, 1982), 212, and Saurel, *Peines et gloires*, 59.

from this moment alone that he is armed by the law regularly to fulfill the functions of an agent of public authority and a representative of the law. Moreover, the words of the oath, which follow, outline the proper mode of conduct for a gendarme: 'I swear to obey my superiors in all that concerns the service to which I am called and, in the exercise of my duties, only to use that force authorized to me for the maintenance of the law and the execution of the laws.'[44]

Forestier, like most military men who came to write their memoirs, was immensely proud of his corps. He had taken his oath 110 years after that corps had been reorganized and given the name 'Gendarmerie'. Over that century, as a military unit, it had won its share of battle honours; yet the day-to-day role of the majority of the men had never been that of the ordinary soldier. From their small barracks the brigades had mounted daily patrols of their districts, maintaining a surveillance of the population for their political masters and, in the broadest sense of the terms, seeking to maintain the peace and preserve good order—both the peace and order dictated by their political masters, and that expected by the population.

The French Revolution had promised equality before the law; the gendarme, whether he and his corps were personally popular or not within a community, was an agent whose presence was, in itself, a promise both to enforce that equality and to ensure a life free from crime and disorder. If the gendarmes had not been present during the nineteenth century, it is unlikely that there would have been a descent into anarchy and/or constant revolution; indeed, the presence of the gendarmes, and of their predecessors, did not prevent the insurrectionary outbreaks which troubled France from the late eighteenth century. Nor would all contemporaries (not to mention subsequent historians) have agreed that, during the nineteenth century, the gendarmes enforced and ensured a uniform equality before the law. Yet none of this is to imply that if they had not been present, French society would still have developed precisely in the way that it did. Gendarmes brought the French state into the provinces. Of course, they were never the sole representatives of the state. There were also *commissaires de police* in the larger towns and schoolmasters—both of these could be outsiders; and the mayors, while local men, appear increasingly to have identified with the French state and with what might broadly be termed the new bourgeois order rather than, first and foremost, with all members of their local community. Together with the activities of these

---

[44] Forestier, *Gendarmes à la belle époque*, 63–4.

other functionaries, those of the gendarmes helped to ensure the greater integration of French society. Most notably in this respect, the gendarmes' presence ensured the collection and protection of taxes, the free flow of foodstuffs, the marshalling of conscripts. At the same time the gendarmes were the physical manifestation of the state's law in the small towns and villages, and on the roads. They were the state's first line of assistance for its citizens when these were the victims of brigands or of other offenders; and they were the first line of assistance provided by the state when these same citizens were threatened by rabid animals, by fire, flood, or other natural or man-made disasters. French citizens, and particularly the peasant-citizens, were both supervised and organized by the gendarmes on behalf of the state, but at the same time they also accepted the state's offer of assistance and used the gendarmes on their own account. At times this acceptance went together with the use of more traditional forms of self-help or community assistance. Yet the greater integration, and the gradual decline of old sources of assistance in the shape of sorcerers and traditional infra-judicial structures, ensured that increasingly the gendarme and, through him the state, became the more usual recourses when offences that could be construed as criminal were involved.[45]

---

[45] Clive Emsley, 'The Nation-State, the Law and the Peasant in Nineteenth-Century Europe', in Xavier Rousseaux and René Lévy (eds.), *Le Pénal dans tous ses états. Justice, états et sociétés en Europe* (*XIIe–XXe siècles*) (Brussels: Publications des Facultés universitaires Saint-Louis, 1997); and see below pp. 252–4 for a more detailed discussion of these issues.

PART III
Europe: *Spreading the Model*

8
HUSSARS, BRIGANDS, AND OTHERS: POLICING RURAL EUROPE BEFORE NAPOLEON

One evening towards the end of 1786 the young Goethe, travelling in Italy, was walking from Assisi to Foligno. He recalled hearing a group of rough voices arguing behind him, and was then surrounded by a four men—two of them brandishing weapons—who asked him what he was doing. His answer bewildered them; why should someone hire a carriage, send it on ahead, and walk? Surely he was a dealer in contraband. Goethe replied that it was curious they should think him a smuggler since he had no bag and empty pockets; he offered to accompany the men back to Assisi and show his papers to the local authorities. This, he believed, satisfied them, and they set off, muttering. Shortly afterwards he was approached again by one of the four who requested a gratuity on the grounds that he had stood up for Goethe, insisting to his comrades that the traveller seemed an honest man. A tip was handed over in the shape of a few silver coins, together with an exhortation similarly to protect any other foreigner visiting Assisi. The man was delighted, urged Goethe to return, especially for the feast of St Francis, and promised that, if he so wished, an introduction could be arranged with a beautiful and respectable woman.[1] This was Goethe's introduction to the *sbirri*, the armed thugs who performed some policing functions in most seventeenth- and eighteenth-century Italian states. Only a few years earlier Charles Dupaty, a French traveller, had summed the *sbirri* up as 'privileged brigands who make war on the brigands who are not privileged.'[2]

---

[1] J. W. von Goethe, *Gedenkausgabe. Der Werke, Briefe und Gespräche*, 24 vols. (Zurich and Stuttgart: Artemis Verlag, 1962), vol. 11, *Italienische Reise*, 128–9.

[2] Quoted in Louis Madelin, *La Rome de Napoléon. La domination française à Rome de 1809 à 1814* (Paris: Plon, 1906), 67.

The heavily armed, generally ill-disciplined *sbirri* were, perhaps, the worst example of policing before the police. In the Papal States they were not functionaries of the state itself, but rather the agents of different courts. Such pay as they received was heavily dependent on fees and rewards. Many of their functions, such as the binding and shackling of captives, were generally regarded as 'vile'; and even their captains, the *bargelli*, appear at times to have sought to disassociate themselves from their subordinates. Not surprisingly, in the land of Cesare Beccaria and where Grand Duke Leopold of Tuscany, in 1786, had introduced a new and liberal Criminal Code, there were some attempts to reform and improve the *sbirri* towards the end of the eighteenth century, but little was achieved before the armies of the French Revolution arrived.[3]

It was not just in Enlightenment Italy that jurists and princes were developing new legislative structures, penal policies, and supervisory systems which involved contemplating new police institutions. Marc Raeff has described attempts in central and eastern Europe to create 'the well-ordered police state' which date back to the early seventeenth century. Police—*Policey*, *Polizei*, and other variants—in this context meant good order within a society. It was the prince's task to maintain *Gute Polizei* in the sense of correcting disorder and ensuring the prosperity of his subjects; to this end the prince, sometimes in co-operation with his Estates, published police ordinances both to ensure the preservation of morality and the established social order, and to foster economic growth.[4] Generally from the mid-eighteenth century absolutist princes, following the pattern set by Louis XIV with his *lieutenant général de police* in Paris, began to appoint their own men to supervise the police administration of their principal cities. As in Paris, the remit of these police administrators was wide, but the supervision of strangers and the repression of beggars and vagrants tended to be high on their list of priorities. The principal focus of these reforms was the situation in towns; there were some developments in the countryside, but these rarely seem

---

[3] Steven C. Hughes, 'Fear and Loathing in Bologna and Rome. The Papal Police in Perspective', *Journal of Social History*, 21 (1987), 97–116; for attempts to reform the police in Tuscany see Carlo Mangio, *La polizia toscana: Organizzzione e criteri d'intervento, 1765–1808* (Milan: Giuffrè, 1988); and for the Kingdom of Naples see Georgia Alessi, *Giustizia e Polizia. Il controllo di una capitale Napoli 1779–1803* (Naples: Jovene, 1992).

[4] Marc Raeff, *The Well-Ordered Police State: Social and Institutional Change Through Law in the Germanies and Russia 1600–1800* (New Haven, Conn.: Yale University Press, 1983); see also, *inter alia*, Roland Axtmann, ' "Police" and the Formation of the Modern State: Legal and Ideological Assumptions on State Capacity in the Austrian Lands of the Habsburg Empire, 1500–1800', *German History*, 10 (1992), 39–61.

to have made much impact on what contemporaries perceived as the problems.

Most eighteenth-century European kingdoms and principalities, much like France, had concerns about beggars and brigands. The population of the continent was growing faster than the economy; there were always tramping artisans on the roads, and every spring witnessed young men and women walking into towns hoping to be hired as labourers or maids. A cautious estimate has suggested that some 5 per cent of the population of the German lands were forced to live on the roads at the beginning of the eighteenth century.[5] Demographic pressure boosted the numbers; and the increase in numbers fed fears of brigands and highwaymen. Of course, some of those who could not find work did slip into criminality, as did soldiers returning from the continent's many wars. There were also marginal groups excluded from society because of their origins and lifestyles, such as gypsies and Jews, or because of their dishonourable trades, such as knackers, and who for a variety of reasons, even in densely populated and relatively well-developed economic regions, became involved in criminal networks.[6] Internal customs barriers, and the customs barriers between states, fostered smuggling. Contraband could be run by individuals, or by armed gangs drawn from the local peasantry, from disbanded or even serving soldiers, or from the marginal groups. The various words for 'bandit', 'brigand', and 'criminal' were employed in sloppy ways to denote all and any such offenders from the marginals to highway robbers and from vagrants to smugglers.

From the middle of the eighteenth century princes in southern Germany began to experiment with different kinds of police to suppress vagrants, beggars, and 'criminals' (*Gauner* or *Jauner*). These police were generally of two types, *Hatschiere* and hussars, though Bavaria also deployed small cavalry units to police its frontiers—*der Militärkordon*. The *Hatschiere*, generally recruited from former soldiers, were directed to patrol the roads and woods, to visit inns and remote farms looking for beggars and vagrants. The effectiveness of the *Hatschiere* varied from principality to principality. In Baden they were commonly recruited from former soldiers; moving men from the military invalid fund to the

[5] Uwe Danke, 'Bandits and the State: Robbers and the Authorities in the Holy Roman Empire in the Late Seventeenth and Early Eighteenth Centuries', in Richard J. Evans (ed.), *The German Underworld: Deviants and Outcasts in German History* (London: Routledge, 1988), 86.

[6] Florike Egmond, *Underworlds: Organised Crime in The Netherlands, 1650–1800* (Oxford: Polity Press, 1993).

paltry pay of a *Hatschier* was seen as one way of saving money in one fund, and the individual *Hatschier* could always increase his pay by collecting a bounty for each offender that he arrested. In Württemberg there is evidence that the *Hatschiere* were sometimes drawn from among the groups that they were designed to suppress. The hussar units were recruited and entrusted with similar duties, but they were fit and active soldiers. Hussars had originated in Hungary; they were light troops who specialized in scouting, skirmishing, and ambush. Those employed on policing duties were often commanded by Hungarians, since the local German gentry saw little honour or prestige in this tough, physical life. Like the French *maréchaussée*, the hussars carried patrol books; these were to be signed by local mayors when an arrest was made, and were to be inspected quarterly. As soldiers, their assistance could only be requested, never demanded by the civil authorities; and in wartime they were called back to the colours to serve with the army. More seriously, the hussars had a reputation for disorderliness and brutality; the extent to which this reputation was deserved remains an open question, but they do not appear to have acquired much trust and respect from the communities in which they served.[7]

During their unification of Spain in the second half of the fifteenth century Ferdinand and Isabella had created a tribunal responsible for the maintenance of law and order in the countryside, the Santa Hermandad. Over the two centuries that followed the executive arm of the tribunal, the Hermandades, was abolished in some provinces and died out in others. By the beginning of the eighteenth century the force had disappeared, and it was replaced piecemeal in the different provinces with a variety of military-style policing units—Guardas and later Fusileros in Aragon, Escuadras in Catalonia, Miñones in Valencia, and so on. These units were burdened with a plethora of tasks; they lacked both unified direction and adequate funding, and were generally ineffective. In May 1781 an officer of the *maréchaussée* based in Avignon wrote to the Spanish ambassador at the French court with a proposal for a French-style *maréchaussée* for Spain. Two months later he repeated his proposal, coupling it with a plan for a fire-brigade for Madrid. It was also clear that the officer was hoping for some significant position in any Spanish equivalent of the *maréchaussée* that was established. Sadly for this individual, his proposal does not appear to have received even an

---

[7] Bernd Wirsing, 'Die Geschichte der Gendarmeriekorps und deren Vorläuferorganisationen in Baden, Württemberg und Bayern, 1750–1850,' Dissertation . . . des Doktors der Philosophie, Universität Konstanz, 1991, chap. 2 *passim*.

acknowledgement from the ambassador, let alone a reply; nor is there any evidence that anyone in authority in Spain seriously considered the proposal.[8] Attempts elsewhere at creating institutions similar to the *maréchaussée* were largely arbortive. During the 1770s and 1780s Count Pergen played a central role in transforming the concept of 'police' in the Habsburg Empire from its broad meaning of general administration and the maintenance of community well-being and order. Under Pergen 'police' came increasingly to stand for an agency of prevention and protection against internal enemies, particularly political enemies. The Habsburgs already had a small institution similar to the French *maréchaussée* in their Belgian provinces; the brigades were principally concerned with policing beggars and vagrants, while a larger company, known as the Prévôté de l'Hôtel and stationed in Brussels, was available to deal with problems of public order. Towards the end of Joseph II's reign Pergen proposed the creation of a gendarmerie for the whole empire; but the proposal foundered on opposition from the military.[9]

In October 1774 Victor Amadeus III had established a special regiment of light troops to preserve the frontiers of Sardinia–Piedmont and check contraband; fifteen years later a second, similar corps was established specifically to combat brigandage commonly linked with smuggling in the hilly wooded districts of the kingdom close to its porous frontiers. The latter regiment, the Corpo Militare di Polizia, became known as the 'Carabini' after the carbines which the men carried. Little research has been done on the effectiveness of these regiments; during the 1790s they were swept up in the war against Revolutionary France, and then dissolved.[10]

Just as revolution and war shaped the French Gendarmerie, so it was to be with the similar corps that were developed across Europe in the early nineteenth century. Although Napoleon himself was to be finally defeated in 1815, the administrative modernization which he brought to his imperial territories, and to his satellites and allies, was continued and

---

[8] Enrique Martínez Ruiz, 'Las Fuerzas de Seguridad y Orden Público en la Primera Mitad del Siglo XIX', *Cuadernos de Historia*, 4 (1973), 83–161; at 84–98 and 111–20.

[9] Friedrich Walter, 'Die Organisierung der Staatlichen Polizei unter Kaiser Joseph II', *Mitteilungen des Vereins für Geschichte der Staat Wien*, 7 (1927), 22–53; at 52. For Pergen's development of the police see Paul P. Bernard, *From the Enlightenment to the Police State: The Public Life of Johann Anton Pergen* (Urbana, Ill.: University of Illinois Press, 1991).

[10] Michele Ruggiero, *Storia del Piemonte* (Turin: Piemonte in Bancarella, 1979), 768. The regiment established in 1774 is regarded by the contemporary *Guardia di Finanza* as its progenitor.

built upon. Even his most implacable continental enemies introduced some administrative changes similar to those in France, and maintained them during the Restoration. Gendarmeries were rapidly perceived as a useful instrument for a centralized state, especially in more peripheral and troublesome areas, or in regions newly acquired. They were national institutions which acted as the executive arm of a unified legal structure. They provided information, surveillance, and a first line of defence against those dangerous ideas ignited by the French Revolution and Napoleon, and not extinguished in 1815. As the century wore on, the gendarmeries were also seen as a first line of defence against the new threats of socialism and organized labour activism. In many instances the political masters of the European gendarmeries continued to be autocratic, but increasingly even those states ruled by autocratic monarchies subscribed to new ideas of law and accountability. Jurists in the German lands began to employ the term *Rechtsstaat*, describing a state based on law in which government bureaucracy was legally accountable, and within which there existed formal legal equality and legally secure property rights. As agents of the central state the gendarmes were subservient to the law and were expected to enforce it in an impartial way; and, following the image created by the commanders of Napoleon's Gendarmerie, morality, nobility, probity, and self-sacrifice commonly figured in officials descriptions of, and proclamations regarding the different corps. But aside from their similar roots, their relationship to the law, and their general military organization, the different economic, political, and social contexts of the individual states and empires helped to mould each gendarmerie variant into a unique national or imperial institution. It is these developments which the following chapters address.

9
'COMPATRIOTS AND FRIENDS': GENDARMES ACROSS THE EMPIRE

The frontiers of France expanded significantly during the revolutionary and Napoleonic period. Before the coup of *brumaire* thirteen *départements* had been added in the north, on the left bank of the Rhine and in what had been the Austrian Netherlands, while another three had been added in the east and south, together with some additional territory between the Haut-Rhin and the Doubs. More *départements* were added with the incorporation of northern Italy into France and, still later, with the addition of the Netherlands and parts of north-west Germany to the Empire. All of these territories acquired the administrative structures developed since the beginning of the Revolution in France. Thus, each *département* had its prefect and subprefects and its own company of Gendarmerie. The policing structure below the gendarmes was also the same, with *commissaires* in the larger towns, and with mayors nominating *gardes-champêtres* elsewhere, though the poverty of several *départements* in northern Italy meant that the *gardes* were not always appointed and, where they were, were few in number as sufficient money to pay them was not available in the communities.[1]

The aims of the Gendarmerie beyond the old French frontiers were the same as within France itself—to enforce and preserve the state's perception of order and tranquillity, to be the eyes and ears of the government in the countryside, and to bring in the conscripts and sometimes also the taxes. The problems were also similar to those faced within the old frontiers. The appearance of gendarmes at a village fête could be unpopular and provoke anti-French feeling directed at gendarmes as

---

[1] AN F²I 1203, Prefect of Gênes, 7 Sept. 1812, and Prefect of Appenins, 17 Sept. 1812. In 1802–3 some of the northern Italian communes were recognized as being so poor that the authorities suspended tax payments: see Michael Broers, *Napoleonic Imperialism and the Savoyard Monarchy, 1773–1821: State Building in Piedmont* (Lewiston, NY: Edwin Mellen Press, 1997), 315.

well as local francophone officals. There could also be divisions and friction with other imperial functionaries, sometimes with prefects but
especially with local mayors. Sometimes such friction seems to have
stemmed from arrogance, brutality, or corruption on the part of an individual gendarme or his brigade; and where such behaviour was proven,
the authorities were keen and quick to bring the offenders to book.
Sometimes it stemmed from clashes over jurisdiction if, for example, a
gendarme ordered an inn to close without first notifying the local *commissaire de police*. Friction also erupted over the arrest of deserters and
the pursuit of refractory conscripts. On 27 *thermidor* Year XII (15
August 1804) the brigade of Moûtiers (Mont Blanc) was attacked by a
crowd in the commune of Cellier. The local mayor backed the crowd,
arresting and imprisoning four gendarmes. The prefect responded by
suspending the mayor and imposing a garrison upon the commune until
the leaders of the disorder were given up.[2] Three years later the entire
brigade of Veilsalm (Ourthe) complained of being attacked at the Fosse
village fête by a crowd led by the mayors of three communes shouting:
'For a long time you have bound the poor conscripts, now you can see
what it's like.' The brigadier was particularly badly beaten, held prisoner until the next day, and given no aid for his injuries. While hostility to the Gendarmerie's involvement in military recruitment provided
the crowd's slogan, there appeared to be other underlying causes to the
affair involving the brigadier's participation in an altercation between
the mayor of Fosse and another individual.[3]

The hostility to conscription led to the occasional subterfuge of pursuing deserters and *réfractaires* in civilian clothes, but this probably
served often to exacerbate friction at the moment of arrest. Gendarmes
Buard and Kinsler, in disguise, sought to arrest the deserter Henry
Clerinx in his native commune in the Meuse-Inférieure in *prairial* Year
XII (June 1804). Clerinx drew a knife; a crowd gathered, armed with
various tools for weapons and led by the mayor, who declared himself
to be Clerinx's brother. The mayor personally manhandled Buard; but
somehow the two gendarmes talked him round, and even managed to
get out of the commune with their quarry.[4] Three years later Gendarme
Quinet of the Charleroi brigade killed a young man whilst in disguise in

   [2] For a general discussion of the situation in Piedmont see Broers, *Napoleonic
Imperialism*, 325–9, 382–6, and 426–32; Ernest d'Hauterive (ed.), *La Police secrète du
Premier Empire*, 5 vols. (Paris: Perrin (later Clavreuil), 1922–64), i., no. 210; and for clashes
with prefects see i., no. 269 (Lys), 521 (Mont Tonnerre), and 806 (Sarre).
   [3] AN AF^{IV} 1156, report to Emperor, 3 Aug. 1807.
   [4] Ibid. 1154, report to Emperor, 20 *prairial* Year XII.

pursuit of a refractory conscript. The incident was the cue for an argument between Moncey and the Prefect of the *département* of the Jemappes. The latter protested that the local authorities had been calling for Quinet's removal for some time on the grounds that he was *un mauvais sujet*. Moncey's response was that Quinet was a good soldier with a good record, and that the problem was the general attitude of the people around Charleroi who sheltered refractory conscripts, sought to bribe gendarmes, and made disguise necessary.[5] It was typical of Moncey that he should leap to the defence of one of his men when criticised, and especially when criticized by a civilian, even if a prefect; but of course this does not necessarily invalidate his defence.

In September 1805 a brigadier and two gendarmes in the Doire disguised themselves as deserters so as to get evidence against the *mayor* of Castelnuovo's deputy, who was suspected of protecting 'brigands'.[6] Civilian clothes were occasionally also worn to infiltrate criminal gangs and when in pursuit brigands. In northern Italy the brigands appear to have taken delight in responding in kind by committing robberies while disguised as gendarmes. When the brigade of Ponte Decimo (Gênes), pursuing a gang of brigands, had their quarry cornered they were assailed by the local populace who took the gendarmes themselves for brigands because of their disguise. The brigade was compelled to return to their residence and change into their uniforms, and by the time they returned to the spot where they had made contact with the brigands these had, of course, disappeared.[7]

As within the old frontiers of France, the word 'brigand' covered a variety of offenders. When the French armies moved into the Austrian Netherlands and the lands on the left bank of the Rhine they also moved deeper into the territory of criminal gangs and smugglers, some of whom had cross-border links into France. The disruption of war and occupation provided new opportunities for some gangs—most notably that of Johannes Bückler, who was metamorphosed into the heroic, legendary Schinderhannes—a few of which, during their raids, claimed to be French soldiers, or declared, in mitigation of their own offences, that French atrocities had launched them on their bandit careers. Again as in France, desertion and draft-dodging, particularly towards the end of the Empire, swelled the ranks of the bandit gangs. The new unity which

---

[5] d'Hauterive (ed.), *La Police secrète*, iii., no. 635. [6] Ibid. ii., no. 273.

[7] Ibid. i., no. 1449 (for an arrest in Dyle brought about by a disguised gendarme); ii., 476, 685, 1254; iii., nos. 238, 286, 392, 421, and 802; AN AF^{VI} 1156, report to Emperor, 11 June 1806.

the French *imperium* brought to the region, together with a more effective legal and police system, combined to undermine brigandage, but this was not the case with smuggling. Indeed, the economic struggle with Britain made smuggling particularly profitable, so much so in fact that even some gendarmes appear to have become involved with customs officials in its promotion rather than its prevention.[8]

Far more bandit-infested than the Low Countries or the Rhineland was the Italian peninsula. Piedmont was noted as a centre of brigandage by the military commander in the region, who was already deploying a short-lived Gendarmeria Piemontese with his troops before the incorporation of the region into France. General Wirion, who was ordered to prepare the plans for establishing the French Gendarmerie in Piedmont, began his report ominously: 'There are in Piedmont around 2,250,000 inhabitants, active, robust, and generally superstitious; the frontier position and above all the political principles of the old government of this country tended to favour rapine, killing, and murder; this people, charged with protecting the routes into Italy always have arms in their hands.' There were, Wirion confidently declared, between 800 and 900 murders a year in the region.[9]

The unification of several different northern Italian territories within France conceivably reduced the opportunities for the old smuggling gangs which had run cattle down to Genoa and brought back salt. But whatever the impact of this unification, the smugglers rapidly found themselves under pressure from the French and found that, in order to survive, they had to adopt more overt forms of criminality such as kidnapping for ransom. Particularly notorious were the bands of Guiseppe

---

[8] T. C. W. Blanning, *The French Revolution in Germany: Occupation and Resistance in the Rhineland, 1792–1802* (Clarendon Press: Oxford, 1983), 289–90 and 293–300; Richard Cobb, *Paris and its Provinces, 1792–1802* (Oxford: Oxford University Press, 1975), chap. 5; Florike Egmond, *Underworlds: Organised Crime in the Netherlands, 1650–1800* (Oxford: Polity Press, 1993), 148–51, especially for the Great Dutch Band; Norbert Finzsch, 'Räuber und Gendarme im Rheinland: Das Bandenwesen in den vier rheinischen Départements vor und während der Zeit der französischen Verwaltung (1794–1814),' *Francia*, 15 (1987), 435–71; id., *Obrigkeit und Unterschichten. Zur Geschichte der rheinischen Unterschichten gegen Ende des 18. und zu Beginn des 19. Jahrhunderts* (Stuttgart: Franz Steiner, 1990), chap. 3 for smuggling and chap. 4 for robbers. For gendarmes involved with customs officials and smuggling see d'Hauterive (ed.), *La Police secrète*, i., nos. 1345 and 1348.

[9] AG X^f 150, Gendarmerie. Italie, Piémont . . . an IX–an XII, General Legrand to minister of war, 6 *fructidor* Year IX and 27 *vendémiaire* Year X; 'Organisation de la Gendarmerie nationale . . . par le Général Wirion'. For the *Gendarmeria Piemontese*, established by the Patriot government in Turin on 1 *thermidor* Year VIII, see Broers, *Napoleonic Imperialism*, 280–3.

Antonio Mayno, 'the King of Marengo and Emperor of the Alps', based in Spinetta (Marengo), and that which followed the Scarzello and Perno brothers from Narzole (Sture), some 50 kilometres south of Turin.[10] The Narzole gang were among those who disguised themselves as gendarmes for robberies, and though less and less could they be regarded as Robin Hoods, the gang developed an arrogance and bombastic pride in their war with the gendarmes. One evening, towards the end of 1807, in the town of Airasca (Pô) some distance from the Narzole gang's home base, the mayor requested gendarmes Fabre and Labrayette, backed up by four National Guards and two *gardes-champêtres*, to investigate the papers of four well-dressed men in a local *cabaret*. On entering the *cabaret* Fabre was shot dead and Labrayette was stabbed to death, at which the guards supporting them fled. The four killers then calmly picked up a coat they had left, took Labrayette's carbine and hat, and walked out into the night firing their guns in the air and shouting: 'We're from Narzole. We're not afraid of gendarmes or you locals.' Several gendarmes were killed in Narzole itself, where the gang had the audacity to ambush a brigade twice in the town centre. At one point Narzole had thirty gendarmes quartered in it at the inhabitants' expense.[11] Further down the peninsula, and especially in Calabria and Basilicata, the French were to find brigandage even more of a problem. Bandit leaders adopted colourful names and personas: Michele Pezza became Fra Diavolo, while Antonio 'King' Correme was 'the shepherd risen to be a king'. In addition to robbery and smuggling, the activities of these men sometimes contained elements of a ferocious guerrilla resistance; prisoners were killed on both sides and cruel vengeance was exacted on men, women, and children. The brigands were sometimes supplied by the British, and were often linked to rich and powerful landowners in what were, for the French, impenetrable bonds of clientage. They were further protected by codes of honour and silence, as well as the fear of reprisal.[12]

But in addition to bringing in the conscripts and suppressing brigandage there was another role for the Gendarmerie beyond the old frontiers of France. Many French administrators considered themselves to be bringing the values and virtues of their civilization, now augmented

---

[10] Michele Ruggiero, *Briganti di Piemonte Napoleonico* (Turin: Le Bouquiniste, 1968), chap. 6 *passim*, and Broers, *Napoleonic Imperialism*, 334–49.

[11] AN AF[IV] 1156, report to Emperor, 9 Jan. 1808. See also d'Hauterive (ed.), *La Police secrète*, ii., nos. 968, 1005, 1476, and 1525.

[12] John A. Davis, *Conflict and Control: Law and Order in Nineteenth-Century Italy* (London: Macmillan, 1988), 71–84.

by the revolutionary and Napoleonic reforms, to other peoples.[13] Gendarmes were seen as being at the forefront of this and able to demonstrate to the conquered the advantages of being French and/or living under French rule. When the Gendarmerie were appointed for the new Belgian *départements* in *frimaire* Year IV (November/December 1795), it was expected that 'if this corps gives an example of morality, of strict discipline and pure patriotism, it will win over hearts; surrounded by public confidence, it will thus Frenchify the new *départements*'.[14] Moncey may not have shared the missionary zeal of the most ardent reformers and administrators of the revolutionary and Napoleonic years, yet he too appears to have considered that the Gendarmerie could play a role in demonstrating the superiority of things French, and of being French. 'Comrades,' he declared in an order of 5 *frimaire* Year XI (26 November 1802), addressed to the men appointed as gendarmes in the '*ci-devant* Piedmont':

From this moment the territory in which the repression of offences is now in your charge has become an integral part of France. You should see only compatriots and friends among the peaceful citizens there.

Secure and consolidate, by your good conduct, the work of Justice. Work to win the hearts and respect of the public when the factious and agitators stir up the means to do harm.

The Gendarmerie of other parts of the Republic is worthy of being your model.

Everywhere its presence is the sign of peace, the guarantee of tranquillity. Learn to merit the same respect.

Show to a people, now French, what a good Gendarmerie is. Prove that it has no other guide but the law, no other passion but public order, and the respect, the confidence that will surround you, will double your authority, even imposing it upon the malevolent, and will be the sweet reward for which you have worked.[15]

Within the new *départements* this bringing of French cultural forms, and the Gendarmerie's role in this, could be popular, particularly when it concerned equality before the law and a general attack on unpopular elements of the *ancien régime*. But in Italy it was resented when it meant

[13] Stuart Woolf, 'French Civilization and Ethnicity in the Napoleonic Empire', *Past and Present*, 124 (1989), 96–120; esp. pp. 105–6.

[14] Quoted in Sylvie Humbert-Convain, 'Le Juge de Paix et la Répression des Infractions Douanières en Flandre et en Hollande, 1794–1815: Contribution à l'histoire du système continental Napoléonien', Doctorat, Erasmus University, Rotterdam, 1993, p. 51.

[15] *Ordres généraux*, Supplément à l'Ordre général du 5 *frimaire* an XI, specialement adressé aux Brigades de la Gendarmerie placées dans le ci-devant Piémont.

the imposition of the Concordat on a population which was still bound to a baroque Catholicism. Gendarmes arrested those clergy who refused to take the oath of loyalty to the regime, and arrested them even on the steps of their altars. They also ensured that regulations banning particular feast days and processions were enforced. A fitting climax to this role came when the order for the apprehension and exile of Pius VII in July 1809 was entrusted to General Radet; and possibly what exacerbated the way in which the Concordat was initially enforced was that many of the first recruits into the Gendarmerie in Piedmont were drawn from the Army of Italy, a force noted for its unreconstructed Jacobinism.[16]

There were usually attempts to fill the Gendarmerie companies established in the new *départements* with a mixture of Frenchmen, both experienced gendarmes and soldiers from the line regiments, and local men who spoke the local language. The first Belgian companies were expected to draw two-thirds of their officers and NCOs from the French Gendarmerie; the remainder was to be composed of two-thirds French soldiers, mainly drawn from the cavalry regiments of the armies of the Nord and the Sambre and Meuse, and one-third Belgians. A council of five officers examined the applications from the former, while the latter were selected from lists prepared by local administrators.[17] When the brigades for the four *départements* on the left bank of the Rhine were set up early in 1799, the applicants were selected by an examining commission presided over by Wirion. The men seeking to be considered for the rank of *maréchal des logis* were even required to take down a brief piece of dictation and respond to questions about the role of an NCO in the Gendarmerie. The questions asked of Louis Dufour, a 33-year-old cavalryman, and his responses are set out below. If nothing else, these show that Dufour had absorbed the rhetoric of command and of the gendarme's tasks; and he was immediately promoted to *brigadier* in Mont Tonerre.

'What means would you employ to establish order and the necessary activity in the brigade which is entrusted to you?'

[16] Michael Broers, 'The Police and the Padroni: Italian Notabili, French Gendarmes and the Origins of the Centralized State in Napoleonic Italy', *European History Quarterly*, 26 (1996), 331–53; at 345–6; Étienne Amadée Combier (ed.), *Mémoires du général Radet, d'après ses papiers personnels et les archives de l'état* (Saint-Cloud: Belin Frères, 1892), 169–250 and 532–57.

[17] AN F7 320 (Dossier 4); Humber-Convain, 'Le Juge de Paix', 51.

'I would impress on subordinates the duties that they are to fulfill and the obligations of their position: show firmness and punish subordinates who deviate from their duties and so on, make reports as required by superiors.'

'Give, succinctly, an analysis of the duties of a brigade commander, the knowledge that he requires, and at what point public considerations influence the success of his operations.'

'He must be well behaved, of good morality and intelligent, and know all the laws relating to his position so as to be able to instruct his subordinates and direct the steps which they must take in different operations.

It is equally indispensible to collect intelligence and precise information on public attitudes in the *arrondissement* where he is stationed and to observe their progress. He and the men of his brigade, must behave in an irreproachable manner and do their duty as men of honour to merit the confidence of the public and to assure the success of the important work with which they are entrusted.'

The surviving records of this examining commission concentrate on the Roër Company. They show (see Table 9.1) that the overwhelming majority of the initial recruits were native Frenchmen, mainly from *départements* in the north-east which were, at the same time, those closest to the new territories and those which, under the *ancient régime*, were noted for providing the majority of recruits to the French army. Men like Antoine Bour and Dominique Duviné, both born in the Meurthe, were noted for their ability to use both the French and German languages; Bour, 'a good soldier, smartly turned out, very intelligent', was immediately promoted brigadier. So too was Sigismund Grabler, whose father had been a captain in a German regiment in French service. Grabler himself, 26 years old, born in Bonn (Rhin-et-Moselle), had been

TABLE 9.1. Départemental *origins of men appointed to the Roër Company*, *February 1799*

Number of men each	Départements
5	Meurthe, Haut-Rhin
4	Seine
3	Calvados, Côte d'Or, Eure, Marne, Moselle
2	Aisne, Ardennes, Jura, Meuse, Nord, Oise, Rhin-et-Moselle, Seine-et-Oise, Somme
1	Hautes-Alpes, Charente-Inférieure, Corrèze, Doubs, Dyle, Gard, Haute-Garonne, Indre-et-Loire, Lot, Haute-Marne, Nièvre, Pas-de-Calais, Bas-Rhin, Rhône-et-Loire, Saône-et-Loire, Haute-Saône, Seine-et-Marne, Switzerland, Tarn, Vosges

Source: AG X^f 23, Gendarmerie: dans la Moselle et le Rhin, 1798–1799.

a sub-lieutenant in the service of the elector of Cologne and subsequently in the Homprech Hussars.[18] Grabler was slightly younger than most of the recruits; the youngest was only 23, the eldest 46, but the overwhelming majority (forty-eight out of sixty-seven) were aged between 26 and 33.

Details of the Roër company collected fifteen years later, some four months after Napoleon's first abdication, are indicative of how the composition of the company had become much like those within the old frontiers of France. Just under a quarter of the men on the roll were natives of the *département*; more than half of the remainder came from the north-east of France, and only five came from neighbouring Belgian and Rhenish *départements* (see Table 9.2). Overall thirty-eight *départements* of the old France were represented in the ranks. The details show how the company had been depleted by war and by other demands: five men were listed as dead, five more were presumed prisoners of war, three had been seconded to the Paris Gendarmerie, six to the elite companies, and fifteen were serving with the armies. The remainder of those

TABLE 9.2. Départemental *origins of men on the roll of the Roër Company, August 1814*

Number of men each	Département
38	Roër
12	Moselle
11	Aisne
8	Bas-Rhin
7	Meurthe
6	Ardennes, Meuse
5	Doubs, Marne
4	Jura, Haut-Rhin
3	Nord, Pas-de-Calais, Seine, Seine-Inférieure, Seine-et-Marne, Somme
2	Calvados, Eure, Manche, Meuse-Inférieure, Nièvre, Orne, Ourthe, Rhône, Haute-Saône, Saône-et-Loire
1	Ain, Ariège, Aube, Aveyron, Bavaria, Cantal, Corrèze, Côte-d'Or, Dordogne, Hérault, Isère, Jemappes, Léman, Loir-et-Cher, Oise, Poland, Rhin-et-Moselle, Seine-et-Oise, Sture, Yonne
4	Unknown

Source: AG X^f 133, Gendarmerie: Pô à Deux Sèvres, 1813–1814.

[18] AG X^f 23, Gendarmerie: dans la Moselle et le Rhin, 1798–99.

fit enough to be kept in service were to be sent to the companies of the Moselle (three men), the Vendée (thirty-four men), and the Yonne (twenty-four men). The details also suggest how the men born in the Roër were facing up to Napoleon's defeat and their own future. Of the thirty-eight men born in the Roër, no fewer than twenty-seven were listed as 'presumed deserters'. No doubt these men had reasoned that it was sensible to leave the service, preferring to stay in their *Heimat* rather than to trust to an uncertain future in France.[19]

Different ratios of Frenchmen to indigenous gendarmes were announced as new companies were formed. The proposed small force that was planned to function in Austria following the battle of Austerlitz was to have fifty-one Frenchmen and 240 Germans.[20] The brigades of the companies announced in February 1811 for the new north German *départements* of the Ems-Supérieur, Bouches-du-Weser, and Bouches-de-l'Elbe were to be composed of two experienced gendarmes, three soldiers from the line, and one *indigène*, if they were mounted, and of one experienced gendarme, four infantrymen, and one *indigène*, if they were not. The experienced gendarmes were to be drawn from the men on detachment to the headquarters of the Army of Germany, as they were expected to have some knowledge of the country. In the strategically important Swiss *département* of the Simplon, annexed in December 1810, the brigades were to be composed of three veteran gendarmes, two soldiers of the line, and one native of the region. The new Gendarmerie for the Netherlands, however, established at roughly the same time, was to be half French and half Dutch. But this decision took little account of the way in which the army of the Kingdom of Holland had developed. Under Napoleon's brother Louis conscription had been rejected in favour of the tradition of a small army largely dependent upon foreign, especially German, mercenaries. In April 1811 the Gendarmerie companies for Holland lacked 181 men of their quota of 740; the problem was diagnosed as the lack of Dutchmen with 'the necessary aptitude'.[21] Fresh from organizing the companies in North Germany, Radet was dispatched to the Netherlands. He recalled:

---

[19] AG X^f 23, Gendarmerie: dans la Moselle et le Rhin, 1798–99 133, Gendarmerie: Pô à Deux Sèvres, 1813–14.

[20] Franz Neubauer, *Die Gendarmerie in Österreich, 1849–1924* (Vienna: Gendarmerie-Jubiläumsfonds, 1925), 536.

[21] AN AF^IV 1157, letter and papers concerning the creation of Gendarmerie legions for Holland and north Germany, Feb. 1811; reports to Emperor, 1 and 10 Apr. 1811. For the Dutch army under Louis see Owen Connelly, *Napoleon's Satellite Kingdoms* (New York: The Free Press, 1965), 185–7.

I looked at things in detail and at the men one by one. I dismissed three-quarters of those recruited, replacing them with men chosen from the line who I combined with a strong nucleus of old and trusted gendarmes requested by me and sent from the Belgian *départements*. The initial organization being defective, and the Dutch who had been recruited being poorly disciplined, had a disastrous impact on the corps which I could only correct with time and a sustained drive.[22]

General Wirion considered 1,400 men to be the absolute minimum for the Piedmontese Gendarmerie. The minister of war proposed only half that number. A compromise was set at 1,000 men, though in the early years at least the numbers did not rise above 760. Based on his experience and practice in Belgium, Wirion wanted the corps to be one-third Pietmontese and two-thirds French. The Frenchmen were to be drawn from the Army of Italy. On 22 *prairial* Year X (13 June 1802) a letter was prepared by the ministry of war to the commanders of the demi-brigades serving in Italy specifying the quota of men to be furnished from their respective commands. The men were to be at least 25 years old, 5 feet 4 inches in height, literate, and of irreproachable conduct; preference was to be given to NCOs. While they did not put their thoughts on paper, it seems reasonable to suppose that the commanders of these units were not keen to lose what would have been many of their best men in this way. A report from Gendarmerie headquarters the following *fructidor* (August/September) lamented that only 228 of the 491 infantry and eighty of the 177 cavalry required under the quotas had arrived in Turin; it declared that reminder letters were being dispatched to the recalcitrant units. Subsequent letters from the demi-brigade commanders outlined the problems faced in finding the quotas after years of campaigning. The commander of the 104th Line protested that, while his quota was eleven, he could only spare five men, 'the demi-brigade having been almost entirely destroyed . . . and rebuilt in Year IX and Year X'. The 72nd also had a quota of eleven. It had even sent this number, but when seven of the men were rejected as unsuitable, the commander complained that he could not make a new selection 'because our resources of men are very limited, those who have the height, the necessary service and standards, lack the other qualities, and those who know how to read and write, lack the height, the age, or the necessary service'.[23] The Piedmontese brigades eventually appear to have had a

[22] Combier (ed.), *Mémoires du général Radet*, 255.
[23] AG X^f 150, Gendarmerie. Italie, Piémont . . . an IX–an XII, and Broers, *Napoleonic Imperialism*, 289–93.

significant percentage of local men in them. There are, unfortunately, no muster rolls for the companies. The surviving lists of officers for the years 1805 to 1806 suggest a possible ratio, in some *départements*, of about three Frenchmen to one Italian—these Italian officers had begun their military service in the Sardinian army. Yet in the *département* of the Pô all the officers were French.[24]

Officers appointed to Gendarmerie companies outside of the old French frontiers were mainly men who owed their advancement to the Revolution, to the wars, and hence to the Napoleonic state. Their position gave them a commitment to, and a stake in, that state. Henry Serre, for example, a lieutenant in the Sture company, was born in Nîmes in 1758, had served in the infantry from 1775 to 1784, and joined the Gendarmerie in his native *département* of the Gard in October 1791, rising to brigadier the following July and lieutenant the following November. He was purged in *vendémiaire* Year VI, but brought back into service in *floréal* Year X. In September 1812 *maréchal des logis* Bouzier, serving in the Haute-Marne, was appointed to a lieutenancy in Montenotte; born in 1756 in the Haute-Marne, he had served as a dragoon from 1778 to 1786, and joined the Gendarmerie in 1792. The officers born in the new *départements* of the Empire similarly had a stake in the Napoleonic regime. These were men like Gabriel Costamagua, born in Bené (Sture) in 1772, who began his military career in 1773 as dragoon in the Sardinian army, and served with the French from the Year VII to the Year IX, suffering wounds which left his right hand crippled; he transferred from a lieutenancy in his native *département* to one in that of the Appenins in *vendémiaire* Year XIV. Camille Borgia, who, aged 36, became captain of the Tibre company in September 1810, began his military career serving on the ships of the Knights of Malta, and had subsequently served in the armies of the Pope and the Habsburgs before entering the French army in the Year VII. He had also acted as a police official for Fouché in the old Papal States. Captain Emmerich, who took command of the company in the Issel-Supérieur in September 1812, had been born in Brussels in 1774 and had begun his military career by enlisting in the Belgian Chasseurs in July 1792.[25]

Whether the ordinary gendarmes drafted to companies in distant parts of the Empire were as keen to go as the men who moved because of

[24] AG X^f 134, Gendarmerie. Somme à Zyderzee, registers for the Tanaro and the Sture; 133, Gendarmerie. Pô à Deux Sèvres, register for the Pô.

[25] Ibid. 134, Gendarmerie: Somme à Zyderzee, register for the Sture; AN AF^{IV} 1157, papers concerning Captain Camille Borgia, 1811; 1158, reports to Emperor, 16 July 1812 and 30 Sept. 1812.

promotion must remain an open question. Moving a man from one brigade to another was, after all, often the common supplementary punishment for a gendarme convicted of an offence. The same question might be posed with reference to men drafted from the army; a posting to a distant part of the Empire was not like returning to their *pays natal* as a gendarme. On at least one occasion a large number of men refused such a draft. When the 283 survivors of the Dromedary Regiment disembarked from Egypt at Marseilles and found themselves destined for drafting into Gendarmerie companies, 113 of them stood out for an absolute discharge. They were threatened with posting to infantry regiments and eventually agreed to join the Gendarmerie, but apparently as the lesser of two evils.[26] While a camaraderie probably did develop within most of the brigades, such a brigade, often under strength, could not provide the wider community of an infantry company or cavalry squadron. Moreover, the men must have felt very isolated within those rural communities, which were at best indifferent and at worst downright hostile. In September 1806 Simon Bachelet, a corporal of grenadiers, was among a group of soldiers seconded to the Gendarmerie companies then being established in the imperial satellite Kingdom of Naples. After six years he had had enough, and requested to be allowed to return to army service.[27]

It may have been that Bachelet disliked the region to which he had been posted, rather than the duties of a gendarme. But that said, gendarmerie duties in the Kingdom of Naples were rather different from the usual, with the sickening violence of the brigandage problem, as well as the threats of landings by British troops or by British-sponsored guerrillas from Sicily. This meant that gendarmes were less likely to be settled in small barracks than working in mobile columns alongside other military units. Just north of the Neapolitan kingdom, in the *départements* of the Tibre and the Transimène, matters were much the same, particularly when, in the spring of 1810, a few months after annexation, the inhabitants found that the benefits of French civilization meant conscription. Brigand bands were swollen by refractory conscripts and deserters; and French religious policy led to priests backing the brigands. In May 1811 the Director of General Police in Rome lamented that 'the brigands were masters of the mountains'—and the mountains covered three-quarters of the Roman *départements*.[28] If the mountains

---

[26] AN AF^IV 1154, report to First Consul, 11 *floréal* Year X.

[27] Ibid. 1158, report to Emperor, 23 Sept. 1812.

[28] Louis Madelin, *La Rome de Napoléon. La domination française à Rome de 1809 à 1814* (Paris: Plon, 1906), 458.

were full of brigands, the plains of the region were notorious for their 'pestilential fevers', which the commander of the 30th Legion of Gendarmerie estimated to be losing him twelve to fifteen men a year. This legion, established by General Radet in 1810, drew roughly a third of its strength from local men, and herein lay a further problem. In March 1813 the legion commander complained that the Romans either had little idea of the requirements of military service, or else were so debauched as to be useless. He considered that at least thirty of his command should be dismissed as being too much like the old Papal police, the *sbirri*, and thus generally loathed by the population.[29]

Equally grim Gendarmerie postings were to Spain or to the Illyrian provinces. In Spain the Gendarmerie, which followed the army into the country in 1809 and which was organized into six distinct legions two years later, was composed of men drafted from French companies. Throughout their existence these legions were embroiled in the ferocious war against the Spanish guerrillas. Here too prisoners were killed and atrocities were committed on both sides. Gendarmes in Spain lived in heavily fortified barracks, and their duties were commonly restricted to actions in conjuction with the army proper or to large patrols on the main roads.[30] The Illyrian Provinces did not have the same dangers as Spain, but their situation made them a bleak posting. The provinces had been put together largely from lands ceded by the Austrians in the aftermath of their defeat in 1809. They had an enormous land frontier to the north and east, prone to incursions from neighbours technically under the authority of the Ottoman empire, and a long sea coast easily raided and easily penetrated by those smuggling British goods. The loyalty of the population was uncertain, banditry was rife, and in some districts the local inhabitants considered weaponry to be a part of their daily dress. This was the very edge of civilized Europe as the French understood it, and the Illyrian provinces were never fully assimilated into the French system of government. Nevertheless, one of the first acts of the French adminstration, early in 1810, was the creation of a Gendarmerie legion of some 420 men divided into four companies. The army and the Gendarmerie were each to send a draft of 164 men; the remainder of

---

[29] AG X^f 133, Gendarmerie: Pô à Deux Sèvres, Rapport pour être joint à la revue passée par Monsr. le colonel commandant le 30e Légion de Gendarmerie, dans le mois de mars 1813.

[30] Henry Lachouque, '1789–1815. Du début de la Révolution à la chute de l'Empire', *Revue Historique de l'Armée*, 17 (1961), 82–118: at 104–9; AG X^f 248, Gendarmerie, Divers, contains a large number of death certificates of gendarmes killed in Spain, noting their origins, their company posting in France, and how they met their death.

the legion was to be made up of local inhabitants. By the following February the legion had been increased to 607 men, with a mere eighty-four of them locals, but it was hard to make up the numbers. Marshal Marmont, who shared responsibility for the provinces' administration, proposed recruiting men from the regiments in Illyria as a 'recompense for old soldiers'; though it is difficult to see why the men would regard this as a 'recompense'. Twenty-nine of the men sent from the Army of Italy were so poorly behaved that they were ordered to be replaced, and there is some evidence that the Legion was seen as a dumping ground for soldiers with fitness or discipline problems.[31]

In most of Napoleon's satellite kingdoms, in contrast, the French system was much more fully established than in Illyria. The Kingdom of Italy, for example, supervised by Napoleon's stepson Eugène de Beauharnais as viceroy, had twenty-four *dipartimenti*, each supervised by a *prefetto*, and each with its own company of Gendarmerie. The latter were based closely on the French model, though the plans for cross-fertilization between the French and Italian corps never got off the ground. Napoleon himself had urged an exchange of gendarmes between Italy and France; the former would receive on-the-job experience in French *départements*, the French gendarmes, on the other hand, could train the Italian brigades to which they were posted. An alternative proposal was to have had the Italian corps trained by 160 gendarmes of all ranks seconded from France for two years. At the top of the Italian Gendarmerie was an *ispettore generale*, Pietro Polfranceschi, responsible to the minister of war. The recruits were to be former soldiers, literate, between 25 and 35 years of age, and with a good conduct record. As well as being organized like its French counterpart, the Italian corps suffered similar difficulties; it was, for example, commonly under strength. The initial establishment, in February 1801, was 1,326 men and in 1804 this was increased to 1,941. Two years later, insisting that he really needed 2,700 men, Polfranceschi complained that there were only 1,517; and in 1808 the numbers had fallen to just 1,400. But there were other

---

[31] Frank J. Bundy, *The Administration of the Illyrian Provinces of the French Empire, 1809–1813* (New York: Garland, 1987), 96 and 493–4, nn. 46–9; AN AF[IV] 1157, report to Emperor, 10 Apr. 1811. There are details of the first officers appointed to the Illyrian Gendarmerie in report to Emperor, 20 July 1810. Of 14 lieutenants, 8 were *maréchaux des logis* serving in Piedmont but who, from the look of their names, were born as French; the remainder were serving in France (2 from the Rhône and the Seine), other new *départements* (2 from Forêts and the Lemone) or in the army (2). The 4 captains came respectively from the Gendarmerie in Piedmont (Marengo) and in Corsica (Golo), one was the commander of the Gendarmes with the army in Illyria, and one, 'Mr Petrowitch', was a native of the region recommended by Marmont.

problems in addition to a lack of numbers, and when the ubiquitous Radet was brought in during the summer of 1805 to make an assessment of the corps, he reported it to be poorly armed and overburdened with paperwork. Radet considered that the NCOs and men had potential, but that there were too many mediocre officers who lacked the appropriate military background and who were easily intimidated by critical local opinion. Moreover, local opinion either could not disassociate the new gendarmes from the corrupt thugs of the old *sbirri* or, in the case of the notables, they disliked the new gendarmes because they were not their creatures like the old *sbirri*. In an exhortation to company commanders Radet urged them to remember the importance of their 'honorable mission', and the necessity of 'moderation, perseverance, mildness, and strict proprieties' in establishing and winning allegiance to new institutions.[32]

Again like its French counterpart, the Gendarmerie of the Kingdom of Italy found its time dominated by the enforcement of conscription legislation. This was no easy task in a kingdom where brigandage was rife and where draft-dodgers and deserters easily slipped into the bandit gangs or formed gangs of their own; where the local officials were generally as lukewarm to the state's military demands as those in the more remote regions of France; and where communal hostility could flare into serious disorder, as was most notable in the insurrection which began in the *département* of Reno towards the end of June 1809 and which, in the course of a month, affected two-thirds of the kingdom's *départements*.

Yet in spite of some gendarmes being less than eager about their postings, of some men behaving brutally and arbitrarily, and of brigades being under strength, the Gendarmerie was perceived as a success. In the Year IV, at the beginning of France's expansion beyond her old frontiers, new functionaries in the Belgian *départements* were desperate for their Gendarmerie companies. Not only were they concerned about

---

[32] Alexander Grab, 'State Power, Brigandage and Rural Resistance in Napoleonic Italy', *European History Quarterly*, 25 (1995), 39–70 (esp. 50–1 for the Gendarmerie); id., 'Army, State and Society: Conscription and Desertion in Napoleonic Italy (1802–1814)', *Journal of Modern History*, 67 (1995), 25–54 (esp. 44–5 for the Gendarmerie); Combier (ed.), *Mémoires du général Radet*, 154–9 and 509–23, quotation at 520. For the training plans see C. A. G. Duchesne de Gillevoisin, Duc de Conegliano, *Le Maréchal Moncey: Duc de Conegliano, 1754–1842* (Paris: Calmann Lévy, 1902), 347–9, and AN AF^{IV} 1155, n.d. [Year XIII] 'Projet d'instruction et de réorganisation de la Gendarmerie du Royaume d'Italie.' The 160 men were to be composed of 1 general, 4 *chefs d'escadron*, 4 captains, 7 lieutenants, 15 *maréchaux des logis*, 28 brigadiers, and 101 gendarmes. The other demands and pressures on the Imperial Gendarmerie appear to have led to the plan being shelved.

robberies, assaults, and killings, and about a general lack of respect for persons and property, but there seemed also to be 'a great number of layabouts who ally themselves with Austrian deserters and other partisans of the infamous House of Austria, continually conspiring and using bribery to hinder our government'.[33] Initially the companies were as feeble as those in France under the Directory; even so, they began to make an impact and some demonstrated a notable courage and zeal in dealing with large gangs of offenders.[34] Once they were more comfortably established, and particularly given the reforms of the Consulate and Empire, even disgraceful behaviour by individual gendarmes or whole brigades did not lead to calls for their removal. In 1803 two brigades of gendarmes clashed with the authorities of the small commune of Villanova (Pô) after three of their number had been arrested for allegedly assaulting the mayor's daughter. The authorities in Paris proposed relocating the local brigade, but the local council opposed this, insisting that they wanted to keep their brigade and that they would be satisfied with the removal of the most culpable men; in the event the mayor settled for the removal of the local brigadier.[35] There was a determination that the gendarmes should appear to represent a moral, non-partisan order in which individuals were equal before the law. Men accused of arbitrary behaviour were suspended from duty and investigated, even when the evidence against them appeared to come from partial sources linked with, or at least sympathetic to, criminal gangs and/or smugglers.[36]

Aggressive or high-handed behaviour on the part of gendarmes across the Empire could stem from a variety of causes. In some instances, notably in the Illyrian provinces and enforcing the Concordat in Italy, gendarmes probably disparaged the locals as ignorant and supersititious. Invariably they must have felt isolated amongst populations hostile to conscription and sympathetic to deserters. There was also the possibility of men failing fully to comprehend their half-military, half-civilian functions and precisely where authority was situated; this latter was compounded by Moncey's desire for the complete independence of his command, and his constant assurances to his men that they were a special elite. Early in 1805 Lieutenant Rapin assembled several brigades in Brussels to go in pursuit of gangs of robbers. Moncey, already under

---

[33] AN F⁷ 3065, folders of Dyle and Escault.
[34] Cobb, *Paris and its Provinces*, 159, 174, and 258.
[35] Broers, *Napoleonic Imperialism*, 426–7 and 430.
[36] Finzsch, 'Räuber und Gendarme im Rheinland', 447–8.

fire from Napoleon over his moves towards independence, was informed bluntly that no officer of Gendarmerie should ever behave as Rapin had done.

It is extraordinary than a simple lieutenant should disorganize the service of a *département*, and bring together fifty gendarmes in a single place, without the authority of the prefect. If the Gendarmerie was thus to have an administrative independence from the civil authority which has responsibility for policing, it would not be advantageous, but harmful to the state. The general commanding the [military] division has complained of having forbidden Lieutenant Rapin, on several occasions, from making these useless shows in the affair of these robbers, and in ordering these fifty gendarmes to mount up in this instance, this officer has persisted in making useless patrols. It is equally astonishing that he had left Brussels without the prefect's order.[37]

The Gendarmerie functioned at the centre of the imperial police machine. When, as National Guards or *gardes-champêtres*, local men were deployed against bandits, smugglers, deserters, or even against landings by enemy troops or seamen, the gendarmes were there to stiffen their resolve. But more usually the gendarmes acted on their own against such offenders, and as the principal coercive force available to the senior civilian administrators charged with policing duties. The crucial moves against Piedmontese brigandage had been made in a period of peace, 1802–3, when troops could be deployed alongside gendarmes with the maximum effect. Significantly, unlike the temporary expedients of the *ancien régimes* against bandits and smugglers, the gendarmes were not recalled after a brief campaign, but remained, permanently established in their small barracks in the countryside, maintaining regular patrols, promising and providing assistance to those who might call for it, and fostering among the indigenous elite an appreciation of a centralized and permanent monopoly of violence. The case is at least arguable that brigandage survived in the south of Italy, and particularly in the Kingdom of Naples, because here the French occupation was of a shorter duration and always much less secure. Rather than being permanently settled in small barracks, the Gendarmerie in the *Mezzogiorno* was generally deployed in numbers alongside the army making periodic sweeps against offenders; it had little opportunity to win the hearts and minds of the local population to the new regime, or to convince local landowners and notables of its utility.

---

[37] *Cor. Nap.*, vol. 10, no. 8,507, to Moncey, 10 *germinal* Year XIII (31 Mar. 1805).

10

'FOR THE GREATER HAPPINESS OF THE STATE': GENDARMES BEYOND THE EMPIRE

In territories both incorporated into and external to the Napoleonic Empire French models of government had a significant impact before and after the Congress of Vienna. Napoleon profoundly influenced the Italian peninsula and the German lands. In the former, where his personal writ ran in many territories, his boundary changes were ephemeral; in Germany his restructuring of states and redrawing of boundaries lasted much longer. A few rulers in both of these geographical entities rejected French models of government and administration simply because they were French, tarred with the brush of revolution and its aggressive imperial offspring. But rather more saw elements in these models which they could shape to their own advantage and use to strengthen the kind of state which they sought to develop. There were enlightened, reforming princes and ministers seeking to centralize and rationalize their systems of government and justice well before the French Revolution, and across the German lands the old notions of *Herrschaft* were under siege.[1] Napoleon's changes generally propelled such reforms forward, possibly faster. New legal structures drew on the Napoleonic Codes, and new institutions for administering the provinces, for enforcing laws, and pursuing offenders looked to what appeared to

---

[1] *Herrschaft* was a concept which located a variety of economic, political, and social powers and privileges within an individual *Herr*. There was no distinction here between 'public' and 'private' spheres of life. These powers and privileges were not acquired from, or granted by any higher authority; they were possessed by an individual as a result of his position, whether it be as a prince or simply as the head of a household. Against this, reformers were seeking to introduce ideas of centralized state administration employing a responsible, hierarchical bureaucracy, economic freedom, and social mobility. For a good introductory discussion see James L. Sheehan, *German History, 1770–1866* (Oxford: Oxford University Press, 1989), 24–41.

be successful French experience and example. But it was never possible, and indeed no monarch or reforming minister ever sought, simply to impose a French model regardless of regional context and traditions.

The larger southern German states of Baden, Bavaria, and Württemberg had all been receptive to Enlightenment ideas and were experiencing varying degrees of change imposed from the top down under enlightened princes and ministers before the French Revolution. Napoleon's reorganization of the Rhineland in 1803 considerably enlarged each of these three states. Of course the rulers seized the opportunity for aggrandizement, but this was often a mixed blessing. Each of these states had debts, and they inherited new ones with their new territories. Participation in Napoleon's wars increased the debts, but fiscal modernization, which was introduced as part of the Napoleonic-style reforms, increasingly separated the prince's purse from the state's treasury. This provided a firmer basis for the latter and, potentially, a more stable reservoir of money to be spent on the military and, where desired, on military policemen. The new populations which these states acquired under Napoleon sometimes had different religious affiliations and different social structures. Charles Frederick of Baden had already experienced, and had largely resolved, this problem when he had unified his Protestant Margravate of Baden with the Catholic principality of Baden-Baden in 1771, but this was a new kind of difficulty for Frederick of Württemberg, as was his acquisition of lands controlled by great nobles as opposed to the essentially town-based elites resting on a subordinate peasant agriculture which predominated in his old territories. The rulers of the expanded states had to grapple with the tasks of protecting the integrity of their new frontiers and constructing some kind of political identity, and broad political considerations were not helped by the fear that internal disorder could be provoked by robbers and vagrants, who were, as ever, indistinguishable in the administrative mind, and who, it was believed, were being forced on to the right bank of the Rhine by new, efficient policing and courts on the French side. Such fears were periodically aggravated by the soldiers discharged from the armies of the southern German states themselves, and by the occasional passage of troops on the march for the next stage of the Napoleonic adventure—such troops were not always well disciplined, while in their wake came the inevitable deserters and stragglers. During the war years Baden, Bavaria, and Württemberg all experimented with reformed policing systems, and all gradually worked towards the creation of gendarmeries modified to their own traditions and developing government structures.[2]

From May 1809 the government of the Grand Duchy of Baden was dominated by the forceful Sigismund von Reitzenstein, who rapidly reorganized the regional administration on a pattern similar to the French *départements*. However, probably because of financial constraints, there was little significant or long-lasting change during the Napoleonic and Restoration periods. In 1812 a new force of some 200 men was created, according to a contemporary report 'in the style of a gendarmerie' ('in der Art einer Gensd'armerie').[3] In reality, the force bore only a passing relationship to most gendarmeries of the period. It had supervisory responsibilities for customs and taxation as well as for the pursuit of vagrants, robbers, and petty offenders. The men had to make patrols and have their patrol books signed by mayors or other local functionaries; they were drawn increasingly from the army, but they were not subject to any military organization or discipline. Moreover, until the mid-1820s they fell under the direction of two civilian ministries, those of finance and the interior, with all the opportunities which such a division provided for friction. Nor, when it came in 1826, did the separation of fiscal and policing duties solve all of the problems; the senior officers of the men who retained responsibility for policing tasks complained regularly that, old soldiers or not, their men were often drunk on duty, took bribes, were too frail, or were just generally unsuitable. From time to time the idea of creating a fully fledged Gendarmerie on the French model was discussed, and then shelved. In 1823, for example, the fear that existing law-enforcement agencies were incapable of dealing with a perceived increase in robberies and assaults prompted serious debate. But it was not until September 1829 that a firm proposal originated from the minister of justice and led to the promulgation of the Gendarmerie Edict on 3 October. The spurs to action appear to have been, first, anxiety about vagrants, particularly large numbers crossing from Switzerland, and second, a conviction that other states which had developed gendarmeries were coping better with the problem of

---

[2] The following discussion draws heavily on Bernd Wirsing, 'Die Geschichte der Gendarmeriekorps und deren Vorläuferorganisationen in Baden, Württemberg und Bayern, 1750–1850', Dissertation . . . des Doktors Philosophie, Universität Konstanz, 1991, chaps. 3 and 4. See also Walter Wannenwetsch, *Das Württembergische Landjägerkorps und die reichseinheitliche Gendarmerie in Württemberg mit einer Rückschau auf die Anfänge der Landespolizei* (Stuttgart: Gewerkschaft der Polizei, 1986), 13–22.

[3] Quoted by Wirsing, 'Die Geschichte der Gendarmeriekorps', 67.

vagrancy and were pushing their undesirables into Baden, which lacked an effective executive instrument for sending them back.

In 1799 Maximilian Joseph became elector of Bavaria and appointed as a minister his advisor Maximilian von Montgelas. An enlightened bureaucrat, whose liberal credentials had made him suspect among some German anti-Jacobins, Montgelas launched a programme of administrative reform, including the creation of a professional civil service. Police reform moved rather faster than in Baden, but initially focused on old practices, namely, the use of troops and, in particular, the deployment of a military cordon along the frontiers to keep out undesirables. In 1803 some 850 men were drawn from the army to form special detachments to combat brigands and vagrants. A new war, two years later, with Bavaria fighting as an ally of Napoleon, led to these *Detachements* being returned to the army and a new experiment with civilian Polizeywachen established as successors to the military Cordonisten. These were local men, responsible to local civilian authority. It was believed that such men would have a better knowledge of local people and places, and that they would see local security as interwoven with their own well-being. But this supposed advantage cut two ways; in 1807 the authorities in Swabia protested that the Polizeywachen never left their home district except when there were church festivals or weddings, and then, rather than protecting people from vagrants, they became a burden on innkeepers, wedding couples, or guests.[4] In addition to the concerns about beggars and vagrants, the Bavarian authorities, like Napoleon's other allies, were expected to enforce the Continental System for regulating trade and, above all, for preventing British imports. In 1811 this prompted the creation of a special customs patrol corps ('Mauthpatrouilleurcorps') of some 240 men.

In May 1808, on Napoleon's advice, Maximilian Joseph, now king rather than elector, published a constitution granting his subjects basic rights and freedoms, together with religious toleration. The constitution also announced a centralized system of government, and included the promise to create a Gendarmerie: 'To maintain the peace in time of war a National Guard is to be created, and to deal with police matters, a Gendarmerie.'[5] In essence, the Bavarian government appears to have felt that the Gendarmerie system was preferable to any further attempts to shore up the old practices; however, the corps was not formally established for another four years. During August and September 1812 there were a series of discussions between Montgelas's finance and interior ministry and the ministry of war about how a Gendarmerie should be organized and controlled. The discussions resulted in compromise; the new corps was to be recognized first and foremost as a military body, but managed by an independent ministerial bureau under the finance and interior ministry. The Gendarmerie Edict of 11 October 1812 provided for a force of 348 mounted and 1,332 dismounted men. There was some continuity between the work of the old Cordonisten and Mauthpatrouilleurs, and some of the personnel from these bodies were incorporated into the Gendarmerie. The duties of the force were very similar to those already developed in France, and even the terms ordinary and extraordinary service ('ordentlichen und außerordentliche Dienst') were employed to differentiate between, on the one hand, the day-to-day patrols along the main roads looking for suspect vagrants, robbers, poachers, checking passports, and with patrol books to be signed by local mayors; and on the other hand responses to the requests for coercive force from civilian authorities. Again like their French counterparts, the Bavarian gendarmes acted as military police, especially responsible for the pursuit of deserters and for the supervision of troops on the march.

Even though the key ministries agreed on the organization and structure, the early years of the Bavarian Gendarmerie were difficult. Officers and men were to be recruited from the army; the former were to be between 25 and 50 years of age with at least four years military service; the latter were to be literate, of good conduct, between 25 and 40 years old, with six years' service and at least one campaign behind them. The initial problem was that the force was created in wartime. While there was a flood of good volunteers, perhaps with many men feeling that they had seen enough of the carnage of Napoleonic battlefields, regimental and battalion commanders had no desire to lose good men to the Gendarmerie. Some of these commanders began threatening and even punishing men who volunteered for the new corps, until ordered by Montgelas to stop it. When discussions began on a new, more liberal constitution for Bavaria in the aftermath of Napoleon's fall, several deputies to the Staatsrat insisted that the Gendarmerie had no place in it, and reference to the corps was duly missing from the constitution of 1818. No one appears to have contemplated abolishing the organization, but there were concerns about its cost. These concerns meant that the deputies only provided sufficient funds for 1,300 foot and 120 mounted gendarmes. In 1825 the budget was cut still further, leading to a significant reduction in the number of officers and a complete reorganization of the entire corps into eight companies, one for each of the kingdom's administrative districts (*Kreis*).

In some respects police reform in Württemberg had moved slightly faster. There was an experiment with a Landreuter corps of 200 men in 1807. This was a mounted body recruited from former soldiers but also from civilians who were literate, courageous, and well-regarded. Two years later the Landreuter corps was replaced by the Landdragoner corps of 320 men, all of whom were to be former soldiers and who were put under a much stricter military supervision. The men carried out regular patrols, with patrol journals that had to be signed by local municipal officials; the journals, and the men themselves, were to be inspected quarterly. The evidence of a Landdragon was expressly indicated as having more weight than that of the accused in court, especially in cases involving vagrancy, and the population was enjoined to assist the dragoons with information. At the same time the dragoons were exhorted never to be too harsh towards offenders, never to interfere with people going about their lawful business, and always to use caution and moderation when dealing with the public. Unfortunately the selection of personnel does not appear to have been particularly successful, and there were a variety of complaints about the dragoons' lack of moral education and honour, and of their bad behaviour and selfishness. In May 1811 the problems led King Frederick to propose new reforms, and a new title, the Gendarmeriekorps. Frederick urged that everything be kept 'strictly military'; he wanted the men serving in the Landdragoner corps who were married or who had civilian backgrounds to be dismissed, and he forbade the senior civil servants in his kingdom from trying to use the men as their personal servants. Above all, he insisted that his Gendarmerie was to avoid any civilian control, and that it should be recognized that 'these men are soldiers chosen for a particular purpose which covers the entire country'.[6] The instructions for the Royal Gendarmerie issued at the beginning of August closely followed Frederick's proposal. Of the 321 Landdragoner, 197 were dismissed as unsuitable. They were replaced by soldiers with good conduct records, all of whom had to be literate. From henceforth any civilian authority needing Gendarmerie assistance had to make a formal application to the senior officers of the men quartered in their district.

[6] Quoted by Wirsing, 'Die Geschichte der Gendarmeriekorps', 61.

'Gendarmerie' was, of course, a French word, and it became unpopular across the political spectrum for precisely that reason. In 1816 the war ministry in Württemberg was urging that any Latin or French terms should be replaced with 'good German expressions'.[7] Liberals linked the Gendarmerie with the French secret police, and given the determination of the Rhineland states, now under Metternich's sway, to suppress all forms of political dissent, this was a suggestive and unpleasant link. At the same time Frederick's successor, William, was swinging rather more towards the traditional aristocracy than the liberals, and in so doing he was keen to disassociate himself with all things French. In October 1821 a reform commission with members from the ministries of the interior, justice, and war was established to investigate the Gendarmerie. Its report, submitted early in 1823, made a variety of proposals which suggested an overall civilianization of the corps. In March 1823 the name was Germanized into the Landjäger-Korps. Recruits were still to be former soldiers, literate, aged between 25 and 40 years, with good conduct records. The Landjägers still performed the same duties, but henceforth they were tied much more closely to the civil authorities, who could give them direct orders and even discipline them. 'Jäger', however, the word for hunter, was also the word used for the light troops deployed for skirmishing and reconnaissance; the notion that gendarmes in the German lands were engaged in a permanent small war against *Gauner*, vagrants, and other undesirables was to be recurrant during the nineteenth century.

In Baden, Bavaria, and Württemberg concerns about order and the threat of vagrants and robbers had been central to the arguments for creating Gendarmeries, but the broader political and administrative contexts were also important. Each of these states experienced major reforms during the Napoleonic period. They had to develop policies to deal with enormous debts made worse by war, and with new populations, often with different religious affiliations, acquired as a result of the Napoleonic reorganization of Germany. To the princes and their ministers, organizing their states into relatively uniform regional blocks and localities, along the French model, seemed a sensible move in the circumstances; the French model appeared to be working well, and besides, Napoleon was their patron. Such organization meant bypassing the old estates and corporations; but this promised a more manageable and, in consequence, more efficient state. Together with these moves,

---

[7] Ibid. 105.

princes and ministers whittled away at many of the privileges of the noble landowners, especially where this was perceived as necessary for undermining the position of powerful men in the newly acquired territories—among the new populations were nobles who had special protection as *Standesherren* under the Confederation of the Rhine. Gendarmerie brigades provided a very public representation of the state uniformly across the territory and, in theory at least, they promised an equitable administration of the prince's justice. In the concluding paragraph of the 1808 constitution, and a few paragraphs below his promise to create a Gendarmerie, Max Joseph proclaimed: 'People of our state! Security, your common welfare, is our aim.'

Similar experiments in gendarmerie-style policing were tried elsewhere in the smaller states of the Confederation of the Rhine. Hussars had been used for policing in Hessen-Darmstadt since 1763; in 1804 these were replaced with a fifty-two-man Landdragoner-Korps, reformed in 1811 and then again in 1822, when it became the Gendarmerie.[8] In March 1808 the ruler of the tiny county of Lippe-Detmold considered that the threats to lives and property from gangs of robbers required extraordinary measures. As a result a Gendarmerie, recruited from the military and consisting of four brigades of three men each, was created. The establishing decree of 19 July 1808 explained:

The duty of the Gendarmerie is the maintenance of public order and security, and to ensure that this important task of the state is fulfilled, the orders [of this corps] must be heeded and obeyed. The authorities are therefore to prosecute, and to demand severe punishment for anyone who resists the Gendarmerie in the execution of its duties, who offends or attacks it. The military, local functionaries and their deputies, and every other inhabitant are obliged to assist it when requested, particularly at markets, at other public gatherings, in visiting inns, stopping disputes, brawls, and disorder, arresting beggars, vagabonds, criminals, people involved in fights, and deserters, as well as in all instances where the Gendarmerie is acting for the maintenance of good order, good government, and public security.

Throughout its existence, like the larger corps, this first Lippe Gendarmerie suffered from a shortage of funding; it also found itself increasingly involved with military tasks, pursuing deserters and assisting with recruiting. In January 1814, as a result of the anti-French feeling which swept across Germany with the 'War of Liberation', the corps was abolished. The rulers of Lippe appear to have seen this as only a

---

[8] Heinz L. Pape, 'Der Säbel der Großherzoglich Hessischen Gendarmerie um 1820', *Archiv für Polizeigeschichte*, 6 (1992), 12–14.

temporary measure, recognizing the value of an executive instrument in the hands of central government for the maintenance of order; however, it was to be twenty-eight years before the Gendarmerie was re-established.[9]

The impact of Napoleon, and the conflict between reformers and traditional upholders of *Herrschaft* had a significant effect on the development of a Gendarmerie in Prussia. The decisive battles of Jena and Auerstadt in October 1806 had threatened Prussia's very survival as a major player in European power politics, and provided an opportunity for the reformers. Though personally indecisive and not especially able, Frederick William III did appoint, successively, two highly competent and imaginative leading ministers in Freiherr vom Stein and Karl von Hardenberg. The two men were very different in temperament and the ways in which they sought to get things done; nevertheless, they were both convinced of the need for a central government bureaucracy within which men held positions that were clearly defined within a hierarchy and which were legally sanctioned. Like other contemporary German reformers, they also shared ideas on civil equality, economic freedom, social mobility, and some limited degree of participation, at least in local government. There was debate amongst reformers about the extent and direction that such changes should be pressed, but the general population in Prussia showed little enthusiasm for the opportunities offered for elections to and participation in municipal government after the edict of November 1808, while the opponents of reform, particularly the Junkers of East Prussia, found a powerful forum for their protests when the old provincial estates were summoned.

In July 1812 Hardenberg issued the *Gendarmerie Edikt*. In the preamble it drew attention to 'the lack of effective state administration in the countryside [*das platte Land*]' and to the continuing disproportionate influence of certain groups within society. A new Gendarmerie corps, subsequently set at 9,000 men, was to mount regular patrols to prevent crime; it was instructed to watch out for and arrest suspicious persons, notably the ubiquitous vagrant. But the organization and structure of the new Gendarmerie was not discussed in the edict until its third part and Section 60. The underlying intention of the document was the creation of a centralized system of provincial government based on the French model. The kingdom was to be divided into new administrative districts based on size and population rather than on traditional

---

[9] Peter Nitschke, *Verbrechensbekämpfung und Verwaltung. Die Entstehung der Polizei in der Grafschaft Lippe, 1700–1814* (Münster: Waxmann, 1990), 171–85: quotation at 176.

boundaries. These districts were to be supervised by centrally appointed officials who were to have responsibility for everything from conscription and tax-collection to the appointment of pastors and the administration of schools. Moreover, peasant uprisings in Silesia in 1811 had convinced Hardenberg that the authority of the local landowners needed to be limited, and this prompted the inclusion of provisions within the edict for the abolition of both the local assemblies that were dominated by the nobility and the patrimonial courts of noble estate-holders. The Junkers were loyal to their king, but they were hostile to such reforms. Of course there was a degree of self-interest in this, but it is always easy to dismiss reactionary protest as selfish. Many Junkers sincerely feared that such reforms would endanger all authority, property, and religion. They understood estate-ownership as an office; their privileges and rights were not private interests but public functions inherent in *Herrschaft*. The Gendarmerie edict was a direct attack on the key institutions of *Herrschaft*—courts, church, and schools—and the Junkers opposed it root and branch. Perhaps without the massive effort required by the German War of Liberation, Hardenberg and the reformers may have been more ready to confront the opposition, though without the earlier war they would never have had the opportunity for reform; as it was, the edict had foundered by the beginning of 1814 and was soon to be abandoned altogether.[10]

The Gendarmerie itself, established under the edict, fared only slightly better. The 9,000 men of the establishment were still seen by the Junkers as a threat to their authority. The army, whose officer corps drew heavily on the same Junkers, resented the Gendarmerie's independent claims on the kingdom's treasury. Moreover, the Prussian debt, which stood at 53 million gulden before the disaster of 1806, had, in spite of Hardenberg's efforts, virtually quadrupled in the following decade. In 1820 pressure from the Junkers and financial stringency forced a reduction of the Gendarmerie to just over 1,300 men, exclusive of officers. At the same time the army command successfully manoeuvred to bring the corps more directly under its control.[11]

[10] *Gesetz-Sammlung für die Königlichen Preußischen Staaten, 1812 (nr. 127) Edikt wegen Errichtung der Gendarmerie*, 30 June 1812. Robert M. Berdahl, *The Politics of the Prussian Nobility: The Development of a Conservative Ideology, 1770–1848* (Princeton NJ: Princeton University Press, 1988), esp. 141–3.

[11] Reinhart Koselleck, *Preussen zwischen Reform und Revolution: Allgemeines Landrecht, Verwaltung und soziale Bewegung von 1791 bis 1848* (Stuttgart: Ernst Klett, 1965), 460–1; Albrecht Funk, *Polizei und Rechtsstaat: Die Entwicklung des staatlichen Gewaltmonopols in Preussen, 1848–1914* (Frankfurt: Campus, 1986), 41–3.

The French may have provided the initial model for the Prussian Gendarmerie, but towards the end of 1815 the Prussian government was seeking information from the Savoyard ambassador in Berlin about the new Piedmontese Carabinieri.[12] The northern Italian state of Piedmont contained territories which had been under Napoleonic control for longer than any others in the peninsula; indeed, the Piedmontese heartland had been fully incorporated into the French Empire in 1802. Here French administration had time to settle in, and the Imperial Gendarmerie had the opportunity to demonstrate its abilities and effectiveness. Victor Emanuel I had succeeded as head of the House of Savoy on his brother's abdication in June 1802, but it was almost twelve years before he could leave the island of Sardinia for his Piedmontese capital of Turin. On 21 May 1814, prompted by a group of *ancien régime* courtiers, Victor Emanuel issued an edict formally re-establishing the old absolutist state; French laws and the notion of equality before the law were abolished, while ecclesiastical and patriarchal prerogatives were restored. Yet less than two months after this edict the law of 13 July established the Carabinieri Reali, a corps strongly reminiscent of the French Gendarmerie. French precedents, not surprisingly, were not acknowledged in the law; there was an *ancien régime* precedent in the shape of the Carabini formed in 1791 to combat brigands, and it was from here that the name for the new corps was taken. Victor Emanuel's Carabinieri were to be a military elite, second only to the royal bodyguard in the hierarchy of the Piedmontese army; in April 1817 the king underlined his high regard for the corps by giving it the highly prestigious task of policing the royal hunting grounds. But at the outset the Carabinieri's duties were stated to be the restoration and maintenance of good order and public tranquillity, and assisting the king in furthering 'the greater happiness of the state, which cannot be separated from the protection and defence of our good and faithful subjects'.[13]

Originally the Carabinieri was to be composed of 800 men, who were to patrol Piedmont proper; the complexities of the state meant that only gradually did the corps take over policing in the other territories ruled by the House of Savoy. A special corps of soldiers policed the island of

---

[12] Archivio di Stato di Torino: Segretaria degli Affari Interni—Serie V [Miscellanea]: Registro Lettere ai Governatori e Commandanti per affari di Buon Governo e Polizia, 1816–1820, Vol. II, Segretario per gli Interni to Conte Lodi, 22 Nov. 1815. My thanks to Michael Broers for this reference.

[13] Michele Ruggiero, *Storia del Piemonte* (Turin: Piemonte in Bancarella), 768; AST, Sezzione Riunite, Categoria: Guerra, Registro 2, 2ᵉ Divisione, Apr. 1817. Quotation from *Regie Patente*, 13 July 1814.

Sardinia; this corps was reorganized in 1818, but Carabinieri did not appear on the island until after the regulations of 1822. When the short lived Republic of Genoa was incorporated into Piedmont in December 1814 its Gardia di Polizia became the Reale Gendarmeria Genovese, and continued as a separate force for another three years. In Piedmont proper the numbers of Carabinieri were gradually increased year by year, but financial constraints, in particular, meant that the corps was kept well below its paper strength. For the anti-smuggling patrols that it mounted along the borders with France and Switzerland the Carabinieri had to be reinforced by troops of the line. In February 1818 the minister responsible for its maintenance complained that, while a revised target strength had been reduced from 2,500 men to 2,000, the Carabinieri could only muster 1,094 men, not counting 183 Gendarmes serving in Liguria.[14] The men were expected to be former soldiers drawn from newly formed Piedmontese line regiments; exceptions were made at particular times, however, enabling recruits to be found in the militia created from Napoleonic veterans and even among the annual conscript levy, providing always that the men met the other requirments.[15] There do not appear to be any personnel or recruitment registers extant, but the details of the first nineteen men killed on internal active service suggest that all, with the exception of Giorgio Priolo and the possible exception of Giovanni Colombatto, were of an age to have been caught by Napoleonic conscription (see Table 10.1). Extrapolating from the same—admittedly slender—details, it appears that around a quarter of the men could have been serving in their province of birth. Some of the first officers were Napoleonic veterans: sub-lieutenant Giacinto Cottalorda had fought at Austerlitz, and sub-lieutenant Count Fabrizio Lazari had volunteered for the army of the Kingdom of Italy in 1812, aged only 15 years; at least two had served in the Imperial Gendarmerie.[16] But there were also officers drawn from

---

[14] Michael Broers, *Napoleonic Imperialism and the Savoyard Monarchy, 1773–1821: State Building in Piedmont* (Lewiston NY: Edwin Mellen Press), 513–14; Alvaro Calanca, 'Le Origini e le Funzioni dei Carabinieri fino al 1848', Tesi di Laurea, Università degli studi di Torino, 1966–67, pp. 119–23 and 195–204. The Ligurian gendarmes, presumably, were those of the old Republic of Genoa who were just in the process of amalgamation.

[15] AST, Sezzione Riunite, Categoria : Guerra, Registro 1, 2ᵉ Divisione, 18 Sept. 1815, and Registro 2, 2ᵉ Divisione, 4 Dec. 1816.

[16] AMSC Cartella 3 (1812–1923), 'Carteggio donato dalla famiglia Frosali', contains various cuttings and biographical details of some of the early officers; Mario Murat, *Il Carabiniere: Storia del Corpo—Avvenimenti dell' Arma* (Piacenza: Edizioni Apuana, 1935), 15, gives very brief details of the previous service of eight officers, of whom two had served in the Napoleonic Gendarmerie.

TABLE 10.1. *Details of Piedmontese Carabinieri killed/died in service, 1815–1822*

Rank	Name	Date and province of birth	Date and province of death
Car.	Giovanni Boccaccio	6/7/1781, Alessandria	23/4/1815, Cuneo
Car.	Gio. Giacomo Costmagna	7/7/1788, Cuneo	26/3/1816, Cuneo
Car.	Pietro Abrardi	15/1/1789, Turin	16/5/1817, Aosta
Car.	Carlo Antonio Patrone	2/8/1786, Vercelli	3/8/1817, Savona
Brig.	Carlo Maestris	4/11/1788, Alessandria	22/9/1817, Pavia
Car.	Giuseppe Arnaud	6/10/1783, Cune	21/11/1817, ?
Car.	Giuseppe Actis-Grande	10/4/1784, Aosta	27/1/1818, Turin
Car.	Bartolomeo Rovere	12/11/1780, Savona	6/10/1818, Genoa
Car.	Andrea Sbarbaro	5/11/1791, Genoa	30/10/1818, Genoa
Brig.	Sebastiano Pezziardi	27/9/1791, Turin	13/2/1819, Alessandria
Car.	Antonio Villanze	3/4/1782, Turin	22/10/1819, Pavia
Car.	Giorgio Priolo	3/10/1794, Turin	6/11/1819, Novara
Car.	Giovanni Colombatto	7/7/1792, Turin	1/1/1820, Savoy
Brig.	Giuseppe Fabaro	21/11/1778, Turin	27/11/1820, Savoy
Car.	Francesco Rivotella	13/10/1782, Turin	1/4/1821, Turin
Brig.	Gio. Antonio Viglione	14/5/1788, Cuneo	20/4/1821, Turin
Car.	Giacomo Laneri	18/9/1780, Alessandria	25/3/1822, Alessandria
Cav.	Cristoforo Bollati	15/9/1779, Cuneo	10/6/1822, Cuneo
Brig.	Domenico Camoletto	9/4/1783, Turin	3/11/1822, Alessandria

Source: AMSC Cartella 10, Registri Morti, Legione . . . di Torino.

members of the nobility who had shunned public life under the French, and there is evidence that in much of the Piedmontese administration and military the opportunities for Napoleonic veterans remained strictly limited.[17] As was common among the Gendarmeries established elsewhere, the men recruited into the other ranks of the Carabinieri were required to be literate; it was specified that they should at least be capable of taking a statement (*processo-verbale*). They were to be aged between 25 and 40 years, with a record of good conduct; in December 1815 the minister of war required also that the men be unmarried. Men who did not measure up to the demands of the job were returned to their regiments, and those who were found guilty of persistent

[17] Michael Broers, 'Policing Piedmont: The "Well-Ordered" Police State in the Age of Revolution, 1789–1821', *Criminal Justice History*, 15 (1994), 39–57; at 49. Massimo D'Azeglio was critical of the way both civil and military offices were filled at the outset of the Restoration. He described men forced to lose rank: corporals became privates, sergeants became corporals, and so on up to captains and colonels. He himself was appointed a lieutenant in the cavary, and was embarrassed to command battle-hardened veterans. Massimo D'Azeglio, *Things I Remember*, trans. and with an introduction by E. R. Vincent (Oxford: Oxford University Press, 1966), 82–3 and 85–6.

misconduct were sent to the punishment battalion, the Corpo Franco, usually reserved for recaptured deserters and serious offenders.[18]

Napoleon's brief return, and the excitement of the Hundred Days, meant that for much of the first year of its existence the Piedmontese Carabinieri was involved in military campaigning. Peace itself brought the drudgery of day-to-day patrolling for the corps, while the bad harvests of 1816 to 1818 brought misery for the peasantry, fostered petty crime, and emboldened a few to try banditry. Significantly, Carabinieri Boccaccio, Costamagna, and Actis-Grande were all killed in clashes with bandits. Yet, thanks in large measure to the Imperial Gendarmerie, banditry in Piedmont was much less of a problem than before. The Carabinieri succeeded in maintaining the security situation which had been inherited from the French, and they were more likely to find themselves ordered to protect people by hunting packs of wolves rather than pursuing gangs of brigands. They also found themselves employed as an instument for policing morality, occasionally being sent off in pursuit of philandering husbands.[19]

To the east of Piedmont were the provinces of Lombardy and Venetia, which were acquired by the Habsburg Empire at the Congress of Vienna. As part of the Napoleonic Kingdom of Italy this region had also had the experience of gendarmerie-style policing, and, while the attention given to conscription legislation had made it far from popular, the Gendarmerie was nevertheless considered an improvement upon its corrupt and often criminal predecessors. Towards the close of 1813 the Gendarmerie companies in Venetia had withdrawn before invading Austrian troops as part of Eugène de Beauharnais's army. In Lombardy, however, the Napoleonic administration remained largely intact after the armistice of April 1814, and the Gendarmerie companies had also remained. Indeed, following the factional disorder in Milan which overthrew the old Napoleonic government, the Austrian General Bellegarde pressed for the retention of the Gendarmerie. It was subsequently fully adopted by the Habsburg regime and incorporated as a regiment of 1,000 men into the imperial army. Men who had learned the role of the gendarme under Napoleon, now carried out the same duties, in the same places, for the Habsburg emperor, and some prospered. Domizio Azzi,

---

[18] AMSC Cartella 13 (1817–1837), *Manifesto concenente il reclutamento per corpo dei Carabinieri Reali, 17 di Giugno 1818*; AST, Sezzione Riunite, Categoria: Guerra, Registro 1, 2ᵉ Divisione, 18 Dec. 1815; and for punishments see AST, Sezzione Riunite, Categoria: Guerra, Segretaria di Guerra . . . Registro: Corrispondenza col Ministero di Polizia e Carabinieri Reale, 1819–1822.

[19] Broers, *Napoleonic Imperialism*, 515; id., 'Policing Piedmont', 50.

for example, had joined the Italian Gendarmerie in 1803 aged only 20. He had reached the rank of sergeant by the fall of Napoleon; he was promoted to sub-lieutenant in 1829, and took a pension in 1843, the Habsburg authorities recognizing him as having given forty years service. Angelo Zecchini was a stonemason from Cremona conscripted into the army in 1803. He transferred to the Gendarmerie in 1812, and was still on the active list as a senior NCO when the Habsburg Empire as a whole established a Gendarmerie in 1849.[20]

A majority of the Central-Organisierungs-Hofcommission, organized to supervise the integration of Lombardy and Venetia into the Habsburg Empire, had favoured an extension of the Lombard Gendarmerie into Venetia; but they faced a stumbling-block in the shape of Lazansky, the commission's president. While not an arch-reactionary in the sense of the *Zelanti* of the Papal States, Lazansky wanted to keep the institutions of the northern Italian provinces as close as possible to those in the other Habsburg lands; no Gendarmerie existed there and therefore, regardless of the situation in Lombardy, there should be no Gendarmerie in Venetia. In consequence, the province found itself with the pre-Napoleonic police re-established, though there was some attempt to improve the quality of the personnel, and a military security guard of 300 men was created for Venice itself.[21]

As far as the rest of the sprawling Habsburg Empire was concerned, at no time during or immediately after the Revolutionary and Napoleonic wars was Count Pergen's plan for an imperial Gendarmerie resurrected. This was in spite of the increasing intrusiveness of the political police which, in 1801, for example, acquired jurisdiction over censorship of everything from the written word to the decoration on artefacts.[22] The potential cost may have been one reason why the proposal remained shelved; the army was swallowing half of the imperial revenue on the fall of Napoleon, and there was a determination to bring costs down.[23] Possibly equally important was the concern to shield the population from all things French, especially after a victorious Napoleon

---

[20] Franz Neubauer, *Die Gendarmerie in Österreich, 1849–1924* (Vienna: Gendarmerie-Jubiläumsfonds, 1925), 28–9; Ka GBBC ABG KL III Box 3084 and Box 3085.

[21] David Laven, 'Law and Order in Habsburg Venetia, 1814–1835', *Historical Journal*, 39 (1996), 383–403; at 387–9.

[22] Donald E. Emerson, *Metternich and the Political Police: Security and Subversion in the Hapsburg Monarchy (1815–1830)* (The Hague: Martinus Nijhoff, 1968), chap. 1.

[23] Gunther E. Rothenburg, *The Army of Francis Joseph* (West Lafayette, Ind.: Purdue University Press, 1976), 10. By 1830 the cost of the army had been brought down to 23% of the revenues.

had himself announced plans for an Austrian Gendarmerie to protect his lines of communication in the aftermath of Austerlitz.[24] But the Habsburg Empire had also had a revolutionary emperor, and the unhappy memory of Joseph II's radical policies of centralization also militated against the development of such a corps. The creation of a Habsburg Gendarmerie, it was recognized, would mean reducing the authority of the gentry by curbing their police powers, and this, in turn, would mean altering their relations with the emperor and the imperial administration. In 1818 Count Joseph Sedlnitzky, the police minister who was to work closely with Metternich until the Revolutions of 1848, briefly contemplated developing a force similar to that in Lombardy across the whole empire. His ministerial colleagues objected on the grounds of what such a change would mean for the gentry. It was nearly thirty years before the issue was to be brought forward again.[25]

While the diplomats at the Congress of Vienna discussed the future of the territories of the Napoleonic Kingdom of Italy, the people on the ground had to cope with the aftermath of war. Thousands of disbanded soldiers flooded the labour market, and many of those who could not find work found it easy to slip into brigandage. The situation was aggravated by the poor harvest of 1814. In Bologna, the principal town of the old Papal Legations, and since then the principal town of the imperial *département* of Reno, former officials of the kingdom, still taking responsibility for the region, sought to maintain order by re-establishing a force on the lines of the old Gendarmerie. By the close of 1814 they had a company of around 200 men, and other legations followed Bologna's lead. In Rome itself the absence of the relatively progressive secretary of state, Cardinal Consalvi, at the Congress of Vienna provided the opportunity for the *Zelanti*, who sought a restoration of the old ways and a destruction of all things French. Cardinal Rivarola brought back the *sbirri*, and with them all the old problems of corruption and of a police force whose behaviour was often little different from the brigands it was supposed to suppress.[26]

Ercole Consalvi had little love for Napoleon. He was furious when, having negotiated the Concordat with the First Consul, the latter made additions to it in the shape of the Organic Articles. He urged the

---

[24] Neubauer, *Die Gendarmerie*, 535–8.

[25] Helmut Gebhardt, *Die Gendarmerie in der Steiermark von 1850 bis heute* (Graz: Leykam, 1997), 25.

[26] Steven C. Hughes, *Crime, Disorder and the Risorgimento: The Politics of Policing in Bologna* (Cambridge: Cambridge University Press, 1994), 23–4.

captive Pope Pius VII to continue his opposition to Napoleon, an action which led to his own imprisonment in Béziers in 1813. Yet Consalvi also perceived a value in reforming the Papal States with a centralized, rational, unified administration. He looked to the French model of *départements* and prefects, and to the French justice system in which there was equality before the law, freedom from arbitrary arrest, and no room for judicial torture. The latter reforms in particular, however, were unlikely to win public confidence as long as the executive arm of justice remained the hated *sbirri*. After some uncertainty, in October 1816 Consalvi abolished the *corpo dei sbirri* and ordered the men to report to the provincial communes as rural guards. At the same time he announced the formation of two special regiments within the papal army; these 1,822 men were to be known as the Carabinieri Pontifici, and their tasks were the maintenance of order and enforcing the laws. The Carabinieri were to be paid at a higher rate than ordinary soldiers. They were directly responsible to the secretary of state via the minister of police. Recruits had to be literate, and aged between 25 and 40 years. Previous military service was not a requirement, but the men who had not been soldiers were to be distributed among the companies so that they might learn from veterans. All recruits had to be able to give proof of moral and political integrity. They were instructed 'to be impartial, attentive, circumspect, prudent, and active; to understand that it is insufficient for a Carabiniere just to have courage, the principal duty of every soldier; to know that in addition to bravery and intrepidity should be added a greater resolve, a transparent morality and a perfect understanding of the state.' They were to be prudent in word, modest about their deeds, and to lift themselves 'above the sphere of everyday life'. Consalvi's stated aim was to create a force which, by its principled, impartial behaviour, would win the esteem of the public both for itself and for the government which it served.[27]

The papal Carabinieri had some success, and villages began to request that brigades be stationed permanently in them as a protection against offenders. But the brigades were thin on the ground; even under Consalvi the corps never reached its intended strength and, whatever the successes, the *Zelanti* still opposed his reforms. In September 1823 the election of Pope Leo XII was a triumph for the old order. Consalvi was removed; Leo and his confidants reverted to a reactionary clericalism and set about dismantling many of the recent changes. The depleted

---

[27] Ibid. 38–9. Quotations from *Sentimenti Morali e Brevi Istruzioni per un Carabinieri* (Rome: 1816?), 4. (This was apparently a supplement to Consalvi's original decree.)

Carabinieri was reduced, partly to save money, but also to fill the ranks of other, more favoured military corps. However, in a relatively short time even the reactionaries surrounding Leo concluded that the Carabinieri provided the best potential for the maintenance of order and security. In September 1827 it was decided to increase the corps to 2,591 men; nevertheless, when revolution struck the Papal States in 1831 it remained 500 men under strength.[28]

---

[28] Hughes, *Crime, Disorder and the Risorgimento*, 99–100.

11

VARIATIONS: CARABINIERI

In Italy the Piedmontese Carabinieri was transformed into the Italian Carabinieri as the peninsula was itself transformed into a united nation state. For most of the first thirty years of its existence the Piedmontese corps was principally concerned with the routine tasks of day-to-day patrolling to maintain the king's peace. Like the French and the German Gendarmeries, it made the same division of its service into ordinary (*funzioni abituali ed ordinarie*) and extraordinary (*servizio straordinario*) duties. Following the successes of the Napoleonic Gendarmerie, clashes with bandits in the mainland part of the kingdom were never particularly frequent and increasingly declined. Nevertheless, between February 1828 and June 1829 the bandit Domenico Adriano left at least four Carabinieri dead around Cuneo and Alessandria, before being forced to surrender following the siege of a village church in which he was holding the local priest hostage.[1] On the island of Sardinia banditry continued to be a serious threat throughout the century.

Dealing with bandits was a traditional problem; dealing with ideas could be considerably more difficult, especially when some members of the Carabinieri themselves were infected with the liberal aspirations fostered by the French Revolution and Napoleon. While Victor Emanuel I had attempted to turn the clock back there was pressure for reform from members of the aristocracy as well as from among men of property and of the professions; representatives of all of these groups mixed in the liberal secret societies, in the Carbonari, and the Freemasons. The attempt to establish a constitution and to declare a Kingdom of Italy which flared in Piedmont in March 1821 began among the military—including some Carabinieri—and professional men in Alessandria, and spread rapidly to Turin. Charles Albert, second in line to the throne and apparently sympathetic to the rebels, was proclaimed regent on the abdication of Victor Emanuel. But Charles Albert's behaviour was equivocal, and after a few days he left the capital with a Carabinieri escort and

---

[1] AMSC Morto in Servizio, schedi 40 (Michele Gastant), 41 (Tommaso Camisass), 45 (Pietro Meinardi), and 46 (Francesco Bourlot).

travelled to Novarra where there were troops loyal to the former regime, and to the heir-apparent, Charles Felix. The members of the Carabinieri left in Turin found themselves in an ambiguous position, especially when the revolutionary government gave them a new commander, Major Camillo Beccaria, a Napoleonic veteran who had served with the corps since its formation. In the relatively mild repression which followed the defeat of the revolution, several Carabinieri officers and men were court martialled for involvement with the rebels. Lieutenant Giovanni Battista Laneri was one of the three rebels executed. Lieutenant Benedetto Allemandi, a Napoleonic veteran like Beccaria and Laneri, was sentenced to twenty years in prison, but found refuge in Switzerland. Beccaria himself was merely dismissed.[2] A few NCOs and men were gaoled and some were transferred, apparently as a punishment, to the unit responsible for policing Sardinia. In general, however, the Carabinieri remained loyal to the Savoyard regime, and in the immediate aftermath of the revolution the minister of war issued instructions for it to act in concert with local authorities and local priests in collecting secret information on political suspects. At the same time there was an attempt to restrict recruitment only to men from the elite regiments; the men were still to be volunteers, but each such regiment was given a quota of Carabinieri to find—a move that does not appear to have been particularly successful.[3] The final legacy of the revolution for the Carabinieri was a new set of regulations published in October 1822. These included an oath which was clearly intended to prevent any future ambiguity as to where loyalty lay: 'I . . . do solemnly swear to be faithful to God and to His Majesty King Charles Felix our Lord, and to His legitimate successors; to sacrifice myself, even my life in defence of His Royal Person, and to sustain His Crown and his Sovereign Authority, even against fellow subjects who seek to subvert the orders of Government.'[4] Further on the individual carabiniere swore never to belong to any proscribed organization; a clause brought about by the

[2] Alvaro Calanca, 'Le origini e le funzioni dei Carabinieri fino al 1848', Tesi di Laurea, Universita degli Studi Torino, 1966–7, pp. 56–82; Mario Murat, *Il Carabiniere: Storia del Corpo—Avvenimenti dell'Arma* (Piacenza: Edizioni Apuana, 1935), 21–32; Pompeo Di Terlizzi, *Quando frammenti di storia si ricompongo. Alle radici culturali e formative dell'Arma dei Carabinieri* (Bari: Levante editori, 1991), 54–84. Murat and Di Terlizzi give slightly different accounts of the numbers of Carabinieri tried for participation in the revolution.

[3] AST, Sezione Riunite, Categoria: Guerra, Segretaria di Guerra . . . Registro: Corrispondenza col Ministero di Polizia e Carabinieri Reale, 1819–1821.

[4] *Regolamento Generale del Corpo dei Carabinieri*, 16 Oct. 1822. The full oath is printed in Murat, *Il Carabiniere*, 34.

involvement of military and Carabinieri personnel in the liberal secret societies before the events of March 1821.

In February 1834 Carabiniere Giovanni Battista Scapaccino, according to the traditions of the corps, obeyed his oath to the letter and became a heroic model held up as an example to future recruits. Scapaccino had ridden into a column of republican volunteers in Les Echelles (Aosta); the republicans, coming from France and Switzerland, were part of an abortive Mazzinian uprising. Called upon to declare himself for the republic, Scapaccino responded 'Long live the King!' and was promptly shot.[5] Whether the events surrounding Scapaccino's death were quite as clear-cut and heroic as the traditional histories imply remains a moot point, but after 1821 the loyalty of the Piedmontese Carabinieri to its monarch was never again in doubt, and the senior officers of the corps prided themselves on a personal bond between the Carabinieri and the king.

The revolutionary wave of 1830–1 largely passed Piedmont by, and Mazzinian threats in the following years disintegrated almost as quickly as they materialized. In 1848, when Charles Albert presented his people with a constitution, the oath of the Carabinieri changed accordingly to reflect the moves towards a *Rechtsstaat*: 'I swear to be faithful to His Royal Sovereign Majesty and his Royal Successors, to observe faithfully the Constitution and the laws of the State' and to carry out all duties relating to my military rank, for the sole purpose of the inseparable good of the King and the Motherland.'[6] Piedmont was spared significant internal disorder in 1848, but Charles Albert's declaration of war on Austria necessitated the temporary closing of some forty-nine Carabinieri posts as 280 men out of an official complement of just over 2,300 were drafted to the army as three cavalry squadrons. When plebiscites in Piacenza, Parma, and Modena opted for unification with Piedmont, plans were rapidly prepared for amalgamation with the Carabinieri of the gendarmerie organizations which these states had been developing. Charles Albert's defeat brought about the collapse of the unification and, consequently, of the amalgamations, but a precedent had been set and was acted upon a decade later. As the Piedmontese and their French allies clashed with the Austrians in the summer of 1859, so Piedmontese troops and officials moved into the duchies on their

[5] Murat, *Il Carabiniere*, 41–6; Francesco Grisi, *Storia dei Carabinieri. Imprese, battaglie, uomini e protagonisti: i due secoli della Benmerita al servizio della gente* (Piemme: Spa, 1996), 31–5.

[6] Quoted in Murat, *Il Carabiniere*, 52.

southern frontier. At the end of May 1859 a proposal had been drafted
to increase the Carabinieri by 400 men, and in the following weeks officials in the newly occupied territories sent request after request for
Carabinieri to help maintain the peace. Three problems were highlighted: it was feared that the local agricultural labourers were 'easily
misled'; some troops of the previous regimes would not disband, or
would not sign up for service with the Piedmontese, and, more seriously, some were roving in the woods as armed bands; finally, to some
of the former regimes gendarmeries were suspect. Yet, in spite of this
latter concern, at the end of August 1859, and more than six months
before the plebiscites which agreed to the duchies becoming part of
Piedmontese Italy, it was generally accepted that any members of the
old gendarmeries who wished were to be incorporated into the
Carabinieri.[7]

The creation of the Gendarmerie forces in Parma and Modena provides a further indication of the way that this policing model was being
adopted elsewhere in the years between Napoleon's defeat and Italian
unification, though such adoptions were not always part of a carefully
worked out policy. Following disorders in Tuscany in August 1847 the
Grand Duke appointed a new, liberal-minded ministry. Cosimo Ridolfi,
a liberal aristocrat with faith in the old Enlightenment philosophies of
reform, became minister of the interior. One of his first moves was to
abolish the administrative department of *Buon-Governo*, which had
responsibility for policing in its widest sense and which co-ordinated
political surveillance. Such a move was popular among liberals, but it
left the old *sbirri* intact and still responsible for day-to-day policing. On
5 October Florentine crowds took matters into their own hands; they
released debtors from prison, burned the guillotine, and hunted down
and attacked the *sbirri*. Ridolfi's response was to abolish the old police
and to make provision for an 800–strong Carabinieri.[8]

In establishing a Tuscan Carabinieri, Ridolfi appears to have been
seeking to find a force which would possess the moral authority sought
by Cardinal Consalvi in his papal police thirty years earlier. While
Consalvi's dominance in the Papal States had been relatively short-lived,
there were some among the papal Carabinieri in the quarter-century
before the events of 1848 who tried to live up to his ideals. There were
instances, notably during the disorders on big estates near Rome in the

---

[7] AMSC Cartella 11 (1815–1860), folder 18, 'Aumento Corpo dei Carabinieri Reali'.
[8] W. K. Hancock, *Ricasoli and the Risorgimento in Tuscany* (New York: Howard Fertig,
1969), 104.

early 1830s, when Carabinieri officers listened to workers' complaints, criticized landowners who appeared less than generous in the food and accommodation allowed to labourers, and sought to mediate when faced with potential conflict.[9] But young recruits to the corps did not always live up to the ideals. Surveillance of the poor and the labouring classes generated unpopularity among those groups. Moreover, the force was was commonly short of funds and, consequently, of men. It was generally considered to have failed miserably in defending the papal regime during the revolutions of both 1831 and 1848, though it is difficult to see what more it could have done in the circumstances. In September 1849 it was abolished in an organizational shambles; some men were kept on in new corps, some were dismissed, and still others were left in limbo. Just under a year later Consalvi's ideas were resurrected with yet another new corps, ultimately named the Gendarmeria. Its activity against bandits appears to have given it a degree of popularity amongst the propertied, but the French military stationed in Rome to protect the Papacy had a very poor opinion of both its personnel and its dependability.[10]

In early nineteenth-century Sicily a first attempt at creating armed companies to combat the problem of banditry appears to have foundered on a recruitment policy which led to a force little different from the bandits themselves. Bandits and the members of the armed companies often had bonds of kinship, close personal ties, or shared factional loyalties. In response to the problem, at the close of 1837 the government in Naples established a mounted corps known as the Gendarmeria Reale. Some members of the old armed companies were permitted to transfer into the new corps, but not those about whom there were any suspicions. But the new gendarmes immediately ran into difficulties. The intensely proud and fiercely independent local authorities in Sicily disliked them for undermining their independence, and were reluctant to co-operate. Local police resented them. Local people, even those who were the victims of offences, did not come forward with information. The situation of the gendarmes was made worse by the usual plethora of tasks and their own small numbers.[11] Overall the experience of the

[9] John A. Davis, *Conflict and Control: Law and Order in Nineteenth-Century Italy* (London: Macmillan, 1988), 140.

[10] Steven C. Hughes, *Crime, Disorder and the Risorgimento. The Politics of Policing in Bologna* (Cambridge: Cambridge University Press, 1994), 114, 139–40, and 220–3; AN MR 2003, 'Gendarmerie Pontificale, posterieur à 1852'.

[11] Giovanna Fiume, *Le Bande Armate in Sicilia (1819–1849). Violenza e Organizzazone del Potere* (Palermo: Annali della Facolta di Lettere e Filosofia dell'Universita di Palermo,

Sicilian Gendarmeria Reale was a foretaste of what was to come for the Carabinieri of united Italy a quarter of a century later.

But even if it the gendarmerie model was being taken up across the peninsula in the decades between Napoleon's fall and before the Unification, and even if the new gendarmes were seen as much preferable to the *sbirri*, many liberals had suspicions. The model was, after all, military. Many European liberals looked to England for their exemplars and during the revolutions of 1848 in Italy, as elsewhere, they sought to develop police organizations which were rather more civilian in orientation and which were based on their perception of the Metropolitan Police of London. In September 1848 the Amministrazione della Pubblica Sicurreza was established within the Piedmontese ministry of the interior; the intention was that this group of civilian officials should link up with the new provincial prefects for the supervision of law-enforcement and security across the kingdom. Two years later the Piedmontese Parliament passed a law establishing the Guardia di Pubblica Sicurreza (PS). This was a civilian force of 300 men for the major cities of Turin and Genoa, and it too was responsible to the ministry of the interior. The debates on the creation of the PS suggest some concern that the Carabinieri was controlled by aristocratic officers, inclined, on occasions, to go their own way irrespective of the directions that they had received from ministers; moreover, it was a major concern to the Piedmontese liberals that, since the events of 1821, the military had acquired a dominance in policing matters. However, while the new force patrolled the principal cities, the Carabinieri were not restricted to countryside, and this worked to the detriment of the PS, particularly when it came to funding, and sometimes rivalry led the two forces to work against each other. The PS guards always lacked the Carabinieri's military glamour and the prestige of having participated in the wars to unite the country. The Carabinieri itself, moreover, had no intention of becoming subservient to officials of the ministry of the interior; it rested its claim to independence on the founding regulations of the corps, which stated that other government agencies could only request, never demand, its assistance, and when such help was deployed it was always to be the senior Carabinieri officer who decided the scale and manner of any action. Following Unification the national Parliament decided to

---

1984), esp. 123–5; and see id., 'Bandits, Violence and the Organisation of power in Sicily in the Early Nineteenth Century', in John A. Davis and Paul Ginsborg (eds.), *Society and Politics in the Age of the Risorgimento* (Cambridge: Cambridge University Press, 1991), 84–6 and 88–9.

spread the dual Piedmontese police system to the whole peninsula permanently, and while there were strong voices calling for local policing based on perceptions of the English model, a parliamentary commission established in December 1861 concluded that the Italian people were not yet ready to take responsibility for policing themselves.[12]

The process of unification during 1859 and 1860 had seen the Piedmontese Carabinieri spread down the peninisula as an instrument for bringing and maintaining peace and order. In some of the territories north of Rome, as noted above, some members of the exisiting gendarmeries were incorporated with the Piedmontese. It was thought unwise to amalgamate the gendarmes in Lombardy as a body since they had served the Habsburg enemy; however, individual veterans from the corps were allowed to enlist in the Carabinieri and to become 'Italian'. At the same time, even though they held on to Venetia until 1866, the Habsburgs dismissed men from their Italian Gendarmerie regiments who had been born in Lombardy.[13] But if there was some concern in Cavour's government about the loyalty of the new Italians in the north, there were much greater anxieties further south. In October 1860 Luigi Farini, appointed Lieutenant General of the new southern provinces, insisted that he urgently needed 200 Carabinieri for Umbria, 150 for the Marches, and 100 more for Naples. The territories were seething with refugees, disbanded and disgruntled soldiers, and Garibaldini, and keeping order in the south did not seem a simple matter at the best of times. To meet Farini's demands, Cavour stripped the north of its Carabinieri, and then proceeded to express concern about an increase in crime and disorder. 'If Piedmont falls into disorder,' he wrote to Farini with a dramatic flourish, 'then goodbye Italy.' Rather more stoically, he explained to Victor Emanuel that the reduction in the Carabinieri in the north had led to a notable increase in crime: 'But never mind. It is obvious that

[12] Richard Oliver Collin, 'The Italian Police and Internal Security from Giolitti to Mussolini', D.Phil., Oxford University, 1983, pp. 12–13 and 16; Steven C. Hughes, 'Poliziotti, Carabinieri e "Policemens": il *bobby* inglese nella polizia italiana', *Le Carte e la Storia*, 2 (1996), 22–31.

[13] See Kriegsarchiv, Vienna Grundbuchblätter 3, ABG KL., Karton 3136. Examples are Guiliano Sala, recruited into the 44th Infantry Regiment aged 22 in Feb. 1851, transferred into the Gendarmerie 11 months later, and dismissed in Sept. 1859, and Martino Testo, conscripted into the 43rd Infantry aged 20 in June 1854, transferred into the Gendarmerie in Oct. 1856, and dismissed in Jan. 1860. In each case their file notes 'Entlassen als Lombarde'; and these were not isolated individuals. Thousands of Italian soldiers serving in the Habsburg army deserted during the 1859 war, and these were mainly from the Lombard regiments who, fighting on their home territory, found it easier to disappear into the civilian population. István Deák, *Beyond Nationalism: A Social and Political History of the Habsburg Officer Corps, 1848–1918* (New York: Cambridge University Press, 1992), 48.

with all the sacrifices being made, the Piedmontese should let themselves be assassinated for the love of Italy.' Piedmontese Carabinieri were also dispatched to Sicily where, for several months, they served uneasily side-by-side with a Sicilian equivalent that had been established by Giuseppe Garibaldi following his lightning campaign against the Bourbon regime. It was with considerable trepidation that the Piedmontese finally authorized amalgamation here.[14]

As with Napoleonic attempts to stamp out brigandage in the *Mezzogiorno*, the Carabinieri alone was incapable of conducting the ferocious campaign of the Brigands' War which followed hard on unification. Throughout the conflict it was deployed alongside the army. At the end of 1861 there were 120,000 troops in the *Mezzogiorno*; the Carabinieri consisted of 16,400 men in total, of whom 4,700 were in the south with the army and another 2,100 in Sicily. If the receipt of medals is an indication of participation in heavy fighting, then the Carabinieri were truly in the thick of it. A total of 2,375 silver medals were awarded and 5,012 men were mentioned in dispatches (*manzioni onorevoli*); Carabinieri won 531 of these medals and accounted for 748 of the honorable mentions.[15] Given the hostility directed towards the military in general during the Brigands' War, it is perhaps understandable that at times the Carabinieri acted more like an army of occupation in an alien land; and members of the corps, and the state that they served, were not blameless in contributing to the scale of violence. From regions other than the south there were complaints that some new recruits to the Carabinieri during the Unification years enjoyed the swank and swagger of the uniform but did not manifest the dignity and probity expected; and there were some officers, especially from the north, who considered banditry as something 'occult, invisible, secret' which permeated the social fabric and the very 'instincts' of southerners, and which had to be eradicated by whatever the means.[16] Such men, and such attitudes,

[14] C. B. Cavour, *Carteggi di Camillo Cavour*, 15 vols., *La liberazione del Mezzogiorno e la formazione del Regno d'Italia* (Bologna: Nicola Zanichelli, 1926–61), iii., nos. 2,147, 2,402 and 2,417, and iv., nos. 2,743, 2,776, 2,782, and 3,118. For a detailed, and traditional, account of the amalgamations of 1859–60 see Mario de Sena, Oscar Scaffardi, Vincenzo Pezzolet, *et al.*, *I Carabinieri, 1814–1980* (Rome: Comando Generale dei Carabinieri, 1981), 103–19.

[15] Cesare Cesari, *Il Brigantaggio e l'opera dell'Esercito Italiano dal 1860 al 1870* (Rome: Ausonia, 1920), 126 and appendix.

[16] Davis, *Conflict and Control*, 233; John Dickie, 'A Word at War: The Italian Army and Brigandage, 1860–70', *History Workshop Journal*, 33 (1992), 1–24; the quotations (at p. 9) are taken from a book by a lieutenant of the Carabinieri, Giuseppe Bourelly, *Brigantaggio nelle zone militari di Melfi e Lacedonia dal 1860 al 1865* (Naples: 1865).

served only to aggravate the situation in the south; and the violence was worsened still further by the licence given to the forces of order by draconian legislation such as the Pica Law.[17]

Sicily too, after Unification, maintained its notorious reputation for banditry and, particularly during the Palermo uprising of September 1866, for violence similar to that of the Brigands' War. During the Palermo uprising the insurgents appear to have singled out the Carabinieri as alien representatives of an unpopular, unwanted state. They were labelled with the hated name *sbirri* while, symbolically, King Victor Emanuel was labelled *capo sbirazzo* (chief cop). On 18 September insurgents attacked the Carabinieri barracks at Misilmeri; at least twenty-one of the defenders were killed and mutilated—some were allegedly captured and tortured before being killed, and there were grisly stories of subsequent butchery and even cannibalism practised on the corpses. The following day a squad of Carabinieri commanded by Brigadiere Remiglio Taroni entered the small town of Ogliastro to assess the situation. They were wearing plain clothes and carrying only concealed revolvers. Detected by the crowd, they took refuge in the town-hall where Taroni appears to have inflamed the situation by waving a tricolour and shouting 'Long live Italy! Long live the King!' Possibly aware of the events at Misilmeri, the survivors of Taroni's squad eventually seem to have opted for collective suicide rather than face the fury of the crowd.[18] The Carabinieri appear to have been the only representatives of the Italian state able to to look back on their role during the Palermo revolt with a degree of pride, and like Scapaccino, Taroni entered Carabinieri mythology as a role-model for recruits. To the Sicilian insurgents the Carabinieri were outsiders, but place of birth of the men killed in the Palermo uprising reveals that, while a majority of the men came from the north, by the mid-1860s it was becoming an Italian, as opposed to merely a Piedmontese, force (see Table 11.1). Significantly, however, when serious disorder broke out in Sicily again during the 1890s, leading government ministers were keen to see that as many as possible of the Carabinieri stationed on the island were local men with a good local knowledge.[19]

[17] The Pica Law of Aug. 1863, and the subsequent modifications of the following Feb. did little more than give legal recognition to the army's policies of detention of suspects, house arrest, exile, summary courts, and reprisals. See Davis, *Conflict and Control*, 179–82.

[18] AMSC Cartella 49 (1862–66 . . . Sicilia), see esp. report to officer commanding Palermo, 14 Oct. 1866. For the Palermo uprising itself see Lucy Riall, *Sicily and the Unification of Italy. Liberal Policy and Local Power, 1859–1866* (Oxford: Clarendon Press, 1998), 198–203.

[19] Richard Bach Jensen, *Liberty and Order: The Theory and Practice of Italian Public Security Policy, 1848 to the Crisis of the 1890s* (New York: Garland, 1991), 142.

TABLE 11.1. *Provinces of origin of Carabinieri killed/died of wounds during the Palermo uprising*

Province	Misilmeri	Ogliastro	Elsewhere	Total
Abruzzi	1	1	–	2
Aosta	–	–	1	1
Campania	–	1	–	1
Emiglia-Romana	–	1	–	1
Lombardy	4	3	9	16
Piedmont	3	1	1	5
Sardinia	5	1	–	6
Sicily	6	–	2	8
Tuscany	2	–	–	2
TOTAL	21	8	13	42

Source: AMSC Cartella 10, Registri Morti, Sicilia. Only 1 of the Sicilians came from the vicinity of Palermo. The others were from Catania (2), Siracusa (2), Agrigento, Enna, and Messina.

On the mainland in the decade following unification hostility to conscription, occasional banditry, and the general scale of popular violence, created similar problems for the Carabinieri to those experienced by their Napoleonic predecessors. In the provinces patrolled by the Legion of Ancona, which encompassed the northern tip of the Abruzzi and the old Papal States of the Marches and Umbria, between 1861 and 1867 seven Carabinieri were killed in fights with deserters or recalcitrant conscripts (*renitenti*), five were killed in conflicts with so-called brigands, four by members of the 'dangerous classes' (*malfattori* or *malviventi*), and another two dealing with brawls. Over the same period the neighbouring legion of Bologna lost fourteen men in confrontations with *malfattori* and four in fights with deserters and *renitenti*.[20] Again like the Napoleonic Gendarmerie, the Carabinieri sometimes sought their quarry in civilian clothes, with unfortunate results on at least one occasion. Carabiniere Settimio Matteini was one of a squad of six men wearing civilian clothes in pursuit of brigands near Chieti in October 1863. While questioning a farmer, the squad was fired upon and Matteini was killed. Depositions taken many years later revealed that the disguised Carabinieri had themselves been taken for brigands by an ambush prepared by National Guards.[21]

But clashes with brigands, deserters, *renitenti*, 'dangerous classes,' or turbulent peasants did not happen every day, and by the last quarter of

[20] AMSC Cartella 10, Registri Morti, Ancona and Bologna.
[21] AMSC Morto in Servizio, scheda 343 (Settimio Matteini).

the century these were much less of a problem, particularly in the north. Successive governments, however, continued to perceive the coercive power of the corps as essential in facing socialist demonstrations and the nascent workers' movement in both town and countryside. Again, as in the Papal States half a century before, Carabinieri officers could be critical of employers and show sympathy for workers, but most appear generally to have mistrusted both workers and peasants. Their sympathy was never translated into anything particularly tangible, and at times it consisted of taking the part of workers or the disenfranchised who claimed, or had it claimed on their behalf, that they were the victims of intimidation by strikers or socialist leagues. A high percentage of police action against strikers and socialists by both the Carabinieri and the PS tended to be violent, brutal, and unrestrained.[22]

It was not only those involved in brigandage, demonstrations, and strikes who experienced rough handling from the Carabinieri; rough handling reminiscent of the brutality of the old, hated *sbirri* appears to have been accepted as unfortunate, but necessary, by the government. In November 1872 William Mercer, an Englishman sick with a lung complaint, was travelling from Sorrento to Castellammare. A landslide on to the road forced him to take a short boat-ride, and he refused to pay what he considered to be an excessive fare demanded by the boatman. He was consequently apprehended by two Carabinieri; he resisted, and during the ensuing struggle one of the Carabinieri bit him on the hand so that he could more easily fit a thumbscrew (*pollici*). The use of the thumbscrew, Mercer's subsequent imprisonment for thirty-six hours, the obstacles put in his way to prevent him from seeing a doctor and getting bail, and his trial for assault eight months later—at which he was acquitted in spite of alleged pressure being exerted on witnesses by the Carabinieri—all provoked outrage among sections of the British and American press. Yet it appeared, first, that his treatment was much like that which a native Italian might expect, and second, that on the evidence of the Italian foreign minister, no less, the use of thumbscrews was a common, if particularly painful, means of restraint. A Neapolitan correspondent of *The Times* reported that a carabiniere had told him that while he, personally, though the thumbscrew brutal and only employed handcuffs (*manetti*), the former were much more convenient. '[T]his

---

[22] Davis, *Conflict and Control*, 284; Collin, 'The Italian Police', 18–19; Jonathan Dunnage, 'Law and Order in Giolittian Italy: A Case Study of the Province of Bologna', *European History Quarterly*, 25 (1995), 381–408.

only proves that Mr. Mercer was treated with the same impartial cruelty as Italians.' The correspondent went on:

The Carabineers are a fine body of men, and are, perhaps, the best guards of public order we have, but they are prompt and sharp and active—at times rough—and would not, I believe, hesitate at a blow. They are composed principally of the Northern element, or were so, and being among a people whom they regard as a somewhat inferior race are disposed to 'lord' it over them.[23]

At the close of the century the Carabinieri continued to be favoured above the Guardia di Pubblica Sicurreza. It was considerably bigger, with 25,000 men as opposed to 5,500—this at a time when the Italian population was about 30 million. It was active in the towns, especially in times of disorder and/or industrial unrest, but as a rule it was deployed overwhelmingly in the countryside, which was where the majority of the population lived. Carabinieri were also to be found disproportionately in the south, which was still regarded as backward and of uncertain loyalty by politicians from the north. At times this deployment left the authorities in northern cities and rural districts exposed when disorder broke out. Prefects protested when their Carabinieri brigades were moved to other provinces, and warned of serious consequences; the government responded by accusing some prefects of overestimating the potential for trouble, and pointing out that the numbers of Carabinieri and soldiers was not infinite.[24] At times, too, the Carabinieri's officers were still inclined to assert their independence from civilian administrators, for example, in omitting to send them information about their public-order activities.[25] Yet the corps prided itself on an ethos of probity, self-sacrifice, loyalty, and an unflinching enforcement of the law.

In 1875 Captain Gian Carlo Grossardi published his *Galateo dei Carabinieri* (*Code of Behaviour for the Carabinieri*); a third edition appeared four years later, and Grossardi himself eventually reached the

---

[23] William Mercer, *How the Police Manage Italy* (Rome: 1876), quotations at 25–6.

[24] Davis, *Conflict and Control*, 232–4; Jonathan Dunnage, *The Italian Police and the Rise of Fascism. A Case Study of the Province of Bologna, 1897–1925* (Westport, Conn.: Praeger, 1997), 29; Jensen, *Liberty and Order*, esp. 5 and 167. Elsewhere Jensen makes the point that the Carabinieri was actually seen as cheaper than the PS primarily because the army was a conscript force; see id., 'Police Reform and Social Reform: Italy from the Crisis of the 1890s to the Giolittian Era', *Criminal Justice History*, 10 (1989), 179–200, at 181 and n. 5, 196.

[25] Dunnage, in 'Law and Order', 399, and also in *The Italian Police*, 56, notes that in Nov. 1908 the *Questore* of Bologna requested that local mayors give him information on public order problems as the Carabinieri were not doing so.

rank of colonel. The *Galateo*, with its introduction for the new recruit entering into the 'family' of the Carabinieri, provides an illuminating insight into the thinking of the officers of the corps towards the end of the nineteenth century. 'Authority' (*l'autoritá*) was seen as the basis of society; it existed in the family, in the commune, and in the state. The goal of authority was to encourage everyone to participate in working for the good of society and in adhering to what was required for popular solidarity; especially since men, who were independent by nature, were easily led astray by foolish theories.[26] The Carabinieri were central to authority. It was their task to enforce the law impartially.

The great political revolutions have destroyed privilege, and every citizen is equal before the law and has equal duties.

For the Carabinieri, therefore, there are no castes, no associations, no rich, no poor, there is nothing other than the citizen who must obey the law without grade or distinction . . .[27]

But the Carabinieri had to remain men apart. They were not to frequent bars or restaurants where they could become beholden to ordinary citizens and thus forced to turn a blind eye to transgressions, however minor. They had to constitute a 'moral influence' on the population. The 'family' of the Carabinieri depended upon men 'who spend the whole of their lives dedicating themselves to the good of others, and their sole recompense is knowing that they have done their duty'.[28] While relations between church and state were icy during the 1870s after the nation state's occupation of Rome, Grossardi could not help but urge the individual carabiniere to think of himself, and to behave, rather like the product of a seminary;[29] and his description of the Carabinieri barracks has echoes of General Ambert's description of that of the French Gendarmerie.

Over the entrance is the Royal insignia with the national flag, and beneath that the name of the corps; this is not like the name of an inn, nor does it indicate solely that this is the residence of the public power; rather, it shows that those to be found here are responsible for order and public safety, for safeguarding private property, for helping the weak, for suppressing the bully, for striking the offender; all of which provides such an elevated image to the carabiniere, that he himself must respect his surroundings, not cause any offence to the building

---

[26] Gian Carlo Grossardi, *Galateo dei Carabinieri*, 3rd edn. (Turin: 1879), 101. For correspondence on the publication of the *Galateo* and Grossardi's other writing see AMSC Cartella 5.

[27] Grossardi, *Galateo*, 112–13.   [28] Ibid. 89 and p. x.

[29] Ibid., xvi–xvii.

nor profane it by unsuitable conduct, but he must increase the reasons for public veneration so that in a small community it will come to represent the principle of authority.[30]

During the turbulent years at the turn of the century, when the country was wracked by the revolt of the Sicilian *Fasci*, as well as by more general violent economic and political disorders, several proposals were put forward for rationalizing the policing structures in Italy. Essentially, the reformers wanted to restrict the Carabinieri to the countryside and to improve the civilian guards. Giuseppe Alongi, for example, a Sicilian and himself a policeman, urged an overall increase in the numbers of police personnel and proposed that the Carabinieri be civilianized and more focused on what he saw as the real requirements of policing. Regularly timetabled military patrols and frequent transfers which prevented men from getting to know their district militated against good police work. Carabinieri generals, jealous of their independence and proud of their military traditions, generally did not bother to respond to their critics, though it was clear that they would vigorously resist any change in the administration and structure of their corps. In the event, no changes were made.[31]

By the last quarter of the century the Carabinieri had developed into the eyes and ears of the unified Italian state, with its officers reporting to their local commander, who in turn reported to the prefect. The reports covered political 'subversives' such as anarchists, socialists, republicans, members of the International, the Catholic political parties, and those seeking a union with the Tyrolian provinces of the Austrian Empire. They reported on the success of the annual conscription process, the electoral candidates who seemed most favoured in their jurisdictions, and any incidents which seemed out of the ordinary, as when, for example, Bulgarian and Romanian railway companies began recruiting workers in the province of Brescia towards the end of 1877.[32]

As in France and elsewhere, assisting the population in times of accident or natural disaster was a way of promoting the state as a guardian of its citizens; it was also a way of building bridges between the Carabinieri and the people, and fitted well with the corps' ideas of

[30] Grossardi, *Galateo*, 25–6. See pp. 136–7 above.

[31] Jensen, 'Police Reform and Social Reform', *passim*; id., *Liberty and Order*, 94, 112–13, and 148–9; see also Collin, 'The Italian Police', 32.

[32] See *inter alia*, AMSC Cartella 92, '1877 Informazioni varie'; Cartella 100, '1880 Partito sovversivi. Italia irredenta'; Cartella 108, '1882–1883, Informazione, Casi varie'; Cartella 122, '1883–1893, Corporazioni religiose, Partito Repubblicano, Mene socialiste fra militari, Elezione politiche, Partito Sovversivi'.

service and sacrifice. They fought fires, often at considerable personal cost; in August 1861, for example, a lieutenant-colonel and four carabinieri were killed rescuing people from a burning building in the centre of Turin.[33] They were sent to assist in times of natural disaster such as floods, and when an earthquake struck Casamicciola (Reggio Calabria) in July 1883.[34] They enforced quarantine regulations during outbreaks of cholera and, as in the more remote regions of France, this could lead to serious confrontations with local populations for whom such epidemics, and the government's attempts at control, had more more sinister origins and meanings.[35] The image of the Carabinieri as the guardian and helper of the people, as well as being impressed on the men by officers like Grossardi, was heavily promoted in press illustrations at the turn of the century. There were graphic pictures of them in action against brigands in Sardinia and Sicily, but they were also shown keeping back crowds from the dangers of volcanic eruptions, helping the injured away from disasters such as an explosion in small factory, a train crash, fires, or floods. The shooting of a dangerous animal may have been a relatively unimportant incident, but when bull ran amok in the small town of Biandrate (Novarra) in June 1907 at least two popular papers seized on the story and carried an idealized coloured representation.[36]

The iconography of power and trust implicit in these pictures may have been aimed deliberately at an illiterate population. Yet these newspaper stories, even when graphically and gorily illustrated, probably had little impact beyond the propertied classes in a country where so few could read. Whatever the assistance offered in times of danger or disaster by the Carabinieri or the PS guards, both forces seem to have remained unpopular among workers and peasants. Of the two forces, the Carabinieri appears to have been the more feared, if also, in some ways, the more respected; though, as an American anthropologist noted much later, a carabiniere could receive *considerazione* (the actual manifestation

[33] AMSC Morto in Servizio, schedi 241–5 (Lt.-Col. Emanuele Trotti, *et al.*).

[34] AMSC Cartella 116 (1883 Grave disastro in Casamicciola).

[35] AMSC Cartella 125 (1884 Dimonstrazioni verificatesi in dipendenza del colera), and for the correspondence of particular legions see Cartella 127 (Varii), 128 (Piacenza, Milano, Firenzi), 129 (Torino), 130 (Napoli). For the 1884 cholera in Italy see Frank M. Snowden, *Naples in the Time of Cholera, 1884–1911* (Cambridge: Cambridge University Press, 1995). For the Carabinieri's role in dealing with the outbreak in 1833 see Murat, *Il Carabinieri*, 37–8.

[36] Paolo di Paolo, *Dalla Cronaca alla Leggenda. I Carabinieri nelle illustrazioni dei periodici popolari italiani* (Rome: Comando Generale dell'Arma dei Carabinieri, 1990, 206–7, and for the Carabinieri assisting in other disasters see, *inter alia*, 74, 81, 104, 107, and 113.

of deference) from a community without *rispetto* (the respect given as a result of informal social rank).[37] In the last decade of the nineteenth century and the years before World War I labour disputes frequently ended in violence; and if, from the turn of the century, Carabinieri reports increasingly stressed the rights and protection of workers as well as those of employers, the men were still rather too inclined to shoot their way out of any confrontation.[38]

While dealing with disasters may have made good news stories in the press, together with combating brigands and repressing strikes, and while the latter and political surveillance may have preoccupied both the politicians and the internal opponents of liberal Italy, these activities rarely had any impact on the men's routine of daily patrols. As with the French Gendarmerie, Carabinieri barracks had registers of daily service which had to be signed by local notables or functionaries as a way of demonstrating that they were carrying out the required patrols. Only one of these books appears to have survived, that for the barracks of Santa Brioni, one of the stations of the Bari legion; it covers the period from 11 April to 29 June 1869. Even though the register lists patrols with soldiers in the search for brigands, it reveals, as might be expected, an overall absence of major incidents. Similarly, the surviving records of arrests suggest a predominance of the mundane.[39]

Perhaps more than anywhere else in Europe, the Italian variant of the Gendarmerie had a central role in building the state. It participated in the Wars of Unification as a military unit. It was seen as having a key role in pacifying and bringing order to territories newly incorporated into Piedmontese Italy. It brought the promise of equality before the law and of good, just government. After unification it became a symbol of the state on the ground, enforcing the state's laws and regulations, protecting the inhabitants on the state's behalf, and sometimes even taking the complaints of the disenfranchised to a higher authority. But the paternalist role was commonly clouded by the popular hostile perception of the corps as, first and foremost, an instrument of repression. In a vicious circle, this perception reinforced the officers' general mistrust of the lower classes and encouraged the men in their inclination to shoot first and ask questions afterwards. The origins of the corps were

---

[37] Sydel Silverman, *Three Bells of Civilization: The Life of an Italian Hill Town* (New York: Columbia University Press, 1975), 106.

[38] Collin, 'The Italian Police', 22, 47, 49, and 52.

[39] The *Registro di Servizio Giornaliero* for Santa Brioni is one of the exhibits in the Carabinieri Museum in Rome. AMSC Cartella 47 (1861–1875 Raccolta di Circulari manuscritti) contains some annual arrest lists, but these are generally in a very poor condition.

Piedmontese, but it also exuded the ethos which Moncey, Wirion, and others had expected from the Napoleonic Gendarmerie and which Consalvi had hoped for in his papal force. Within united Italy the Carabinieri rapidly became a national institution, drawing its men from all over the country, though apparently increasingly from the south as the century wore on. United Italy was a land of clientalism in which local elites controlled jobs and land and determined most taxes; they often also controlled the small electorate and demanded that deputies to the national parliament prioritize regional and local issues. The Carabinieri could not help but find itself used to defend the interests of these regional and local elites against popular protest and economic unrest. Yet in structure, composition, and deployment the Carabinieri was a truly national force, with notions of service and sacrifice for the nation rather than a focus on region and locality.

12

VARIATIONS: LANDJÄGERS AND GENDARMES

The states of nineteenth-century Germany differed from each other in economic structure as well as in cultural, political and social traditions. As outlined above in Chapter 10, during the Napoleonic period and its immediate aftermath Gendarmeries were created in most of the German lands, though not those of the Habsburgs. The reasons for this were largely similar: central governments wanted a positive extension of their authority into, and stricter supervision of, their provinces, both of which were linked with conscious attempts to build a specific national or state identity among the inhabitants. There was also a belief that there was a need for some kind of state authority to safeguard what were often new territorial frontiers, and to check the movement and possible depredations of vagrants and other suspect characters whose whose numbers were growing as a result of the disruption of war and economic change.[1] The German Gendarmeries were intended to be rural police, but were easily sucked into the towns during emergencies. Yet if their origins were much the same, significant contrasts were to be found between the different national corps.

Prussia became the dominant state in Germany from the 1860s, and much nineteenth-century German history has tended to be

---

[1] Tangentially, it is interesting to note that when a member of the Bavarian royal house became King of Greece in the 1830s there was an assumption among his entourage that the Greeks needed western administrative and technical help in creating their state. Amongst the modernizing institutions introduced was a Gendarmerie, commanded by a French philhellene. While Bavarians stiffened the Greek army, however, the bulk of the Gendarmerie, established for the maintenance of internal order, was to be recruited from young Greeks. The new corps played an important role in the conflicts with brigands, but there were also concerns that it enforced the law in traditional ways, and that the men slipped into brigandage themselves and even swore blood-brotherhood with the brigands and migratory shepherds they were meant to control. John Anthony Petropulos, *Politics and Statecraft in the Kingdom of Greece, 1833–1843* (Princeton NJ: Princeton University Press), 1968, 163 and 170; John S. Koliopoulos, *Brigands with a Cause: Brigandage and Irredentism in Modern Greece, 1821–1912* (Clarendon Press: Oxford, 1987), 78–9, 157–8, 240, and 264.

Prusso-centric. The Prussian Gendarmerie, however, remained a relatively small force throughout the ninteenth century. Reduced from a nominal compliment of 9,000 to around 1,300 NCOs and men in 1820 by pressure from the Junkers and the army, its numbers scarcely changed until the Revolution of 1848, and this in spite of an increase of some 46 per cent in the Prussian population over the same period. In 1848, with a Gendarmerie of 2,700 men, Prussia had roughly one gendarme for every 12,000 inhabitants; this gave it the lowest ratio of gendarmes to population of any significant German state (see Table 12.1). By 1890 the numbers in the Prussian Gendarmerie had increased to just over 4,600; they had reached 5,600 at the outbreak of World War I.[2] The smaller, more compact states of south Germany had a much greater presence of gendarmes proportionate to their populations, even when, as in the case of Bavaria, the Gendarmerie numbers were reduced in the second half of the century (see Table 12.2).

TABLE 12.1. *Number of gendarmes per 100,000 of population in the German states in 1848*

State	Number
Baden	37
Bavaria	52
Brunswick (1839)	40
Hanover	23
Prussia	8
Saxony	10
Württemberg	25

Source: Ralph Jessen, *Polizei im Industrierevier: Modernisierung und Herrschaftpraxis im westfälischen Ruhrgebiet 1848–1914* (Göttingen, Vandenhoeck & Ruprecht, 1991) 353.

Financial considerations helped to keep the Prussian Gendarmerie small, especially in the early years. In February 1825, for example, the minister of the interior warned of the problems already created for the state's pension fund because of men being retired from the Gendarmerie; he urged that men due for their pension be kept on if they

---

[2] Elaine Glovka Spencer, *Police and the Social Order in German Cities: The Düsseldorf District, 1848–1914* (De Kalb, Ill.: Northern Illinois University Press, 1992), 6 and 87.

TABLE 12.2. *The size of the South German Gendarmeries*

State	Number of gendarmes	Ratio to population
(a) 1830		
Baden	225	1 : 5,129
Bavaria	3,071	1 : 1,314
Württemberg	417	1 : 3,715
(b) 1864		
Baden	492	1 : 2,748
Bavaria	2,700	1 : 1,775
Württemberg	536	1 : 3,363

Source: Wirsing, 'Die Geschichte der Gendarmeriekorps', 181.

were fit enough to continue in post, and that any recruit be rejected if it seemed likely that he would only to be able to serve for a short period. A decade later another interior minister was advising that, mainly for financial reasons, gendarmes were supposed to supervise the local police and not substitute for them.[3] At the same time in Baden it was suggested that pension money might be saved by transferring men who, for one reason or another, could no longer cope with the rigours of the gendarme's life, to be policemen in small towns. Such men, it was urged, would be preferable to other ex-soldiers who commonly took these positions, since gendarmes had police experience and training. But while it was seen as a financial saving and potentially beneficial to send former gendarmes into the town police, there was a reluctance to let serving gendarmes be drawn into local policing more generally. Gendarmerie officers denigrated local policing. 'In many places the police are without uniform and arms,' complained one inspecting officer of Gendarmerie; 'or, which is quite preposterous, they are of such a kind as to need looking after themselves. One finds men who are deaf, aged, lame, weak, and more often drunk than sober; in one place the policeman has already been reported for theft and penalized.'[4]

Many of the Rhenish districts which Prussia acquired at the Congress of Vienna had lived under the French legal codes supervised by

[3] Landesarchiv Magdeburg, LHA Rep C 20 I, 1b Nr. 2059 1, minister of interior, 4 Feb. 1825; Alf Lüdtke, *Police and State in Prussia, 1815–1850* (Cambridge: Cambridge University Press, 1989), 76.

[4] Bernd Wirsing, 'Die Geschichte der Gendarmeriekorps und deren Vorläuferorganisationen in Baden, Württemberg und Bayern, 1750–1850', Dissertation . . . des Doktors Philosophie, Universität Konstanz, 1991, pp. 173 and 184.

imperial gendarmes for more than a decade. The Rhinelanders were keen to keep French law and, apart from a brief period at the beginning of the Restoration, the Napoleonic Codes were maintained. The Rhenish burghers appear generally to have supported the Imperial Gendarmerie in its campaigns against bandits and vagrants; they may even have looked back on it with some affection and have preferred it to its Prussian replacement, not least because it was so much thicker on the ground. The French *département* of the Rhin-et-Moselle, for example, had initially been given a Gendarmerie company of 130 men for a population of 280,000; after the reorganization of the Prussian Gendarmerie in 1820 the same district, now with a population of around 400,000, had a mere sixty-three gendarmes. During unrest in the textile trades in November 1828 there were complaints that the gendarmes around Krefeld were insufficient to cope with the problem.[5] Nothing was done, and again, a decade later in 1839, the Oberpräsident of the Rhine province complained to the interior ministry about what he saw as a continuing shortage of men:

The 2–4 Gendarmes in the large border counties, with a population of 30–40,000 souls each, represents the most obvious insufficiency when one considers that they are virtually fully occupied with the need to observe aliens and other border business, and that their effect on internal policing is virtually nil. There is almost no control of public houses, annual markets and other gatherings. However, the lack of restraint over the lower popular classes on such occasions encourages minor excesses which, if they were to become commonplace, could all too easily lead to greater excesses.[6]

One key difference between the French Gendarmerie and its German namesakes, which clearly had an impact on the way in which men could be deployed in emergencies, was in their distribution across the national territory. Whereas the French were located in small barracks containing four to six men, it was usual for German gendarmes to live singly, or with their families, in rented accommodation. Only towards the end of the century was there an abortive proposal to establish barracks for the Prussian Gendarmerie, and this stemmed from a greater concentration on the task of maintaining order in regions of rapid industrial and urban development. This deployment put the pressure of finding and paying for suitable accommodation on the German gendarmes themselves, and

---

[5] Heinrich Rösen, 'Der Aufstand der Krefelder "Seidenfabrikarbeiter" 1828 und die Bildung einer "Sicherheitswache": Ein Dokumentation', *Die Heimat: Zeitschrift für Niederrheinische Heimatpflege*, 36 (1965), 32–61; at 41–2 and 45.

[6] Quoted in Lüdtke, *Police and State*, 77.

it also meant that transfers were unpopular with the men because of possible additional expense. A Landjäger in Württemberg was dismissed and sentenced to three years imprisonment for embezzlement in 1828; he had a wife and three children, and he claimed that six transfers in two years had impoverished him and driven him to despair.[7] This, of course, was an extreme case, but the problem was allowed to continue well into the second half of the century. In July 1884 Gendarme Henriegel was ordered to move immediately from Heiligenstadt to Wahlhausen in Thuringia; at the end of August he found himself paying rent to two landlords, and he requested assistance from his superiors.[8] Moreover, since individual gendarmes were isolated in their districts and living in private lodgings there could be problems of supervision for the NCOs and officers. Towards the end of 1842 Wachtmeister (sergeant) Giebelhausen requested an additional allowance given the distances that he had to cover in supervising his district. While the regulations stipulated that patrols were only to cover some three to four miles, Giebelhausen complained that he was having to make journeys sometimes over twenty, and even over forty miles from his station at Erfurt. These journeys could require overnight rests and, during the winter, even day-long rests for his horse—all of which had to be paid for. He claimed that, until her death, his mother had helped to support him, but now both her savings and his own were exhausted. The authorities accepted the complaint and were sympathetic, but they could not afford another Wachtmeister, so Giebelhausen was given an additional annual allowance for expenses, out of which it was suggested he should pay another NCO periodically to assist him. In addition to the supervision by NCOs and officers, considerable reliance was also put on the comments made in the gendarmes' duty journals by the senior local civilian authority, the Landrat.[9]

In the German lands in the early nineteenth century, borders, especially new borders, often created problems since they meant little to local people. Though not to the extent that the Prussians had hoped, the Congress of Vienna redrew the frontiers of Saxony in Prussia's favour. In 1817 Saxon gendarmes created a minor international incident when they pursued two Prussian subjects across the new border and

---

[7] Walter Wannenwetsch, *Das Württembergische Landjägerkorps und die reichseinheitliche Gendarmerie in Württemberg mit einer Rückschau auf die Anfänge der Landespolizei* (Stuttgart: Gewerkschaft der Polizei, 1986), 29.

[8] Ibid., Nr. 1694/3246, Aug. 1884.

[9] Thüringisches Staatsarchiv, Gotha, Kasten 394 Nr. 1699/711, correspondence Feb.–Apr. 1823, and Nr. 1701/859 correspondence Sept. 1842–Jan. 1843.

arrested them in the village of Moritz. The Prussians insisted that the Saxon officer who ordered his men into their territory be punished. The Saxons responded by protesting that the people of Moritz were abusing their customary rights to gather wood on their side of the frontier. Five years later threats to burn customs houses on the border led to a strengthening of the Gendarmerie on the Prussian side of the frontier around Merseburg.[10] Significantly, when in 1828 a customs agreement was signed between Bavaria and Württemberg, it was the elite units of the respective Gendarmeries which were entrusted with the supervision of the borders.[11] But, of course, the supervision of new frontiers was only one of a multiplicity of tasks.

Section 81 of the 1812 Prussian Gendarmerie Edict specified that as 'executors of the public force' members of the Gendarmerie were to patrol their district for, amongst other things, the prevention and investigation of crimes and other offences. They were particularly instructed to watch out for suspicious and dangerous persons who could be arrested without either a warrant or first seeking the authority of a superior. Across the German lands during the *Vormärz* the gendarmes appear to have arrested many more 'beggars' (*Bettler*) than 'criminals' (*Gauner* or *Jauner*), though the precise understanding given to these terms, which prompted first suspicions and then arrest, and the problem of not knowing the incidence of rearrest, particularly among 'beggars', make it difficult to draw any precise conclusions about whom the gendarmes regarded as their targets.[12] As elsewhere, they were expected to get to know their districts; in 1818 the Prussian gendarmes were instructed to collect statistical information for the government, and this was seen as having the added value of helping them to 'expand their local knowledge'.[13] When disorder flared in the Prussian countryside it was the gendarmes who were brought in first, and as quickly as possible. The fact that they were thin on the ground and lived in single-man posts meant that they were only available in small numbers, usually from two

---

[10] Landesarchiv Magedeburg, LHA Rep C 28 I f, Nr 1078, letters 20 Mar. 19 Apr., and 8 Sept. 1817; LHA Rep C 20 I b, Nr. 2056, letter Feb. 1822. Attitudes towards the pursuit of a serious criminal offender across borders were probably rather different. Gendarme Hehl pursued a notorious *Gauner* in both his native Württemberg and Baden, apparently without a problem; Wannenwetsch, *Das Württembergische Landjägerkorps*, 22.

[11] Manfred Teufel, 'Das Württembergische Landjägerkorps, 1807–1934', *Archiv für Polizeigeschichte*, 6 (1992), 14–23; at 18.

[12] Lüdtke, *Police and State*, 88–9; Wirsing, 'Die Geschichte der Gendarmeriekorps', 186–8.

[13] Landesarchiv Magdeburg, LHA Rep C 28 If, Nr 1933, quotation from Schwarzenburg to Royal Government I Division, 26 Apr. 1818.

to four men. Yet they usually appear to have coped, which suggests suggests both courage and relative efficiency on the part of the gendarmes, and a measure of fear and respect for them on the part of the local communities. In similar disorders in towns without garrisons the small squads of gendarmes provided a back-up to civilian police or to citizen militias. Nevertheless, in nineteenth-century Prussia considerable reliance continued to be placed on the army when it came to dealing with popular disorder.[14]

Across the length and breadth of Germany local authorities had more confidence in gendarmes than in their own local police when it came to dealing with serious outbreaks of disorder. In particular, gendarmes were seen as more dependable and as being regarded with more respect by the labouring classes.[15] But this greater confidence did not necessarily mean that the relations between the military gendarme and the representatives of the civil power were warm. The hierarchies of the gendarmeries were jealous of their military standing and independence, something which rubbed off on many of the rank and file. Nowhere was the civil power able to issue a direct order to a gendarme; in early nineteenth-century Bavaria it was stated that if, on any occasion, any civil servant was allowed to give such an order without a proper written requisition, then the personal freedom of the population could be severely threatened.[16] However, the possibilities for argument and misunderstanding between gendarmes and the civil power were plentiful, not least because of the requirements that the civilian authorities sign duty journals and that the local Landrat write a periodic comment on a man's behaviour in his duty journal.

Gendarmes brought more work for local mayors. The insistence of a gendarme on a night patrol that a mayor get out of bed to sign his duty book could be an infuriating inconvenience. Beggars and vagrants brought before the mayor for examination and sentencing were another, and took up time. In southern Germany, especially during the first third of the century, some mayors sought to avoid the latter inconvenience by promptly releasing the offenders brought before them by gendarmes. In an attempt to eradicate this behaviour, from 1838 the Baden authorities began requiring that the gendarmes prepare lists of every offender

---

[14] See Lüdtke, *Police and State*, *passim*; also id., 'The Role of State Violence in the Period of Transition to Industrial Capitalism: The Example of Prussia From 1815 to 1848, *Social History*, 4 (1979), 175–221.

[15] Spencer, *Police and the Social Order*, 21.

[16] Wirsing, 'Die Geschichte der Gendarmeriekorps', 158.

apprehended and the punishment inflicted, so that the responses of mayors could be inspected and those who were lax could be prompted into action. Those mayors who were shown to be particularly lax or incompetent could find a squad of gendarmes or soldiers quartered on their community, with the community forced to bear the costs.[17] But the gendarmes themselves were not paragons of virtue. When Baden introduced a bounty for every beggar who was arrested there were gendarmes who saw this as an opportunity for making extra money by arresting tramping artisans as vagrants.[18] The records of the Württemberg Gendarmerie reveal men being punished for visiting taverns when on duty and failing in their duties and responsibilities.[19] Even some Prussian gendarmes seem to have been as keen on a quiet life as some south German mayors. During the unrest among the Krefeld silkworkers in 1828 Gendarme Tanton was described as 'an honest man who has served for some years, but who prefers peace and quiet to effort'. At the same time his comrade, Gendarme Wirtz, was noted as having enlisted when the corps was first established, 'when men were put into uniform with little regard for their physical and moral qualifications, and while he is talkative, physically he is not up to the job'.[20] In the Münster district for five years running one Brigadier filled in his men's annual arrest statistics using identical figures from the previous year; no one appears to have noticed, though regulations required that duty journals be checked regularly and reminders to this effect were sent out.[21]

But while some men were lax, others were quite the opposite, and this could lead to problems in police relations with the public. Members of the German Gendarmeries, schooled in the military, continued to think in military terms and to believe that they were engaged in a war against the internal enemy. Oberstleutnant (lieutenant-colonel) Schact, who commanded the company of Swabia and Neuberg in Bavaria, wrote in precisely such terms in a memorandum drafted in May 1848. The 'small war' of the Gendarmerie required 'cunning and cleverness, bravery and determination, mobility and stamina'. Five years later the administration in Arnsberg proposed to the Prussian ministry of the interior that the Gendarmerie should exchange their white belts for black so that they

[17] Ibid. 167.   [18] Ibid. 163 and 189–90.
[19] Teufel, 'Das Württembergische Landjägerkorps', 19.
[20] Rösen, 'Der Aufstand Der Krefelder "Seidenfabrikarbeiter" 1828', 41.
[21] Lüdtke, *Police and State*, 88; Thüringisches Staatsarchiv, Gotha, Kasten 394 Nr. 1699/1612, July 1828, and Nr. 1692/5803, Aug. 1868.

would be less visible on their daily patrols and investigations; the parallel was drawn with soldiers in wartime who blackened the brass on their helmets, and 'the Gendarmes are *always* facing the enemy'.[22] The military mentality, and the belief that they were engaged in a war, probably contributed to the lack of discretion and blind obedience to orders which some men showed in their attitudes towards individuals, regardless of class or status. If a man looked suspicious or could not produce the appropriate papers he was considered by gendarmes as their property. Such attitudes led, for example, to the arrest of a professor of minerology in the Swabian Alps early in 1838. The professor was suspected because he was spotted, while engaged in his research, wearing dirty clothes and carrying a hammer.[23] On the other side, even in Prussia, such behaviour led to gendarmes being resisted and insulted, with resulting jurisdictional problems over whether or not these incidents should be investigated first by the civil authorities or left to the Gendarmerie.[24]

In general, the liberals in Germany during the first half of the nineteenth century had no objection to the deployment of gendarmes in the countryside against beggars and vagrants who were readily identified both as criminals and as threats to the social order. Yet they disliked the military nature of the different corps, their often rigorous enforcement of what seemed petty regulations, and what appeared to be their unshakeable loyalty to their prince and the existing form of government. The liberals found allies among local authorities, who had no wish to see their policing powers usurped by an institution of the central state, and at times protests could be successful. Events in the university town of Tübingen provide an extreme, but telling example of the way in which such frictions could develop and be resolved. Both the town and the university had their own police organizations, and these police were rather more lax in enforcing police regulations than the Württemberg Landjägerkorps. Trouble came to a head during the political excitement generated by the revolutionary wave of 1830 to 1831. On 16 January 1831 Landjäger Michael Hanse confronted a group of men whom he considered to be in breach of the peace; he drew his sabre and injured Ludwig Kost, a local winegrower. Demonstrations erupted in the town.

---

[22] Wirsing, 'Die Geschichte der Gendarmeriekorps', 203; Lüdtke, *Police and State*, 77.
[23] Wirsing, 'Die Geschichte der Gendarmeriekorps', 205.
[24] Landesarchiv Magdeburg, LHA Rep C 28 If, Nr. 1568, minister of the interior to Oberpräsident in Magdeburg, 8 Feb. 1841, repeating a circular of 30 Apr. 1838, and an explanation of how such investigations should be undertaken of 25 May 1839.

Hanse was court-martialled, sentenced to six months in prison, dismissed from the elite Landjäger corps, and returned to the army. But this did not appease the residents or the students. A deputation from the town administration was sent to the king and, while he had generally resisted demands for reform throughout 1830, the king was persuaded permanently to withdraw his Landjägerkorps from Tübingen.[25]

In the years before 1848 the German Gendarmeries had kept a watchful eye on 'democrats', liberals, and radicals.[26] In early March of that year gendarmes in the southern states kept their superiors informed of the worsening internal situation. But, as rural *charivaris* linked up with urban disorder to become revolution, the gendarmes increasingly became objects of suspicion and their orders were ignored except where these coincided with popular requirements or desires. In Württemberg some elements of the Landjägerkorps were themselves caught up in the revolutionary excitement and petitioned against autocratic officers and regulations which, among other things, restricted marriage and forbade men from wearing civilian clothes when off duty. Other men remained fervently loyal to the old regimes, often showing remarkable courage, like the Württemberger who halted an anti-Semitic demonstration by standing in front of the crowd and shouting: 'I stand here in the name of the King, and who is for the King, join me!' Such courage could border on stupidity, as with the Baden brigadier who entered a tavern full of revolutionaries and proposed a toast to his prince. Attempts to report local officials for revolutionary behaviour or to supervise the policemen of revolutionary communes were asking for trouble, and many small detachments probably spent the period of revolutionary effervescence keeping their heads down; there was little else they could do. However, in the military repression that followed, like the French Gendarmerie, German gendarmes were called upon for their local knowledge and were accordingly deployed to assist the armies.

In the immediate aftermath of the revolutions of 1848 the German Gendarmeries reverted to their old tasks. Besides their regular patrols they also made occasional, large-scale sweeps of the countryside, sometimes linked with army units, to pick up vagrants and any suspicious characters. In the repressive atmosphere of the decade following the year

---

[25] Bernd Wirsing, ' "Gleichsam mit Soldatenstrenge": Neue Polizei in süddeutschen Städten. Zu Polizeiverhalten und Bürger-Widersetzlichkeit im Vormärz', in Alf Lüdtke (ed.), *'Sicherheit und Wohlfahrt:' Polizei, Gesellschaft und Herrschaft im 19. und 20. Jahrhundert* (Frankfurt-am-Main: Suhrkamp, 1991), esp. 79–82.

[26] The following account of 1848 is drawn principally from Wirsing, 'Die Geschichte der Gendarmeriekorps', 248–61.

of revolutions, 'democrats' continued to be on their list of suspects. In 1852, for example, an off-duty soldier was arrested by a gendarme in Munich on the grounds that he was wearing the coat and hat of a 'democrat'. Social change and technological development brought new tasks, such as the surveillance of passengers at railway stations; this also brought the possibility of new frictions, with train conductors objecting to gendarmes trespassing on the private property of their trains. The pursuit and arrest of offenders was popular with the victims of crime or vandalism and might earn a gendarme a present or private reward.[27] But gendarmes could also still be deployed in force in areas where disorder was expected; their military nature often evoked fear and resentment, and they could respond with arrogance and contempt for the local people. Such was the case, for example, with the Prussian gendarmes deployed in Marpingen during the excitement following reported visitations of the Virgin Mary in July 1876. Similarly, any gendarme's determination to enforce regulations precisely and by the book provided the potential for provoking popular hostility and friction with the local civilian authorities.[28]

Of course, bending or breaking the rules, either by accident or design, meant that a gendarme could be disciplined or reprimanded. Sometimes the bureaucratic red tape of the police probably appeared to some men as an impediment to doing the job. Early in 1892 Gendarme Bosse found himself in trouble for entering a miners' barracks in the Neuhaldensleben district and arresting a worker. Bosse's error was in failing to inform the local police and the gendarme resident in the district of the mine; he had asked the barrack supervisor to inform the local gendarme, but this was regarded as insufficient.[29] Other offences were similar to those noted in other Gendarmeries. Gendarme Ziermann was punished in October 1866 for falsifying entries in his duty journal, for accepting free drinks, and for drunkenness. In September the following year he was again punished for accepting drinks and for drunkenness. His local commander wanted to get rid of him as a disgrace to the corps; Ziermann himself requested his pension, claiming that he was unfit because of rheumatism. However, the local Landrat was unwilling to see him go, describing him as 'one of the most comptent gendarmes in the

[27] See e.g. Thüringisches Staatsarchiv, Gotha, Kasten 394 Nr. 22855/219, May 1874.

[28] Wirsing, 'Die Geschichte der Gendarmeriekorps', 165–6 and 205; David Blackbourn, *The Marpingen Visions: Rationalism, Religion and the Rise of Modern Germany* (London: Fontana, 1993), 267–73; Lüdtke, *Police and State*, 101.

[29] Landesarchiv Magdeburg, LHA Rep C 30, Haldensleben I, Nr. 759/4774, Staatsanwallschaft to Landrat in Neuhaldensleben, 19 Apr. 1892.

district of Erfurt'.[30] And even though Prussia was a militarisitic state and its Gendarmerie was, by definition, a military police, the *Rechtsstaat* meant something to the people. While some may have been overawed by the gendarmes, others had no qualms about protesting and demanding redress for what they considered to be improper behaviour.[31]

Such complaints were probably irksome to the gendarmes and their superiors and, on occasions, the regulations of the *Rechtsstaat* must have appeared particularly pettifogging. Towards the end of 1890 a local government bulletin in the Merseburg district announced that a Polish worker called Janzak, whose address was unknown, had been sentenced to a fine of 10 marks or to two days in prison. But while the local government may not have known Janzak's whereabouts, a local court did, and the Pole appeared before this court on a second petty charge. Gendarme Daniel, present as a witness in this second case, arrested Janzak and handed him over to the local prison. The County Court of Mersberg demanded that Daniel be reprimanded on the grounds that, while Janzak's earlier sentence had been announced, there was no actual warrant for his arrest. The arguments continued well into the following year. In August 1891 the exasperated Regierungspräsident of Merseburg wrote to the Oberpräsident of the province of Saxony:

. . . I still do not accept the application for reprimanding the gendarme. Gendarme Daniel is . . . one of the most competent gendarmes and his enthusiasm and loyalty will suffer as a result these allegations. He did nothing but arrest, temporarily, an errant Polish worker . . . and then pass him to the prison warden. . . .

If you disregard the legal side and just look at the practicalities, the complaint is almost incomprehensible. One would have expected the courts to be pleased that they are supported in the execution of justice by such an efficient Gendarmerie, and they should not create difficulties for any gendarme who, in his eagerness, may perhaps for once have acted not quite legally. In the matter in hand, particularly where a vagrant Polish worker agreed with the way in which his case had been conducted, it seems unnecessary to burden oneself, as well as other authorities, with additional work simply for the sake of reprimanding a gendarme.[32]

---

[30] Thüringisches Staatsarchiv, Gotha, Kasten 394 Nr. 1692/2743, Apr.–Aug. 1868.

[31] See e.g. the claim against Gendarme Gross for allegedly breaking a lock in 1846 (Thüringisches Staatsarchiv, Gotha, Kasten 394 Nr. 1693/1984) and Theresa Kruse's claim against Gendarme Schliecher for tearing her clothes and damaging her property while arresting her in Jan. 1855—a case which took two years to resolve (Thüringisches Staatsarchiv, Gotha, Kasten 394 Nr. 1693/578).

[32] Landesarchiv Magdeburg, LHA Rep C 20 I, Ib, Nr. 2066/1, Regierungspräsident to Oberpräsident, 21 Aug. 1891.

Of course, the same defence might be raised in instances of more dubious behaviour.

In the last third of the century economic development and urban growth in Germany, and Prussia in particular, accelerated changes in policing structures and brought a shift in the focus of the gendarmes' activities. While there were experiments with state-appointed police directors, the Prussian Police Law of 1850 had the effect of returning to the municipalities the control and recruitment of police in most towns and cities. However, gendarmes were funded from state coffers, and in addition to calling them in to deal with the occasional serious problem of public order, some parsimonious municipalities, in an attempt to save money, appear also to have tried to use them to support their patrolmen in ordinary day-to-day patrolling. As earlier in the century, this brought friction with locals accusing the gendarmes of military arrogance and an attitude of superiority, while gendarmes accused the municipal police of sloppy habits, smoking in the streets, frequenting pubs, and taking tips. In 1881 the minister of the interior confirmed that the Gendarmerie was not to be deployed for ordinary municipal policing, and nine years later, while contemplating an augmentation of the corps in the industrial districts, he urged that the burdens of the regular patrols might be reduced so as to give more time for addressing the problems of the fast-changing society. In the two decades before World War I some municipalities in the booming Ruhr turned to the royal state police, the Königliche Schutzmannschaft, for everyday order maintenance. The royal Schutzmann (literally 'protection man'), established initially for Berlin in 1848, was recruited from the army, and with his *pickelhaube* and accoutrements he had a distinctly military appearance; but unlike the gendarme he was no longer a soldier, and the possibility of civil–military conflict was thereby averted. Like the gendarme, however, he was attractive to cost-conscious burghers because the central government picked up a significant percentage, though not all, of his costs.[33] But if municipal and royal police were responsible for day-to-day patrolling in the urban districts, the Gendarmerie was seen by many as the best instrument for confronting industrial agitation and disorder.

During the liberal phase of the Prussian Revolution in 1848 consideration had been given to the possibility of doubling the Gendarmerie

[33] Spencer, *Police and the Social Order*, esp. 36, 49, 87 and chap. 9; Ralph Jessen, *Polizei im Industrierevier; Modernisierung und Herrschaftspraxis im westfälischen Ruhrgebiet 1848–1914* (Göttingen: Vandenhoeck & Ruprecht, 1991), 69–70; Landesarchiv Magdeburg, LHA Rep. C20I, Ib Nr. 2062/I 3101, minister of the interior to *Oberpräsident* in Magdeburg, 9 May 1890.

to 5,400 men. This had been welcomed by the authorities in the Ruhr, who were concerned about the unemployed becoming vagabonds or resorting to crime and extortion. The plan was dropped, partly because the unrest of the spring and early summer declined and partly too, it would appear, because of the cost. During the 1860s, however, at a time when the Gendarmerie was increasingly moving out of the towns and cities, it was increasingly seen as the most effective instrument for over-awing recalcitrant workers. At the end of the decade industrialists were seeking to entice gendarmes into providing their premises with special attention by offering them cheap housing and arranging well-paid factory jobs for their children. Some industrialists requested that gen-darmes be stationed in their factories, and in return took over the costs of pay, pensions, and equipment; in 1875 the Krupps Works in Essen had six gendarmes employed on such terms. These practices were ended in 1883, but industrialists still sought to have gendarmes posted perman-ently in the vicinity of their works and provided them with privileges.

The number of gendarmes in the Ruhr increased more than fourfold between 1848 and 1889, but the population grew even faster. The min-ers' strike of 1889 saw gendarmes and troops drafted into the affected area from all over Prussia. In the aftermath, the military commander urged that the army should not be called upon for such emergencies in future, and that the number of police and gendarmes deployed in the region be augmented to an appropriate number. At the same time, the minister of the interior concluded that 'the Gendarmerie, by virtue of its organiza-tion, is the best qualified to prevent outrages against the public peace, security, and order by an agitated population'. The miners' strike, and the fear of subsequent unrest, prompted a general plan for the reorganization of policing which included instituting a ratio of twenty-eight gendarmes for every 100,000 of the population, provision for gendarmes to patrol in pairs, and the creation of Gendarmerie barracks to enable at least four men to be stationed in the same location. The plan never came to fruition, though as Ralph Jessen has pointed out, its very existence points to a growing camp- and siege-mentality among Prussian policy-makers; they wanted to confront workers' unrest without recourse to the army, but could only contemplate doing this by an increasing militarization of the police. On the eve of World War I 45 per cent of Prussia's Gendarmerie was based in the vicinity of the kingdom's major industrial districts.[34]

[34] Jessen, *Polizei im Industrierevier*, 58–9, 64, 74, 77–82, 88, and 119–20; quotation at 80; Albrecht Funk, *Polizei und Rechtsstaat: Die Entwicklung des staatlichen Gewaltmonopols in Preussen 1848–1914* (Frankfurt: Campus, 1986), 234.

For the gendarmes of the German states showing the flag was a far less important role than it had been for Napoleon's imperial force or than it was for the Italian Carabinieri. In the years shortly after their formation the corps in southern Germany were one of the elements with the new state frontiers which contributed to people's identity as Bavarians, Württembergers, or whatever. But such a role was scarcely needed in the second half of the century; and German unification was never as dependent on internal military enforcement and surveillance as the Italian. Like other Gendarmerie corps, those in Germany were established to sweep the countryside clear of undesirables who appeared to threaten social peace and order, the beggars and vagrants who, in the perceptions of the propertied and the respectable, were easily transformed into criminals. As such, the German Gendarmeries had their antecedents in older, often temporary bodies organized to arrest beggars and vagrants. The boost to their creation as regular agents of the state came with the example of the efficient, centralized Napoleonic model. Such a state met with hostility from opposite ends of the political spectrum—from traditional gentry, like the Prussian Junkers, and from progressive liberals. This opposition, and the resulting negotiation with governments, helped shape the structure of the policing which emerged during the nineteenth century. In the final analysis, German gentry, liberals, and governments could agree on the value of gendarmes for general order maintenance against undesirables in the countryside, and later against economic organization and protest by workers in the burgeoning industrial cities.

13
VARIATIONS:
THE HABSBURG LANDS

In February 1846 the Polish gentry in the Habsburg provinces of Galicia rose in revolt. The uprising, with the authorities already alerted, was a disaster, but the aftermath was especially bloody, since the peasants in those areas where seigneurial obligations had remained particularly oppressive took the side of the monarchy and wreaked a terrible revenge on their landlords. A rumour spread that the Emperor had abolished the Ten Commandments, thus permitting the killing of the gentry; over 400 manors were plundered, between 1,100 and 1,200 seigneurs, seigneurial agents, and priests were killed. The Habsburg authorities were both appalled by the savagery of the peasantry's response and encouraged by its support for the monarchy against the landlords. The events strengthened the hope that, across the Empire, the Emperor could rely on the peasantry for support against demands from the gentry and from liberals, and this in spite of the bad harvests of the mid-1840s which were fostering unrest in the countryside as well as the towns. The authorities were not prepared to introduce land reform and emancipation but, nevertheless, considered it expedient to issue decrees outlining the existing possibilities for the commutation or redemption of obligations to the landlord; this, it was hoped, would help cement peasant loyalty to the monarchy.[1] At the same time Metternich began seriously to consider extending the Habsburg Gendarmerie from Lombardy into the other provinces of the Empire. In August his subordinates were approaching the governments of France, Bavaria, and Prussia for information on the organization of their Gendarmeries. A report of 9 December expressed Metternich's belief that it was 'desirable and necessary' to establish such a corps, 'particularly in Galicia'.[2] However, it was not until the Empire

---

[1] Jerome Blum, *The End of the Old Order in Rural Europe* (Princeton NJ: Princeton University Press, 1978), 340 and 364; Alan Sked, *The Decline and Fall of the Habsburg Empire, 1815–1918* (London: Longman, 1989), 63–4.

[2] Staatsarchiv, Vienna, Staatskanzlei Vorträge (1846) Folie 33–7 V, Karton 294 1846 (Metternich), letters of 18 Aug, and 10 Nov. 1846, Report of 9 Dec. 1846.

had been profoundly shaken by the events of 1848 and Metternich himself had been forced into exile, that a Gendarmerie was eventually established for all of the Habsburg territories.

By the spring and early summer of 1849, while fierce fighting continued in the Hungarian and Venetian lands, radical revolution in
Vienna had been suppressed. However, moderate reform still appeared
possible and the new young Emperor, Franz Joseph, had himself
endorsed the movement for constitutional change. A constitution was
promulgated in March declaring equality before the law and a long list
of civic freedoms. Towards the end of June a new legal structure was
introduced which separated the judiciary from the executive and,
equally significantly, also from landholding. These changes suggested
the need for some sort of police institution to implement and maintain
them, and a month before these legal reforms Alexander Bach, the minister of the interior, put such a proposal before the Emperor. Even
under the old regime, Bach argued, the gentry was beginning to perceive a need for a centralized police organization; the need was even
greater now when the new political freedoms could foster licence:

A *Rechtsstaat*, to which the Austrian Monarchy is converting, cannot be successful without a strengthening of the judicial power, without proper guardians
of the law, and respected executors of state authority. The creation of public
prosecutors and courts therefore necessitates the creation of a state security
guard which is charged with the investigation of crimes, the pursuit of offenders, and the execution of judicial decisions.[3]

Franz Joseph agreed to the proposal on 8 June, and while it was another
six months before a formal bill was presented and twelve months before
service regulations were drafted, an Inspector-General of Gendarmerie
had been appointed by early autumn.

Johann Kempen had been born in 1793, the son of an officer in the
imperial army. He began his own military career in the wars against
Napoleon and then, for thirty years, served in a variety of posts across
the Habsburg Empire. He distinguished himself in subordinate roles
during the suppression of the revolution in 1848 and 1849, particularly
in Hungary. In May 1849 he was involved in discussions among the military over the possible creation of an internal security corps. He seems
to have been suggested to Franz Joseph for the position of Inspector-
General of Gendarmerie by General Haynau, the man who had finally

---

[3] Quoted in a summary kindly forwarded to me by the Austrian Ministry of the
Interior, 27 Sept. 1994, 'Österreichische Bundesgendarmerie, Ref II/4/Ausb'.

smashed the Hungarian revolution. Kempen took up the post on 1 November 1849, though much to his annoyance, apparently for financial reasons, his pay did not start until mid-January the following year. Kempen was an energetic administrator. His diary entries for the period of the initial organization reveal both the young Emperor taking an intense interest in the new corps and the potential for friction already emerging between the ministries of war and of the interior and the new Gendarmerie.

Franz Joseph believed that the army had saved the empire in 1848. In consequence, the army was to be fêted during his reign; this produced a crippling financial burden for the Empire even though the army itself never succeeded in achieving the numbers that it had on paper. Franz Joseph was determined that his new Gendarmerie should be organized on military lines, but the early years of his reign were dominated by innovative rather than restorative ideas. 'It would not be a bad idea', he told Kempen in May 1849, 'if people who were not normally appointed as officers were appointed as such in the Gendarmerie.' Similarly, he wanted the different regiments of the corps to have a national mix; even though the constitution of 1849 was rapidly shelved, the idea prevailed of a single, uniform citizenship for the peoples of the Empire, within which ethnicity was secondary and largely irrelevant.[4]

Within a week of taking up his appointment as Inspector-General Kempen was expressing concerns about being responsible to two ministries. While interior minister Bach continued to be particularly helpful in developing the Gendarmerie, Kempen was advised to lean towards the war minister. In the end he succeeded in carving out a significant degree of autonomy for himself between the two. There were also problems with other institutions within the Empire. Some army officers were jealous of the elite status of the new corps, which was made manifest by its distinctive spiked helmet, the *Pickelhaube*. Josip Jellacic, the ruthless and single-minded Ban of Croatia, sought unsuccessfully to keep the corps out of his jurisidiction. There were clashes with the judiciary, notably in the Steiermark during the summer of 1850 when a judge ordered gendarmes not to bring their weapons with them into his court. Here, as in many of the other clashes, the new Gendarmerie was

[4] Joseph Karl Mayr (ed.), *Das Tagebuch des Polizeiministers Kempen von 1848 bis 1859* (Vienna: Österreichischer Bundesverlag, 1931), entries for 3 May and 23 Sept. 1850; for a discussion of the innovative ideas behind the first two decades of Franz Joseph's reign see R. J. W. Evans, 'From Confederation to Compromise: The Austrian Experiment, 1849–1867', *Proceedings of the British Academy*, 87 (1995), 135–67.

favoured; in September the ministry of justice issued a decree to the effect that gendarmes had not only the right but the duty to attend court proceedings with their weapons.[5]

Apologists for the new Gendarmerie stressed its disinterest and probity in much the same way as those speaking or writing in favour of the similar corps established elsewhere in Europe. Paul Aloys Klar, for example, an imperial official in Bohemia, celebrated the Gendarmerie moving into a new barracks in Prague in 1857 with a short booklet in which he explained the guiding principles instilled into the men. Gendarmes were to fulfill their duties conscientiously, without fear or favour, and were always to consider mild persuasion and warnings before resorting to arrest.

New recruits are told that the gendarme should never take advantage of his position, should seek to gain the trust and love of the people, and should not appear as a watchdog or a strict disciplinarian but as a mainstay of the public welfare. He is not supposed to interfere in private lives and with families, for the Gendarmerie is only supposed to deal with the citizen's public affairs, and has nothing in common with the functions of the secret police.[6]

Unfortunately this was not always how matters seemed to the population of the Empire, both civilian and military, over all of whom the gendarmes had authority. 'It was an open question', wrote one soldier, 'whether the military of all grades or the civilians hated the gendarmes more.'[7] Initially there appear to have been concerns among people that the Gendarmerie was a way of quartering the army on them at their expense; and the army had not been noted for its good behaviour in dealing with order maintenance in the past. The end of revolutionary disorder, coinciding as it did with the creation of the new corps, gave the Gendarmerie a general aura of success in its first years, at least amongst the propertied classes; though the gendarmes were unable to eradicate the banditry, sometimes tinged with nationalist aspirations, which continued, especially in Hungary. Regulations which privileged a gendarme's evidence in court, together with the imperial decree of April 1854 which authorized gendarmes and policemen to order a fine, fourteen days imprisonment, or even in some instances a whipping to any-

---

[5] Mayr (ed.), *Das Tagebuch*, 24–8, see also, for example, diary entries for 5, 6, 17, and 30 Nov. and 1 Dec. 1849 (ministries), 9 Feb., 3, 10, and 24 June 1850 (Jellacic), 23 and 24 Aug. 1850 (weapons in court).

[6] Paul Aloys Klar, *Denkschrift der Gendarmeriekaserne in Prag* (Prague: 1857), 47–9.

[7] Quoted in Gunther E. Rothenberg, *The Army of Francis Joseph* (West Lafayette, Ind.: Purdue University Press, 1976), 46.

one who challenged their authority, did not contribute greatly to their popularity. Nor did Kempen's elevation to head of the imperial police in April 1854, a role which he combined with that of commander of the Gendarmerie and military governor of Vienna.[8] Whatever the protestations of men like Klar, this unity of roles in Kempen's person meant that the Gendarmerie became associated with the spies and informers deployed against both liberal constitutional reformers and radicals. Kempen was dismissed in 1859 and the Gendarmerie was, once again, separated from the police, but the damage had been done.

Originally the Gendarmerie was to be composed of sixteen regiments of 900 men each. The number of regiments was increased to nineteen in 1854, but the loss of the Italian provinces, the *Ausgleich* by which Hungary gained autonomy in 1867, and the constant need for financial stringency within the Empire led to a series of reorganizations and cutbacks during the 1860s and early 1870s. From 1866 the Regiments-Kommandos were given the more civilian name Landesgendarmerie-kommandos (LGK). After the reorganizations of 1876, and until the end of the monarchy in 1918, there were fourteen such LGKs. Each regiment or, later, LGK was responsible for a particular province or set of provinces. It had its own headquarters which also served as a training depot, but most of the men were deployed in small barracks spread throughout their province. The Gendarmerie never had its full quota of men; it reached a peak of 18,985 officers and men, of whom 1,517 were mounted, in 1857 when the Empire's population was around 30 million. By the mid-1870s the population had grown to about 35 million, but the Gendarmerie had shrunk to a mere 5,700 men. Thereafter it was increased gradually until, on the eve of World War I, there were 14,400 gendarmes for an imperial population of almost 50 million.[9]

Unlike most similar institutions in Europe, service in the Habsburg Gendarmerie was generally undertaken during, and as a part of, a man's military career rather than at the conclusion of it. Before 1845 different provinces of the Empire required different periods of service from conscripts. The regulations of 1845 established a uniform service period of eight years; this was altered in 1852 to eight years with the colours and two in the reserve. But there were a variety of exceptions and filters.

---

[8] Helmut Gebhardt, *Die Gendarmerie in der Steiermark von 1850 bis heute* (Graz: Leykam Verlag, 1997), 63 and 69–71; Gendarmerieoberst iR Franz Hesztera, *Die Kommandostrukturen der Gendarmerie von 1850 bis 1993* (Vienna: Leiro, 1994), 13 and 16.

[9] Clive Emsley and Sabine Phillips, 'The Habsburg Gendarmerie: A Research Agenda', *German History* 17 (1999), 241–50.

Conscription was by lot, and some communities, notably in Hungary, used this as an opportunity for getting rid of misfits and undesirables. Everywhere the propertied were able to exempt themselves from conscription. This, and the poor standards of education across the Empire, meant that conscription always fell on the poorest, and fewer than one in ten conscripts were literate. The generals preferred long-service soldiers, believing them to be less susceptible to subversive civilian influences; this, together with the requirement to keep costs down, led to the practice of furloughing most conscripts in the infantry after eighteen months and most conscipts to the artillery and engineers after three years; only conscripts in the cavalry generally served the full eight years. Such recruitment policies and military practices combined to make it difficult to get and keep good NCOs; it also limited the pool of men available for the Gendarmerie—the ordinary gendarme was, after all, equivalent in rank to an army corporal.[10]

Men moved from the army to the Gendarmerie, and sometimes back again. Transfer back to the army might be at at a man's personal request when he found that the life of a gendarme somehow did not measure up to his expectations; but each man was on probation for his first six months of service, and sometimes transfer back into the army was because an individual was considered by his superior's to be unsuitable for Gendarmerie tasks. From a sample of 526 men taken from the corps' personnel registers there are details of the length of service of some 402 men joining between 1849 and 1889; for 480 of these men there are also the reasons for departure from the first Gendarmerie regiment in which each served. Just under 5 per cent of the men served for six months or less. A slightly larger percentage served for more than eight years (see Table 13.1); indeed, a few had very long periods of service, especially those who got promotion. Johann Ober Mueller, for example, a comb-maker born in Rhind, Upper Austria, in 1851, joined the artillery at the age of 20, had risen to senior NCO by 1875, and transferred to the LGK of his native province in March 1877. Initially he signed up as a gendarme for four years; in 1882 he was promoted to acting Postenführer (station commander), and the rank was confirmed four years later. In 1888 he was promoted to Wachtmeister. He died in post in April 1891. For most men, however, service in the Gendarmerie continued for between one and six years. Around 40 per cent of the men went back into the army, and another 16 per cent transferred to different

---

[10] For Habsburg recruitment policies and practices see Rothenberg, *The Army of Francis Joseph*, esp. 13, 42, and 61.

TABLE 13.1. *Period served in the Habsburg Gendarmerie*

Period	Number of men	%
6 months or less	24	4.7
6 months to 1 year	44	8.6
1 to 2 years	49	9.6
2 to 3 years	53	10.4
3 to 4 years	56	10.9
4 to 5 years	52	10.2
5 to 6 years	38	7.4
6 to 7 years	26	5.1
7 to 8 years	27	5.3
More than 8 years	32	6.3
Unknown	110	21.5

Source: Samples from Kriesgarchiv, ABG KL, Kartons 2814–3148; see Emsley and Phillips, 'The Habsburg Gendarmerie'.

Gendarmerie units (regiments or LGKs), or appear as transferring to different units because of an internal reorganization of the corps (see Table 13.2). Thus, Josef Ivancie, born in the Steiermark in 1841, joined the army in September 1862 and transferred to the 6th Gendarmerie Regiment, with its headquarters in Pest, the following August. The internal reorganization of 1866, when the ten regiments became fifteen Kommandos, had him transferring to the 6th LGK with its headquarters in Groß-Wardein, also in Hungary; at the end of the year he transferred back into the cavalry. Johann Lepniak, noted in the personnel registers as a Serb-speaker, was born in Hungary the year after Ivancie, and followed a similar military career—from the infantry to the 6th Regiment, thence to the 6th LGK, and in 1867 back to the infantry.

The original regulations required gendarmes to be between 24 and 36, though men transferring from the army were sometimes allowed to be both younger and much older; and while possible, it was very exceptional for men to be recruited directly from civilian life after their military service was over. In 1857 the minimum age for entry was formally reduced to 21. The ages are recorded of 509 men in the sample recruited between 1849 and 1889. Roughly half of these joined between the ages of 21 and 25; the twenty-seven officers in the sample were rather older— none of them was under 25, thirteen were between 30 and 39, and seven were over 40 (see Table 13.3). The result of these recruitment policies meant that the Habsburg Gendarmerie was generally younger than its

TABLE 13.2. *Reasons for leaving the Habsburg Gendarmerie*

Reason	Number	%
Transfer to army	196	37.9
Transfer within Gendarmerie	86	16.6
Transfer to reserve	22	4.3
Discharged	68	13.2
Dismissed	26¹	5.0
Invalided	43	8.3
Died	26	5.0
Suicide	8	1.5
Deserted	9	1.7
Unknown	33	6.4

Note: ¹ Includes 9 men dismissed as Lombards in 1859 and 2 dismissed as Italians in 1866.
Source: Samples from Kriegsarchiv, ABG KL, Kartons 2814–3148; see Emsley and Phillips, 'The Habsburg Gendarmerie'.

TABLE 13.3. *Ages of men joining the Habsburg Gendarmerie, 1849–1889*

Age (years)	Number (officers in brackets)
20 and under	17
21	43
22	71
23	74
24	62
25	41 (plus 3)
26	41 (plus 2)
27	19
28	25 (plus 1)
29	16 (plus 1)
30	10 (plus 4)
31	9 (plus 1)
32	8
33	10 (plus 1)
34	9 (plus 2)
35	6 (plus 1)
36	3
37	2 (plus 2)
38	1 (plus 1)
39	3 (plus 1)
40 years and over	12 (plus 7)

Source: Samples from Kriegsarchiv, ABG KL, Kartons 2814–3148; see Emsley and Phillips, 'The Habsburg Gendarmerie'.

counterparts elsewhere in Europe. Moreover, there were restrictions on the men's opportunities for marriage. Initially the Habsburg gendarmes were required to be single or widowers, though it was possible for men to marry with the permission of their superiors officers. The sample shows that the majority of the rank and file were single, but no fewer than twelve of the twenty-seven officers were married and yet another was a widower. The concern appears to have been that a wife and, subsequently, children would be a financial burden on a man. In September 1876, for example, the commander of the 3rd LGK based in Innsbruck was concerned that while Postenführer Giuseppe Ober's intended, Maria Zenatti, was of good family—her father was the clerk of a court— and had a good reputation, she had very little dowry and would not, therefore, improve 'his material existence'. In contrast, when a woman was noted as bringing a substantial dowry the officers were much more sympathetic to the match.[11] While it would be difficult to measure, it seems probable that the age and marital status of the Habsburg gendarmes had some impact on their general conduct. They were much closer to being regular soldiers than, for example, the settled gendarmes of provincial France, military veterans who were often married men with families. And there were other problems.

The plethora of languages spoken in the Empire created difficulties within the Habsburg army; NCOs were supposed to know any language that was spoken by 20 per cent of the men in their unit.[12] Gendarmes were expected to know the language of the region in which they were serving, and this made it sensible to deploy men in the region of their birth. However, gendarmes were not always local; perhaps half of the men serving in Bohemia and Galicia were natives to those provinces, as were a third of those serving in Upper Austria and Hungary, but rather less than this in Croatia and Dalmatia. Manifestly gendarmes did not always know the local language. In January 1874 Wachtmeister Simon Geretzberger was sentenced to fifteen days imprisonment for getting involved in an argument in a tavern. Geretzberger appears to have been insulted first, but he responded with 'tactless shouting and provocative behaviour'. His complaints about his officers following the sentence were given short shrift, and his regimental commander lamented that

[11] Kriegsarchiv, KKfLV, Karton 293, Nr. 1424; and for officers much more sympathetic because of larger dowries see, *inter alia*, Nr. 2476 (Gendarme Nicolodi Dominik) and KKfLV, Karton 296, Nr. 19581 (Postenführer Josef Gastner).

[12] Gebhardt, *Die Gendarmerie*, 39; István Deák, *Beyond Nationalism: A Social and Political History of the Habsburg Officer Corps, 1848–1918* (New York: Cambridge University Press, 1992), 99.

'with his experience he should have behaved strictly in all situations according to the regulations . . . and after serving almost ten years in this command [he] has shown no ambition to learn even one of the local languages'.[13]

Problems of finance dogged the Gendarmerie in the same way that they affected the army proper and the Empire as a whole. Military defeat in 1859 necessitated financial retrenchment and led to cuts in the Gendarmerie in addition to the abolition of the now-redundant Lombardy Regiment; the same thing happened following defeat by Prussia in 1866. However, perceived needs of order maintenance in border regions, market towns, and around factories, and the increased mobility provided by the spread of the railways all contributed to demands for new or restored brigades, and an increase in Gendarmerie numbers. All of these issues came together in, for example, Hohenau, some 50 miles north-east of Vienna, early in 1869. The town's Gendarmerie post had been closed with the cutbacks of 1860, but now the local council and the owners of a sugar factory in the town saw a case for reopening it. The town was close to the Hungarian border; the population was regarded as rough and uneducated, and there was a problem with cross-border cattle-rustling. There was a new railway station, and the sugar factory was expanding, indeed the factory owners offered accommodation for the restored brigade. By the end of May 1869 a brigade of four men had been re-established in Hohenau, when the neighbouring market town of Dürnkrut also began demanding a brigade, listing similar reasons and adding the problem of cross-border robberies; again local factory-owners offered accommodation. The new brigade for Hohenau had been created by depleting others, and the Council of Lower Austria warned that this could not be done to establish a brigade in Dürnkrut since the local Kommando was already undermanned and severely stretched. In the event the money was found for a temporary brigade of three men in Dürnkrut, but the brigade commander (Postenführer) was to be paid at less than the usual rate.[14] But if local councils in the Habsburg Empire requested gendarmes for protection, as in other states, those same councils were not always keen to

---

[13] Kriegsarchiv, KM, Sonderreihe, Karton 25, Nr.14, Nr.16, and Nr. 263. Geretzberger's previous career did not mark him out as a model NCO. In May 1869 he was ordered to pay 3.5 gulden to Aloysin Wirth, the cook of a local priest, for an assault, and he was confined to barracks for eight days for abusing his subordinates; Karton 18, Nr. 308. For the national mix in the Gendarmerie, see Emsley and Phillips, 'The Habsburg Gendarmerie'.

[14] Niederösterreichische Landesregierung, 1869 Statthalterei, Nr. 93 (18) 2349.

put their full support behind the gendarmes. This was even noted as a problem in Lower Austria, at the very heart of the Empire.[15]

The Habsburg soldier was possibly slightly better-off than a factory worker or labourer in the Empire, and the Habsburg gendarme generally had better pay and quarters than the ordinary soldier.[16] A few men were tempted to steal, even from their own comrades; and Vinzenz Rupprecht, serving in the headquarters of the 13th LGK at Czernowitz (Cernauti, Bukovina), devised and, between 1873 and 1877, ran an unpleasant scheme compelling men to pay him before he handed them their private letters. But the most common offences committed by Habsburg gendarmes were, as elsewhere, neglecting their duties and drunkenness; and, again as elsewhere, occasionally NCOs were disciplined for not keeping their barrack books in satisfactory order.[17] While breaking the rules could lead to punishment and/or dismissal, courage and determination could bring rewards. Following a break-in at a Petersdorf paper factory and the theft of 900 gulden on the night of 22 December 1873, Postenführer Ignaz Spitkopf and Gendarme Andreas Frank set off in pursuit of the offenders. Travelling for three days with virtually no rest they succeeded in arresting two men, who were handed over to the local court, and recovering most of the money. The paper factory offered a reward of 60 gulden for Spitkopf and 40 gulden for Frank—more than their monthly pay; their commander had no objection to the rewards and urged also that the men be given certificates of merit.[18] Of course, not every gendarme was able to win such rewards, but at the end of a man's service there was the chance of a pension or, if his service had been good but, for whatever reason, cut short,

---

[15] Ibid. 16964.

[16] Deák, *Beyond Nationalism*, 106; Rothenberg, *The Army of Francis Joseph*, 46.

[17] Kriegsarchiv, KM Sonderreihe, Karton 17, Nr. 295; in Nov. 1868 Gendarme Georg Toth was stripped of his silver medal, dismissed from the Gendarmerie, and sentenced to a month in prison, with two weeks in solitary confinement, for stealing from comrades in the 8th LGK; in the same month in the 10th LGK Postenführer Josef Talapka was reprimanded for not having kept his barrack journals properly, and Wachtmeister Karl Geissinger was punished for falsifying facts, neglecting his duties as a post commander, and, in particular, not keeping to the proper schedule in training his men. For the Rupprecht case see KK MfLV, Karton 293, Nr. 14952. Rupprecht was dismissed and denied his pension.

[18] Kriegsarchiv, KM Sonderreihe, Karton 25, Nr. 5. The pay of a Postenführer in 1873 was 600 gulden a year, that of a Gendarme 400 gulden. Franz Neubauer, *Die Gendarmerie in Österreich 1849–1924* (Vienna: Gendarmerie-Jubiläumsfonds, 1925), 336–48, relates a similarly successful story of a squad of gendarmes making a long night-time trek to an alpine village in Nov. 1859, where they arrested seven deserters in the face of fierce local opposition.

he could receive a one-off payment; and if he died in service his family could receive such benefits as were due.[19] In addition to the possibility of the pension or one-off payment, as with NCOs retiring from the army, gendarmes had the right to be appointed to some low-level position in the public service such as doorman, a courier, or civilian policeman.

As was the experience of men in other Gendarmeries, the pursuit of thieves, brigands, or deserters was not an everyday occurrence for Habsburg gendarmes. The growth of socialism and scares about industrial unrest were not as marked as in many other states, but the Empire did experience popular disorder arising from the claims of its various nationalities; and such disorders often proved too big a problem for the small brigades of gendarmes. While collateral services, such as the pursuit of rabid animals and runaway horses, the fighting of fires, and assistance in cases of flood or other disaster, could, as elsewhere, foster tolerance of and a degree of respect for the gendarmes, fervent nationalists within the Empire scorned their ethnic brothers who chose to wear the Habsburg eagle on a gendarme's helmet.[20] At the same time, and rather as senior officers of the Napoleonic Gendarmerie had seen their men as the standard-bearers of French civilization, so some Habsburg officers saw the gendarmes as bringing the benefits of western civilization to the remote peasantries. In 1910, for example, the gendarmes stationed in Bukovina were advised of the importance of their role as representatives of western culture in a territory overlooked by the orient.

Here [the gendarme] acts as a constant advisor, as the provider of the thousand needs of the population. Here he is a friend and the authority to whom people frequently look for support . . . whether it is in instances of personal conflict, to ask for advice on legal matters, for protection and safety, or just to write an address on an envelope.[21]

The Habsburg Gendarmerie was established in a period when there

---

[19] The is, for example, the tragic case of Postenführer Giovanni Agostini who died in service in Mar. 1881 leaving a pregnant wife. It was agreed that Osola Agostini should receive a one-off payment of just over 500 florins (three months' salary plus a bonus). Sadly, two months after her husband's death Osola died in childbirth, together with her baby. Postenführer Agostini's father then received the payment. Kriegsarchiv, KK MfLV, Karton 296, Nr. 4638.

[20] Alfred Alexander, *The Hanging of Wilhelm Oberdank* (London: London Magazine Books, 1977), 107–9.

[21] Quoted in Colonel Leopold Kepler (ed.), *Die Gendarmerie in Österreich 1849–1974. 125 Jahre Plichterfüllung* (Graz: Leykham Verlag, 1974), 167.

were hopes of shaping a uniform, imperial citizenship which tran-
scended ethnicity. The gendarmes were intended to play a role here, in
particular by fostering love of the Emperor and respect for his law. The
Italian Carabinieri, perhaps rarely as heroically and altruistically as its
apologists have claimed, played a significant part in establishing a united
Italy and in the process of moulding peasants into Italians. The pre-
sumption that a similar process was impossible for the ethnic mix of the
Habsburg Empire was not something that Franz Joseph or any of his
ministers would have countenanced; and historians who deny the possibility are, perhaps, rather too influenced by hindsight and the knowledge
of the dramatic route taken by events during and in the immediate aftermath of World War I. That said, however, the odds were generally
stacked against the Habsburg gendarmes, both as crime-fighting
imposers of imperial order and as unifiers of the Empire. Young, generally single men serving for a relatively short period, they were much
more like regular soldiers than the gendarmes in other states. Thus,
while they assisted individuals and communities fearful of or menaced
by crime, or faced with national disaster, the Habsburg gendarmes, as
individuals, probably never developed a separate gendarmerie culture, as
opposed to a military one. Moreover, their numbers remained small;
regiments, then LGKs, were always spread thinly across vast territories
occupied by a large, ethnically mixed population which had the potential, if not the inevitability, of pulling apart.

14

VARIATIONS: ELSEWHERE

The French Gendarmerie's precursor, the *maréchaussée*, had become a national force under the *ancien régime* when a dynamic minister seized on the potential of the disparate companies scattered across the kingdom and acted upon the occasion of concern about beggars and vagrants. Developments in France during the Revolutionary and Napoleonic periods were again the result of seizing upon the perceived potential of the institution and acting upon the occasion of a multiplicity of anxieties. The development of gendarmerie forces elsewhere had different individual causes. In some old regimes both rulers and peoples were dissatisfied with existing police structures, but the finances and the determination to press through significant changes were lacking. The Revolutionary and Napoleonic periods liberated some state administrations and replaced others. In territories where the old order was replaced the French set out to impose their own style of Gendarmerie in the same way that they sought to impose other elements of their new administrative structure. France's allies took up the system because, like other elements of the French state, it appeared to work effectively and to undertake a multiplicity of tasks. Gendarmes pursued vagrants and malefactors, but they also brought in the conscripts, pursued deserters, protected frontiers, showed the flag to peasants of uncertain loyalty, and provided both information on what people thought and a first line of defence against popular disorder. The comparisons discussed above demonstrate the variety of elements which helped to foster the origins and developments in the Italian and German lands. The brief survey of experiences elsewhere which follows reinforces this picture of a similar police system favoured for different reasons in different contexts and at different times.

At the Congress of Vienna Belgium was united with the Netherlands under the House of Orange. The king, William I, was more than happy to take over as ruler of a state which, thanks to the French, was far more centralized than during the pre-Revolutionary period. He also enjoyed an absolutist authority far greater than that of his forebears who had been stadholders in the old Dutch Republic; again, this was the result of French imperialism. As described above, both the Netherlands and Belgium had been patrolled by Napoleonic gendarmes, and parts of the Belgium provinces even had an experience of such policing going back to the *ancien régime*. At the end of February 1814, as Napoleon's armies withdrew within the pre-Revolution frontiers of France, the allied powers occupying Belgium had established a *maréchaussée* to maintain peace in the region, though recruitment was difficult and it does not appear to have been popular with the local population. Eight months later William established his own Koninklijke Marechaussee in the southern provinces of his kingdom, namely, Belgium and Dutch Limburg. These regions were suspect for two reasons: they had reputations as centres of banditry and smuggling, at least before the French came; and, being largely Catholic, they were confessionally different from much of the rest of his kingdom. The new corps was organized on the lines of the French Law of 28 *germinal* Year VI (17 April 1798); it was recruited from Belgians and Dutch, though most of the officers were Belgian.

After the Belgian Revolution of 1830 the newly independent kingdom opted to keep a centralized military police on the French model, changing its name to the Gendarmerie Nationale. In the early years of independence special units of the corps were deployed along the northern frontier to keep partisans of the Dutch in check. But generally, Belgian gendarmes were stationed in small barracks spread across the country and they functioned alongside other police organizations in a system very similar to that in France; there were burgomasters (mayors), *commissaires*, municipal police, and *gardes-champêtres*. The rural burgomasters and *gardes-champêtres* were commonly perceived as ineffective, particularly when it came to closing *cabarets* and dealing with issues in which they might be partial. There were proposals that the latter should be replaced by gendarmes, but these foundered on the potential expense. However, if the *gardes* continued to exist, they were increasingly displaced by the gendarmes in bringing cases to court; between roughly 1840 and 1885 the percentage of cases brought to court by burgomasters and *gardes-champêtres* virtually halved, while that brought by gendarmes tripled. As industrialization developed, and with it anxieties about worker and socialist activism, so the Belgian gendarmes found themselves increasingly called upon for the policing of strikes and popular demonstrations. The Dutch also maintained their gendarmerie corps in the aftermath of Belgian independence. The Koninklijke Marechaussee was a centralized military organization functioning alongside the police of the independent local authorities. In the after-math of the Belgian Revolution it remained principally in the southern provinces of Limburg, North Brabant, and Sealand; there was a fear amongst the Netherlands' Protestant rulers that the Catholics in the region might seek to secede and join Belgium. However, before the end of the 1830s the Marechaussee also proved its worth in the northern provinces, where a new land tax provoked resistance and the gendarmes were deployed to protect tax-collectors. As concerns grew about social unrest towards the end of the nineteenth and beginning of the twenti-eth centuries, so the Marechaussee was deployed more extensively and permanently in the northern and western provinces also.[1]

Similar anxieties prompted the development of the only national gen-darmerie in Scandinavia. Denmark had created two small military polic-ing institutions in the middle third of the century. The tiny Grænsegendarmeriet was established in 1839 to patrol the customs bor-der with Germany. In 1851, after the fighting over the duchies of Schleswig and Holstein, the slesvigske Gendarmerikorps was set up to patrol the areas of Schleswig which, because of their German popula-tion, appeared suspect to the government in Copenhagen. Then, in 1885, the militære Gendarmerikorps was established to police the rural areas of the kingdom. The occasion of the creation of this corps had little to do with concerns about crime and/or vagrancy or with the per-ceived need to unify the national territory; rather, it was the result of a worsening conflict between Left and Right in parliament. The Left, which drew its support principally from small farmers and minor pro-fessional men such as schoolmasters, had a comfortable majority in the lower house, the Folketing, and demanded a share of government com-mensurate with this majority. The Right, dominated by big landowners and the old administrative elite, clung to power by virtue of their major-ity in the upper house, the Landsting. Concerned about the radical rhetoric of the Left, and the proliferation of patriotic rifle associations created by the Left, the Right's response was to establish the new corps of professional soldiers to intimidate its opponents in the countryside. The impact of the gendarmes is difficult to assess; probably the

[1] My particular thanks to Axel Tixhon and Vincent Sleebe for sharing with me their knowledge of the Belgian Gendarmerie and the Koninklijke Marechaussee. See also Lode Van Outrive, Yves Cartuyvels, and Paul Ponsaers, *Les Polices en Belgique: Histoire socio-politique du système policier de 1794 à nos jours* (Brussels: Editions Vie Ouvrière, 1991), 18, 29–33, and 56–60; for a guide to the literature on the history of the Koninklijke Marechaussee see Cyrille Fijnault and William Voss, *Bibliografie van de Politie in Nederland 1813–1988* (Lochem: Van den Brink, 1992), section 1.3, pp. 34–7.

intimidation was not needed, as the Left's rhetorical bark was far worse than its bite, and in the event the gendarmes were never engaged in political conflict. In 1894 the corps was dissolved as the first of a series of political compromises which took the heat out of the situation.[2]

The short-lived Danish Gendarmerie was an instrument forged out of, and for use in, political conflict. In Russia the Gendarmerie was established as part of a vision for the good and efficient management of an absolutist regime. From 1811 there had been independent companies of internal security forces acting under military discipline and organization which were responsible for escorting and training troops, for the pursuit of deserters, runaway serfs, and criminal offenders, and for protecting public buildings. In 1815 a regiment of dragoons was transformed into the Gendarmerie Regiment specifically as a police for the Russian army of occupation in France; two years later this regiment was given authority over Russian civilians. Following the Decembrist Revolt of 1825 the new Tsar, Nicholas I, fused elements of the internal security companies with the latter to make his Corps of Gendarmes. In many respects Nicholas I's gendarmes were like their namesakes elsewhere in Europe. The rank and file came from the army, usually the cavalry; they had to be men of exemplary character and behaviour, and officers were warned that they would be responsible for bearing the costs of a replacement if any man with their personal recommendation did not come up to scratch. It was possible for NCOs with unblemished records to win commissions within the corps, but Nicholas hoped to encourage young men from the best families and from his personal entourage to serve as senior officers. However, while the Corps of Gendarmes was responsible for the pursuit of offenders and the maintenance of public order and decorum at public assemblies such as fairs and feast days, it was also linked with the Third Section of the Tsar's Private Imperial Chancellory, the political police. Initially this link was through Count Alexander Benckendorff in his capacity as head of the Third Section and commander of the Corps of Gendarmes. However, increasingly the gendarmes were absorbed into the section as its executive arm, and they were fully incorporated under a single chain of command in 1842.[3]

---

[2] Jens Jensen, *De danske Gendarmerikorps 1839–1939* (Haderslev: Winds bogforlag, 1938); E. O. A. Hedegaard, 'Det militære Gendarmerikorps 1885–1894', *Krigshistorisk Tidsskrift*, 2 (1967), 5–50. My thanks to Gunner Lind for information on the Danish Gendarmerie.

[3] P. S. Squire, *The Third Department: The Establishment and Practices of the Political Police in the Russia of Nicholas I* (Cambridge: Cambridge University Press, 1968), chap. 3 and esp. 80–1 and 93–5; John L. H. Keep, *Soldiers of the Tsar: Army and Society in Russia*,

Benckendorff had served in the Russian embassy in Paris after Napoleon's meeting with Tsar Alexander I at Tilsit. While in Paris he had had the opportunity of seeing Napoleon's police at work under Fouché, and had begun to develop his own ideas about protecting the Russian peoples from what he perceived as error and oppression. In 1821, in a memo to Alexander on the potential threat from secret societies, he proposed the creation of a French-style Gendarmerie.[4] Alexander was not interested. But Nicholas, who aspired to run the Empire with the kind of efficiency that he detected in Prussia and in the manner of a colonel commanding a regiment, was much more receptive. The Third Section was to root out corruption within the imperial bureaucracy as well as sedition, wherever it might be found; the gendarme, with his distinctive pale blue uniform, was to be an example of impartiality, morality, and probity, protecting the Tsar's people from local, selfish vested interests as well as from political subversives. While some young gentlemen were reluctant to join the Gendarmerie because they disliked the idea of being branded informers and busybodies, others embraced the idea and shared Nicholas's vision of ensuring the people's wellbeing. The flag of the Moscow Gendarmes carried the motto 'Le bien-être général en Russie', which a local wit allegedly translated as 'It is good to be a general in Russia',[5] but throughout the nineteenth century the Russian Gendarmerie continued to perceive itself as the moral physician of the people and the necessary instrument of autocracy. The problem for the gendarmes, as for the regime as a whole, was that a fiercely paternalist autocracy was not to everyone's taste; and the methods of preserving the regime easily slipped beyond the limits of probity and fairness, especially given that the concept of a *Rechtsstaat* was rejected and the law itself was regarded by many close to the crown as the emanation of the will of a divinely appointed autocrat. At times the Third Section interfered with the courts and even ordered the gendarmes to decide cases for themselves.[6] Moreover, if the gendarmes were ever properly to have enforced morality and probity on the local officials and petty functionaries of the ramshackle Tsarist bureaucracy, there would have had to have been many more of them. Nicholas I does

1462–1874 (Oxford: Clarendon Press, 1985), 313–14; see also Sidney Monas, *The Third Section: Police and Society in Russia Under Nicholas I* (Cambridge, Mass.: Harvard University Press, 1961).

   [4] Monas, *The Third Section*, 93–4; Squire, *The Third Department*, 50.

   [5] Monas, *The Third Section*, 286.

   [6] Richard S. Wortman, *The Development of a Russian Legal Consciousness* (Chicago: University of Chicago Press, 1976), 180.

not appear to have set a limit on their numbers, but by the mid-1830s there appear to have been just over 4,000 men in the corps,[7] a pitifully small number given the enormous size of the Empire and of the tasks expected of them. Half a century later a French traveller noted that the gendarmes did bring important men before the courts and had even arranged for governors to be replaced, but they also looked the other way and ignored minor pecadilloes, since their principal concern was always with the opponents of the regime:

The officers of the *gendarmerie* . . . picked and well paid, have always been above suspicion or reproach: a *gendarme* who once abuses the trust reposed in him loses his place. But the integrity which characterizes this select corps it has unfortunately not been able to introduce, in any marked degree, into the administration placed under its control. Had they undertaken to expose all the abuses that went on around them, and to repress all the abuses they exposed, the *gendarmes* would have found the work beyond them.[8]

In the early 1890s a new liberal government in Spain proposed that their own gendarmerie variant, the Guardia Civil, might investigate corrupt practices by local functionaries, notably regional governors, rather on the lines of the Russian Corps of Gendarmes. If the functionaries were found to be manipulating elections or employing other illegalities, then they were to be prosecuted.[9] The intention behind this proposal, however, was a long way from the Romanov aspiration of using the gendarmes to maintain and enhance the regime of a divinely appointed autocrat. The intention of the Spanish liberals was to bring civil peace and establish the rule of law; they failed, and partly, perhaps, because of the way in which the Guardia Civil itself had developed.

Like the Habsburg Gendarmerie, the Guardia Civil was established a generation after most of the European gendarmeries and in the wake of insurrection and war, though the latter troubles in Spain were far more extended than the Galician revolt of 1846 and the revolutions of 1848 in Franz Joseph's Empire. During the reign of Joseph Bonaparte and the French occupation the royal and imperial gendarmes had never been able to settle down as a regular service for policing and surveillance; at the same time, in those territories not under French occupation there had been some experiments in the deployment of military police units

[7] Squire, *The Third Department*, 95.

[8] Anatole Leroy-Beaulieu, *The Empire of the Tsars and the Russians*, 3 vols. (New York: Putnam, 1902), ii. 148–9.

[9] Robert W. Kern, *Liberals, Reformers and Caciques in Restoration Spain, 1875–1909* (Albuquerque, N.Mex.: University of New Mexico Press, 1974), 76.

to deal with banditry, but these were ephemeral. In the aftermath of the war with Napoleon, and the withdrawal of his gendarmes, the pursuit of bandits and the maintenance of public order in Spain had been left in the hands of the Captains General, the army, the local militia, and the vestiges of the old regional police forces. In July 1820 the Marqués de las Amarillas, minister of war in a liberal government, proposed the creation of a Legión de Salvaguardias Nacionales. This was to be a corps of 5,320 men recruited from the army, but dependent upon the civil authorities. Its main objective was the extermination of banditry so as to ensure safe travel throughout the country. However, the proposal was withdrawn after only twenty-four hours, on the grounds that it threatened the liberty of the country's militia.[10]

Militias had largely been supported by different shades of liberal opinion since the beginning of the conflict with Napoleon, but from the 1820s, and especially in the aftermath of the new National Militia Law of 1822, sharp disagreements developed between the two branches of liberalism over who should be allowed to enlist. The Moderates (*Moderados*) wanted to restrict membership to the relatively well-to-do; their more radical opponents, the *Progresistas*, were prepared to extend membership much further down the social scale. During the turbulent 1830s, against the background of the Carlist War, of urban radicals agitating for the re-establishment of the liberal constitution of 1812, and of extremists turning violently on churches, monasteries, and the clergy, the radicals met with success as the ranks of many units of the Militia filled with urban workers. At the same time, the Moderates grew increasingly concerned about the local ties of the Militia, which often made units resistant to control from Madrid and encouraged them to participate in party conflicts. In the summer of 1843 a new government under the Moderate General Ramón Narváez took power; the Militia was disarmed, and in March the following year the Guardia Civil was established.

The turbulence of the 1830s had convinced Narváez and his ministers of the need for some centralized instrument of public order other than

---

[10] Enrique Martínez Ruiz, 'Las Fuerzas de Seguridad y Orden Publico en la Primera Mitad del Siglo XIX', *Cuadernos de Historia*, 4 (1973), 83–161; at 149–52. In 1813, in response to complaints about murders and robberies in the unoccupied region, the Regency issued orders for the creation of military units to deal with banditry, to protect tax convoys, and to carry dispatches. These were to be largely recruited at local expense, but were to pay for their own provisions out of the unclaimed goods taken from bandits. See, *inter alia*, *El Imparcial: Diario político y mercantil de la ciudad de Alicante*, 27–9 Dec. 1813; my thanks to Charles Esdaile for this information.

regular recourse to the army. The plan was for the Guardia Civil to provide a civilian alternative to the army and a disciplined, dependable alternative to the Militia. The Duke of Ahumada, the son of the Marqués de
las Amarillas whose Salvaguardias had received such short shrift in 1820,
was approached to be the first director of the corps. However, Ahumada
insisted that he would only accept the command if, rather than a 'civil
guard', the new force was to be placed under the minister of war, militarized, and housed in barracks. Narváez agreed, and the Guardia Civil
came into existence under two virtually contradictory decrees. The first
was that initially agreed by the government; the second was a decree
issued by Narváez himself which accepted the structure demanded by
Ahumada and which actually shaped the way in which the corps would
develop. Both the ministry of the interior and the ministry of war issued
regulations regarding the corps, but while the Guardia Civil could be
requested to act by the civil authorities, the civil power never achieved
any real measure of direct control. It was not, however, until the new
Army Law of November 1878 that the institution was formally integrated
into the army and the ambiguity was finally resolved.[11]

Along the Pyrenees the Guardia Civil co-operated with the French
Gendarmerie; and during the 1850s one of its journals, the *Mentor del
Guardia Civil*, saw the two forces as united in a common aim—'the
extinction of crime'—and as members of a police family which included
the Dutch Marechaussee, the Carabinieri in Piedmont and the Papal
States, and which might, in time, cover the whole of Europe. At the
same time the *Mentor* lamented that the Spanish government failed to
match the generosity of the French in the treatment of the families of
guardias killed in the line of duty.[12] The similarities between the different corps were clear: they were military men, generally regarded as an
elite; they were usually housed in barracks, and conducted patrols of
their districts in pairs—in Spain this led to the nickname *la pareja*.[13]

[11] For the origins of the Guardia Civil see Diego López Garrido, *La Guardia Civil y
los orígenes del Estado centralista* (Barcelona: Editorial Critica, 1982), esp. chap. 2; and
Enrique Martinez Ruiz, *Creacion de la Guardia Civil* (Madrid: Editora Nacional, 1976),
chap. 1, and the appendix which contains the decrees that established the corps.

[12] Ruiz, 'Las Fuerzas de Seguridad', 145–7.

[13] Gerald Brennan, *The Spanish Labyrinth: An Account of the Social and Political
Background of the Civil War*, 2nd. edn. (Cambridge: Cambridge University Press, 1950),
157, states that the *guardias* patrolled in twos for safety's sake. It probably was safer to
patrol in pairs, and there is little doubt that the Guardia Civil was not a favoured institution among the populace in pre-civil war Spain, but the fact remains that two-man
patrolling was common to many gendarmeries and was instituted among the French
maréchaussée during the eighteenth century (see above, p. 20).

Like the gendarmes in Paris during the first two-thirds of the century, the *guardias* in Madrid demonstrated a ferocious loyalty to regimes under threat; they were, for example, the last men to surrender in the 1854 July Revolution, and the insurrectionary crowds singled them out as the men who had to be disarmed.[14] The growth of the labour movement in Spain towards the end of the century, as elsewhere, meant that the *guardias* were increasingly deployed during strikes and popular demonstrations. But different national contexts meant significant differences.

The Guardia Civil did not have the Carabinieri's role as an instrument of unification; Spain had long been a unity. But the *guardias* were an instrument of a centralizing state which increasingly looked to the army for support and which whittled away at traditional regional privileges, particularly those relating to taxation and military service. The corps's growth and deployment, as the minister of war, General Leopoldo O'Donnell, put it in a circular of September 1854, was seen as 'a fully military *occupation* of the entire national territory'. Regions like Catalonia and Valencia struggled against the tide to maintain a local, non-military police, but Spanish soldiers, unlike their French counterparts, were heavily involved in politics throughout the nineteenth century. They commonly saw themselves as the saviours of the state, and in the last quarter of the nineteenth century the state was increasingly prepared to sanction this perception, even giving military courts the authority to try cases which had hitherto been taken before civilian judges. As soldiers, the *guardias* were both part of, and profited from this military ascendancy; from 1878 anyone who insulted or resisted the *guardias* was subject to military jurisdiction. At the same time *guardias* were encouraged to take a suspicious attitude towards the majority of the population and specifically to identify with and to support the wealthy, the 'honourable', and the people who held positions of authority. Those with wealth and position reciprocated: both landowners and industrialists sometimes paid to have Guardia Civil barracks built on their land or where it suited them; and some also contributed towards the men's equipment, living costs, and medical expenses. The original legislation establishing the corps had authorized volunteers from the army to serve in their province of birth, yet this appears to have been one of the earliest regulations to disappear under the policies pursued by Ahumada and his successors; the *guardias* were forbidden to

---

[14] V. G. Kiernan, *The Revolution of 1854 in Spanish History* (Oxford: Clarendon Press, 1966), 63 and 64–5.

associate familiarly with the locals where they were stationed, or to marry local women. They were strangers to, and remained largely outsiders in, the communities that they policed.[15]

The Guardia Civil may have liked to see itself as part of an international brotherhood of similar police forces, and its development may have been 'the foremost example of the growth of the liberal state in Spain',[16] yet its style of policing was not the one which most nineteenth-century liberals tended to hold up as a model. As noted earlier, liberals in Italy and Germany, and even Napoleon III, spoke highly in favour of, and sometimes experimented with, a model based on their perception of London's Metropolitan Police. The Metropolitan Police had been constructed to look very different from French police. The English disliked and feared the spies who appeared to predominate in the Paris police under Fouché and afterwards; and while many, like Sir William Mildmay, might admire the *maréchaussée*/Gendarmerie, they nevertheless believed that military policing was quite out of keeping with English traditions of liberty. The structure of the English state and the manner in which it had developed also militated against a centralized police, military or not. This was a decentralized state, yet by no means feeble for that. Power in the provinces was exercised by local elites, closely interlinked with the national elite. They held their local offices, notably as magistrates, from the crown; members of parliament, both lords and commons, and even ministers could be in the commission of the peace for their county and act as local magistrates. There was little inclination to change the system which had evolved in its nineteenth-century form most notably from the Glorious Revolution of 1688. It had helped bring in recruits for the Revolutionary and Napoleonic wars; it had seen off food riots and other popular disturbances, as well as the Napoleonic threat. Not all of the provincial police of nineteenth-century England were modelled directly on the Metropolitan Police, but the men in the counties and municipal boroughs who made the final decisions about what kind of police they were going to have were essentially conservatives who saw the counties and, at a pinch, the municipal boroughs as the basic units of local government and who jealously guarded local independence. The system appeared to have worked well and it suited both national and local elites; aside from a few Benthamite enthusiasts, centralization was not on the agenda, nor, with occasional, very brief

[15] López Garrido, *La Guardia Civil*, esp. 142–70; quotation from O'Donnell at 164.
[16] Adrian Shubert, *A Social History of Modern Spain* (London: Routledge, 1990), 181.

exceptions, was paramilitary policing. Wales was generally considered as fully integrated with England, and Scotland was similar; Ireland, however, was different.

While eighteenth- and early nineteenth-century Irish magistrates liked to equate themselves with their English cousins, they proved themselves supine and/or ineffective in dealing with disorder. This was not always their fault, since holding down a dissatisfied, largely Catholic peasantry for the Protestant English crown was no simple task. In 1814 Sir Robert Peel, then chief secretary for Ireland, introduced the paramilitary Peace Preservation Force which could be recruited and moved into a troubled county as and when needed, and supported at that county's expense. But the system was expensive and impermanent, while the alternative, the Yeomanry, was as expensive. Moreover, since its members were volunteer, part-time soldiers, the Yeomanry could not be long maintained in a turbulent area, and since the yeomen were predominantly fiercely Protestant Ulstermen, the prospect of deploying them in Catholic communities was seen as likely to inflame a situation. Charles Grant, Peel's successor, searched for a permanent solution, but was worried by the prospect of 'a vigorous system of police . . . a Gendarmerie'. Henry Goulburn, who replaced Grant in December 1821, had no such qualms. He rapidly drafted a bill for a centralized, permanent, armed constabulary linked to salaried police magistrates, and was then surprised by the hostility of the Whig opposition and the Anglo-Irish representatives in parliament. Even Grant condemned what he considered as an attempt 'to place the whole of Ireland under an armed police, to subject it to a species of gendarmerie'. This was something alien to English policy and could hardly be imposed on the Irish if it would never be imposed on the English. Goulburn made a few minor amendments, but the bill, which he introduced on 24 May 1822, received the royal assent on 5 August.[17]

Goulburn's act left some anomalies. The Peace Preservation Force continued to be seen as an important aid to the civil power during emergencies. Senior officers of the Constabulary were centrally appointed, but appointment to the lower ranks was, initially, in the hands of local magistrates; the senior officers, backed by the administration in Dublin Castle but without legislative authority, began to take over this responsibility in the early 1830s. The local magistrates also claimed the right to deploy the Constabulary as they thought fit, and squabbled with

[17] Stanley G. Palmer, *Police and Protest In England and Ireland, 1780–1850* (Cambridge: Cambridge University Press, 1988), 238–45; quotation at 242.

Dublin Castle over the interpretation of the law in this respect. Deployment by landowning magistrates, however, particularly during the Tithe War of 1830–3 and with permanently smouldering agrarian discontent, did not help the Constabulary's claims to, and aspirations of, impartiality. Nor did the fact that, ten years after the force's creation, while the number of Catholic constables was increasing, they still only constituted just over a third of the men. A new Constabulary bill was introduced by the Whig government in 1835, and finally became law the following year. Tory and Anglo-Irish opposition did not raise the spectre of a French Gendarmerie in their criticisms, but preferred to focus upon the expense and the destruction of local independence. It also voiced religious anxieties and what was seen as a potential threat from a Catholic-dominated Constabulary.

The act of 1836 merged the remains of the Peace Preservation Force with the Constabulary to make a new body of 7,700 officers and men by the beginning of the following year. The Constabulary was now fully centralized, with an Inspector-General and a deputy based in Dublin Castle at the heart of the British administration in Ireland. Appointments and promotions were centralized, and Catholic recruits were carefully sought. Moreover, to underline the claims of impartiality, a policy was immediately introduced of clamping down on both the marches of Protestant Orangemen and the faction fights of the rural Catholic communities.[18]

Unlike its continental European counterparts, the Irish Constabulary, or Royal Irish Constabulary (RIC) as it became in 1867, was not subject to a duality of ministerial control; there was only one superior authority, and while the Inspector-General might be a military man his post was a civilian one, based in the civilian administration in Dublin Castle. The constables were not soldiers, though they were armed and equipped like soldiers and, during the Crimean War, about 100 of them served as the nucleus for a military police with the army.[19] The Constabulary's *modus operandi* was much the same as that of the French Gendarmerie; the men were based in small barracks at strategic points in towns and on the main roads, and conducted regular patrols through the districts of their jurisdiction. The deployment of the Constabulary against peasant protest and disorder has figured prominently in the histories of nineteenth-century Ireland, yet their role went far beyond this. 'Everything

[18] Palmer, *Police and Protest*, 353–68.
[19] R. J. Sinclair and F. J. M. Scully, *Arresting Memories: Captured Moments in Constabulary Life* (Coleraine: Royal Ulster Constabulary, 1982), plate 7.

. . . from the muzzling of a dog to the suppression of rebellion, is done by the Irish constabulary', claimed one of its apologists in 1881.[20] Indeed, the Crime and Occurence Register for the remote district of Derrypark in County Mayo, covering the period from November 1879 to December 1897, suggests that, with the exception of the excitement generated by the appalling Maamstrasna murders of August 1882, most offences—almost nine out of ten—dealt with by the men stationed there were petty infringements of government rules and regulations. The most serious recurrent problem was enforcing the annual payment of the dog tax each spring.[21]

Most of the Constabulary were drawn from the country's predominantly agricultural community. There was a conscious, and successful effort to recruit from the Catholic population, and this resulted in a force in which the number of Catholics was very close to the proportion recorded in the population itself. Indeed, when the RIC replaced the Belfast Borough Police in that fiercely sectarian city in 1865, working-class Protestants condemned their new policemen as 'papists', and some of their middle-class co-religionists also had reservations. RIC men found their wives in the areas to which they were posted. A constable could not serve in his native district, nor in that of his wife, but he commonly served in his native province, as it was felt that he was in touch with the local community and its way of life.

[I]n terms of its organisation, public posture and day-to-day duties; and in terms of its personnel . . . the RIC was by the early years of the twentieth century very much a civil police force, reflecting very accurately in its composition the socio-economic structure of Irish society and in its operations the needs of small, relatively law-abiding, rural communities.[22]

This was not a linear development, in the sense of the RIC becoming progressively more accepted as the nineteenth century wore on. There

[20] Henry A. Blake, 'The Irish Police', *The Nineteenth Century*, 9 (Jan.– June, 1881), 385–96: at 390.

[21] Ian R. Bridgeman, 'Policing Rural Ireland; A Study of the Origins, Development and Role of the Irish Constabulary, and its Impact on Crime Prevention and Detection in the Nineteenth Century', Ph.D, Open University, 1993, pp. 191–201. Until 1881 the Derrypark district was in County Galway. Probably the Maamstrasna massacre is the reason why the official weeders considered that the Derrypark Register should be preserved.

[22] W. J. Lowe and E. L. Malcolm, 'The Domestication of the Royal Irish Constabulary, 1836–1922', *Irish Economic and Social History*, 19 (1992), 27–48; at 27. For the deployment of the RIC in Belfast see Brian Griffin, *The Bulkies: Police and Crime in Belfast, 1800–1865* (Dublin: Irish Academic Press, 1998), 139–40. One of the concerns, if not the main concern of the middle-class Protestants in Belfast, was that they were giving up what was an essentially English-style borough police for an armed, 'unconstitutional' force.

is evidence that some men were fitting in well with the communities they policed during the 1830s—in the eyes of senior officers rather too well, since they were enjoying regular drinks and card-games with their civilian neighbours. The most widespread antipathy towards the institution appears to have come with the Land War of the early 1880s, but by the turn of the century even some Irish nationalists had good words for the men. 'If our sons did not join,' a French visitor was told in 1907, 'would not England at once import twelve thousand Englishmen to do the work? In that case we should only have helped to Anglicize and Protestantize Ireland a little more.'[23]

At the beginning of the twentieth century there continued to be broad similarities amongst the European gendarmeries, as well as significant national and imperial differences. Gendarmeries everywhere were primarily stationed in rural areas, though increasingly they were brought into towns to deal with new forms of popular disorder. But looking across nineteenth-century Europe, there is not always a simple, clear-cut urban–rural divide; Sicily, for example, was a rural economy, yet most people lived in large, often hilltop agro-towns. The structure of the gendarmeries was everywhere military, though the extent to which different individuals and the different national and imperial institutions stressed their military nature varied. In Ireland the military elements were in eclipse, as constables of the RIC became more and more like members of a civilian police. In Italy and Spain, in contrast, the military aspects of the institutions tended to become paramount. In Italy, Spain, France, and indeed in most states where they had been created, the gendarmes followed the same practice of leaving their barracks for their patrols in pairs. Yet in Germany the men were commonly stationed, and consequently acted, on their own; it was usually only during an emergency that they were brought together to act in groups. The Irish Constabulary became more and more like a civilian police, and had no local rivals; the Dublin Metropolitan Police was confined to the

---

[23] Brian J. Griffin, 'The Irish Police, 1836–1914: A Social History', Ph.D, Loyola University of Chicago, 1991, chap. 8, quotation at 690. The quotation raises the issue of the RIC as an imperial police. It used to be confidently asserted by historians of British policing that while the Metropolitan Police provided the model for England, Wales, and Scotland, and urban police in general, the RIC provided the model for much of the empire. The idea has been challenged by Richard Hawkins, 'The "Irish Model" and the Empire: A Case for Reassessment', in David M. Anderson and David Killingray (eds.), *Policing the Empire: Government, Authority and Control, 1830–1940* (Manchester: Manchester University Press, 1991), and re-emphasized as significant for the Canadian experience by Greg Marquis, 'The "Irish Model" and Nineteenth-Century Canadian Policing', *Journal of Imperial and Commonwealth History*, 25 (1997), 193–218.

capital, but with central control there was no serious conflict over juris-diction or the distribution of finance. In France, in contrast, as the cen-tury wore on the Gendarmerie tended to be neglected in comparison with other police officials and, particularly, with the civilian police in Paris. It was the same in Germany, where the gendarmeries had always been relatively small. However, in response to the rise of labour move-ments and socialist parties, attention periodically swung back to the gen-darmeries as a potent first line of defence against popular disorder and revolution.

Every police institution is to some extent political, given that it is required to enforce laws made by political actors and to maintain a par-ticular socio-economic structure. In this sense all gendarmeries, as police institutions, were political, but some had a much more explicit political role than others. The short-lived Danish Gendarmerie provides an example of an institution devised with specific political intent, even though it was never deployed for the ends that had been envisaged. The Russian Corps of Gendarmes provides an example of a police institu-tion whose *raison d'être* was a consciously defined political one. Yet putting representatives of different nineteenth-century gendarmeries together, they could probably have agreed, as the *Mentor del Guardia Civil* claimed, that they shared *modus operandi* and common aims—the repression of crime and the maintenance of order. Few, if indeed any of them would have recognized any potential for debate or disagreement over the broad concepts of 'crime' and 'order'.

15
'THE MAN PRAISING ORDER'

In one of the dialogues in Diderot's *Supplément au voyage de Bougainville*, character B asks:

But do you want man to be happy and free? Then do not interfere in his affairs: there are enough unexpected chances in the world to lead him to enlightenment or vice; and always remember that it was not for your sake but for theirs that cunning legislators molded and misshaped you as they have done. Look at all the political, civil, and religious institutions; study them with care; and I am much mistaken or you will find Man, century after century, the yoke-ox of a handful of knaves. Mistrust the man who comes to you praising 'order;' creating order always means bullying others to their own discomfort. The Calabrians are almost the only people left, unseduced by the flattery of legislators.[1]

State jurists and apologists for the nation state would not have understood the satire. For them the state and its law were instruments of progress, bringing rationality and civilization where they had not existed before. While to some commentators, notably in France and Germany, the peasant might be the simple preserver of earlier, purer traditions of the nation, to others, particularly in Italy, he was ignorant, devious, and at times downright dangerous—Cesare Lombroso claimed to have found the inspiration for his theory of criminal man while serving as a military doctor during the Brigands' War in Calabria. In contrast to state jurists and apologists for the nation state, people on the Left, including a number of historians, have been inclined to see the state and its law as instruments of class authority, designed to impose the will of a social group and protect the needs of a means of production. At the same time, the work of anthropologists has suggested how, in peasant eyes, the laws of the nation state can appear as bizarre and wrong-headed as peasant practices are to the jurist. But whatever perspective is taken, the

---

[1] Denis Diderot, *This is Not a Story, and Other Stories*, trans. with an introduction by P. N. Furbank (Oxford: Oxford University Press, 1993), 109.

nineteenth-century gendarme was manifestly a man who came praising, and at times enforcing, order on behalf of the state and its legislators.[2]

The nineteenth century is commonly seen as a major period of modernization in the European countryside, when inward-looking, isolated rural communities became more integrated into the wider world of nation states or multinational empires. A clutch of economic, political, and social developments contributed to this, not the least of which was the increased whittling-away of the old relationships between seigneur and peasant. While there could be conflict between central government and rural elites, and while some gentry, notably the Junkers in East Prussia, resisted the encroachments of the state better than others, the state's penetration of the countryside became marked by its power to appoint influential figures in the communities, such as mayors, and by the deployment of its own emissaries, such as schoolmasters and gendarmes.

Rural communities had their own means of dealing with offenders and minor trouble before the arrival of the gendarmes. This could involve using the law. But the law was costly and time-consuming, and at times was seen more as an instrument for perpetuating a feud than for the quick resolution of an offence. A quick resolution within the community was much preferred, especially if the offender was known. Sometimes problems were resolved through individual or community violence; sometimes there was recourse to magic, or more often, to agreements negotiated by influential figures within the community, possibly the seigneur, but more likely his agent, the curé, or the mayor. While measurement is impossible, it seems generally accepted that during the nineteenth century these methods of settling offences within rural society declined. The presence of the gendarmes contributed to this. The physical chastisement of an offender by another individual, victim of the initial offence or not, could be construed by the man of order as an assault. A *charivari*, or its Italian or German equivalents— *scampanate*, *Katzenmusik*—by which an individual who had offended against community norms was the subject of boisterous ridicule, could similarly be labelled as an unlawful assembly or riot. Some gendarmes, as simple men themselves, possibly from a peasant background and from

---

[2] For a more detailed discussion of the issues raised here and in the next three paragraphs see Clive Emsley, 'The Nation-State, the Law and the Peasant in Nineteenth-Century Europe', in Xavier Rousseaux and René Lévy (eds.), *Le Pénal dans tous ses états: Justice, états et sociétés en Europe (XIIᵉ–XXᵉ siècles)* (Brussels: Publications des Facultés universitaires Saint-Louis, 1997).

close to the community in which they were serving, may occasionally have turned a blind eye to such incidents. Also, if they were aware of it, they may have ignored a peasant's recourse to the local 'cunning' person or sorcerer to solve misfortunes, from animal sickness to theft; though some gendarmes probably considered an approach to a sorcerer in a case of theft as an affront to their authority. As for the accords between victims and offenders, or their families, it seems that in the early nineteenth century, in France at least, it was becoming increasingly difficult to find men with traditional authority who were prepared to act as infra-judicial negotiators. Seigneurs and their agents were now less inclined to act, and so too were mayors. This seems to have been partly due to an increasing division between social groups and an end to the old paternalism; also, mayors increasingly appear to have seen themselves less as community headmen, and to have accepted the authority and dominance of the state, identifying themselves with it more and more. With fewer men of authority prepared to administer the informal, infra-judicial practices, such accords as were reached were negotiated by people with less social standing, and consequently they became less respected and less binding. All of which encouraged victims to turn to the gendarme for redress. But people did not necessarily do this because they wanted him to enforce the state's law; rather, it was because he appeared to carry some authority and weight within the community by the very nature of his role; he was permanently in the community, if not necessarily perceived as an integral part of it, and stood out as distinctive by nature of his uniform and his trade. NCOs in charge of small local barracks were probably happy to go along with this. A century after Italian unification an American anthropologist working in a small town in Umbria found the *maresciallo* (sergeant-major) of the local Carabinieri perceiving of himself as the local patron, and being used by members of the community as a medium in interpersonal conflicts:

People with grievances often find reason to denounce their offender before the maresciallo. This has the effect of announcing the grievance publicly and confirming its seriousness, while allowing the parties to avoid face-to-face confrontation. The maresciallo is not actually an arbitrator. The conflict itself must be resolved by other means, either informally or by resort to lawsuit; in many instances (such as an accusation of sexual misconduct with one's spouse) the accuser clearly does not intend the maresciallo to settle the conflict.[3]

---

[3] Sydel Silverman, *Three Bells of Civilization: The Life of an Italian Hill Town* (New York: Columbia University Press, 1975), 141, and see also 242 n. 7.

None of this is to suggest that the peasantry willingly and eagerly embraced the new legal structures which gradually developed across Europe from the period of the Enlightenment, and particularly after the French Revolution. Nor does it mean that peasants readily accepted and understood concepts such as the *Rechtsstaat*. A profound suspicion remained towards lawyers and sometimes towards the law itself. Moreover, questions about precisely how peasants gained information about the law and about changing legal rights and liberties have rarely been explored by historians. At times it fell to the parish priest, to a schoolmaster, to a gendarme or other local police agent, to make new law public. Sometimes explanations were probably garbled, and especially when translated into a patois or different language. Sometimes peasant interpretation could be at odds with what politicians and jurists intended, notably over questions of land reform in periods of revolutionary upheaval and over the law of proof in jury trials. In the former, peasants might take the abolition of seigneurial rights and privileges more literally and, in consequence, much further than was intended; in the latter, peasant juries might make decisions based on old community norms and on their attitudes to accuser and accused, rather than on the evidence. Peasants were pragmatists who sought to use the law when it suited them and in their own interest; yet the very use of the law, and the use of its agents such as the gendarmes, served increasingly to integrate the peasantry further into state or empire.

If small communities wanted to use gendarmes in their own way, few gendarmes were likely to complain too much. After all, it was sensible to establish a live-and-let-live relationship as far as possible with the community in which they lived and worked. Towards the end of the nineteenth century there was even a popular term for such a relaxed barracks in the RIC—'home rule'.[4] It was a similar attitude that encouraged some old sweats among the gendarmes to turn a blind eye to poaching in those areas where the rural communities accepted it as an everyday, acceptable occurrence.[5] Recent participant observation studies of routine police practice have noted how police officers commonly conceive of two forms of trouble—'on the job' and 'in the job'.[6] The

---

[4] Brian J. Griffin, 'The Irish Police, 1836–1914: A Social History', Ph.D, Loyola University of Chicago, 1991, pp. 537–42.

[5] Ludwig Thoma, *Kaspar Lorinser*, in *Gesammelte Werke*, 8 vols. (Munich: R. Piper, 1956), v. 11–12; Regina Schulte, *The Village in Court: Arson, Infanticide and Poaching in the Court Records of Upper Bavaria, 1848–1910* (Cambridge: Cambridge University Press, 1994), 124–5.

[6] See e.g. M. R. Chatterton, 'The Supervision of Patrol Work Under the Fixed Points System', in Simon Holdaway (ed.), *The British Police* (London: Arnold, 1979).

former arises from the problems that may be confronted during routine patrols, and encompasses the difficulties sometimes faced in making an arrest, handling a minor disorder, dealing with challenges to personal authority, and so forth. Such difficulties are generally accepted and recognized by the police officers as going with the job. 'In the job' trouble is different. It arises from relationships with superior officers; it can be more unpleasant and, in the long run, more serious than a minor fracas on patrol. Men seek to avoid such trouble by careful mangement of the information about what they have done and are doing. Occasionally, as has been noted above, men were caught and disciplined for falsifying barrack books and service journals; probably many more got away with it, and carefully selected what they thought their superiors needed to know, balanced by a recognition of what their superiors wanted and expected to see in the reports.

There were, of course, men filled with their own importance or determined to treat local people like sloppy soldiers in need of discipline, and who were determined to enforce laws and regulations to the letter. As discussed above, the tactless behaviour of *maréchal des logis* Midel caused disorder on La Croix Rousse in February 1870, and the behaviour of Brigadier Liotard in Bédarieux cost him his own life together with that of some of his men.[7] But not all regulations were unpopular with rural communities. When gendarmes stopped, questioned, and demanded to see the papers of travellers and strangers, especially shabbily dressed ones, suspicious rural dwellers were unlikely to regard their behaviour with anything other than sympathy. Direct orders to enforce particular laws and regulations were less easy to accommodate within the lax remit of 'home rule'; and there were always some roles undertaken by the gendarmes which, while overt hostility towards them may have declined over the nineteenth century, were never popular—the marshalling and marching off of the annual quotas of conscripts is the obvious example.

Conscription helped the integration of rural communities into the nation state or empire; it also helped, indirectly, in the recruitment of gendarmes. Generally gendarmes were soldiers or former soldiers, often NCOs with records of good conduct; the principal exception here being the Royal Irish Constabulary which never recruited directly from the army. In some instances men used the gendarmerie institution as a way to get back to the region of their birth. Perhaps the regulated military life suited them and they had absorbed the new ideas of the importance

---

[7] See above pp. 124 and 129.

of, as well as loyalty to, the state. Possibly their time in the army had led them to disparage civilian life, or perhaps they had lost their patrimony while serving as conscripts. In some instance the gendarmeries may have been seen as providing opportunities for social advancement; there were opportunities to rise from the ranks, and the corps were attractive to officers who did not have the kind of personal fortune required by line regiments, especially cavalry regiments. But even if a man never rose above the rank of gendarme or junior NCO, the hierarchical gendarmeries provided a steady, regular wage and, in most instances, a lodging. The job held out the promise of a pension on retirement, or some provision for a widow and orphans, at a time when many peasants and labourers too old to work were forced to depend on their children or on charity. While serving, a man with a good record could apply for, and be granted, extended leave with pay and even some expenses to enable him to sort out family problems.[8] But it is, of course, impossible to assess how far such considerations were weighed up in any individual's mind when he requested appointment as a gendarme. Furthermore, it would be wrong to think of the life of a gendarme as an easy option during the nineteenth century. The pay may have been regular, but at times it might fall below the average in the locality where a man was serving. Patrols were expected to be made in all weathers, whether in the temperate climate of northern France, the snows of the Alps, or the blazing heat of a Sicilian summer.

The gendarme may have been serving in his province of birth, may have married a local woman, may have spoken the local language, but he was marked out from the local community in a variety of ways. His regular patrols, and his superiors' attempts to check up on these with the use of service journals and reports, made him closer to a regulated, supervised industrial worker than to the peasantry. Not for the gendarme the local annual calendar of village feasts or saints' days—even though he was expected to supervise them; and even in a barracks where 'home rule' had become the order of the day, the chances of indulging in the artisans' traditional 'St Monday' were remote.[9] Rather, the gen-

---

[8] See e.g. the case of Wachtmeister Josef Karl stationed in Klausenburg (Hungary), who was given compassionate leave, with expenses, to deal with family problems in his native Bohemia in 1874; he had also received similar leave in 1862 (Kriegsarchiv, KM Sonderreihe, Karton 25, Nr. 58); and the case of Carabiniere D'Ecclesia, given extended leave from his posting in Piedmont following the earthquake in his family town of Casamicciola in 1883: AMSC, Cartella 16 (1883, Grave disastro in Casamicciola).

[9] In the RIC Christmas appears to have been an exception. It seems to have become an unwritten rule of the Constabulary that officers did not inspect barracks or stations in the

darmes had their own calendar, a national or imperial one; in addition
to the regular patrols, they were expected to mark, for example, the
monarch's birthday or other days of national celebration. The gendarme
added a touch of military splendour to the peregrinations of the state's
representatives in his region, to the visits of others, and to the ritual of
the state's justice at the principal lawcourts and public executions. He
was clearly distinguished by his uniform; at times this may have become
weathered and worn, but it was quite different from the homespun of
the peasantry and differed also from the amalgam of a uniform, or simple armband or badge worn by the local village or small-town policeman. Clothing provides a means of differentiating and identifying. It is
both moulded to, and shaped by the wearer; it affects the ways in which
people move, carry themselves, and gesture, and it can give a message
of what is expected of the wearer. And in addition to his distinctive
clothing, in some of the more remote districts, particularly in central
and eastern Europe, the gendarme also stood out because of his use of
soap and his barbered hair and whiskers.[10] But wherever he was stationed in the towns and villages, the uniform isolated the gendarme and
identified him as the man of the state rather than just a member of the
community. It might also mark him off from other men of the state: the
Pickelhaube of the Habsburg Gendarmerie, for example, was a jealously
guarded symbol of the inviolable privileges of the force; the distinctive
hats of the Carabinieri and the Guardia Civil were similar; in France, in
contrast, the bicorne and boots of the gendarme were, by the end of the
nineteenth century, considered to have become simply too old-
fashioned. Even in the least militarized of the gendarmeries, the RIC,
the passion for smart uniforms, and shining belts, boots, and buttons
was seen by some as seriously reducing the time available for the prevention and detection of crime.[11]

The gendarme had sworn an oath to the state or to the monarch. This
was in itself a rite of passage. It was taken by a man who had opted vol-
untarily for the life. Political oaths had become very important during
the French Revolution. In 1791, when the Gendarmerie Nationale was

---

days immediately before and after Christmas. During this period duties were commonly
'suspended' and replaced by dances, card parties, and drinking: Griffith, 'The Irish
Police', 519–20.

[10] As late as the 1890s, for example, recruits to the Habsburg army from Transylvania
had long hair, heavily greased and parted in braids, and they had never heard of soap. See
István Deák, *Beyond Nationalism: A Social History of the Habsburg Officer Corps,
1848–1918* (New York: Cambridge University Press, 1990), 105.

[11] Griffin, 'The Irish Police', 47–8.

established and when the first oath for the corps was drafted, the radical journal *Révolutions de Paris* could criticize fanatical—that is, religious—oath-taking, but it warned also that 'the common people do not make light of the sacred bond'.[12] During the nineteenth century religious practice remained a part of everyday experience, and ritual solemnity was important in rites of passage such as weddings and funerals.[13] In this context the ritual oath taken when enlisting as a gendarme was no small, idly taken step, and appears to have been commonly seen as a significant moment in a man's service and, indeed, his life. Giovanni Frosali was one of the men for whom the army, and the gendarmerie, was a means of social mobility. He volunteered for the Tuscan infantry as a private soldier in 1830, rose to the rank of lieutenant, transferred to the Tuscan Gendarmerie in November 1849, and from thence to the Carabinieri of a united Italy in March 1860, where he reached the rank of lieutenant-colonel. The record of service donated by his family to the Carabinieri archive singles out the fact that he took his oath of loyalty in Florence in June 1860.[14] Ignace-Émile Forestier's stress on the significance of the oath of a French gendarme was quoted earlier.[15]

Swearing an oath which was regarded as important, solemn, and as a defining moment in a man's military career was one thing, but a question remains as to exactly what some of the men understood by the words of the oath. The situation in France presents the most complex case. In 1791 the gendarmes swore to enforce the law and to maintain public order; under the Directory they also swore fidelity to the republic together with a hatred of both royalty and anarchy. In less than a decade it was fidelity to the Emperor and the constitution of the Empire. Subsequently they swore allegiance to other regimes. The Emperor in February 1815, in whose armies most had fought, was the 'usurper' by the summer. Some men, like Lieutenant La Roche and Gendarme Touret, stayed loyal to an ousted regime when it was changed—though Touret, in his time, had served many different manifestations of the French state.[16] Arguably most men took as their guides to action the example of their comrades, obedience to their immediate superiors, and

---

[12] Quoted in Timothy Tacket, *Religion, Revolution and Regional Culture in Eighteenth-Century France: The Ecclesiastical Oath of 1791* (Princeton NJ: Princeton University Press, 1986), 17; and see in general, Lynn Hunt, *Politics, Culture and Class in the French Revolution* (Berkely, Cal.: University of California Press, 1984), 20–1 and 27.

[13] Eugen Weber, *Peasants into Frenchmen: The Modernization of Rural France, 1870–1914* (Stanford, Cal.: University of Stanford Press, 1976), 339–40.

[14] AMSC, Cartella 3, 'Carteggio donato dalla famiglia Frosali.'

[15] See above pp. 144–5.　　　　　　　　[16] See above p. 103.

perhaps too the honour of their corps and the maintenance of the law as they understood it. This was a pragmatic choice too; after all, what kind of job could an ordinary gendarme find when he resigned because of a change of regime, possibly hundreds of miles away from his post? His chance of a pension would be forfeited, and, if he had a wife and children, what would become of them? There is evidence that members of the RIC intensely disliked their coercive role during the Land War. The authorities suspected that some would prove unreliable, and there was an increase in resignations.[17] But most men stuck it out, probably because of the difficulties and problems involved in finding and growing accustomed to another job.

Pragmatism dictated the extent of 'home rule', the way in which many men responded to changes of regime and to distasteful duties. Most labour groups, including soldiers and police officers, develop a work-place mentality which enables people to shape their working lives at least in part to suit themselves, as well as their superiors. Indeed, some even seek to shape their superiors. When Brigadier Forestier took command of the brigade at Neuillé-Pont-Pierre (Indre-et-Loire) he found two old sweats who had their own, very clear ideas about how the brigade should be run and what patrols should be made; one of them even thought nothing of reading the confidential papers in Forestier's desk.[18] Franz Dukovsky, a brigade commander in southern Hungary, thought that he could enjoy himself gambling in a private house and that it would be sufficient to send a scrap of paper to his men ordering them out on patrol. Unfortunately his men walked into a confrontation which they were unable to handle, and Dukovsky found himself punished by four weeks imprisonment, one week to be on a diet of bread and water.[19]

General inspections, and discipline and punishment books reveal a multitude of offences: absence without leave, insubordination, fighting, drunkenness, and other acts of 'immorality' such as gambling or getting into debt. Totalling up these offences, however, would be unlikely to give any precise picture of the behaviour of different companies or different national forces. Much probably depended upon local commanders and deployment. Hermannstadt (Sibiu) and Kronstadt (Brassó) were

---

[17] Griffin, 'The Irish Police', 682–8.

[18] Ignace-Émile Forestier, *Gendarmes à la belle époque* (Paris: Editions France-Empire, 1983), 78–80 and 84–5; and for examples of men intriguing against their superiors see Captain Louis Saurel, 'La Gendarmerie dans la société de la Deuxième République et du Seconde Empire', Thèse pour le doctorat, Université de Paris, 3 vols., 1964, vol. ii., pp. 403–5.

[19] Kriegsarchiv, KM Sonderreihe, Karton 17, Nr. 295.

German districts on the south-eastern edge of Transylvania, patrolled
in the late 1860s by men of the 14th Habsburg Gendarmerie. Their punishment records suggest that they could have been very different organizations in very different regions. Hermannstadt was the regimental
headquarters, which meant there was a greater concentration of officers,
probably leading to better overall discipline and a much tighter regime
when it came to the supervision of petty offences. In May 1869, for
example, eleven men were punished, generally for being absent without
leave or drunk; the punishment was rarely more than eight days confined to barracks, sometimes with the deprivation of tobacco. Kronstadt,
in the same month, witnessed five men punished. Their offences were
disobedience and insubordination; their punishments were imprisonment for eight days (for a man with a previously good record), six weeks,
two months, three months, and four months, with various additions of
no tobacco, of bread and water for a fixed period, or of solitary confinement.[20] These, of course, were offences for which men were disciplined and punished and for which, in consequence, a record has
survived. Even in the Habsburg Gendarmerie, however, there was probably flexibility, with officers and NCOs overlooking some offences and
simply warning men to behave better in future. Moreover, men bound
by bonds of work, camaraderie, and an *esprit de corps* were quite likely
to cover up for each other in instances of minor, and even major, pec-
cadillos.

But if there was camaraderie amongst the gendarmes there was also
the potential for tension within the barracks. In their different ways
cameraderie, the boredom of the daily grind of patrols, and personal tensions probably contributed to the heavy drinking which appears to have
been common in most gendarmeries. Some officers and NCOs were
domineering and bullied their men; some men swore at their superiors,
argued, and sometimes fought with each other. Sub-inspector Hayes of
the RIC at Edenderry, King's County, was reported in 1856 to be always
upsetting his men by abusing them publicly in front of civilians; while
a leading Fenian attributed his escape, eight years later, from the police
barracks at Tralee to the friction existing between the constables.[21] In
November 1868 the Habsburg Gendarme Johann Biro was sentenced to
eight days imprisonment for getting drunk, being insubordinate, and
then abusing his comrades, while Gendarme Mathias Juznic was given
four weeks in irons, with a fast day each week, for having created a

---

[20] Ibid., Karton 18, Nr. 308.   [21] Griffin','The Irish Police', 534 and 543.

'public scandal' by drinking, gambling, and assaulting a comrade.[22] Weapons were part of the gendarme's daily equipment, and this meant that, on occasions, violence within the barracks could be mortal. The death registers of the Carabinieri are peppered with incidents of men killing their comrades and superiors during arguments. In June 1836 Carabiniere Giuseppe Allasia began the amorous pursuit of a young woman in the town where he was stationed. The woman's father complained to Brigadiere Bruneti, who ordered Allasia to stop visiting the woman and instructed Carabiniere Casazza to keep an eye on him. A subsequent confrontation between Allasia and Bruneti resulted in the former shooting dead both his *brigadiere* and Carabiniere Casazza. In October 1849 Micheletto Onorata died as a result of three slashes from a comrade's sabre. 'Jealousy' was reported as the cause for Umberto Seri shooting dead his *brigadiere* in August 1882. Nearly a decade later Vincenzo Schilardi shot and killed his *brigadiere*, who had seized his love letters, accused him of 'flirting', and recommended an investigation into his love life. Paolo Viscusi also shot dead his *brigadiere*, apparently fearing disciplinary action over the loss of insignia.[23] The incidents of such killings in Italian barracks, and particularly among the Carabinieri, were even taken up by the London *Times* in the spring and summer of 1884.[24] But while such incidents appear to have be more apparent among the Carabinieri, this may in part be because of the way in which the records have been preserved; and if contemporaries considered Italy, and southern Europe in general, to be more violent,[25] barrack violence among gendarmes which resulted in death was not unique to the Carabinieri.[26]

[22] Kriegsarchiv, KM Sonderreihe, Karton 17, Nr. 295.

[23] AMSC, Cartella 10, Registri Morti, Torino (1836 and 1849), Bologna (1882), Bari (1890); Morto in Servizio, schedi 63 (Giovani Brunetti), 64 (Pietro Casazza), 1168 (Eugenio Martinelli), and 1172 (Paolo Volonte).

[24] *The Times*, 15 Apr. 1884, p. 3; 30 May, p. 5; 31 May, p. 7; 23 June, p. 7; 2 July, p. 5; 7 July, p. 5; 15 July, p. 9; and 19 Aug., p. 5.

[25] *The Times* correspondent, commenting on the execution of Carabiniere Marino in Naples, quoted the journal *Roma* on the sad impression left by events which appeared to contradict the century's scientific and political progress, and added: 'I adhere perfectly to this latter statement, for while Italians see daily with comparative indifference the blood of their countrymen shed in trifling quarrels, they resist the Law which interferes to maintain order and save life' (*The Times*, 15 July 1884, p. 9). Ten years later an essay in comparative criminology demonstrated statistically the greater incidence of violence compared with the states of northern Europe: Enrico Ferri, *Atlante antropologico-statistico dell'omicidio*, published as an appendix to Enrico Ferri, *L'omocidio nell'antropologia criminale* (*Omicida nato e omicido pazzo*) (Turin: 1895).

[26] Saurel, 'La Gendarmerie . . .', ii. 402–3.

Sometimes the violence took the form of suicide, as men found themselves unable to cope with being disciplined or with the pressures that were building up on them. In June 1874 Gendarme Josef Trait, serving with the 8th Habsburg Gendarmerie in the province of Slovenia, was ordered to ride as guard on a mail-coach. He fell asleep and lost his rifle; apparently too scared to face the consequences, at the end of the journey he went into the barracks, took the gun of a sleeping comrade, and shot himself. Four months later Gendarme Georg Säffer, serving in the same regiment, also shot himself. Säffer had a bad reputation as a wastrel and had accumulated large debts; his superiors concluded that it was this which drove him to suicide. There are no overall suicide figures for the Habsburg Gendarmerie, but the imperial army as a whole had a higher suicide rate than the population of the Empire.[27] During the second quarter of the nineteenth century suicides among the relatively small Württemberg Gendarmerie were running at an average of two a year. The French statistics also suggest that gendarmes had a higher suicide rate than the overall population.[28]

Gendarmes were expected to be tough and courageous; on occasions they needed to be, and sometimes, in some regions more than others, an ordinary patrol or request for assistance could turn into something violent and dangerous. On the evening of 21 February 1876 Gugliemo Occhiena was called to an inn in Bussolino (Turin), where there was an argument between the proprietor and some of his customers over a broken carafe. Possibly because Occhiena was new to the Carabinieri he may have been unsure of the best way to handle the situation. Matters got completely out of hand; angry customers turned on Occhiena and killed him with his own sabre. In August 1890, while patrolling a road after dark in Gioiosa Ionica (Bari), Carabinieri Antonio Bova and Marcello Olivetti stopped a coach being driven without lights. An argument ensued and the coach-driver drew a knife, killing Bova and wounding Olivetti before the latter overpowered him.[29] Violence of this sort may well have encouraged some gendarmes to get their retaliation in first, and/or to adopt a tough and aggressive way of addressing or otherwise dealing with people, especially those whom they considered suspect. Arrogance, officiousness, and violence on the part of French gendarmes

---

[27] Kriegsarchiv, KM Sonderreihe, Karton 25, Nr.1176 and Nr. 776; Deák, *Beyond Nationalism*, 107

[28] Walter Wannenwetsch, *Das Württembergische Landjägerkorps und die reichseinheitliche Gendarmerie in Württemberg mit einer Rüchshau auf die Anfänge der Landespolizei* (Stuttgart: Gewerkschaft der Polizei, 1986), 30; Saurel, 'La Gendarmerie . . .', ii. 161–2.

[29] AMSC, Morto in Servizio, schedi 1057 (Occhiena) and 1171 (Bova).

under Napoleon has been attributed to the recruitment of poor-quality men.[30] In the Prussian context similar behaviour could be put down to a general militaristic arrogance on the part of policemen both civilian and military; and while, at times, such an attitude was deplored, more often it was sanctioned by the respectable classes so long as it was directed against drunks, idlers, prostitutes, vagrants, and suspected thieves.[31] Yet perhaps there was something in the very nature of the nineteenth-century gendarmeries which could both foster arrogance and lead to any form of local civilian indifference being read rather too easily as insult.

The gendarmeries were considered to be elite institutions; generally, elite military institutions. The literature prepared by the creators of the gendarmeries and by officers for their subordinates commonly portrayed the institutions in heroic mould and the men as honest, modest, courageous, and generally as single-minded defenders of the law. The high-flown verses written by some of the men themselves commonly followed suit, as the following examples from France and Italy demonstrate:

> Armé de mille bras, d'une forte poitrine,
> Esclave du devoir et de la discipline;
> Lorsqu'il sert son pays, tel est son dévouement,
> Qu'il ne doit, après Dieu, que chérir son serment.
> Soldat plein de bravoure et plein de vigilance,
> Ne transigeant jamais avec sa conscience,
> Bras droit de la Justice . . .

> Del Re custodi e della Legge, schiavi
> Sol del dover, usi obbedir tacendo
> E tacendo morir, terror dei rei,
> Modesti, ignoti eroi, vittime oscure
> E grandi, anime salde in salde membra,
> Mostran nei volti austeri, nei securi
> Occhi, nei larghi lacerati petti,
> Fiera, indomata la virtù latina—
> Risonate, tamburi: salutate,
> Aste e vessilli—Onore, onore ai prodi
> Carabinieri![32]

---

[30] Eric A. Arnold, jr. *Fouché, Napoleon and the General Police* (Washington, DC: University Press of America, 1979), 108–9; Frank J. Bundy, *The Administration of the Illyrian Provinces of the French Empire, 1809–1813* (New York: Garland, 1987), 96 and 494, n. 49. However, much of Arnold's evidence comes from Fouché; and Bundy notes that men were reluctant to serve in the Illyrian Provinces.

[31] Richard J. Evans, 'Polizei, Politik und Gesellschaft in Deutschland 1700–1933', *Geschichte und Gesellschaft*, 22 (1996), 609–28; at 619–20.

[32] 'Armed with a thousand arms, with a brave heart, | Slave to duty and discipline; |

Military pride and *ésprit de corps*, however, commonly meant that, even though the ideal members of these institutions saw themselves as self-sacrificing defenders of the law, they often vigorously resisted subservience to civilian officials. Military pride and independence could easily slide into military arrogance, especially when other elements were brought into play, such as, for example, a wide degree of autonomy. In France the Gendarmerie's independence was curtailed during the nineteenth century, and from the Second Empire the military increasingly found themselves with less influence in policing matters. By the closing decade of the nineteenth century the generals were working closely with the civilian authorities in matters of public order, and the Gendarmerie, while a military body, was accepted as essentially an instrument readily available to the interior ministry and its representatives. In consequence, the potential for the kind of friction which had existed under the first Napoleon had all but disappeared. In united Italy the liberals aspired to a similar arrangement, but the Carabinieri was allowed much a much greater degree of independence than the Gendarmerie of the Third Republic. The corps prided itself on its role in Unification and its special relationship with the King, which it used to keep the liberals at arm's length. At the same time Carabinieri officers subscribed to the elite's fears and suspicions, first of the peasantry—especially that in the

When he serves his country, such is his devotion, | That he cherishes his oath of allegiance next only to God. | Soldier full of gallantry and full of vigilance, | Never having to compromise with his conscience, | The right arm of Justice . . .'

'Guardians of king and law, slaves | To duty alone, used to obeying in silence | And dying in silence, terror of criminals, | Modest, unsung heroes, martyrs obscure | But great, steadfast hearts and strong limbs, | With severe regard and steady | Gaze, breasts capable of pain, yet | Proud, indomitable Latin virtue— | Beat drums: salute | With lances and banners—Honour, honour to the courageous | Carabinieri!' The first of these poems was written by Gendarme Marconnis, who produced several such verses during the Second Republic and Second Empire; see Saurel, 'La Gendarmerie . . .', ii. 370–1; the second was reproduced in Gian Carlo Grossardi, *Galateo del Carabinieri*, 3rd edn. (Turin: 1879), p. xv.

I have used the words 'generally as single minded defenders of the law' advisedly since the law appears to be given rather less emphasis by, e.g. the Guardia Civil. 'Recuerdos de un veterano', for example, published in Don Enrique Ceballos Quintana, *Libro de el Guardia Civil* (Madrid: 1873), 26–7, has a veteran advising his son about joining the corps and stressing the importance of *Ordenanza* (military ordinances) rather than law:

'Yo mi sangre derramé, | yo vi mi frente tostada, | yo sufrí mil privaciones | de todo género, y nada | pudo hacer nunca variar | esta divisa estimada, | que da calma á la conciencia | y consuelo le da al alma. | El honor fué mi divisa, | el honor y la Ordenanza . . .' | (I shed my blood, | I was scarred on the front, | I suffered a thousand privations | Of many kinds, yet nothing | Would ever change | This emblem I love | Which brings calm to the conscience | And counsels the soul. | Honour was my emblem, | Honour and also the ordinances . . .').

south and in Sicily, which seemed alien and scarcely human rather than Italian—and subsequently of urban workers; from the scale of violence at the turn of the century, it would appear that such attitudes rubbed off on the rank and file. In Spain, where the army saw itself as the guarantor and preserver of the state, attitudes within the Guardia Civil seem to have developed along similar lines. In Prussia there was not the same suspicion of the native German peasant, though in the east the Poles were branded as ignorant and likely to be criminal or troublesome. But in nineteenth-century Prussia, where a military uniform seems generally to have instilled an aggressive sense of superiority among officers and NCOs, the myriad of police regulations gave numerous opportunities for friction between members of the public and gendarmes, as well as between the public and ordinary civilian policemen.

There is, however, a danger in assuming that hostility and violence were the norm in relations between gendarmes and those whom they policed. There were dramatic clashes in times of revolution and rebellion. There were smaller, but no less ferocious confrontations in times of food shortages and conscription ballots. Food riots and confrontations over conscription appear to have declined in much of Europe as the century wore on; the supply and distribution of the former improved, while the latter, though still often resented, was seen to be an inevitable part of life as citizens—peasants and others—became increasingly integrated into their national or imperial states. There were, of course, other opportunities for confrontation as newer forms of economic and political activity by the lower classes generated anxieties among governments and led to the deployment of gendarmes against this activity. Yet these were never daily events, and nor were the equally dangerous tasks of helping people faced with natural disasters, of pursuing brigands or rabid animals, or of trying to stop runaway horses. The gendarme's day was generally taken up with patrolling, writing reports of the patrols, taking details of accidents and petty regulatory offences, and cleaning his barracks. Rather than always living side-by-side in a constant state of tension, it seems more probable that in many, perhaps in most instances outside of the more turbulent areas of southern Italy and Spain, peasants and gendarmes, and townsmen and gendarmes, learned to live with each other. Peasants and poor townsmen were pragmatic enough to learn rapidly when and how they could use the gendarmes to protect their persons and property; gendarmes, with the exception of individuals keen to work by the book and peculiarly sensitive of their own authority, recognized when discretion was more sensible than confrontation. Moreover, while the gendarmes were present as an arm of the state to nip trouble in the bud, maintain a steady surveillance of what was going on in the provinces, and provide information for the centre, they also served to integrate people closer with the state or empire in which they lived. As, during the nineteenth century, new roads and railways facilitated the development of regional and national markets, and as new schools and schoolteachers helped to establish national cultural identities, so gendarmes were the living manifestation of the state and, particularly, of its law, a law which generally promised (even if the state did not necessarily ensure) that all were equal before it. Gendarmes enforced the state's demands for taxes, conscripts, and obedience to its regulations; but there was supposed to be reciprocity in the relations between state and citizen, and consequently, in the name of the state, the gendarmes also provided various forms of assistance and protection to the citizen in times of emergency.

This explanation of the gendarme's role in the development of the nineteenth-century state is, of course, an inference based on a comparative study of the day-to-day tasks of the men and a recognition of how societies, particularly rural societies, changed over the period. It is not an explanation of why the gendarmeries were created. While many of the rulers of *ancien régime* Europe aspired to establishing well-ordered police states, few ever possessed the capabilities for effectively enforcing their police ordinances. Yet there are no archival sources from the late eighteenth and early nineteenth centuries, in which principal ministers, ministers of the interior, ministers of war, or any other ministers, consistently and persistently argue for the creation of a gendarmerie because of a belief that such an organization will assist in the spread and maintainance of the state. The model, established in France under the *ancien régime*, was adopted by the rulers of states in the early nineteenth century because, like other elements of the Napoleonic state, it appeared to work well in handling a variety of practical problems—apprehending beggars and vagrants, rounding up conscripts, suppressing brigandage and minor disorder—while, at the same time, helping to concentrate power at the centre. Even those who were consistently opposed to Napoleon recognized this, though it was to take a new wave of upheaval during the 1840s to convince the rulers of Spain and the Habsburg Empire that they too should adopt the model. The fact that, in part at least, gendarmes were soldiers was perceived both as natural and as an advantage by governments. Soldiers were the traditional defenders of regimes; increasingly, they were seen as disciplined and controlled; and they were armed, which, in rural societies where so many had access to weaponry, was no bad thing.

Paradoxically, almost at the moment when gendarmeries were becoming established across continental Europe an alternative model of police was created. Partly because of a hostility to things French and a dislike of deploying the military internally, the British government insisted that police should be civilian—except, of course, in the backward, turbulent territory of Ireland and in various wildernesses of the empire. Just as absolutist states in the early nineteenth century saw advantages in the centralized Napoleonic system of administration, together with the Gendarmerie, so many European liberals saw the future to lie with English models, among which was included that of London's Metropolitan Police. Moreover, as the century wore on politicians and administrators who were not necessarily liberal in their outlook increasingly saw military organizations as instruments which should be reserved for international and external conflict; they were to be used internally only as a last resort. By the end of the century such attitudes, often reinforced by the reluctance of civilian ministers to yield any authority to generals, contributed to limitations on, even curtailments of, the gendarmeries in preference to civilian policemen.

BIBLIOGRAPHY

ARCHIVAL SOURCES

Austria

Staatsarchiv, Vienna

Staatskanzlei Vorträge (1846) Folie 33–7 V Karton 294 1846 (Metternich).

Kriegsarchiv, Vienna

ABG KL Kartons 2814–3148 (These cartons contain information on Gendarmerie personnel during the nineteenth century).
KK MfLV, Gendarmerie LA, Kartons 293 and 296.
KM Sonderreihe, Kartons 17, 18, and 25.
Niederösterreichische Landesregierung, Vienna.
1869 Statthalterei, Nr. 93 (18).

France

Archives Nationales, Paris

Série BB¹⁸ Correspondence générale de la division criminelle.
Cases sampled from files 1–85 (conscription and recruitment, Year VII–1814) and from 943–1036 (criminal cases, 1814–26).
Série F7 Police générale.
This is an enormous collection, but included among its cartons are various 'Rapports de Gendarmerie' from the First Empire through to the Second. Several *départements* were followed throughout the whole period, others were sampled periodically. The principal cartons consulted were: 3917–19 (Basses-Alpes); 3947–49 (Cantal); 3993–6 (Eure-et-Loir); 3997–4002 (Finistère); 4009–11 (Gers); 4103–6 (Nord); 4119–22 (Puy-de-Dôme); 4143–6 (Rhône). Reports on particular events during the 1830s and 1840s can be followed up in cartons 6780–4.
Other useful cartons in the series are:
Carton 3065, containing the responses to the Ministry of Police circular of 19 *nivôse* Year IV, on the state of crime, begging, the National Guard and the Gendarmerie.
Carton 3053 with correspondence between Prefects and Gendarmes, Year XIII–1807.

F²I 1203–4 Police Rurale (Objets généraux) Year III–1830 has useful material on the *gardes-champêtres*.

F⁹ 320–6 Affaires militaires, Gendarmerie, contains a variety of correspondence particularly relating to the Revolutionary period.

AF^{IV} Secrétairerie d'Etat Impérial, cartons 1154–8, Ministre de la Guerre: Gendarmerie et police militaire, are central to any study of Napoleon's Gendarmerie.

Archives de la Guerre, Vincennes

Série E⁵ Correspondence Militaire, Générale et Divers, 1830–61 (various volumes sampled, notably 152, Troubles occasionés par la cherté des grains, 1839–40, and 160, Innondations, 1846).

Série F¹ Révolution de 1848 (various cartons sampled, notably the Rapports quotidiens de 1848 (esp. nos. 16 and 17) and the Correspondence générale 1849–52 (esp. nos. 29, 31, 37, and 65).

Série X^f Gendarmerie (this is the key series of documents for the Gendarmerie from the Revolution to the Second Empire, though the material becomes much thinner after 1815. The principal cartons consulted are listed below):

X^f 4 Correspondence, 1791–Year II.

X^f 9 Organisation général.

X^f 10–11 Decisions ministerielles rendues sur les rapports du jury d'organisation.

X^f 23 Dans les 4 départements de la rive gauche du Rhin, Year VII.

Xf 92 Revues d'inspection, an X–1807.

X^f 97 Idem, 1808–11.

X^f 98 Idem, 1812.

X^f 104 Compagnies départementales, affairs particulières, etc. Year XII–1814.

X^f 128–34 États nominatives des sous-officiers et gendarmes (for the First Empire, by *département*, and the information is variable).

X^f 150 Italie, Piémont, correspondence, rapports, Year IX–Year XII.

Xf 210 Compagnies de Reserve, 1830–76.

X^f 234 Voltigeurs algériens (includes also Meurthe review, *fructidor*, Year V).

X^f 244 Divers, 1701–1814.

X^f 246 Recrutement, Year II–1806.

X^f 248 Divers, correspondence Year IX–1827.

X^f 250 Officiers, dossiers d'affairs particuliers, 1830–48.

X^f 252 Dépens d'entretien, 1830–76.

X^f 254 Divers, jugements.

X^f 256 Revues d'inspection, 1813–14.

X^f 257 Idem, 1819.

Série Y^b (A key series for any study of the *marechaussée*). For this volume I have used only the inspection reports listed below):

Y^b 787 Revue de Maréchaussée 1771.
Y^b 788 Idem.
Y^b 789 Idem.
Y^b 790 Idem.
Y^b 800 Revue de Marechaussée 1799.
Y^b 801 Idem.
Y^b 802 Idem.
Y^b 803 Idem.
Y^b 804 Idem.
Y^b 805 Idem.
G^8 180–3 Rapports de Préfets (Second Empire).
MR 1957 Gendarmerie, 1770s–1840s.
MR 2003 Garde nationale mobile. Gendarmerie.

Musée de la Gendarmerie national, *Melun*
Correspondance of Marshal Moncey (principally with Colonel Martin-Charly, commandant of the 8th Legion) 1805–9. (The museum also contains a printed copy of Moncey's *Ordres généraux*, various printed instruction manuals, and a run of *Le Journal de a Gendarmerie*.)

Germany

Landesarchiv Magdeburg
Landeshauptarchiv LHA Rep. C.20 1b, Oberpräsidium der Provinz Sachsen, I Allgemenie Abteilung. IV Landjäger und Gendarmerie.
Landeshauptarchiv LHA Rep. C.28 If, Regierung Magdeburg Polizeiregistratur.
XVIII Landeshoheits-Sachsen.
XXVII Polizei-Sachsen a) Generalia.
XXXII Statistische-Sachsen.
Landeshauptarchiv LHA Rep. C.30 Polizeiverwaltung: Haldensleben I.

Thüringisches Staatsarchiv, Gotha
Regierung Erfurt, Kasten 394, Landespolizei und Gendarmerie.

Italy

Archivio del Museo Storico dell'Arma dei Carabinieri, Rome
This archive has been scarcely used by historians. The principal cartons consulted were:
3 Varia, 1812–1923.
10 Varia (includes *Registri morti*, lists, by legion, of men who died or were killed in service).
11, Varia 1815–60 (includes correspondence on the Carabinieri during unification).

13, Varia 1817–37 (a useful collection of printed laws and regulations).

47, 1861–75, Raccolta di Circolari manuscritti.

49, 1862–6, Sicilia.

92, 1877, Informazioni varie (Brescia, Milan Legion).

100, 1880, Partito sovversivi, Italia irredenta (Brescia, Milan Legion).

108, 1882–3, Informazione, Casi vari (Brescia, Milan Legion).

116, 1883, Grave disastro in Casamicciola.

122, 1883–93, Corporazioni religiose, Partito Repubblicano (Avellino, Naples Legion).

125, 1884, Dimonstrazioni verificatesi in dipendenza del colera.

Also useful were the *Morto in Servizio* files which contain reports, sometimes in considerable detail, of men who were killed, or who died on duty.

Archivio di Stato di Torino

Sezzione Riunite, Categoria: Guerra.

Segretaria di Guerra e Marina, poi Ministero di Guerra: Uffizio di Gabinetto e protocoli, Registro: Correspondenza col Ministero di Polizia e Carabinieri Reali, 1819–22.

2e Divisione: Registro della Corrispondenza per Reggimenti Provinciali e Milizie, Registro 1, Registro 1 bis, Registro 2.

PRINTED PRIMARY SOURCES

A l'Assemblée Nationale, par addition au Mémoire présenté, le dix-neuf de ce mois, par les Brigades de la Maréchaussée de l'Îsle de France, le 25 septembre 1790: A l'Assemblée Nationale, pour seconde addition au Mémoire présenté le 19 septembre et augmentée d'un plan economique de 2,005,233 liv. sur le traitement annuel de la Maréchaussée de l'Îsle de France, même nombre de Chefs de Brigades et Cavaliers, avec augmentation de paie, le 14 octobre 1790 (Paris, 1790).

ANON., *Précis important sur les maréchaussées* (Paris, 1791).

—— *Réflexions sur le Corps de la Maréchaussée, addressées, en forme de lettre, à l'auteur du livre intitulé: Défense du système de guerre moderne* (Geneva, 1781).

AZEGLIO, MASSIMO D', *Things I Remember*, translated with an introduction by E. R. Vincent (Oxford: Oxford University Press, 1966).

CAVOUR, C. B., *Carteggi di Cavour*, 15 vols. (Bologna: Nicola Zanichelli, 1926–61).

CHÉNIER, LOUIS-JOSEPH-GABRIEL, *Éloge historique du Maréchal Moncey* (Paris, 1848).

[CONSALVI, Cardinal ERCOLE?] *Sentimenti Morali e Brevi Istruzioni per un Carabinieri* (Rome, 1816?).

COURSON, Vicomte AURÉLIEN DE (ed.), *Souvenirs d'un officier de gendarmerie sous la Restauration*, 3rd. edn. (Paris: Plon, 1914).

FORESTIER, IGNACE-ÉMILE, *Gendarmes à la belle époque* (Paris: Editions France-Empire, 1983).

FOUCHÉ, JOSEPH, *Les Mémoires de Fouché*, ed. Louis Madelin (Paris: Flammarion, 1946).

FOURASTIÉ, VICTOR (ed.), *Cahiers des doléances de la sénéchaussée de Cahors* (Cahors, 1908).

Mémoire présenté au temps par M. Gauthier d'Auteville, à Paris, ce 13 juillet 1791, suivi d'une lettre à M. Duportail, Ministre de la Guerre (Paris, 1791).

GROSSARDI, GIAN CARLO, *Galateo dei Carabinieri*, 3rd. edn. (Turin, 1879).

GUICHARD, AUGUST-CHARLES, *Manuel de la Gendarmerie nationale* (Paris, 1791).

GUILLAUTE, M., *Mémoire sur la réformation de la police de France* (1749), introduction and notes by Jean Seznec (Paris: Herman, 1974).

HAUTERIVE, ERNEST D' (ed.), *La Police secrète du Premier Empire*, 5 vols (Paris: Perrin (later Clavreuil), 1922–64).

KLAR, PAUL ALOYS, *Denkschrift der Gendarmeriekaserne in Prag* (Prague, 1857).

LE MAY, A. (ed.), *Cahiers des doléances des corporations de la Ville d'Angers et des paroisses de la Sénéchaussée particulière d'Angers*, 2 vols. (Angers, 1915).

MAYR, JOSEPH KARL (ed.), *Das Tagebuch des Polizeiministers Kempen von 1848 bis 1859* (Vienna: Österreichischer Bundesverlag, 1931).

MÈGE, FRANCISQUE (ed.), *Les Cahiers des paroisses d'Auvergne en 1789* (Clermont-Ferrand, 1899).

MERCER, WILLIAM, *How the Police Manage Italy* (Rome: Italo-American School Press, 1876).

MILDMAY, Sir WILLIAM, *The Police of France: Or, an Account of the Laws and Regulations established in that Kingdom for the Preservation of Peace, and the Preventing of Robberies* (London, 1763).

Correpondance de Napoléon 1re (Paris, 1862).

PASQUIER, ÉTIENNE-DENIS, *Souvenirs de Chancelier Pasquier 1767–1815*, introduction and notes by Robert Lacour-Gayet (Paris: Hachette, 1964).

RADET, ÉTIENNE, *Mémoires du Général Radet, d'après ses papiers personnels et les archives de l'état*, ed. Etienne Amadée Combier (Paris: Belin Frères, 1892).

SMOLLET, TOBIAS, *Travels through France and Italy*, ed. Frank Felstein (Oxford: Oxford University Press, 1979).

BOOKS

ALESSI, GEORGIA, *Giustizia e Polizia. Il controllo di una capitale Napoli 1779–1803* (Naples: Jovene, 1992).

ALEXANDER, ALFRED, *The Hanging of Wilhelm Oberdank* (London: London Magazine Books, 1977).

ARNOLD, ERIC A., *Fouché, Napoleon and the General Police* (Washington, DC: University Press of America, 1979).

AUBUSSON DE CAVARLAY, BRUNO, HURÉ, MARIE-SYLVIE, and POTTIER, MARIE-LYS (eds.), *Les Statistiques criminelles de 1831 à 1981*. *La base Davido, séries générales* (Paris: Cesdip, 1989).

BAYLEY, DAVID H., *Patterns of Policing: A Comparative International Analysis* (New Brunswick, NJ: Rutgers University Press, 1985).

BERDAHL, ROBERT M., *The Politics of the Prussian Nobility: The Development of a Conservative Ideology, 1770–1848* (Princeton NJ: Princeton University Press, 1988).

BERNARD, PAUL P., *From the Enlightenment to the Police State. The Public Life of Johann Anton Pergen* (Urbana Ill.: University of Illinois Press, 1991).

BERTHAUD, JEAN-PAUL, *La Révolution armée. Les soldats-citoyens et la Révolution française* (Paris: Robert Laffont, 1979).

BESSON, GENERAL JEAN and ROSIÈRE, PIERRE, *La Gendarmerie nationale* (Paris: Xavier Richer, 1982).

BIASE, LUIGI AMADEO DE, *Carabinieri contro Briganti e Banditi 1814–1934* (Rome: Museo Storico dell'Arma dei Carabinieri, 1995).

BLACKBOURN, DAVID, *The Marpingen Visions: Rationalism, Religion and the Rise of Modern Germany* (London: Fontana, 1993).

BLANNING, T. C. W., *The French Revolution in Germany: Occupation and Resistance in the Rhineland, 1792–1802* (Oxford: Clarendon Press, 1983).

BLUM, JEROME, *The End of the Old Order in Rural Europe* (Princeton, NJ: Princeton University Press, 1978).

BOUTON, CYNTHIA A., *The Flour War: Gender, Class and Community in Late Ancien Régime French Society* (University Park, Pa.: Pennsylvania State University Press, 1993).

BRENNAN, GERALD, *The Spanish Labrynth: An Account of the Social and Political Background of the Civil War*, 2nd. edn. (Cambridge: Cambridge University Press, 1950).

BROERS, MICHAEL, *Napoleonic Imperialism and the Savoyard Monarchy 1773–1821: State Building in Piedmont* (Lewiston, NY: Edwin Mellen Press, 1997).

BUISSON, HENRY, *La Police: son histoire* (Vichy: Imprimerie Wallon, 1949).

BUNDY, FRANK J., *The Administration of the Illyrian Provinces of the French Empire, 1809–1813* (New York: Garland, 1987).

CAMERON, IAIN A., *Crime and Repression in the Auvergne and the Guyenne, 1720–1790* (Cambridge: Cambridge University Press, 1981).

CARROT, GEORGES, *Le Maintien de l'ordre en France depuis le fin de l'ancien régime jusqu'au 1968*, 2 vols. (Toulouse: Presses de l'Institut d'études politiques de Toulouse, 1984).

CESARI, CESARE, *Il Brigantaggio e l'opera dell'Esercito Italiano dal 1860 al 1870* (Rome: Ausonia, 1920).

COBB, RICHARD, *The Police and the People: French Popular Protest 1789–1820* (Oxford: Oxford University Press, 1970).

COBB, RICHARD, *Paris and its Provinces, 1792–1802* (Oxford: Oxford University Press, 1975).

CONNELLY, OWEN, *Napoleon's Satellite Kingdoms* (New York: The Free Press, 1965).

COULIN, Colonel R., *Historique et traditions de la Gendarmerie nationale* (Melun: École des Officiers de la Gendarmerie nationale, 1954).

DIAMANT-BERGER, MARCEL, *Huit siècles de la gendarmerie* (Paris: J.F. Editions, 1967).

DAVIS, JOHN A., *Conflict and Control: Law and Order in Nineteenth-Century Italy* (London: Macmillan, 1988).

DEÁK, ISTVÁN, *Beyond Nationalism. A Social and Political History of the Habsburg Officer Corps 1848–1918* (New York: Cambridge University Press, 1992).

DIEU, FRANÇOIS, *Gendarmerie et modernité. Étude de la spécifité gendarmique aujourd'hui* (Paris: Montchrestien, 1993).

DUCHESNE DE GILLEVOISIN, C. A. G., Duc de Conegliano, *Le Maréchal Moncey: Duc de Conegliano, 1754–1842* (Paris: Calmann Lévy, 1902).

DUNNAGE, JONATHAN, *The Italian Police and the Rise of Fascism: A Case Study of the Province of Bologna, 1897–1925* (Westport, Ct.: Praeger, 1997).

EGMOND, FLORIKE, *Underworlds: Organised Crime in The Netherlands, 1650–1800* (Oxford: Polity Press, 1993).

EMERSON, DONALD E., *Metternich and the Political Police: Security and Subversion in the Hapsburg Monarchy (1815–1830)* (The Hague: Martinus Nijhof, 1968).

EMSLEY, CLIVE, *The English Police: A Political and Social History*, 2nd edn. (London: Longman, 1996).

FIJNAULT, CYRILLE and VOSS, WILLIAM, *Bibliografie van de Koninklijke Marechaussee 1813–1988* (Lochem: Van den Brink, 1992).

FINZSCH, NORBERT, *Obrigkeit und Unterschichten. Zur Geschichte der rheinischen Unterschichten gegen Ende des 18. und zu Beginn des 19. Jahrhunderts* (Stuttgart: Franz Steiner, 1990).

FIUME, GIOVANNA, *Le Bande Armate in Sicilia (1819–1849). Violenza e Organizzazone del Potere* (Palermo: Annali della Facolta di Lettere e Filosofia dell'Universita di Palermo, 1984).

FORD, CAROLINE, *Creating the Nation in Provincial France: Religion and Political Identity in Brittany* (Princeton, NJ: Princeton University Press, 1993).

FORREST, ALAN, *Conscripts and Deserters: The Army and French Society During the Revolution and Empire* (Oxford: Oxford University Press, 1989).

FUNK, ALBRECHT, *Polizei und Rechtsstaadt: Die Entwicklung des staatlichen Gewaltmonopols in Preussen, 1848–1914* (Frankfurt: Campus, 1986).

GALLEY, J. B., *Saint-Étienne et son district pendant la Révolution*, 2 vols. (St Étienne: Imprimerie de la Loire Républicaine, 1904–06).

GARRIDO, DIEGO LÓPEZ, *La Guardia Civil y los orígenes del Estado centralista* (Barcelona: Editorial Critica, 1982).

GEBHARDT, HELMUT, *Die Gendarmerie in der Steiermark von 1850 bis heute* (Graz: Leykam Verlag, 1997).

GRIFFIN, BRIAN, *The Bulkies: Police and Crime in Belfast 1800–1865* (Dublin: Irish Academic Press, 1998).

GRISI, FRANCESCO, *Storia dei Carabinieri. Imprese, battaglie, uomini e protagonisti: i due secoli della Benemerita al servizio della gente* (Spa: Piemme, 1996).

HANCOCK, W.K., *Ricasoli and the Risorgimento in Tuscany* (New York: Howard Fertig, 1969).

HESZTERA, Gendarmerieoberst iR FRANZ, *Die Kommandostrukturen der Gendarmerie von 1850 bis 1993* (Vienna: Leiro, 1994).

HOLDAWAY, SIMONY, *Inside the British Police: A Force at Work* (Oxford: Basil Blackwell, 1983).

HUFTON, OLWEN H., *The Poor of Eighteenth-Century France, 1750–1789* (Oxford: Clarendon Press, 1974).

HUGHES, STEVEN C., *Crime, Disorder and the Risorgimento: The Politics of Policing in Bologna* (Cambridge: Cambridge University Press, 1994).

JENSEN, JENS, *De danske Gendarmerikorps 1839–1939* (Haderslev: Winds bogvorlag, 1938).

JENSEN, RICHARD BACH, *Liberty and Order: The Theory and Practice of Italian Public Security Policy, 1848 to the Crisis of the 1890s* (New York: Garland, 1991).

JESSEN, RALPH, *Polizei im Industrierevier: Modernisierung und Herrschaftspraxis im westfälischen Ruhrgebiet 1848–1914* (Göttingen: Vandenhoeck & Ruprecht, 1991).

KEEP, JOHN L.H., *Soldiers of the Tsar: Army and Society in Russia 1462–1874* (Oxford: Clarendon Press, 1985).

KEPLER, Colonel LEOPOLD (ed.), *Die Gendarmerie in Österreich. 125 Jahre Plichterfüllung* (Graz: Leykham Verlag, 1974).

KERN, ROBERT W., *Liberals, Reformers and Caciques in Restoration Spain 1875–1909* (Albuquerque, N.Mex.: University of New Mexico Press, 1974).

KIERNAN, V. G., *The Revolution of 1854 in Spanish History* (Oxford; Oxford University Press, 1966).

KOLIOPOULOS, JOHN S., *Brigands With a Cause: Brigandage and Irredentism in Modern Greece, 1821–1912* (Oxford: Clarendon Press, 1987).

KOSSELECK, REINHART, *Preussen zwischen Reform und Revolution: Allegemeines Landrecht, Verwaltung und soziale Bewegung von 1791 bis 1848* (Stuttgart: Ernst Klett, 1965).

LARRIEU, General L., *Histoire de la Gendarmerie depuis les origines de la Maréchaussée jusqu'à nos jours*, 2 vols. (Paris: Charles-Lavauzelle, 1927–33).

LEFEBVRE, GEORGES, *The Thermidorians* (London: Routledge & Kegan Paul, 1964).

LEWIS, MICHAEL, *Napoleon and his British Captives* (London: Allen & Unwin, 1962).

LEROY-BEAULIEU, ANATOLE, *The Empire of the Tsars and the Russians*, 3 vols. (New York: Putnam, 1902).

LORGNIER, JACQUES, *Maréchaussée, histoire d'une révolution judiciaire et administrative*, vol. 1, *Les juges bottés*; vol. 2, *Quand le gendarme juge* (Paris: L'Harmattan, 1994).

LUCAS, COLIN, *The Structure of the Terror: The example of Claude Javogues and the Loire* (Oxford: Clarendon Press, 1973).

LÜDTKE, ALF, *Police and State in Prussia, 1815–1850* (Cambridge: Cambridge University Press, 1989).

MACLEOD, R. C., *The North-West Mounted Police and Law Enforcement, 1873–1905* (Toronto: University of Toronto Press, 1976).

MADELIN, LOUIS, *La Rome de Napoléon. La domination française à Rome de 1809 à 1814* (Paris: Plon, 1906).

MANGIO, CARLO, *La polizia toscana; Organizzazione e criteri d'intervento, 1765–1808* (Milan: Giuffrè, 1988).

MARGADANT, TED W., *French Peasants in Revolt: The Insurrection of 1851* (Princeton NJ: Princeton University Press, 1979).

MARX, KARL, *The Eighteenth Brumaire of Louis Napoleon*, in Karl Marx, *Surveys from Exile: Political Writings, vol. 2*, edited and introduced by David Fernbach (London: New Left Books, 1973).

MERRIMAN, JOHN M., *The Agony of the Republic: The Repression of the Left in Revolutionary France, 1848–1851* (New Haven, Conn.: Yale University Press, 1978).

MIQUEL, PIERRE, *Les Gendarmes* (Paris: Olivier Orban, 1990).

MONAS, SIDNEY, *The Third Section: Police and Society in Russia under Nicholas I* (Cambridge, Mass.: Harvard University Press, 1961).

MURAT, MARIO, *Il Carabiniere: Storia del Corpo—Avvenimenti dell'Arma* (Piacenza: Edizioni Apuana, 1935).

NEUBAUER, FRANZ, *Die Gendarmerie in Österreich, 1849–1924* (Vienna: Gendarmerie-Jubiläumsfonds, 1925).

NITSCHKE, PETER, *Verbrechensbekämpfung und Verwaltung. Die Enstehung der Polizei in der Grafschaft Lippe, 1700–1814* (Münster: Waxmann, 1990).

PALMER, STANLEY G., *Police and Protest in England and Ireland, 1780–1850* (Cambridge: Cambridge University Press, 1988).

PAOLO, PAOLO, DI, *Dalla Cronaca alla Leggenda. I Carabinieri nelle illustrazioni dei periodici populari italiani* (Rome: Comando Generale dell'Arma dei Carabinieri, 1990).

PAYNE, HOWARD C., *The Police State of Louis Napoleon Bonaparte* (Seattle: University of Washington Press, 1966).

PERROT, JEAN-CLAUDE and WOOLF, STUART J., *State and Statistics in France, 1789–1815* (Chur, Switzerland, and London: Harwood Academic Publishers, 1984).

PETROPULOS, JOHN ANTHONY, *Politics and Statecraft in the Kingdom of Greece, 1833–1843* (Princeton NJ: Princeton University Press, 1968).

PILBEAM, PAMELA M., *The 1830 Revolution in France* (London: Macmillan, 1991).

PINKNEY, DAVID H., *The French Revolution of 1830* (Princeton, NJ.: Princeton University Press, 1972).

RAEFF, MARC, *The Well-Ordered Police State: Social and Institutional Change Through Law in the Germanies and Russia 1600–1800* (New Haven Conn.: Yale University Press, 1983).

RAMSAY, CLAY, *The Ideology of the Great Fear. The Soissonais in 1789* (Baltimore: Johns Hopkins University Press, 1992).

REINHARDT, STEVEN G., *Justice in the Sarladais, 1770–1790* (Baton Rouge, La.: Louisiana State University Press, 1991).

REITH, CHARLES, *The Blind Eye of History* (London: Faber, 1952).

REY, ALFRED and FÉRON, LOUIS, *Histoire du corps des gardiens de la paix* (Paris, 1894).

RIALL, LUCY, *Sicily and the Unification of Italy: Liberal Policy and Local Power, 1859–1866* (Oxford: Clarendon Press, 1998).

ROTHENBERG, GUNTHER E., *The Army of Francis Joseph* (West Lafayette, Ind.: Purdue University Press, 1976).

RUGGIERO, MICHELE, *Briganti di Piemonte Napoleonico* (Turin: Le Bouquiniste, 1968).

—— *Storia del Piemonte* (Turin: Piemonte in Bancarella, 1979).

RUIZ, ENRIQUE MARTINEZ, *Creacion de la Guardia Civil* (Madrid: Editora Nacional, 1976).

SAHLINS, PETER, *Forest Rights: The War of the Desmoiselles in Nineteenth-Century France* (Cambridge, Mass.: Harvard University Press, 1994).

SAMSON, R., *Marginaux, délinquents et séditieux dans le beauvaisis 1765–1791*, vol 1, *Vagabonds et mendiants à la veille de la révolution de 1789* (Beauvais: Centre départemental de documentation pédagogique, 1980).

SAUREL, Colonel LOUIS, *Peines et gloires des gendarmes* (Paris: Lavauzelle, 1973).

SCHULTE, REGINA, *The Village in Court: Arson, Infanticide and Poaching in the Court Records of Upper Barain, 1848–1910* (Cambridge: Cambridge University Press, 1994).

SCHWARTZ, ROBERT M., *Policing the Poor in Eighteenth-Century France* (Chapel Hill, NC: University of North Carolina Press, 1988).

SELIGMAN, EDMOND, *La Justice en France pendant la Révolution (1789–1792)*, 2 vols. (Paris, 1901–13).

SENA, MARIO DE, SCAFFARDI, OSCAR, PEZZOLET, VINCENZO, *et al.*, *I Carabinieri, 1814–1980* (Rome: Comando Generale dei Carabinieri, 1981).

SHEEHAN, JAMES L., *German History, 1770–1866* (Oxford: Oxford University Press, 1989).

SHUBERT, ADRIAN, *A Social History of Modern Spain* (London: Routledge, 1990).

SILVERMAN, SYDEL, *Three Bells of Civilization: The Life of an Italian Hill Town* (New York: Columbia University Press, 1975).

SINCLAIR, R. J. and SCULLY, F. J. M., *Arresting Memories: Captured Moments in Constabulary Life* (Coleraine: Royal Ulster Constabulary, 1982).

SKED, ALAN, *The Decline and Fall of the Habsburg Empire, 1815–1918* (London: Longman, 1989).

SNOWDEN, FRANK M., *Naples in the Time of Cholera 1884–1911* (Cambridge: Cambridge University Press, 1995).

SPENCER, ELAINE GLOVKA, *Police and the Social Order in German Cities: The Düsseldorf District, 1848–1914* (De Kalb, Ill.: Northern Illinois University Press, 1992).

SQUIRE, P. S., *The Third Department: The Establishment and Practices of the Political Police in the Russia of Nicholas I* (Cambridge: Cambridge University Press, 1968).

STURGILL, CLAUDE C., *Claude Le Blanc: Civil Servant of the King* (Gainesville, Fla.: University Presses of Florida, 1975).

—— *L'Organisation et l'administration de la maréchaussée et de la justice prévôtale dans la France des Bourbons, 1720–1730* (Vincennes: Service Historique de l'Armée de la Terre, 1981).

TERLIZZI, POMPEO DI, *Quando frammenti di storia si ricompongono. Alle radici culturali e formative dell'Arma dei Carabinieri* (Bari: Levanti, 1991).

TILLY, CHARLES, *The Vendée* (London: Edward Arnold, 1964).

TRAUGOTT, MARK, *Armies of the Poor: Determinants of Working-Class Participation in the Parisian Insurrection of June 1848* (Princeton NJ: Princeton University Press, 1985).

TULARD, JEAN, *La Préfecture de police sous la monarchie de Juillet* (Paris: Imprimerie Municipal, Hôtel de Ville, 1964).

—— *Paris et son Administration (1800–1830)* (Paris: Ville de Paris Commission des Travaux Historiques, 1976).

VAN OUTRIVE, LODE, CARTUYVELS, YVES, and PONSAERS, PAUL, *Les Polices en Belgique: histoire socio-politique du système policier de 1794 à nos jours* (Brussels: Editions Vie Ouvrière, 1991).

VIALA, S., *Marseille Révolutionaire, l'armée nation (1789–1793)* (Paris: Chapelot, 1910).

WANNENWETSCH, WALTER, *Das Württembergische Landjägerkorps und die reichseinheitliche Gendarmerie in Württemberg mit einer Rückschau auf die Anfänge der Landespolizei* (Stuttgart: Gewerkschaft der Polizei, 1986).

WEBER, EUGEN, *Peasants into Frenchmen: The Modernization of Rural France, 1870–1914* (Stanford, Cal.: Stanford University Press, 1995).

WILLIAMS, ALAN, *The Police of Paris, 1718–1789* (Baton Rouge, La.: Louisiana State University Press, 1979).

WOLOCH, ISSER, *The New Regime: Transformations of the French Civic Culture, 1789–1820s* (New York: Norton, 1994).

WORTMAN, RICHARD S., *The Development of a Russian Legal Consciousness* (Chicago: University of Chicago Press, 1976).

ARTICLES

AXTMANN, ROLAND, ' "Police" and the Formation of the Modern State: Legal and Ideological Assumptions on State Capacity in the Austrian Lands of the Habsburg Empire, 1500–1800', *German History*, 10 (1992), 39–61.

BLAKE, HENRY A., 'The Irish Police', *The Nineteenth Century*, 9 (1881) 385–96.

BROERS, MICHAEL, 'Policing Piedmont: The "Well-Ordered Police State" in the Age of Revolution, 1789–1821', *Criminal Justice History*, 15 (1994), 39–57.

—— 'The Police and the Padroni: Italian Notabili, French Gendarmes and the Origins of the Centralized State in Napolenic Italy', *European History Quarterly*, 26 (1996), 331–53.

BROWN, HOWARD G., 'From Organic Society to Security State: The War on Brigandage in France, 1797–1802', *Journal of Modern History*, 69 (1997), 661–95.

CHATTERTON, M. R., 'The Supervision of Patrol Work Under the Fixed Points System', in Simon Holdaway (ed.), *The British Police* (London: Arnold, 1979).

DANKE, UWE, 'Bandits and the State: Robbers and the Authorities in the Holy Roman Empire in the Late Seventeeth and Early Eighteenth Centuries', in Richard J. Evans (ed.), *The German Underworld: Deviants and Outcasts in German History* (London: Routledge, 1988).

DICKIE, JOHN, 'A Word at War: the Italian Army and Brigandage, 1860–70', *History Workshop Journal*, 33 (1992), 1–24.

DUNNAGE, JONATHAN, 'Law and Order in Giolittian Italy: A Case Study of the Province of Bologna', *European History Quarterly*, 25 (1995), 381–408.

DYONET, NICOLE, 'La Maréchaussée et la culture judiciaire française au temps de Beccaria', in Michel Porret (ed.), *Beccaria et la culture juridique des lumières* (Geneva: Droz, 1997).

—— 'La Maréchaussée et la ville en France au XVIIIᵉ siècle', in Xavier Rousseaux and René Lévy (eds.), *Le Pénal dans tous ses états. Justice, états et sociétés en Europe (XIIᵉ–XXᵉ siècles)* (Brussels: Facultés universitaires Saint-Louis, 1997).

EMSLEY, CLIVE, 'La Maréchaussée à la fin de l'ancien régime: note sur la composition du corps', *Revue d'histoire moderne et contemporaine*, 32 (1986), 622–44.

—— 'Policing the Streets of Early Nineteenth-Century Paris', *French History*, 1 (1987), 257–82.

—— 'The Nation State, the Law and the Peasant in Nineteenth-Century Europe', in Xavier Rousseaux and René Lévy (eds.), *Le Pénal dans tous ses états. Justice, états et sociétés en Europe (XIIᵉ–XXᵉ siècles)* (Brussels: Facultés universitaires Saint-Louis, 1997).

—— 'A Typology of Nineteenth-Century Police', *Crime, histoire et sociétés/Crime, history and societies* 3 (1999), 19–24.

EMSLEY, CLIVE, and PHILLIPS, SABINE, 'The Habsburg Gendarmerie: A Research Agenda', *German History* 17 (1999), 241–50.

EVANS, RICHARD J., 'Polizei, Politik und Gesellschaft in Deutschland, 1700–1933', *Geschichte und Gesellschaft*, 22 (1996), 609–28.

EVANS, R. J. W., 'From Confederation to Compromise: The Austrian Experiment, 1849–1867', *Proceedings of the British Academy*, 87 (1995), 135–67.

FINZSCH, NORBERT, 'Räuber und Gendarme im Rheinland: Das Bandenwesen in den vier rheinischen Départements vor und während der Zeit der französischen Verwaltung (1794–1814)', *Francia*, 15 (1987), 425–71.

FIUME, GIOVANNA, 'Bandits, Violence and the Organisation of Power in Sicily in the Early Nineteenth Century', in John A. Davis and Paul Ginsborg (eds.), *Society and Politics in the Age of the Risorgimento* (Cambridge: Cambridge University Press, 1991).

GONNET, PAUL, 'Esquisse de la crise économique et sociale en France de 1827 à 1832', *Revue d'histoire économique et sociale*, 33 (1955), 249–92.

GRAB, ALEXANDER, 'State Power, Brigandage and Rural Resistance in Napoleonic Italy', *European History Quarterly*, 25 (1995), 39–70.

—— 'Army, State and Society: Conscription and Desertion in Napoleonic Italy (1802–1814)', *Journal of Modern History*, 67 (1995) 25–54.

HAWKINS, RICHARD, 'The "Irish Model" and the Empire: A Case for Reassessment', in David M. Anderson and David Killingray (eds.), *Policing the Empire: Government, Authority and Control, 1830–1940* (Manchester: Manchester University Press, 1991).

HEDEGAARD, E. O. A., 'Det militære Gendarmeriekorps, 1885–1894', *Krigshistorisk Tidsskrift*, 2 (1967), 5–50.

HOUSE, JONATHAN M., 'Civil–Military Relations in Paris, 1848', in Roger Price (ed.), *Revolution and Reaction: 1848 and the French Second Republic* (London: Croom Helm, 1975).

HUGHES, STEVEN C., 'Fear and Loathing in Bologna and Rome: The Papal Police in perspective', *Journal of Social History*, 21 (1987), 97–116.

—— 'Poliziotti, Carabinieri e "Policemens": il *bobby* inglese nella polizia italiana', *Le Carte e la Storia*, 2 (1996), 22–31.

JAUFFRET, JEAN-CHARLES, 'Armée et pouvoir politique. La question des troups spéciales chargées du maintien de l'ordre en France de 1871 à 1914', *Revue historique*, 547 (1983), 97–144.

JENSEN, RICHARD BACH, 'Police Reform and Social Reform: Italy from the Crisis of the 1890s to the Giolittian Era', *Criminal Justice History*, 10 (1989), 179–200.

KENNEDY, BENJAMIN, 'Crisis in the Borderlands: General Moncey in the Western Pyrenees, 1794–1795', *Proceedings of the Annual Meeting of the Western Society for French History*, 19 (1992), 139–47.

LACHOUQUE, HENRI, '1789–1815. De début de la Révolution à la chute de l'Empire', *Revue Historique de l'Armée*, 17 (1961), 82–118.

LAVEN, DAVID, 'Law and Order in Habsburg Venetia, 1814–1835', *Historical Journal*, 39 (1996) 383–403.

LUC, JEAN-NOËL, 'La revalorisation de la Gendarmerie nationale sous la Monarchie de Juillet (1841–1847), *Revue Historique des Armées*, 213 (1999), 15–25.

LÜDTKE, ALF, 'The Role of State Violence in the Period of Transition to Industrial Capitalism: The Example of Prussia from 1815 to 1848', *Social History*, 4 (1979), 175–221.

LOWE, W. J. and MALCOLM, E. L., 'The Domestication of the Royal Irish Constabulary, 1836–1922', *Irish Economic and Social History*, 19 (1992), 27–48.

MACKRELL, JOHN, 'Criticism of Seigneurial Justice in Eighteenth-Century France', in J. F. Bosher (ed.), *French Government and Society 1500–1850* (London: Athlone Press, 1973).

MACPHEE, PETER, 'Une meurtre dans le Sud de la France en 1830: violence, mémoire et tradition démocratique', *Bulletin du centre d'histoire contemporaine du Languedoc Méditerranéan Roussillon*, 56 (1995), 3–30.

MARQUIS, GREG, 'The "Irish Model" and Nineteenth-Century Canadian Policing', *Journal of Imperial and Commonwealth History*, 25 (1997) 193–218.

MARTIN, DANIEL, 'La Maréchaussée d'Auvergne face aux authorités administratives et judiciaires au XVIIIᵉ siècle (1720–1780)', *Cahiers d'histoire*, 18 (1973), 337–49.

O'BRIEN, PATRICIA ANN, 'The Revolutionary Police of 1848', in Roger Price (ed.), *Revolution and Reaction: 1848 and the French Second Republic* (London: Croom Helm, 1975).

PAPE, HEINZ L., 'Der Säbel der Großherzonlich Hessischen Gendarmerie um 1820', *Archiv für Polizeigeschichte*, 6 (1992), 12–14.

PATRICK, ALISON, 'French Revolutionary Local Government, 1789–92', in Colin Lucas (ed.), *The French Revolution and the Creation of Modern Political Culture*, vol. 2, *The Political Culture of the Revolution* (Oxford: Pergamon Press, 1988).

PETIT, JACQUES-GUY, 'Marianne en Anjou: l'insurrection des ardoisiers de Trélazé', *Annales de Bretagne et des Pays de l'Ouest*, 104 (1997), 187–200.

PRICE, ROGER, 'Techniques of Repression: The Control of Popular Protest in Mid-Nineteenth-Century France', *Historical Journal*, 25 (1982), 859–87.

REGNAULT, Chef d'escadron DOMINIQUE, 'Les convictions du Maréchal Moncey', *Revue historique des armées*, 4 (1991), 15–21.

REINHARD, MARCEL, 'Nostalgie et service militaire pendant la Révolution', *Annales historiques de la Révolution Française*, 30 (1958), 1–15.

ROBISHEAUX, EARL, 'The "Private Army" of the Tax Farms: The Men and their Origins', *Histoire Sociale/Social History*, 12 (1973), 256–69.

ROSEN, HEINRICH, 'Der Aufstand der Krefelder "Seidenfabrikarbeiter" 1828 und die Bildung einer "Sicherheitswache": Ein Dokumentation', *Die Heimat: Zeitschrift für Niederrheinische Heimatpflege*, 36 (1965), 32–61.

RUIZ, ENRIQUE MARTÍNEZ, 'Las Fuerzas de Seguridad y Orden Público en la Primera Mitad del Siglo XIX', *Cuadernos de Historia*, 4 (1973), 83–161.

RULE, JAMES and TILLY, CHARLES, 'Political Process in Revolutionary France, 1830–1832', in John M. Merriman (ed.), *1830 in France* (New York: New Viewpoints, 1975).

SAUREL, Colonel LOUIS, 'Regards sur l'histoire de la Gendarmerie', *Revue Historique de l'Armée*, 17 (1961), 9–49.

STORCH, ROBERT D., 'The Plague of Blue Locusts: Police Reform and Popular Resistance in Northern England, 1840–1857', *International Review of Social History*, 20 (1975), 61–90.

—— 'The Policeman as Domestic Missionary: Urban Discipline and Popular Culture in Northern England, 1850–1880', *Journal of Social History*, 9 (1976), 481–509.

STRIETER, TERRY W., 'Drinking on the Job: *Ivresse* among the French Gendarmerie in the Nineteenth Century', *Proceedings of the Annual Meeting of the Western Society for French History*, 13 (1986), 173–81.

—— 'The Faceless Police of the Second Empire: A Social Profile of the Gendarmes of Mid-Nineteenth-Century France, *French History*, 8 (1994), 167–95.

TEUFEL, MANFRED, 'Das Württembergische Landjägerkorps, 1807–1934', *Archiv für Polizeigeschichte*, 6 (1992), 14–23.

WALTER, FRIEDRICH, 'Die Organisierung der Staatlichen Polizei unter Kaiser Joseph II', *Mitteilungen des Vereins für Geschichte der Staat Wien*, 7 (1927), 22–53.

WEGELIN, PETER, 'Die Bayerische Konstitution von 1808', in Werner Näf and Ernst Walder (eds.), *Schweizer Beiträger zur Allgemeinen Geschichte*, 16 (Bern: Herbert Lang, 1958), 154–206.

WIRSING, BERND, ' "Gleichsam mit Soldatenstrenge:" Neue Polizei in süddeutschen Städten. Zu Polizeiverhalten und Bürger-Widersetzlichkeit im Vormärz', in Alf Lüdtke (ed.), *'Sicherheit und Wohlfahrt:' Polizei, Gesellschaft und Herrschaft im 19. und 20. Jahrhundert* (Frankfurt-am-Main: Suhrkamp, 1991).

WOOLF, STUART, 'French Civilization and Ethnicity in the Napoleonic Empire', *Past and Present*, 124 (1989), 96–120

THESES

BERLIÈRE, JEAN-MARC, 'L'Institution policière sous la Troisième République, 1875–1914', Thèse pour le doctorat, 3 vols., Université de Bourgogne, 1991.

BERTIN-MOUROT, ELIANE, 'La Maréchaussée en Bretagne au XVIIIᵉ siècle (1720–1789)', Thèse pour le doctorat, Université de Rennes, 1969.

BRIDGEMAN, IAN R., 'Policing Rural Ireland: A Study of the Origins, Development and Role of the Royal Irish Constabulary, and its Impact on Crime Prevention and Detection in the Nineteenth Century', Ph.D, The Open University, 1993.

CALANCA, ALVARO, 'Le origini e le funzioni dei Carabinieri fino al 1848', Tesi di Laurea, Università degli studi di Torino, 1966–67.

COLLIN, RICHARD OLIVER, 'The Italian Police and Internal Security from Giolitti to Mussolini', D.Phil., Oxford University, 1983.

GARNIER, CATHERINE, 'La Gendarmerie dans le Maine-et-Loire de 1791 à 1815', Mémoire de maîtrise, Université d'Angers, 1996.

GRAND, GÉRARD, 'La Maréchaussée de Provence (1554–1790)', Thèse pour le doctorat en Droit, Université d'Aix-Marseille, 1956.

GRIFFIN, BRIAN J., 'The Irish Police, 1836–1914: A Social History', Ph.D., Loyola University of Chicago, 1991.

HESTAULT, ERIC, 'La Maréchaussée dans la lieutenance de Nantes à la fin de l'Ancien Régime (1770–1790)', Mémoire de maîtrise, Université de Nantes, 1992.

HUMBERT-CONVAIN, SYLVIE, 'Le Juge de Paix et la Répression des Infractions Douanières en Flandre et en Hollande, 1794–1815: Contribution à l'histoire du système continental Napoléonien', Doctorat, Erasmus University, Rotterdam, 1993.

O'BRIEN, PATRICIA ANN, 'Urban Growth and Public Order: The Development of a Modern Police in Paris, 1829–1854', Ph.D, Columbia University, 1973.

RENAULT, Captain DOMINIQUE 'L'Inspection Générale de la Gendarmerie au début de l'Empire', Mémoire de Diplôme Technique, Enseignement militaire supérieur scientifique et technique, 1986–7.

SAUREL, Captain LOUIS, 'La Gendarmerie dans la société de la Deuxième République et du Second Empire', Thèse pour le doctorat, 3 vols., Université de Paris, 1964.

WIRSING, BERND, 'Die Geschichte der Gendarmerikorps und deren Vorläuferorganisationen in Baden, Württemberg und Bayern, 1750–1850', Dissertation . . . des Doktors Philosophie Universität Konstanz, 1991.

INDEX